TRANSNATIONAL CHICANX PERSPECTIVES ON ANA CASTILLO

LATINX AND LATIN AMERICAN PROFILES

FREDERICK LUIS ALDAMA, EDITOR

TRANSNATIONAL CHICANX PERSPECTIVES ON ANA CASTILLO

EDITED BY
BERNADINE M. HERNÁNDEZ
AND KAREN R. ROYBAL

UNIVERSITY OF PITTSBURGH PRESS

Published by the University of Pittsburgh Press, Pittsburgh, Pa., 15260
Copyright © 2021, University of Pittsburgh Press

Manufactured in the United States of America
Printed on acid-free paper
10 9 8 7 6 5 4 3 2 1

Cataloging-in-Publication data is available from the Library of Congress

ISBN 13: 978-0-8229-4667-0
ISBN 10: 0-8229-4667-X

Cover art: Suzy Gonzalez, *Nature Nurtures*, 2019. Acrylic, dyed corn husks, and oil on canvas, 48 × 36 in.
Cover design: Melissa Dias-Mandoly

For all the Chicana feminists who have inspired us, and for our moms and *abuelas* who remain with us always

CONTENTS

PART III. GIVE IT TO THE GLOBE

PART IV. MAMÁ, MIJXS, AND ME

PART V. TEACHING AND PEDAGOGY

PART VI. AN INTERVIEW WITH ANA CASTILLO

ACKNOWLEDGMENTS

First and foremost we would like to thank all the contributors to *Transnational Chicanx Perspectives on Ana Castillo* for their hard work, diligence, and faith in this project. This book would not have been possible without their dedication. We would also like to thank Ana Castillo, whose work over the past forty-plus years has inspired us all. We cannot believe this tribute had not happened before.

We would also like to thank Frederick Luis Aldama, editor of the Latinx and Latin American Profiles series; Josh Shanholtzer, acquiring editor; Alex Wolfe, editorial and production director; and Amy Sherman, managing editor, at the University of Pittsburgh Press. We would also like to thank copyeditor Emily Jerman Schuster for her patience and sharp eye.

Thank you, also, to the anonymous readers for their time, insight, attention to detail, and support for this project. This book is much stronger because of their careful criticisms and suggestions. We are grateful to all the hardworking staff at the University of Pittsburgh Press for helping us turn this manuscript into the beautiful collection you now hold in your hands.

We would be remiss if we did not thank the Hulbert Center for Southwest Studies at Colorado College for their support. Thank you, also, to Eric Perramond, Santiago Guerra, and Nancy Ríos, for being great colleagues and for supporting this project. Special thanks to Carol Hernández for arranging travel and attending to the details—we could not have done this without your help. Thank you, also, to Jenn Sides, for arranging work space for us at Tutt Library at Colorado College during the early stages of this project. Thank you to our dear friends and colleagues at the University of New Mexico, Melina Vizcaíno-Alemán and Jesse Alemán, for their continued support over many, many years; Jesse, your mentorship has been invaluable to us. We owe a debt of gratitude to Francisco J. Galarte, for his help with research, editing, inspirational conversations about the project, and overwhelming support throughout the entire process. Thank you to Maylei Blackwell, for sharing formatting strategies with us as we began this project.

This project began at the 2017 American Studies Annual Meeting, where we organized and presented on a panel entitled "Political Prowess in Ana Castillo's Chicanx Literature of Dissent." Thank you to our colleague and friend Norma Valenzuela, who presented with us that year, and again to Ana Castillo, who served as the respondent and who generously listened to and approved of our idea to produce this collection.

Finally, thank you to our families for their unending support, and to each of you for reading and using this collection in your classrooms and in your research.

OUR COLLECTIVE DREAMING AND WORLD SHAPING WITH ANA CASTILLO

FREDERICK LUIS ALDAMA

I have always loved words. In my idealized sense of my infant self, I could read before I could talk. I love the way their careful planning and patterning can conjure up new ways of seeing, hearing, touching, tasting, and feeling. I love the way creators can build edifices—worlds—for me to step into, explore, and be shaken to my core. Ana Castillo is one such creator.

Growing up, I spent hours in our local library reading nearly anything I could get my hands on. Of course, at that time I had no idea about a nascent formation of Latinx literature; I had no idea that an Ana Castillo or a Sandra Cisneros existed. Thanks to a gracious librarian and letters from an autodidact *papá*, I did know well Faulkner, Borges, Cortázar, and García Márquez. I had no idea either that one could choose a life of professionally reading, teaching, and publishing on authors of fiction. If one got into college, it was a go-for-broke study to become a doctor or engineer.

I pre-med tracked at Berkeley: O-chem, biology, and math. In the fall of 1990, however, I woke to another possibility. The fall of 1990 I followed a buzz on campus among us Latinx undergrads. A freshly minted assistant professor, Alfred Arteaga, had arrived and would teach an entire course just on Chicano literature. The course changed everything for me.

For an entire semester I would deep-dive into the very varied storyworlds of Tomás Rivera, Oscar "Zeta" Acosta, Arturo Arias, Sandra Cisneros, and Denise Chávez, among others. One author especially captivated me: Ana Castillo. *The Mixquiahuala Letters* built worlds on both sides of the US/Mexico border that resonated deeply with the stories my *mamá* had shared of our past; how at eighteen years old she decided to save enough for a bus ride to Guatemala City to meet relatives she'd only heard of growing up in California and Texas. How she got off the bus in Mexico City, fell in love (with the city and a proverbial *chilango*), and had a family instead—me included. *The Mixquiahuala Letters* showed me that I wasn't alone, finding that I could feel a sense of *belonging* on both sides of the border. And, the work's flexible narrative structure—the order in which one chose to read the chapters determined if you imagined the story as a "Conformist," a "Cynic," or a "Quixotic"—deeply satisfied my proclivity for puzzle-solving stories.

As I carved a path forward to become a professor, Castillo's words *and* worlds became some of my close traveling companions. With *Sapogonia* (1990) I continued to step into the shoes of Latinxs shaped by a hemispheric Americas sensibility, often struggling to come to terms within internalized residues of coloniality of power: *machista* and *casta* systems of oppression. In other of her novels and poetry, I would meet powerful women of all sorts such as artists, activists, healers, and everyday workers who, like the *tías*, *madrina*, and *mamá* in my life, would stand up to different forms of physical and spiritual domination and abuse. I would see the women in my life for what they were: resilient superheroes of Maya and Aztec descent. And, Castillo's constant experimentation with form along with her "verses of witness" (her words) continued to energize and wake me to the limitless possibilities of imagining such characters and their worlds. Castillo's rich, complex, and exquisitely shaped Latinx hemispheric and queer imaginaries would weave their way into my early scholarly forays into identifying decolonial narrative practices.

I'm not alone, of course. Castillo's words and worlds have been traveling companion to a legion of Latinx readers, creators, and scholars. A clear testament to this: Karen Roybal and Bernadine Hernández's curating of this extraordinary volume on Castillo. In a call-and-response fashion, we encounter a myriad of scholar-creators who deepen our knowledge, pleasure, and love of Castillo's splendorous storyworlds and multitudes. They wake us to the marvelous and magical ways that Castillo's words powerfully weave into our ideas and dreams of our better selves. They invite us to see how Castillo's words build storyworlds that clear milky film from eyes to see how we might push forward as warrior-healers to make a future free of the shackles of the coloniality of power.

TRANSNATIONAL CHICANX PERSPECTIVES ON ANA CASTILLO

INTRODUCTION

KAREN R. ROYBAL AND BERNADINE M. HERNÁNDEZ

When Ana Castillo sent the literary world into a frenzy with her 1993 novel *So Far from God*, her first published poem, "Otro Canto," was already sixteen years old (1977), not to mention that her first genre-bending novel, *The Mixquiahuala Letters*, was seven years old (1986). The timeline of her first writings compared to her worldwide literary "success" is the foundation of this edited collection. Castillo has been a key literary figure in Chicana/o/x and American literary history for more than four decades, yet there is no critical collection examining her works to date. So why embark upon a journey that is long overdue and why focus this edited collection on the transnational Chicanx context? This question has two answers. First off, Castillo's writing offers us many roadmaps for how we can begin to navigate our current political and social moment. That is, Castillo's work offers readers speculative trajectories through a Chicana feminist praxis, which creates a language within her novels that interrogates real world trauma and racialized violence (ongoing today) while simultaneously blending, breaking, and challenging genre conventions. Castillo is a Chicana feminist writer who deals with global issues. Secondly, and most importantly, there is a direct gap of interpretation between Chicana feminist literature and theory and that of other third world feminist theories and writings. Castillo deals directly with transnational and global issues in her literature; her work is read in an array of literature courses. This edited collection strives to expand the reach of her work by suggesting we broaden our categorization of her work as solely Chicana and acknowledge that it can and should also be read as a significant contribution to Latina/o/x studies, especially in how it fosters new conversations in gender/sexuality studies that help trace how early Chicana feminism contributed to the genealogy of work in Latinx feminist politics. Considered in this way, Castillo's work transcends borders of literature *and* theory. In this collection, we refer to Castillo as Chicana; however, we honor the ways in which she identifies as Xicana, Mexic Amerindian, mestiza, *and* Chicana. We also employ the "x" in the spirit of acknowledging the ways this category makes a bold statement about identity politics as noted by Nicole Guidotti-Hernández, who says it "carries the excessive and diverse affective load of a population in ways that other ethnonationalist and pan-Latina/o terms cannot."[1] As this collection hopes to show, Castillo's work has contributed to the discussions of culture, politics, history, and positionality across disciplines and across time.

A transnational Chicanx perspective is evident in much of Castillo's writing in the way she turns genre on its head, traverses space and place, and combines literary movements. She does this beautifully in her groundbreaking novel *So Far from God*, published in 1993 by W. W. Norton and Company. When the novel begins, the youngest daughter of Sofia/Sofi, three-year-old La Loca, has "passed away" of an epileptic seizure. Without explanation, La Loca rises from the dead, alive and well during her funeral. Before this happens, Father Jerome, the Catholic priest giving the funeral mass, questions Sofi's faith in God and says, "As devoted followers of Christ, we must not show our lack of faith in Him at these times and in His, our Father's fair judgment. Who alone knows why we are here on this earth and why He chooses to call us back home when He does."[2] Father Jerome calls upon Sofi to have faith, but the faith he is forcing upon her is based on institutionalized religion: a religion of conquest, a religion that ties the Americas together in interdependent ways. As Sofi shows her aggravation and sadness, "The [coffin] lid pushed all the way open and the little girl inside sat up, just as sweetly as if she had woken from a nap, rubbing her eyes and yawning."[3] La Loca flies to the top of the church but is not able to fly completely away from it, because she is restricted by the male-dominated space of the church. And it is in this moment that Castillo counters this male dominance by bending genre convention by subverting male authority represented by Father Jerome. She opens her novel with this scene of magical realism that can only be explained by Father Jerome as something to do with possession by the devil. Magical realism, a twentieth-century literary movement originating in Latin America, is marked by depictions of "the real" alongside depictions of the fantastical; Castillo pushes the boundaries of this Latin American genre made most popular by male Colombian writer Gabriel García Márquez and Argentinean writer Jorge Luis Borges, and coined as *lo real maravilloso* by Cuban novelist, essayist, and musicologist Alejo Carpentier.

Whereas a general readership would—for potentially racist reasoning and ignorance of certain geopolitical locations—categorize Castillo in this Latin American boom, we read Castillo as taking the political form of magical realism as building off Latin American writers deliberately to play on the device's popularity of the "fantastic." She certainly moves transnationally through literary genres and geopolitical spaces. Wendy B. Faris defines magical realism as "an 'irreducible element' of magic, something we cannot explain according to the laws of the universe as we know them. In the terms of the text, magical things 'really' do happen."[4] Through the lens of realism, magic details the phenomenal world through what we come to know as 'reality.' The phenomena of what cannot be explained in reality are narrated with a matter-of-fact tone in the texts. However, it was Alejo Carpentier who coined the term *lo real maravilloso*, which brought magical realism from German art criticism to Latin American literary criticism. In his essay "On the Marvelous Real in America," originally published in 1949 in the preface to Carpentier's novel *El reino de este mundo*, and later published in English translation as *The Kingdom of This World* in 1957, he suggests that the New World is intrinsically marvelous and cannot be fully and accurately represented by Western realists' literary "ruse of Surrealism."[5] For this very reason, his novel depicts the French colony of Saint-Dominique and later Haiti through the presence of ghostly phantoms and animal metamorphosis, which are all taken as fact by the Black characters in the novel. This highly political move to adjust how readers conceptualize "rational" Western thinking and "magical" Afro-Caribbean thinking makes room for a rejection of colonialism and conquest and opens up a space for readers to envision what "reality" might look like for non-Western thinkers, characters, and representation. Carpentier gave rise to the Latin American "Boom" fiction of the '60s and '70s that is associated with the term *magical realism*. In *So Far from God*, Castillo is building off this political genre, not to add a "Latin American" voice to the already burgeoning canon, but to playfully will readers in the United States to think about *how* the political informs the literary. It would be wise for us *not* to read Castillo as a part of the Latin American Boom, but as utilizing the literary technique to unsettle a US-centered readership. Marta Caminero-Santangelo notes that to lump simplistic paradigms of "magic" into magical realism is to essentialize Chicana/o/x "as part of its larger commodification within mainstream U.S. culture."[6] Castillo borrows from the literary tradition of magical realism that blurs the lines between natural and supernatural and elasticized notions of time and space, but utilizes different narration styles to turn the genre on its head.[7] This collection brings together issues and questions of collective Latinx subjectivity through Chicana feminist literary history and culture, as we will later explain.

Father Jerome cannot fathom how or why La Loca could fly to the top of the church roof with such fervor and fierceness. However, as a narrative that is rooted in oral storytelling, the novel utilizes gossip to convey major events and characters. The novel begs readers to ask: Did La Loca *really* fly to the top of the church? How? Who is the narrator telling us the story of this flying resurrection in the first place? In an attempt to play with genre convention through magical realism while challenging the male-dominated church, Castillo turns magical realism on its head as we consider that there is nothing magical about gossip. The narration of this event and all preceding events is told by the *señora* neighbor, who probably heard about it from another neighbor, as is common practice in impoverished neighborhoods. These women celebrate the highs and the lows together and talk about everything as survival strategies.[8] Readers are forced to read this scene for its literalness and symbolism combined. In an attempt to "fly," La Loca symbolizes the female character that attempts to leave home. While Castillo gives us a magical realist component, she simultaneously undercuts it through narrative strategy. "Don't you dare!' She [Sofi] screamed at Father Jerome, charging at him and beating him with her fists. 'Don't you dare start this about my baby . . . hombre necio, pendejo . . . !'"[9] In this moment readers see, as Theresa Delgadillo notes, "Castillo's narrative undoubtedly creates Chicana characters who actively participate in the construction of their world, yet the text goes beyond questioning to confront."[10] Juxtaposing the entire genre of magical realism with the transnational conquest of the church in tension with female-centered spirituality, the female characters in the novel are (re)presented to readers in different shapes and forms as a way to link death with larger structures of power that link Chicana subjects across locales, places, and oceans, and Castillo does this in the first few pages of the novel.

Born in Chicago, Illinois, on June 15, 1953, Castillo is a copious writer of poetry, novels, short stories, essays, collected editions, plays, and more. She utilizes what she terms as "conscienticized poetics" in her novels. This particular political poetics and Chicana feminist positionality works to raise people's awareness and political consciousness while revealing the interconnectedness of diverse cultural traditions. Castillo strives to create a language within her novels that interrogates real world trauma and violence such as racialized and gendered violence while simultaneously blending, breaking, and challenging genre conventions. B. J. Manríquez reminds us, "Although Castillo experiments with generic form in each novel, she explores the same aesthetics of confrontation: the masculinized politics of power; the ineffectuality of racism specific to minorities under capitalism; and the complex nature of romantic love, its sexual expression, and its relation to the prevailing ideologies of social power."[11] Castillo's writing imagines queer, women of color–centered spaces as a direct comment upon a dystopian society that connects with larger cultural, political, and transnational concerns. As a practitioner of Xicanisma and a self-identified Mexic Amerindian, mestiza, and Chicana, Castillo hopes that Chicana feminism will be "rescued from the suffocating atmosphere of pedantry and carried out to our work places, social gatherings, kitchens, bedrooms, and the public sphere."[12] Castillo's concept of Xicanisma is more than an expression of feminism in nationalism. Her Chicana feminist politics are instead better categorized as a "critique of Chicano nationalism [that] thus operate[s] as a powerful critique of neoliberalism that incorporates oppositional nationalism," as Grace K. Hong notes in her discussion of Chicana feminist praxis in this era.[13] By the release of the twentieth-anniversary edition of *Massacre of the Dreamers* in 2014, Castillo's Xicanisma also evoked a more transnational articulation of feminism in which gender politics must transcend national borders because they operate from unfixed and diverse positions. This shift in our conception of Chicana feminism is what has, in part, inspired this collection.

Castillo was one of the first Chicanas to be published by a New York publishing firm. As literary agents began to see success with Latin (American) literature, they needed a strategy to make Chicana literature consumable for a mainstream audience. Castillo was one of the first authors to be published on the heels of the "chica lit" boom. Chica lit, an extension of Latina literature, resulted from a definite shift away from Chicana literature (of the late '80s and beyond); it was an attempt to make Chicana literature seem more foreign and not domestic, to seem more magical and less political.[14] This marketing strategy attempted to make the political Chicana more consumable to the mainstream public. Castillo took conventional genre and form and made it palpable for a mainstream audience, while simultaneously interrogating issues that Chicana/o and Latina/o subjects were experiencing.

Her various uses of literary form and genre make Castillo a transnational feminist with a Chicana feminist praxis, because quite frankly, she juxtaposes normative literary convention with more oral traditions of folklore from Mexico and across other international borders. This allows her not only to stretch genre and form to its absolute coherency, but it also allows her to play with convention, meaning she satirically brings to light transnational issues. Daniel Cooper Alarcón coins the term *literary syncretism* in thinking about how Castillo's novel *So Far from God* "selectively draws on, combines, and reconfigures the conventions of her numerous source materials" in order to combine canonical texts and popular literary traditions that range from the "Bible and *Don Quixote*, to hagiography and Catholic legends, to popular Mexican American proverbs, folk legends, and remedies."[15] This combining of different literary genres, conventions, and forms is a classic Castillo move. Through literary syncretism, she mirrors social commentary on racism and sexism in her novels and poetry. Castillo is able to explore many social issues in her novels because she is not wedded to a particular literary form or genre. For example, as Alarcón states, Sofi rejects and recasts the tale of La Llorona in *So Far from God*, which sheds light on how sexism runs rampant not only in the small community of Tóme, but also within the institution of the Catholic church. Castillo's narrator tells readers: "The Weeping Woman astral-traveled all throughout old Mexico, into the United States, and really anywhere her people lived, wailing, in search of her children whom she drowned so as to run off with her lover. For that God punished her forever on earth."[16] The La Llorona folktale puts all the burden and blame on the female figure, but Castillo is quick to counter this historic folktale through her narrator, who states, "The idea of a wailing woman suffering throughout eternity because of God's punishment never appealed to Sofia, so she would not have repeated it to her daughters."[17] When Sofi's oldest daughter, Esperanza, a journalist, is held hostage while she is reporting and then dies in the Middle East, La Llorona appears to La Loca to inform her of her sister's death, and Sofi, her daughter Fe, and La Loca all weep for Esperanza. This weeping is *not* because Sofi "had left her children, much less drowned them to run off with nobody. On the contrary, she had been left to raise them by herself."[18] The three of them weep because war and nation-state violence took their family member. Castillo recasts the La Llorona folklore to put the onus on histories of war, not on the woman of color. Castillo employs literary syncretism to exemplify the interweaving of the "literary" and the pragmatic, of convention and the mundane.

This type of reading of Castillo's form would fit into a postmodern literary technique that elucidates a disjuncture of form, but pushes against the postmodern form because Castillo is a writer who is deeply connected to history.[19] The literary syncretism that Alarcón coins that takes into consideration this disjuncture functions along the same lines as Tereza M. Szeghi's concept of literary didacticism, meaning that Castillo's poetry and novels emphasize the idea that different forms of literature ought to convey information and instructions. In her 2008 novel *The Guardians*, she offers a raw political message that "effectively aim[s] to combat the cognitive defenses readers of human rights literature experience, which prevent them from taking action."[20] Castillo utilizes Regina, the narrator and protagonist, as a call to action on the borderlands. In fact, this postmodern form of disjuncture and theorizing its own condition of possibility was how Castillo crafted her novels *Sapogonia: An Anti-Romance in 3/8 Meter* (1990) and *So Far from God*, which originated in short story form; *Sapogonia* as "Anti-hero" and *So Far from God* as "Loca Santa." We see this exact form of the combination of many literary forms, genres, and conventions in Castillo's novel *The Mixquiahuala Letters* (1986). For example, letter thirty-two in the novel is one of two letters in which poet Teresa writes about herself in third person. The shift from first to third person is an obliteration of her sense of self. But as Lesley Larkin states, Teresa also becomes multiple in these letters. "There are at least three Teresas here: the self-possessed, feminist Teresa of 'another life' who speaks with 'muffled shouts'; the shattered Teresa, attempting to piece herself together again; and the Teresa writing retrospectively about the act of recovery in which the second Teresa is engaged."[21] In doing this, Castillo allows Teresa to be reader, writer, and subject of the text. These examples point to Castillo's vastness and her expanse in the literary field. Just as Sandra K. Soto suggests, Castillo's form explores "transcultural forms of belonging and desire," meaning that Castillo's narrative forms and characters are "constantly negotiating various forms of travel: outward journeys that move her characters across literal and figurative time, space, and sometimes even dimension."[22] This edited collection was born where Castillo's varied form and her varied transnational space meet.

The collection considers the large span and scope of Castillo's body of work, from her beginning poetry and formidable novel *The Mixquiahuala Letters* to her critically acclaimed novel *So Far from God* to her raunchy aesthetics in *Give It to Me* (2014) to, finally, her gripping nonfiction piece *Black Dove: Mamá, Mi'jo, and Me* (2016). We are asking: What are the connections to be made between Castillo's work, the US Chicanx/Latinx context, and the larger transnational and global context that considers Brown bodies and cultures to lay at the margins in the current moment? How does Castillo's work allow a conversation to emerge between Chicana feminists and transnational feminists? In what ways does Castillo's themes and language connect to a larger body of work, and in what ways is she solidifying Chicana feminism as a foundational theoretical body of work?

A LITERARY GENEALOGY OF CASTILLO WITHIN CHICANA AND AMERICAN LITERATURE

Tracing a literary genealogy of Castillo in relation not only to Chicana literature, but also to broader American literature and the transnational feminist canon seems overambitious at first; however, upon further examination, it becomes a critical mapping project that is the foundation of this collection. This mapping begins with recognition of the integral work early Chicana feminists underwent to make their voices heard—a journey that begins as early as the 1960s. As Dionne Espinoza, María Eugenia Cotera, and Maylei Blackwell assert in their 2018 anthology, *Chicana Movidas: New Narratives of Activism and Feminism in the Movement Era*, Chicanas in the 1960s "enact[ed] a new kind of *política* (politics) at the intersection of race, class, gender, and sexuality, they developed innovative concepts, tactics, and methodologies that in turn generated new theories, art forms, organizational spaces, and strategies of alliance."[23] This foundation, or the *movidas* of women in the Chicano movement era described by Espinoza, Cotera, and Blackwell, worked to deepen resistance against the oppressive social, racial, political, and personal spaces within which these early Chicana feminists maneuvered and were forced to navigate. Liberation from oppression was a common goal for Chicanos and Chicanas alike during the 1960s and 1970s, but as Sonia Saldívar-Hull reminds us, "A split also came between traditional, male-identified Chicanas who refused to recognize women's struggles as legitimate areas of dispute, and feminist Chicanas, who insisted on liberation from oppressive cultural traditions."[24] Saldívar-Hull's assertion makes clear that the Chicana feminist movement was not based on a homogenous group of women; instead, the movement symbolized a moment of significant change that included the acknowledgment of the heterogeneity of women's issues even within groups of Chicana feminists. In other words, the Chicana feminist movement brought to light the issues that came with classifying the Chicano movement as solely a fight based on nationalism and race. Movement rhetoric and actions that drove it neglected sex and sexuality—issues Chicanas faced daily. This absence motivated Chicana feminists to forge their own movement that acknowledged the importance of these issues in the national narrative; they created a political movement that propelled them into the public eye as dynamic subjects who contested the internalization of what we now identify as neoliberalist modes of power. Grace K. Hong reminds us, "Rather than attempting to resolve or compensate for the losses wrought upon Chicana/o communities by the racial state and capital and in this way overcome the state of abjection, Chicana feminism instead politicized abjection."[25]

Castillo's writing in the 1970s speaks directly to this politicized abjection. Alternativa Publications published her first chapbook of poetry titled *Otro Canto* in 1977. Coincidently, this was the same year that the Combahee River Collective published their statement on Black feminism that stated their collective was "committed to struggling against racial, sexual, heterosexual, and class oppression, and see as our particular task the development of integrated analysis and practice based upon the fact that the major systems of oppression are interlocking."[26] *Otro Canto* was the beginning of a call to form alliances between Latinas/os in the United States and was a coalitional model that stood among statements like the Combahee River Collective Statement in that moment of civil rights, nationalist movements, and activism by radical groups across the nation. Just two years after her first chapbook publication, Castillo published another chapbook, *The Invitation*, in 1979. Castillo was among the first Chicana novelists to be published, including Sandra Cisneros, who published *The House on Mango Street* in 1984 (Arte Público Press), and Margarita Cota-Cárdenas, who published *Puppet: A Chicano Novella* in 1985 (UNM Press); Castillo's first novel, *The Mixquiahuala Letters*, saw print in 1986 (Bilingual Press/Editorial Bilingue). These foundational authors set the stage for a Chicana literary canon that examined not only issues of gender, but also how race, sexuality, and class were intersecting structures of violence that second-wave feminism would never attend to or accept. Around this time, Puerto Rican poets were also establishing their literary voice in New York City with the opening of the Nuyorican Poets Cafe, where Sandra María Esteves was putting out her first book of poetry called *Yerba Buena: Poems & Drawings* (1980).

Simultaneously, Black feminists Barbara Smith and Audre Lorde were establishing Kitchen Table: Women of Color Press. The women of color feminist anthology *This Bridge Called My Back*, published by Kitchen Table in 1982 (1981 by Persephone Press) and edited by Cherríe Moraga and Gloria Anzaldúa, is still a foundational text that mixes genres, essays, poems, and short stories to create a genealogy of women of color activism. Women of color feminists continue to recognize Moraga and Anzaldúa's *This Bridge* as one of the most notable dialogues about transborder feminism. When the collection was originally released in 1981 on the heels of the Chicano and the women's movements of the 1960s and 1970s, it influenced feminist thought in important ways. This collection opened dialogue between women of color feminists that transformed feminist theory and practice in the most radical way when it emphasized the important role of collaboration and community building between and among feminists of color across the nation to contest neocolonial ideologies that continued to render them invisible or as second-class citizens. The women of color feminists who contributed to *This Bridge* aligned their own work with third world communities and cultures, though some scholars would say this was done erroneously, as the distinction between first and third world women of color was major. However, this coalition ensured political solidarity that further expanded Chicana feminist concerns as *transnational* feminist concerns.

When prominent Chicana feminist scholars responded by using politicized and gendered writing through such venues as Third Woman Press, spearheaded by prominent Chicana feminist scholar Norma Alarcón, then a graduate student at Indiana University, they began to fashion a space through which "written and visual expressions" and "intellectual activism" of women of color could be published and distributed to a broader audience and, in turn, created an alliance through which women of color from around the nation and globe could "imagine a new political class centering sexuality, race, and gender."[27] In fact, in 1980 Castillo was present at the Midwest Latina Workshop where Alarcón decided to create Third Woman Press.[28] In 1993, Castillo joined forces with Alarcón and Cherríe Moraga to coedit their own collection through Third Woman Press that examined the state of the Latina and Chicana in the United States (*The Sexuality of Latinas*). In 1996, Castillo edited her own collection, *Goddess of the Americas: Writings on the Virgin of Guadalupe / La Diosa de las Américas: Escritos Sobre la Virgen de Guadalupe*, published by Riverhead. Both collections examine the performativity of gender and sexuality in the Americas through colonialism and imperialism.[29] And while the Chicana feminist canon is foundational and rooted in our theoretical politics of liberation today, this edited collection aims to break open the essentialist notions of womanhood and lesbianism, appropriated terms of indigeneity, and how "third world" is located and theorized in these early Chicana writings and through the work of Ana Castillo specifically. If we are truly looking toward liberation and writings that can give us a roadmap to liberation, we must be critical and engage in the nuances of the works that brought us to the moment we are in right now.

At the peak of this multiethnic art renaissance, Castillo began publishing at a steady pace. She wrote *Women Are Not Roses* in 1984 (Arte Público Press) and her most popular book of poetry, *My Father Was a Toltec and Selected Poems, 1973–1988* (W. W. Norton & Company), in 1995. In between those two, she published *Sapogonia: An Anti-Romance in 3/8 Meter* (Bilingual Press) in 1990 and her short story collection *Loverboys* (W. W. Norton & Company) in 1996, with her famous novel *Peel My Love Like an Onion* (Doubleday Press) coming out in 1999. But it really was her first novel, *The Mixquiahuala Letters*, published in 1986 (Bilingual Press), that set the stage for all her future novels to come. Castillo dedicates the book to Argentine writer Julio Cortazar's *Hopscotch* and tells the reader, "Dear Reader: It is the author's duty to alert the reader that this is not a book to be read in the usual sequence. All letters are numbered to aid in following any of the author's proposed options."[30] This subversion of genre to express Xicanisma through a male Latin American writer begs the reader to ask, is this parody or pastiche in a novel? In American literature, postmodern parody finds itself without a trajectory. It has lived and that strange new thing, the pastiche, slowly comes to take its place. Pastiche is, like parody, the imitation of a peculiar or unique, idiosyncratic style, the wearing of a linguistic mask or speech in a dead language. But it is a neutral "practice of such mimicry, without any of parody's ulterior motives, amputated of the satiric impulse, devoid of laughter. . . . Pastiche is thus blank parody, a statue with blind eyeballs."[31] Castillo uses and circumvents the literary tradition of postmodernism in her novels as she breaks down reality as a strategy to invoke not only literary history, but the materiality of history. In her latest novel, *Give It To Me*, which was published in 2014 by the Feminist Press, Palma, the main protagonist, functions against the norms of American integration discourse through multiple scenes of sexual vignettes that take readers on a journey with Palma but do not follow a plot; the narrative, therefore, does not allow us to become invested.

Give It To Me rejects a tidy plotline and follows its forty-three-year-old Chicana protagonist, Palma, on more than twenty sexual escapades transnationally. Palma, a bisexual Chicana, grows up in Chicago, where she lives with her seemingly judgmental grandmother after her parents leave her to work on the migrant trail. Her parents end up in Los Angeles, where Palma finds them in her quest to fill a certain void in her life. While her roots are in Chicago, she moves to Albuquerque, New Mexico, with her ex-husband Rodrigo who gets a job there in education. When Rodrigo's brother calls to tell him his mother is ill and ailing, the couple flies to Medellín, Colombia, only to find out that Rodrigo's brother is disappearing people and is at odds with the cartel, a "family business" Palma knew had taken the two to Colombia in the first place. She lives most of the novel in Albuquerque, where she finds odd-end jobs and ends up in Rio de Janeiro, Brazil. Palma becomes the embodiment of what cannot be contained within the Chicana body, but at the same time she seems disinterested in her position as a racialized woman, her sexual excess, or her community at large. However, a closer look into her "empty" characterization allows for a generative supplement to the discourse of postmodernism that deems Palma without profound knowledge of herself. For Castillo, the postmodern splitting of the subject is the very condition of the conquered and colonized Westerners under all eras who utilize survival skills and is not particular to the conventional postmodern condition of the twentieth century. Castillo again turns movement and genre on its head.

WHERE X MEETS THE HISTORICAL POSITION OF THE CHICANA

As Chicana feminism is met with the changing landscape of the studies (Chicana/o/x studies, Latina/o/x studies, and feminist studies), the debate within labeling continues. And just as Chicana feminism must contend with the ways it overlaps with transnational feminism and hemispheric Latina/o/x political conditions, it also must contend with the ways in which people of color are attempting to transcend the restraints of markers of differentiation: race, gender, sexuality, class, and ethnicity. Castillo coined the term *Xicanisma* in *Massacre of Dreamers* published in 1994 by University of New Mexico Press. As Suzanne Bost writes, "In *Massacre of Dreamers* (1994), she traced the 'strength and endurance' of Chicana feminism back to ancient Mesoamerican spirituality, taking the 'X' from the Mexica tribe (whom the Aztec people claimed as ancestors) and creating an opposition between the patriarchal and hierarchical cultures imposed by European conquest and a supposedly more peaceful and egalitarian indigenous worldview."[32] The way Castillo employs the X centers the power of the female and interrogates the colonial gender binary. In her writings, while she examines the X, we are convinced that Castillo is dedicated to a Chicana feminist praxis, which as Guidotti-Hernández tells us is "nationalism in feminism [that] called for a politically active social feminism that relied on the recuperation of Mexic-Amerindian women's experience."[33] Through evoking wholeness, Castillo coins the term Xicanisma to reclaim subjectivity during a struggle for political recognition within Anglo society and her own community of patriarchal Chicanos.

Castillo articulates gendered sexual and violent politics that navigate and circumvent the X through textual poetics. She utilizes death in her novels as a vehicle to comment upon the social maladies that plague women of color. In *So Far from God* (1994) when Caridad, one of Sofi's middle daughters and the most beautiful of the four, is physically attacked after she was out drinking one night at bar, she is left completely unrecognizable. The police blame Caridad for her situation as a consequence of her sexual promiscuity, and no one is ever held responsible for her physical attack and mutilation. Instead of a "man with a face" that attacks Caridad, it is the "malogra . . . a thing, both tangible and amorphous. A thing that might be described as made of sharp metal and splintered wood. . . . It held the weight of a continent and was indelible as ink, centuries old and yet as strong as a young wolf."[34] Francisco, the Penitente and man who rapes Esmeralda (the woman with whom Caridad falls in love), is indirectly linked to the malogra. In this indirect link, the novel comments on the Spanish conquest of the Americas and the soulless methods used to colonize, specifically the gendered violence of colonial and imperial violence. Gender and sexuality in Castillo's writings are defined within the context of the social constructions of patriarchy and heteronormativity. After her restoration, Caridad enters a new spiritual life with curandera Doña Felicia and eventually meets Esmeralda during a pilgrimage in northern New Mexico. Caridad's queerness, not just in regard to her sexuality, but in the way she positions herself in direct opposition to institutional religion and violent systems of power, allows her to form alternative kinships and women-centered spaces that are in direct contrast to her neoliberal sisters. While the identifying category of Latinx came after much of Castillo's own work and is defined as "a person of Latin American origin or descent used as a gender-neutral or non-binary alternative to Latino or Latina," Castillo interrogates and undoes the performativity of gender and sexuality within white supremacist boundaries.[35] The distinct violence that Chicanas experience in the world is the focus of much of Castillo's writing. Chicanas embody the histories of colonialism, migration, and displacement/dispossession and historical legacies of sexual violence as tied to positions of domination and servitude. This is not to say that there are not nuanced positions of power that Chicanas hold within history that maintain white supremacy, patriarchy, and capital; however, Castillo's representation and stereotypes interrogate and procure the "excessive" Chicana female body that is voluptuous, open for sex, overproducing, yet not productive.

While we use Chicanx in this collection to build upon the "X" that has become so popular in contemporary popular culture, we are well aware that the "X" in Chicanx is relational to Latinx. We want to open up a discussion not only on the "X" in relation to Chicana feminism, but also on how Chicanx can be in critical conversation with Latina/o/x studies. Becoming popular by Latino millennials in the late 2000s, Latinx has come to mean the diverse and those whose subjectivity cannot be verbalized within the naming of Latina/o and Chicana/o. In *Latinx Literature Unbound: Undoing Ethnic Expectation* (2018), Ralph E. Rodriguez encourages literary scholars to challenge their own assumptions about identity and to embrace the diversity of Latinx writers, who, he argues, are better categorized as heterogenous.[36] Claudia Milian in *Latining America: Black-Brown Passages and the Coloring of Latino/a Studies* (2013) traces the same critical thought as Rodriguez, in that she acknowledges the importance of a Latino identity, but she also engages the ways in which the Latino literary canon misses the epistemological and ontological differences of the many peoples who fall under Latino.[37] However, Rodriguez's work encourages us to shift away from, rather than embrace, Latinx solely as a strategic category that effects political outcomes. Instead, he says, we must "evaluat[e] the very rubric under which we do our work," which, for Rodriguez, is returning to understanding the importance of genre in literary studies. This edited collection takes both Milian's and Rodriguez's arguments one step further to ask not only *what* is particular about Latinx aesthetics, but *how* the X forms aesthetics *and* genre.

We also take into consideration Antonio Viego's discussion of Latinx, which he states is the general indeterminacy that marks the moment with respect to conceptualization of the human subject.[38] Latinx makes room for the subject with the understanding that it is an impossibility to do so. The "always becoming" subject is that with which Castillo's work reckons. The Latinx body is always already becoming through the term *Latinx*, which gives us the space to imagine what possibilities are ahead for the liminal body. Guidotti-Hernández wrestles with the historical position of Chicanas/os and Latinas/os when she utilizes José Esteban Muñoz's (2000) notion of Latino affect to state that we need to move beyond the notions of ethnic identity as fixed and instead understand it as performative; in other words, brownness is what people do.

If we examine the breadth of Castillo's cultural production, it is evident that she does not shy away from bringing to the forefront of her work issues pertinent to communities of color, including women of color feminists; she has addressed sexuality and bisexuality and the various ways in which they are represented are significant to queer communities; she has challenged normative conceptions of the family and discrimination against peoples of color; and she has emphasized the importance of cross-border perspectives and critically focused on the border space and its subjects. Over time, Castillo has remained committed to these issues. The genealogy of her work also reveals how she transcends the borders of genre, gender, and space. From her 1984 book of poetry, *Women are not Roses*, in which she demarcates how women defy societal and cultural norms, to her 1990 novel, *Sapogonia*, where she vividly details the destructive powers of civil unrest, misogyny, and how issues of racial identity impact geographical and physical bodies, to her 2014 novel, *Give It to Me*, in which her protagonist faces all the makings of complex family life because of divorce, pseudo incest, and the ways the protagonist defies the boundaries placed around sex and sexuality, to her 2016 memoir, *Black Dove: Mamá, Mi'jo, and Me*, where she shares personal stories about motherhood, family life, and being a bisexual Chicana feminist—we get a glimpse of the ways Castillo's work confronts, reveals, and attempts to makes sense of our constantly changing world: the becoming of X that we see in Chicanx. She has, over time, considered how local, regional, national, and global geographies intersect with gendered, sexualized, racialized, and politicized subjects and how those intersections have impacted subject positions. Through her own process of identity formation and conviction as a Mexic Amerindian woman, she has rejected the confines of a heteropatriarchal society that has historically rendered her race, culture, gender, and sexuality invisible. Castillo's attention to bisexuality is both public and private. As Aldama (2005) notes,[39] she "self-reflexively clears a space for the story of a Xicana lesbian border-erotic to unfold," which can be seen in her short story collection, *Loverboys*, and in many of her novels, including *So Far from God*, *The Mixquiahuala Letters* (addressed by Ximena Keogh Serrano, Szeghi, and Liliana González in this volume), and *Give It to Me* (addressed by Cruz in this volume). Her work continues to resonate with contemporary scholars, who embrace ideas such as the one expressed in Castillo's assertion that "the very act of self-definition is a rejection of colonization," a statement that conveys the shifts that have occurred in women of color feminism and queer/transnational feminist theory and praxis.[40]

TRANSNATIONAL CHICANX FEMINIST POLITICS AND DECONSTRUCTING BORDERS

There is a cross-national concern in Castillo's writing that constructs links between the United States and Latin America, establishing the most evident transnational connection her work confronts. *The Guardians* published in 2007 is a prime example. Set on the Juarez border towns of Cabuche and El Paso where people live in constant danger and crossing the border often results in disappearance or murder, *The Guardians* is a story told from four perspectives: Regina, Miguel, Gabo, and Abuelito Milton. Following a journey to find Regina's missing brother Rafa, the novel is a critique of how state and global structures function on the space of the border, where transnational goods and tariff policies are sent back and forth every day; however, bodies are also watched, managed, and killed every day. Transnationalism is theorized by, as Katharyne Mitchell states, "Capitalism, money, information, and a hegemonic narrative of modernity . . . [a] narrative that privileges a singular, western-centric vision of capitalism, information or modernity."[41] To think about this term void of "placeness" puts strict limits on its connectivity and how locales are implicated in the homogenizing capitalist machinery. Transnationalism also runs the risk of taking the nation as an undisturbed framework where one does not question the effects of economies, migration, or hierarchy. However, the Chicanx transnational focus in this collection interrogates, examines, and unsettles how Castillo's texts form, circulate, and mitigate by focusing on several zones of contact and discussing the ways in which her different genres—the novel, short story, poem, critical essay, and autobiography—knit the extended Americas and the globe together in complex narratives of interdependence. Focusing on how literature produces meaning through the interconnected relations of different sites, we seek to unravel how Chicanx (and other people of color) transnational connections are possible forms of coalition.

For Castillo, situating herself physically along the US/Mexico borderlands enables this type of interconnectedness. The author moved to southern New Mexico in 2005, which she describes as "right on the border of Land Management. It's almost Texas, but El Paso, Texas, and El Paso almost considers itself part of New Mexico because El Paso has been so disenfranchised by the rest of Texas."[42] This geopolitical border space within which Castillo resides has influenced much of her writing, and especially, the settings in some of her most recognized works, including her novels *So Far from God* and *The Guardians*. The former is set in the village of Tóme, situated twenty-five miles from Albuquerque, and part of the Town of Tóme land grant settled in 1739 when the grant was issued by the Spanish crown to early settlers of the region. *The Guardians* is also set in New Mexico, along the border region between New Mexico, El Paso, and Ciudad Juárez. These select New Mexico settings are significant because they trace a long line of border politics—both demarcated by racial and political lines that reveal the importance of transnational politics addressed in Castillo's work. Tóme is situated along El Camino Real de Tierra Adentro, the route taken by Spanish colonizers as they made their way from Mexico City to Ohkay Owingeh, New Mexico, from 1598 to the late 1800s; in other words, it is a space that traces the path of settler colonialism in what is now New Mexico. The US/Mexico border space in *The Guardians*, on the other hand, is tied to other forms of border crossing. At the time of this writing, the border community in El Paso is still healing from an August 3, 2019, incident in which one of the deadliest mass shootings that targeted immigrants occurred at a

local Walmart. This act of domestic terrorism was fueled by white nationalist and anti-immigrant attitudes. More recent immigration stories are present in texts like *The Guardians* (addressed by Sandra Ruiz in this volume);
however, Castillo traces a longer line of migration in other works, including
her memoir *Black Dove* (addressed by Elena Avilés in this volume).

Transnationalism was already always central to Castillo's life and the
narrative she shares with us about her mother in *Black Dove*; it serves as
a stark reminder that the borderlands from which her family departed are
defined by a legacy of colonialism and imperialism that begins with the
genocide and dispossession of Indigenous peoples from their homelands.
Embedded within her fictional and nonfictional work, Castillo incorporates pieces of this significant history and draws attention to its broader
implications to our national and transnational narratives. When westward
expansion drove settlers west and southwest, dispossession continued for
minorities, and like the Indigenous peoples who suffered at the expense
of colonialism before them, the identities of Mexicanas/os also changed
almost overnight in matters of citizenship, national identity, and belonging.[43] The US/Mexico border space thus became a ubiquitous symbol of
erasure—a place in which Anglo domination reigned superior and any other identities and cultures were shattered and reshaped to fit the imperialist
project that guided the forming of the US nation-state.

During their moves north, many Mexicanas/os, like Castillo's family,
settled in Chicago, where a vibrant immigrant, working-class community
emerged. Even though Chicago is considered a global city, sociopolitical
borders were present in very visible ways. As Castillo recollects her experiences growing up, the reader sees that despite Chicago's multiculturalism,
multilingualism, and internationalism, she was exposed there to ongoing
resistance to unequal social, political, gendered, and cultural injustices occurring around her and told to her by her mamá. As she came of age in the
"Windy City," Castillo recognized the fact that "racial tensions were high
then" and that "color and ethnicity were important . . . , particularly in a
white-dominated city" where she was constantly reminded, "I wasn't white.
You had only to ask what any European-descended individual thought of
me. With my reddish-brown hue, indigenous features, and dark hair I inherited mostly from my mother, the usual comment was that I couldn't
even be American."[44] This passage in Castillo's memoir, *Black Dove*, and
most of the chapter entitled "Peel Me a Girl," renders visible the ways in
which the author was already always contemplating not only the role of
identity in understanding her own place in the world as a woman of color,
but also the ways in which her feminist praxis was always transnational
as it was influenced by the move her mother made to protect herself and
her children. Castillo's feminist discourse—influenced significantly by her

mother's journey north—serves as a reminder that feminist practices travel across geographical and cultural locations. Considering Castillo's work in this way reveals how she pushes temporal and spatial boundaries of Chicana feminism and Latina/o/x and Chicana/o/x literature and how her feminist praxis intersects with and impacts identity formation.

What Castillo articulates in the short passages that describe her mother's migration north and her own coming to consciousness about race invokes a transnational feminist frame from which she makes connections between gendered identity, race, culture, and nation, and the ways that patriarchy—stemming from its colonial roots—impacted her mother and then *her* inherited place within the US nation-state. With all of its global culture, and despite its physical location in relation to the US/Mexico border, Chicago becomes a space within which Castillo is demarcated by her gender and the color of her skin and where she becomes even more cognizant of the various forms of borders that surround her. Her family story of migration across the US/Mexico border and her experiences in Chicago and later, in New Mexico, also emphasize how gender, space, race, and place came to shape her work. These experiences also reveal what Caren Kaplan, Norma Alarcón, and Minoo Moallem describe as "feminist practices as part of the transnational circulation of cultures and politics as well as material goods."[45] This type of feminist production is influenced by "spatiality (territoriality/deterritorialization), temporality (time of national culture, timelessness of the nation), nationalist body politics (national body, body as landscape, landscape as feminized body, national hero as masculinized body), and nationalist heterosexual and kinship metaphors of state fatherhood and motherhood."[46] This collection interrogates and uncovers how Castillo's work functions in these ways.

Castillo's autobiographical writing gestures toward the ways these zones of contact have impacted her family history of migration, especially evident when she relays in *Black Dove* that her mother moved to Chicago with her two older siblings from the Texas/Mexico borderlands—a move her mother made because of her need to escape the older and married man who had taken advantage of her when she was just a teen. Although she experienced the impacts of patriarchal violence while still in Mexico, her mother, armed with a "machete in hand," made her way north with her children to establish her life away from Nuevo Laredo and within the bustling city of Chicago to provide for her family and to escape her traumatic past.[47] It is almost ironic that Castillo returns to the borderlands in New Mexico in her adult life to further address the politics of border subjectivity in this politically significant moment in the twenty-first century.

In *Chicana Feminisms: A Critical Reader* (2003), editors Gabriela F. Arredondo, Aída Hurtado, Norma Klahn, Olga Nájera-Rámirez, and Patricia Zavella remind us that Chicana feminists have long been interrogating the relationship between geographical space and especially the US/Mexico border space, and their histories and lived realities. They argue, "The particularities of the histories of Mexico and the United States and the realities of continuous movement within and across social locations mean that Chicanas increasingly deploy a transnational perspective that enables us to confront the clash and confluence of cultural, political, and economic disparities."[48] Castillo employs this transnational perspective and also contributes to the growing body of queer scholarship in the ways she addresses the politics of identity, gender, and sexuality that continue to impact our transborder publics. Working in tandem with Moraga's and Anzaldúa's "theory in the flesh," what they describe as

> one where the physical realities of our lives—our skin color, the land or concrete we grew up on, our sexual longings—all fuse to create a politic born out of necessity. Here, we attempt to bridge the contradictions in our experience.
> We are the colored in a white feminist movement.
> We are the feminists among the people of our culture.
> We are often the lesbians among the straight.
> We do this bridging by naming ourselves and by telling our stories in our own words.[49]

Castillo uses her fiction and nonfiction to confront and acknowledge the multidimensionality of Chicana/o/x identity. In *Black Dove* for instance, Castillo bridges the personal and the political, as she provides readers with particulars about her familial and romantic relationships, bookended by a critique of current immigration issues and her experience living along the US/Mexico border in southern New Mexico. This memoir offers confirmation of the complexity of Chicana/o/x identity, including a testimony to what it means to be a queer woman of color.

Recent studies that link American literary history, Chicanx studies, and transnationalism, such as William Orchard and Yolanda Padilla's edited collection *Bridges, Borders, and Breaks: History, Narrative, and Nation in Twenty-First-Century Chicana/o Literary Criticism* (2016), argue for the need to "loose[n . . .] commitments to nationalism that animated an earlier generation of Chicano thinking and politics."[50] Orchard and Padilla's collection builds on Ramón Saldívar's foundational 1990 study, *Chicano Narrative: The Dialectics of Difference*, in which he honors Américo Paredes's early methods and theoretical contributions to border studies. Paredes's work is identified by many border studies scholars such as Saldívar as the first scholarly intervention that emphasized a "transnationally oriented approac[h] to US literary studies."[51] Paredes grounded his discussion of border studies in Greater Mexico, emphasizing how Chicanos remain connected to and influenced by place, even when they are not physically anchored to it. Post-Paredes's early work, in the 1960s and 1970s, Chicano nationalism became grounded in a cultural and nationalist paradigm. As Marissa K. López asserts, "Chicana/o nationalism is often understood as an ethnic nationalism that makes specious claims to indigeneity, working-class roots, the myth of an Aztec heritage, and the patriarchal family."[52] This volume demonstrates how much of Castillo's work responds to the limits of the ideologies guiding this Chicano nationalist paradigm while also acknowledging the historicity and transnational construction of Chicana/o identity itself.

Like other scholars who consider Chicanx studies beyond the confines of a physical border or who understand Aztlán as "part of a broad geographic and historical continuum,"[53] in this volume, we too call for thinking beyond the boundaries of nation when we define Chicanx studies. We examine Castillo's oeuvre to demonstrate how place is but one component of Chicanx identity; however, she also challenges us to reconsider belonging in relation to place through characters who embody multiple subjectivities and who are often unbounded to place. Re-envisioning Chicanx studies as transnational allows for embracing Paredes's original emphasis on Greater Mexico as integral to border studies, while simultaneously acknowledging the ways in which Chicanx-identifying peoples transcend borders and are also connected to Latin America more broadly. This transborder approach expands how we understand the politics, culture, traditions, and memories associated with Chicanx identity. Castillo's subject matter aligns with this broader transborder focus, as she often addresses global topics such as mestizaje and environmental, economic, social, and racial (in)justice, but she also expands these discussions by drawing attention to transnational feminism, queerness, gender, and sexuality not only across the US/Mexico border, but also beyond and into the greater Américas.

Castillo's literary contributions can thus be read as transnational *and* Chicanx, or as Chicanx transnationalism, as she develops characters who build and maintain (sometimes very complex) relationships across borders. As Olga Herrera reminds us, these exchanges occur *beyond* borders, not in the service of reinforcing them.[54] In other words, national borders are designed to be dismantled. We might better characterize Castillo's Chicanx transnationalist approach as one way through which she renders visible an opening for what Saldívar labels the "transnational imaginary," a metaphor for the "complex differential double bind that the socially symbolic and the historically real always enact in the space of the transnation."[55] The transnational imaginary is a form of consciousness rooted in acknowledging the diaspora of peoples (in the case considered here, Chicanx/Latinx peoples) from their homelands, which results in cultural hybridity that transcends physical borders. Marissa K. López's assertion that "the Chicana/o struggle in the United States is intimately connected with the global struggle against oppression"[56] is useful here for better understanding why we urge reading Castillo's work through a transnational Chicanx sensibility that extends beyond Greater Mexico and into Latin America and beyond. Castillo also connects her characters, plots, and critical essays to her own experiences in which she was part of a large cadre of Chicana feminists, many of whom are queer, who united with the third world feminist movement, an important move for many feminist scholars/activists of color. The "transnational turn in Chicana/o studies," as literary scholar John M. González emphasizes, " . . . is the powerful lesson of Chicana feminism and queer studies in their own transformations of Chicana/o studies, challenging the field's imaginary of a universal Chicano subject through the specifics of bodily experience and social positionalities."[57] As we consider how and why Castillo's feminist solidarity extends beyond borders, we must understand that for Chicana feminists like her, the transnational turn extends to including what Sergio A. Gallegos identifies as transversal politics that acknowledges the need for solidarity between feminists of varying identities and perspectives of/against oppressive systems.[58] Castillo's fiction, critical essays, and memoir illustrate a distinct Chicana consciousness, one that challenges Chicano nationalism's limits around issues of gender, queerness, and sexuality. Importantly, Castillo also employs her literary work and critical scholarship to connect her plots and characters to political and cultural concerns in Latin America *and* emphasizes her commitment to rooting her work in a transnational Chicanx feminist sensibility.

For Castillo, and many Chicana authors including Gloria Anzaldúa, Cherríe Moraga, Sandra Cisneros, Lucha Corpi, Demetria Martinez, Denise Chávez, Norma Alarcón, Emma Pérez, Norma E. Cantú, Alicia Gaspar de Alba, and Yvonne Yarbro-Bejarano, to name but a few, gender and the US/Mexico borderlands are an inherent part of their identities and their narratives. In this critical moment in time, this border space is a geopolitical one embedded with diversity in the ways that Chicana/o/x, Latina/o/x, and Latin American authors theorize and translate this space and its impacts on identity formation and gender politics. Together, their work contributes to a transborder feminist political network that has engaged in transnational feminist dialogue for decades.

SO HOW DO WE TEACH CASTILLO?

Our experiences teaching Castillo's corpus of work inspired this collection a great deal. Her writings invite the exploration of constructs of gender, sex, class, and race that can be traced through multiple lenses of inquiry. Castillo's writing invigorates the curriculum with an interdisciplinary pedagogy that takes historical, political, social, and cultural context into consideration while "elasticizing" the text through multimedia forms and "mapping" the geography of the text. When introducing students to Castillo's novel *The Guardians*, for instance, it is crucial to introduce them to the 1965 Border Industrialization Program in conjunction with *The Borders Trilogy* by Alex Rivera. Looking at the history of the border in relation to the cultural production of Rivera's short films that examine the border through technology, familial ties, and transnationalism, students map the material spaces of the border in the novel and consider how filmic and historical representations of the border work in conjunction with state-sanctioned violence, racialized labor through globalization, and patriarchal violence from the text.

Along similar though not identical lines, transnationalism is also central to Castillo's 1990 novel, *Sapogonia*. Although it is less frequently taught in literature courses than her other novels, *Sapogonia* connects the United States to the broader "Americas" and the state-sanctioned violence that surged during civil wars in Central and most of Latin America in the 1970s and 1980s. Through her antihero, Maxímo Madrigal, a character students love to hate, Castillo reveals how, for Maxímo, the concept of "nation" carries with it an inherent conflict of identity and state of mind. When taught from an interdisciplinary perspective, this novel encourages discussions about what Kimberlé Crenshaw (1989) coined as intersectionality,[59] as it can be used to interrogate colonial histories and their residual effects, to examine sexuality, gender, and patriarchy, and to understand how Castillo's use of place and time is symbolic of nationalism, identity, and belonging. *Sapogonia* can also be discussed in relation to Chicana feminist theories, such as Gloria Anzaldúa's new mestiza consciousness. In this vein, Castillo's narrative can be used to demonstrate to students how the author dissolves borders to forge a new mestiza/o world, Sapogonia, where characters like Pastora Velásquez Aké reflect Indigenous, Mexican, and Spanish identity. Essays in the Teaching and Pedagogy section of this collection similarly explore the diverse ways Castillo's fiction and nonfiction work has contributed to curriculum across disciplines.

The breadth of Castillo's work is evidence of the consciousness with which she writes and lives—knowledgeable, critical, and truthful. This collection is designed to illustrate the multifaceted ways she has contributed to our understanding of literature, Chicana/o/x identity, Chicana and transnational feminism, sexuality, gender, race, and class. It is organized into five sections: I. The Chicanx Letters: Transnational Poetics, Language, and Form; II. So Far from Nation: Borders and Immigration; III. Give It to the Globe: Considering Gender and Sexuality; IV. Mamá, Mijxs, and Me: Connecting Chicana Feminism and Transnational Feminism in the Era of Globalization; and V. Teaching and Pedagogy. The essays in this collection are written by scholars from diverse fields, with differing ideological lenses and perspectives, and provide a robust and dynamic perspective of Castillo's work. To cultivate an even richer discussion, we invited foundational Chicana feminist respondents to dialogue with the authors to demonstrate the diversity of Chicana/o/x identities and the ways in which scholars across generations and gendered identities have cognized Castillo's cultural production.

CHAPTER SUMMARIES

Essays in section I of the collection, "The Chicanx Letters," address how Castillo expands boundaries around traditional literary form when she leads readers to actively engage with her work and the concepts of identity formation, nationhood, memory, and gender. Authors in this section emphasize how Castillo employs a defined Xicana feminist praxis that reveals how she navigates and responds to gender politics, sexism, and the colonial histories that have dictated our national and transnational narratives.

In her essay, Ximena Keogh Serrano calls attention to the important role that memory plays in Castillo's cultural production. Her essay, "Lettered Encounters: Ana Castillo's Poetics of Spilling in *The Mixquiahuala Letters*," centers on Castillo's 1986 novel by considering how *The Mixquiahuala Letters* reflects a "narrative style of self-weaving" that Keogh Serrano identifies as a theoretical praxis of a "poetics of spilling" that which cannot be contained. In her reading of Castillo's work, Keogh Serrano describes how letters written by one of the novel's protagonists, Teresa, to her friend, Alicia, are evidence of how Castillo creates an epistolary production that becomes a site of self-making and a record of a "*fronteriza* state of being." Keogh Serrano's engagement with Castillo's work contributes to the transcultural and trans-feminist debates of other Chicana/o/x feminist scholars, including Norma Alarcón (1989), Emma Pérez (1999), Chela Sandoval (2000), Sandra K. Soto (2010), among others.

In "For the Pleasure of the Chicanx Poet: Spatialized Embodied Poetics in Ana Castillo's *My Father Was a Toltec*," Shanna M. Salinas offers a nuanced reading of Castillo's poetry, in which she considers how it can be read as a response to the pervasive sexism and racism that exists in intellectual and academic institutions, as well as in the mainstream literary market. By claiming and making space for Chicanx poetics, Salinas argues, Castillo "remakes the Chicanx body as a *poetic* body on her own terms, as informed by pleasure and desire." This examination of Castillo's poetry reveals how she establishes a legacy of literary work deeply informed by racialized and gender-coded spaces that challenges Western paradigms. She uses the poem "A Christmas Gift" not only to introduce her argument, but as a guiding mechanism to interpret Castillo's poetry collection, *My Father Was a Toltec*.

In her reflection "Unbounded and Limitless: Ana Castillo's Poetics of Place and the Body," literary scholar and Castillo's fellow Chicagoan Olga L. Herrera addresses the ways the authors whose work comprises this section of the collection culminate in a critical assessment of the importance Castillo places on form and language in her work and the ways the transnational border space inherently permeates within her poetics; she also challenges the fixity of reading Castillo and her work as transnational, and instead suggests the author's "work is deeply invested in notions of unbounded place, nation, and belonging." As Herrera notes in her reflection on Salinas's and Keogh Serrano's essays, the authors articulate how the Chicana figure can be read as a site for negotiating subjectivity. For Castillo, this embodied Chicana subjectivity is one that transcends borders to give emphasis to women's experiences across a globally shared experience for women of color. Together, the essays in this section give new readings of Castillo's contributions to "Chicanx letters."

Section II, "So Far from Nation: Borders and Immigration," brings attention to current conversations about citizenship, national and transnational border space(s), and "border subjects'" methods of survival and resistance. The essays included in this section call attention to the ways Castillo uses her fiction and nonfiction to emphasize how the historical malleability of geographical borders impacts language, culture, and identity for those whose lives are intimately intertwined with contested border spaces.

In his essay "'¿A'ca'o qué, comadre?': Border Languages and Xicanisma in Ana Castillo's *So Far from God*," Ayendy Bonifacio engages Alfred Arteaga's theory of the linguistic borderland to emphasize the intersections between border languages and *ciudadanía* (citizenship) in Castillo's 1993 novel. Although Tóme, New Mexico, appears to be far from the US/Mexico border, Bonifacio reads the space as a linguistic contact zone, one in which Castillo introduces her readers to a larger geopolitical history that destabilizes how we conceive of nationality and citizenship. Read in this way, Bonifacio argues, the narrative guiding *So Far from God* reveals a new way to understand border languages and how they function as "transnational and malleable cultural heuristics subject to change and hybridity" that is distinctly embraced by the women in the novel.

Adding to the conversation about the complexities of border space, Tereza M. Szeghi addresses the idea of the porousness of borders in her essay, "Identity Formation and Dislocation: Transnationalism in *The Mixquiahuala Letters* and *The Guardians*." Szeghi argues that though the characters' experiences in these two seemingly diverse novels render border crossing visible in different ways, they emphasize Castillo's conviction that transnational migration is a basic human right. In *The Mixquiahuala Letters*, Teresa crosses the border with relative ease, while in *The Guardians*,

Gabo is prohibited from crossing because he lacks the legal documentation that allows him to do so. Written in 1986 and 2007, respectively, the novels appear to forecast the attempt through current "zero-tolerance" policy to reinforce fixed borders, and as Szeghi reveals, through her narratives, Castillo argues that we should instead advocate for making borders more fluid by transcending the concept of the nation. Electra Gamón Fielding also considers the porousness of borders in her essay, "Selling the 'Authentic': Performance and Hybridity in Carlos Saura's *Carmen* and Ana Castillo's *Peel My Love like an Onion*." In her analysis of Saura's and Castillo's work, Fielding both challenges and seeks to understand how "authenticity" impacts identity in a dynamic global world. She situates flamenco as a performative act that has been understood as a symbol, or "true representation of Spain" and Spanish identity, and then reveals how in *Carmen* and *Peel My Love Like an Onion*, Saura and Castillo challenge the idea of "authenticity" when they suggest through their narratives that flamenco is really a symbolic performance of identity. Fielding's essay calls our attention to the need to recognize that hybridity, rather than authenticity, is the means for survival in today's global society.

In her response to the essays in this section of the collection, Chicana scholar and fiction writer Amelia María de la Luz Montes stresses the importance of recognizing, as do the authors in this section, how Castillo calls her readers to acknowledge the complexities of nationhood and identity for those who live in the liminal space of the borderlands. In this discussion that is more pressing than ever, de la luz Montes expands the conversation to also address how Castillo, like Gloria Anzaldúa, gestures in her work toward the idea that to analyze oppressive power structures, develop a "new consciousness," and in fact survive, we might remain "far" from and, perhaps, on the margins of the nation.

"Give It to the Globe: Considering Gender and Sexuality," section III of the collection, calls attention to the ways that Castillo's cultural production transcends geographical, gendered, and sexualized borders. Thinking beyond a US Chicanx context, the essays in this section address how her work can be read as a significant contribution to both US and third world transnational feminist theory, especially in the way Castillo employs an epistemology rooted in oppositional consciousness that fashions queer spaces designed to defy boundaries.

In his/their essay "Queering Space in Ana Castillo's *Give It to Me*," Daniel Shank Cruz contends that Castillo's 2014 novel can be read as much more than an illustration of bad pornography. Rather, through this narrative, Castillo creates a "conceptual queer space" that is both political and sexual in the way it defies boundaries and archives queerness—what Sara Ahmed calls "an archive of rebellion"—through her acknowledgment of queer history, spirituality, and theory. Cruz emphasizes the importance of acknowledging Castillo as a Latinx queer author, one whose literary production traces a "transnational landscape that teaches readers how to live intersectional lives."

In her essay, Elena Avilés examines Castillo's most recent publication, *Black Dove: Mamá, Mi'jo, and Me* (2016), to make visible how the author centers motherhood through queerness, and specifically, bisexual motherhood, in her memoir. Avilés connects her discussion to the borderlands, which she argues make visible the ways Castillo revises narratives of "sex, gender, and sexuality for border-crossing women through the lens of desire." Considered in this way, Castillo's memoir can be read as a form of new poetics that calls our attention to the important relationship between motherhood, queerness, and place, and outside the "borderlands" of the straight-gay paradigm.

Liliana González continues the discussion of desire driving much of Castillo's work through her examination of *The Mixquiahuala Letters*. González plays on the notion of nostalgia as a way to look not only at the past, but also to a future envisioned by the character Teresa, one in which queer desire, social justice, and sexual futures merge. González heeds the calls of José Esteban Muñoz and Juana María Rodríguez, who note that often, queers of color are "framed as non-existent and as limited," as she addresses queer and sexual futurity by emphasizing how the letters in Castillo's novel articulate lesbian erotics and desire that offer hope for intimate connections across time and space, even in the current contested geopolitical space of the US/Mexico borderlands.

Chicana borderlands historian and gender studies scholar Emma Pérez comments on the essays in this section of the collection, especially in their treatment of the ways Castillo's novels and critical essays confront dominant ideologies about queerness, transnational feminist theory, motherhood, and gendered and sexed history. In her scholarly work over the past three decades, Pérez has similarly called attention to the fact that we need to further consider sexuality and queerness as central to our discussions of theory and resistance; in other words, she, too, leads us into a queer futurity that liberates Chicanx/Latinx generations through a potential "undoing" of heteropatriarchal constraints.

The essays that comprise the collection's section IV, "Mamá, Mijxs, and Me: Connecting Chicana Feminism and Transnational Feminism in the Era of Globalization," bring nuanced readings of Castillo's work and its contributions to female spirituality, ancestral memory, and transnational feminist solidarity. Authors included in this section also address the significant role of social justice and injustice that guides Castillo's theoretical framework.

In her essay, Laura Elena Belmonte compares Castillo's novel *So Far from God* with María Amparo Escandón's novel *Esperanza's Box of Saints* to reveal how Castillo's work is in dialogue with transnational feminist works in its representations of religion and culture across the borderlands. Through her interrogation of these two significant novels, Belmonte also demonstrates the healing and saving powers of "la madre," as she explains how Castillo and Escandón re-center women's spiritual roles and challenge the patriarchal institution of male headship in Mexican and Mexican-American religious life and culture, and across the US-Mexico border.

Rebecca Kennedy de Lorenzini's essay examines how Castillo's concept of Xicanisma can be understood within other transnational feminist and racial/ethnic experiences of the broader "Americas," especially in her poetry. In "The Unbreakable Link": Ancestral Memory in Xicanista and African Diasporic Women's Poetry," Kennedy de Lorenzini reads Castillo's poetry alongside African Diasporic poetry and explicates the connections between the two approaches to poetic expression by linking memory, border crossing, and transcultural dialogues alongside the physical and spiritual connections that are guided by "ancestral memory." Kennedy de Lorenzini's reading of Chicana and African Diasporic poetry makes clear the global contexts that bond African and ethnic Mexican women and imagines the possibilities of a more liberated future of the Americas.

Continuing this discussion and establishing a global feminist perspective that traverses transnational borders, Araceli Esparza's essay, "Feminist Imaginaries of Justice: Ana Castillo, Sister Dianna Ortiz, and Political Violence in Guatemala," considers how Castillo's poem "Like the people of Guatemala, I want to be free of these memories" and her collection of plays, *Psst . . . I Have Something to Tell You, Mi Amor*, center the disappeared as a form of justice-making, especially in how Castillo narrativizes the disappearance and torture of Sister Dianna Ortiz at the hands of the Guatemalan military. In addition to analyzing Castillo's writings, Esparza examines Ortiz's testimonio, *The Blindfold's Eyes* (2002), in which Ortiz recounts the violence she endured. Further, Esparza problematizes the contradictions of desire for solidarity and justice across geopolitical borders, and cautions against US-centered writers and scholars marginalizing and appropriating the experiences of histories of violence of Central Americans.

In her response to the essays in this section, multiethnic literary, Chicanx, and gender and sexuality studies scholar Ellie D. Hernández highlights how the authors noted above draw attention to how Castillo's oeuvre of literary production renders visible transnational subjectivity as a movement that reorients us within a new world—one in which motherhood, love, politics, justice, and identity intersect. Together, Hernández argues, the essays further contribute to discussions about how feminist of color scholarship has, historically, employed political activism and theory to disrupt systems of power. In this way, Castillo's writings reveal her commitment to a transnational feminism that is both resistant and collaborative.

The large array of Castillo's work has been taught across the nation and across the globe. Section V, "Teaching and Pedagogy," highlights four essays that address how the authors employ her novels, memoir, poems, and critical essays to expand students' understanding of transnational feminism, linguistic hybridity, identity formation, Chicana/o/x and Latina/o/x literature, and regionalism. In her essay, "Replanting You as *Winyan, Uarhiti, Kwe*: Transnational Indigena Mothering from Michoacán to Mni Sota Makoce," Gabriela Spears-Rico uses *testimonio* to reflect on her experiences as a P'urhepecha/Matlatzinca woman and mother whose personal and pedagogical work contributes to a Xicanista feminism guided by Indigenous epistemologies that allows her to reclaim traditional knowledge and embodied experiences. As she reflects on her personal history and "Xicana motherwork," Spears-Rico also describes how, as an Indigenous feminist, she employs Castillo's philosophy of Xicanisma alongside Indigenous epistemologies in what she calls a "radical feminist praxis" for which we have a pressing need, especially in our current political moment. This radical feminist praxis, Spears-Rico argues, is demonstrated in the ways Castillo encourages Chicana/o/x and Indigenous women to empower themselves through embracing ancestral, spiritual, and medicinal knowledge.

Leigh Johnson continues the conversation about the ways in which Castillo's cultural production contributes to a growing transnational feminist epistemology that challenges and confronts social constructions of family and gender identities. Using what she labels "transvisionaria poetix," in her essay, "Teaching Ana Castillo: Transnational Feminist Theory, Transvisionaria Poetix, and Practical Tips for the Classroom," Johnson argues that this praxis imagines and then enacts ways of being that are not dependent on white- or Western-dominated feminisms. For Johnson, literature is significant to this "transnational, hemispheric feminist movement and the possibilities for agency." The practical classroom tips she offers detail how she pairs Castillo's novels *So Far from God* and *Give It to Me* with her memoir, *Black Dove*, her stories in *Loverboys*, and her play, *Psst . . . I Have Something to Tell You, Mi Amor,* to render visible the agency Castillo's characters inhabit that influences them to fight for economic and political power, or her transvisionaria poetix.

Sandra Ruiz's essay reminds us to "never *stay* silent" about political issues around immigration, such as those with which we are currently faced: "mixed-status families, transborder politics, faith, and intergenerational trauma." Ruiz describes how she uses Castillo's novel *The Guardians*, alongside Héctor Calderón's notion of California as part of "Greater Mexico," to connect her students' experiences in Southern California to ways for them to better understand how marginalized and transnational communities are forced to confront these political issues in their daily lived realities. In *The Guardians*, Ruiz suggests, Castillo humanizes the experience of anxiety and trauma experienced by those who migrate, and Ruiz details how she employs new and emerging technologies and social media platforms in her classes to guide her students to become content creators who use Castillo's literature, classroom lectures, and historical documents to challenge systems of oppression.

In her essay on teaching *So Far from God*, Danizete Martínez addresses how she uses this unique and effectual novel to introduce students in the Southwest to regional writing, to have them consider the significances of folklore in contemporary literature, and also to help them understand Chicana/o/x literary production from a Chicana perspective. This approach to teaching Castillo's work from a regional perspective does not solely focus on the local, as Martínez emphasizes. The issues confronted by the characters in the novel are based on long-standing national and transnational discussions that center race, class, and gender in a global context that expands discussion of Latinx identity more broadly. Martínez's essay interrogates the challenges of teaching from this global perspective in a regional community college setting.

Chicana/o/x and Latina/o/x cultural studies scholar Norma E. Cantú brings her expertise in US Latina/o literatures and creative writing to the forefront of her response to the essays in this section of the collection. Cantú recognizes the vast contributions Castillo's work has made on pedagogical approaches to Chicana/o/x and Latina/o/x literature, Indigenous/Chicana feminisms, and identity across various campuses and addresses how the authors included in this section build on the pedagogical approaches to teaching Castillo's broad range of work. She notes that the authors whose work comprise this section also incorporate first-person narratives in their essays—perhaps a gesture to the way Castillo draws her readers into the life stories of her characters. Cantú notes that the essays in this section leave us "at a crossroads," and she reminds us that further examination of Castillo's work in our classrooms and in our scholarship will continue into the foreseeable future.

PART I

THE CHICANX LETTERS

Transnational Poetics, Language, and Form

LETTERED ENCOUNTERS

Ana Castillo's Poetics of Spilling in *The Mixquiahuala Letters*

XIMENA KEOGH SERRANO

Where, I wonder . . . is the shadow of the presence from which the text has fled?

—Toni Morrison, "Unspeakable Things Unspoken"

In Ana Castillo's 1986 epistolary novel, *The Mixquiahuala Letters*, the letter-page emerges as a space for self-weaving. It is a space of movement, and drifting habitations. In its capacity to mediate between space and time, self and other, absence and presence, the letter becomes a site of theoretical inquiry for the Chicana writer, who tactfully adopts the fictional realm of the epistle to engage with questions of boundaries and border formations.

The Mixquiahuala Letters presents a compendium of letters written from Chicana poet Teresa, to her friend Alicia, who is a New York visual artist of Spanish Gypsy roots. In her unidirectional address to Alicia, Teresa draws upon their shared experience while traveling across the United States, Mexico, and briefly through Puerto Rico in their twenties. The letters relate the formation of these two young women who are bound by friendship, cultural hybridity, and emergent desires for embodied freedom and the pursuit of the arts. Through shifting methodologies of expression, Teresa's letters interrogate the violence emitted by patriarchal codes and gendered conditionings. They express the ambiguities that emerge from cultural expectations set on women, and the psychic effects of defying expected models of behavior.

This chapter explores Teresa's modes of critical reflection and dialogic exchange over the page. In examining Teresa's narrative style of self-weaving, I argue that her traversed epistolary cartography negotiates and resists structured boundaries in cultural identity, womanhood, national belonging, and kinship. In this way, Castillo's use of the epistolary form creates a strategic space through which to question border formations vis-à-vis what I call a "poetics of spilling." I utilize the metaphor of "spilling" as a way through which to understand the epistle's rich and symbolic acts of articulation. A poetics of spilling points to what emerges outside of the confines of recorded speech. Emotion, resonance, and silence are but a few of the ungraspable elements that emerge in acts of "spilling." Here, "spilling" points to that which cannot be contained. It registers the quality of both fluidity and mess, as it evidences a form of excess. It also defies structures of legibility by its mode of revealing that which has come undone. In this way, Castillo's epistolary framing enacts a theoretical praxis wherein the epistolary form becomes the mode of embodying, shaping, and creating a record of transnational feminism, informed by her transcultural, *fronteriza* state of being.

As Teresa recounts her and Alicia's real and symbolic border crossings, she makes apparent and archives their modes of subjected fragmentation. Thus, in the process of narration, Teresa becomes both witness and cocreator of emerging scenes of the past. Meanwhile, the page also retains the affective residues that seep out of Teresa's recorded return. In this sense, that which "comes to light," as the etymological root *emergere* denotes, is a blistered understanding of the past, one that reveals itself also to be incomplete, another fragment. Through the act of crossing, however, we come to see a poetics that embraces the porous conditions of skin, space, place, and time.

READING PATHS

Set across and between the United States, Puerto Rico, and Mexico, Teresa's thirty-eight letters arrive to the reader undated. The letters are numbered, and the opening pages offer the book-holder possible reading trajectories—be it Conformist, Cynical, or Quixotic. Following Julio Cortázar's 1966 novel *Hopscotch*,[1] the reader enters the bounded cartography to thereon choose her path.

The divergent reading possibilities Castillo proposes in the novel's opening pages succinctly speak to the desire for unbounded readings. They problematize the lines of authority, cutting any possibility of wholeness to the narrative. Instead, this call onto the reader performs the idea of a self, being, and culture (always) *in the making*. Nevertheless, narrative coherence is still made possible through the letters, even through different sites of entry.[2]

In choosing to break with a single narrative path, Castillo also gestures toward the ways in which all readings are subject to continual interpretation, following a particular lens of engagement with the world. I bring attention to this dissolution of unitary path as a mode through which to engage with transnational belongings. That is, in offering up the text as an entity "in formation," Castillo plays with the notion of fixed territories and the arbitrary drawing of lines and limits. Here, the author's suggestively framed reading routes—Conformist, Cynical, or Quixotic—become loaded signifiers. Although the reader is not obligated to follow any of these organized paths, any engagement with the book-form will lead to incomplete and irresolute encounters with chrononormative time-mapping. With this, Castillo demonstrates a desire to question accustomed practices of entry. In this case, it is a matter of reimagining points of entry *into* the text and pursuing a nonlinear navigation through its pages. The book operates as an inviting territory, one wherein the reader does not have to participate in acts of expected behavior in order to access the story. Thus, the linear model of reading from one page to the next becomes denaturalized here. This is crucial to point out given the narrative conventions enacted by novels and the ways in which they call for the reader to perform a whole system of acts as they engage with the storyline.

Castillo's reimagined engagement with the epistolary form thus works to destabilize the reader's often unquestioned attunement to both the real and symbolic borders that follow suit in all reading encounters. The letters shift across space and time in order to break with the reader's spatiotemporal compass. The absence of marked chronology, which comes by the refusal to date the letters, suggests that time flows and circulates outside of a teleological bordering of time. Instead, we imagine a coexistence of the past and present, here converging, as though in a perpetual crossing.

The letters redraw the lines of experience, augmenting the texture of the past, through its reformulation in the present. In the act of reading, we come to experience new frequencies of emotion that emerge through the inscription of memory. The partial transcription of letter 2 (below) enacts this relation. Upon immediate view, the reader witnesses a defiance of convention, where the epistle appears textually in the form of a poem. In narrative prose, the text produces a summary of the years Teresa and Alicia shared while traveling in their twenties. In wishing Alicia a happy thirtieth birthday, Teresa writes:

Dear Alicia,

Finally we end the cesspool
twirl of our 20s
that will be remembered always
untainted by today's designer jeans
camouflaged makeup, sculptured fingernails
pampered feet and glittering teeth. We
shared a jar of Noxema. In the music halls
of a sacrificial temple at the ruins of Monte Albán
you changed your tampon
before the eyes of gods, ghosts, scorpions

while i watched for mortals. [. . .]
[. . .]
Finally men
no longer can
deposit memories of past love affairs
with their dirty underwear in our hampers. Our
art is not a handkerchief to wring out with sobs of
my man done gone and left me over and again
like a warped Billie Holiday record. (Just when
one thinks she can forget, the ass is knocking
on the door again.)[3]

Moving across the bounds of the present in relation to the past, the line in parenthesis points to that which returns. Like an interruption, the parenthesis seeks to explain that which lies outside of the borders of a sentence. It lies in-between, as a marker of explanation and readdress to the main line of argument. In this case, the assertion of a felt reality becomes undone gesturally through the parenthetical break. It shows how in attempting to determine the present, which happens through the pronouncement of a renewed womanhood in relation to men, a spilling occurs. The acknowledgment of this fact can even appear as Walter Benjamin's theoretical elaborations on the "angel of history" and the shattering of the past, that cannot but return as debris in the present.[4] As Benjamin's theoretical framing on historical materialism establishes, "To articulate the past historically does not mean to recognize it 'the way it really was.' . . . It means to seize hold of a memory as it flashes up at a moment of danger."[5] The historical materialist thus acknowledges that "moment of danger" and grabs hold of it, making it a scene of knowledge and recognition. In the case of Teresa here, her written line in parenthesis takes note of the past and its ever-shifting dynamic in the present. The preceding reference to a "warped Billie Holiday record" furthermore instantiates a spatiotemporal distortion, wherein the voice of *Billie's Blues* echoes over the present retelling.

WRITING THE SELF

Existent scholarship on the epistolary form points to the possibilities of self-formation through letter writing. As Paul J. Eakin asserts, "all letters represent an intent, conscious or not, of constructing the I, even if writing to construct the other."[6] Similar attitudes are held in relation to the letter's ability to preserve the self in history. Following the historical practices that have prevented women from participating in the public production of history and/or its preservation outside of the private home, letters have been seen to be important spaces through which women could relate their experiences in the world.[7] In addressing the very materiality of the letter, we come to see the way it can be understood as a living document that in some form or another marks a passing. The letter leaves a trace, becomes the symbolic habitus of experience—one that importantly travels, making its way out of the physical body and into an external world. Hence, this too invigorates my argument as it performs a "spillage."

For Anne Bower, "the epistolary heroine . . . creates a material object—the letter—that not only speaks the self, but metonymically, is the self."[8] In this material self-configuration, the letter becomes a drifting body, willing to travel and to be dispersed. In other studies on epistolary writing, the letter has also been seen as opening up a unique space through which to construct what Rebecca Earle nominates "fictions of the self."[9] In this sense, the letter permits a refashioning of the self, a making of the self, separated from the exterior forces that often aim at a facile modality of containment. That is, of an other's gaze—especially when it happens that she is routinely spoken for, by hegemonic powers. A woman's decision to express the self through the epistolary mode illuminates another theoretical approach to the woman's intent for the conservation and telling of her own history: "The letter-writing female protagonist uses the pen not only to affirm herself, not only to bridge the gap between self and other, but often to *rewrite* the self, presenting a personal self-definition that contradicts, supersedes, or supplements the identity others have assumed her to have."[10]

Teresa documents and archives a history yielded on *her* terms, operating within a logic of transgression and affective corporeality. This method of writing and history-making makes claim to feminist models of knowledge production that aim to locate intersectional struggles, and work to account for embodied subjectivities. Chicana theorists Cherríe Moraga and Gloria Anzaldúa conceptualize these forms of knowledge-making as "theory in the flesh."[11] In writing of the self, expanding upon the ways in which the writer's body enters into contact with others, and is perceived by others, Anzaldúa and Moraga make visible the gendered, racial, sexed, and cultural politics that structure personal experience.

Through Teresa's written record, the reader witnesses an intersectional framework of writing, wherein her personal subjectivity permeates the text. She speaks in her own way, one that applies to her multidimensional forms of embodiment. Beyond her corporeal registry, Teresa shifts between the styles of writing poems, offering critical analysis of past events, and serving as documentarian, to design her own mode of being read. It is here where its poetics of spilling comes to be, as a mode of theoretical purpose and feminist positioning. Teresa's thoughts and remembrances spill across the letter pages—they appear in disjointed recollections, taking on different styles of speech and form. This authorial registry by way of Castillo works to reveal the slippery factions of the self, vis-à-vis her created character, Teresa. In this way, access to a complete and unified vision of our Chicana speaker, Teresa, is purposefully made null.

While the letter-writer engages with an interlocutor via the page, she is also textually composing her multidimensionality, thereby performing a dialogue not only with the addressee, but importantly with herself. In this way, I examine Teresa's letters through a lens of self-creation and self-recognition.

Teresa fashions her epistolary writing outside of the typical form that characterizes a letter. Letters often speak from the present moment, even if conjuring scenes of past occurrences. That is, their "point of departure" tends to be the present. With Teresa, however, the temporal habitus of the present, in other words, the writing space of the "now," is oftentimes absent. Instead, the letters produce retellings of past experiences—wherein her interlocutor, Alicia, receives memory-scenes of their past. I highlight this information because it often escapes critique.[12] Yet in that lapse of consideration lies the theoretical model I argue Castillo advances with this epistolary novel. Ruptures in form, content, and style reinforce Castillo's embrace for disintegration through which she models the very idea of movement across space and time—a proposition made possible through the letter as a unique trans-operative medium. By holding onto scenes of the past and reworking them into the present page, we come to see a challenge to linear modalities of time that cohere to social values of narrative expectation. Teresa plays with the modes of expectation attached to the letter-page, as already seen by the absence of dates in all of the letters. Bordering outside the fictional frame, we also come to see Castillo's positionality on the case of reading engagements with her novel.[13]

Teresa's modes of articulation also work rhetorically to make her interlocutor a participant in the scenes of memory-making and self-weaving. This occurs in more explicit ways by means of interpellation—that is, by calling Alicia into question. In a number of instances, Teresa cuts her narrative exposition to directly engage with Alicia: "Do you know the smell of a church?" (letter 4); "There were three of us then, remember?" (letter 10); "Do you remember that tepid afternoon in Washington Square?" (letter 8).

Another way in which Castillo's lettered index breaks with the provisions of lettered correspondence is by its discontinuous, unstructured, and divergent styles of invocation and farewell. Teresa's letters do not follow a model of salutation upon the entry to the page, nor do they pursue a formulaic approach to addressing her friend in writing. Ranging between modes of address, which include the conventional "Dear Alicia," and its direct form "Alicia," Teresa also plays with her interlocutor's participatory reading, by introducing lines outside of the quotidian models of etiquette.

The variation in context and form (as seen in the chronological selection below) delivers a deliberate refashioning of the epistolary form:

Letter	Mode of Address
Six	Remembrances on a January day,[14]
Seven	Alicia,[15]
Thirteen	Alicia, why i hated white women and sometimes didn't like you,[16]
Fourteen	Hermana,[17]
Fifteen	So Alicia, as you may reluctantly recall:[18]
Eighteen	In Mexico[19]
Nineteen	You wanted to decipher one day,[20]
Thirty-Five	Oh Alicia,[21]

In parallel form, Teresa's signature is often slippery, unbound to a sole enunciation. She signs with "Tere" or "Teresa" or "T.," and many times the letters conclude without a signature, producing therein another form of unboundedness and discontinuity. These shifting styles in writing exemplify Teresa's unwillingness to submit to one sole way of being, pointing instead to a perpetual dissolution of self, a self unwed to fixity, always in the making.

IN SPILLING

Letters gather as much linguistic production as they do unconscious revelation. As such, we might say that in the act of dialogic transcription, *desvíos*[22] (detours), or insightful readings, emerge.

Acts of spilling also point to the unsaid, to the tone through which the words emitted linger after reading. They point to the residues that emerge from the (un)written. Here lies a gestural presence marked by its absence. The letter-page becomes a site shaped by its own bordered registry. Forms of desire are bordered from linguistic production, thereby suggesting a propensity for succumbing to expectations in speech and written behavior. Letter 11 plays with these felt realities, as Teresa introduces her thoughts on her relationship with Alicia, to then shift the course of the letter entirely. It opens with the assertion:

Dearest Alicia,

When i say ours was a love affair, it is an expression of nostalgia and melancholy for the depth of our empathy.

We weren't free of society's tenets to be convinced we could exist indefinitely without the demands and complications one aggregated with the supreme commitment to a man.

> Even greater than these factors was that of an ever present need, emotional, psychological, physical . . . it provoked us nonetheless to seek approval from man through sexual meetings . . . [23]

Then, the letter shifts in tone and content (visually rendered in a cursive font), where Teresa captures an erotic meeting between Alicia and a man:

> You lay flat on your belly
> [. . .]
> closed your eyes and waited
> [. . .]
> with the help of his confident hands
> worked past thighs horizontally
>   clumsily
> over calves and each naked foot
> on the sofa
>   across the room
> i closed my eyes
>   went on
> with my nap[24]

Although Teresa does not participate in this encounter, she exposes her knowledge of the event, as she lies "napping" somewhere in the vicinity. Just as the scene turns sultry in Teresa's exposition of minute details between her friend and the man of "expert fingers"[25] and "confident hands,"[26] it quickly cuts desire cold. In recalling the nap, the letter ends with a sense of undoing, and closes with a curt "T."—nothing else. This quick and inadvertent gesture marks a form of longing that reverts to the idea of their friendship like "a love affair," one that appears cut off by unnamed, but arguably traceable, social codes.

Although at times Teresa willingly breaks with normative codes of behavior prescribed to her being, she also inadvertently reproduces the structured bounds that organize female public life. A knowledge of this oscillation appears through the novel's epigraph from Anaïs Nin's *Under a Glass Bell*: "I stopped loving my father a long time ago. What remained was the slavery to a pattern." Castillo's election here is purposeful. With it, she points to how patriarchal codes mark social formulations of self and webs of relation. They are embedded in social structures and become naturalized through gendered norms of behavior.

In calling upon the fluid connotations attached to a poetics of spilling, I point to the letter's capacity to exhibit the porous and shifting qualities inherent (albeit structurally obscured) to state and social constructs of border control. Important to note are the ways in which the contours of skin, and its corporeal racialization and gendering, constitute a form of bordered control. By this, I point to the ways in which Teresa and Alicia's bodies are read across the varying geographies of their joint transit. Of equal importance is the way they each inhabit the geographical spaces through which they move—thereby relating the experience of cultural formation and internalized codes of behavior. Throughout her letters, Teresa exposes her struggles with subscribing to the gendered models of Latinidad imposed upon her. She marries young and, upon later leaving her husband, is subject to harsh social critique. Meanwhile, Alicia's "partially white" lineage, along with her liberal upbringing in Manhattan, engenders a different kind of political identity and socialization. Teresa registers these differences time and again:

> i hated white women.   You knew when we first met
> sensed it all over my Antarctic pose: i didn't want to be
> your friend—you, some WASP chick or JAP from Manhattan's
> west side and we could not possibly
>> relate.
> But i was only half right. You were partially white
> raised moderately comfortable.[27]

Furthermore, in relating the known and recurrent forms of female competition in heterosexual realms, Teresa notes: "You had been angry that i never had problems attracting men. You pointed out the obvious, the big breasts, full hips and thighs, the kewpie doll mouth. Underlining the superficial attraction men felt toward me is what you did not recognize. i was docile."[28]

The brusque closing line here serves as a lens through which to understand a kind of wounded recognition, a knowledge that arrives through a close study and reflection of the ways cultural upbringing traverses the self, in consciously unwanted ways.

In letter 9, Teresa recalls her arrival to the summer institution in Mixquiahuala. She is twenty, and visibly banded in marriage, which in many ways seems to perplex Alicia:

"Since we met that summer in Mexico you believed I'd no business being married, eyed my wedding band as if it were a shackle, found it incomprehensible that any woman of your generation would willingly commit herself to slavery. I don't think I ever told you the story of when I reached the cracks of my dilemma and finally made a break for it."[29]

In writing Alicia, Teresa is also able to work through cultural aspects of their being that were seemingly unaddressed in the past, not in a way that would be clear and decisive as the letters point to in the present. Letter 3 bears the imprint of this retrospective look: "Now I think I know how you saw me that first summer, although at times I was ethereal to you. I was part of the culture that wouldn't allow me to separate. You, on the other hand, saw your sign isolated, even unwanted by men and their world, observed me from that reality."[30] The marked distance between the moment in time from their original encounter to the present remembrance provides a space to articulate the societal codes to which these two women *felt* and were subjected.

The conditions that mark female subjectivity at a young age are present in almost all *The Mixquiahuala Letters*. The politics of womanhood, race, gender, and sexuality surface in ways that are important to address here, for they instantiate layered visions through which to unveil the psychosocial violence(s) that become naturalized in women's formation and everyday living. Through her letters, Teresa is able to capture the social tensions that inhabit and surround young women's bodies. In their case, they are two young, attractive women in their twenties, who time and again become subject to varying degrees of objectification. On one occasion Teresa notes, "What was our greatest transgression? We traveled alone."[31] Lines like this one subconsciously reveal, or consciously reproduce, the patriarchal language that deems the travel of two women together as equal to "traveling alone." Linguistically, this line points to the nullification of female sovereignty, as registered within a patriarchal view.

In traveling together, Teresa and Alicia challenge the models of "staying in place" that had fervently dictated social norms for women of their time.[32] Although Teresa is married, in traveling outside of her country of residence (the United States) and in choosing to travel without her husband, she defies the bounds of behavior dictated within the social habitus.

During these years, Teresa and Alicia experience the harsh realities of young womanhood proffered by sociocultural systems that force them to fit into models of desirability. Alicia unknowingly falls in love with a married man, who is only interested in her "white, North American" status. At one point, Teresa is jilted at the altar by a man who calls off their wedding via a telegram.[33] In the middle of Washington Square, a pimp tries to sell Teresa on the opportunities of sex work. Scenes of an often male predatory gaze accumulate over the pages and demonstrate what Teresa at one point names as "the constant affront to our beings."[34] These experiences illustrate what scholar Norma Alarcón deems to be Teresa and Alicia's failed "erotic quest": the disappointed search for romantic love under the regime of heteropatriarchy.[35] Meanwhile, critic Sandra Soto importantly notes the racialized component of this erotic quest.[36] Both women's ethno-racial positionality (Teresa's Indigenous roots and Alicia's mixed heritage) account for their often conflicting and uneven romantic pursuits.

In the majority of the letters, the theme of romance and failed heterosexual love come to surface. Through their various routes of transit, men enter the scene in pursuit of Teresa and Alicia—in trains, on the beach, and other liminal zones—sometimes with conflicting intentions. Anne Bower's critical analysis of *The Mixquiahuala Letters* identifies Teresa's epistolary writing as a "site of remapping," wherein *"remapping"* serves to respond to "the historic link between conquest of land and conquest of the female body that has characterized patriarchal societies."[37] Other critics have similarly drawn upon themes around Teresa and Alicia's homosocial bond and its relation to their contested national filiation.[38]

The retelling of encounters with men make evident the women's struggles for valorization. Furthermore, these accounts reveal Teresa and Alicia's ability to navigate the patriarchal world and its codes of female domination. We come to see their strategies of resistance, their tools of engagement within a system that continually undermines their wit and independence. Hence, these letters function as modes of working through the patriarchal harms that have come to inhabit the body. The histories of experience contained in the letters, the critiques, the making sense of what happened all work as a form of building an archive. In written form, the letters draw upon a mestiza consciousness that, following performance studies scholar Diana Taylor, *"tells* a history and . . . *embodies* a history."[39] Thus, the narrative record of the past *spills* from Teresa's embodied memory. It constitutes an extension of the self, *reaching out* to the other (Alicia), enacting a space for remembrance and unbounded kinship.

In a letter that details Teresa and Alicia's encounter with two engineers on a train, we learn about the ways in which they grow cynical of male interest. Contending with their own erotic desires, they participate in the play of romantic quest often attached to these heterosexual encounters. Yet it serves to point out the ways in which desire enters Teresa and Alicia's friendship. On occasion, Teresa's letters utter words imbued with notes of romance toward Alicia. In recollecting aspects of their travel and critiques of their environment, her tone shifts in admiration: "In our room at the boarding house, we laughed. This, above all, i've treasured in having known you. How you made me laugh behind the closed door, away from critical strangers. You told me of your lover, Rodney, back home with big yellow eyes."[40] In these scenes, the unconscious pen slips over paper and records that which drifts from linear recollection. Staggering acts of admiration clutter the page, which on some occasions result in the letter closing without signature.[41] This gestural absence could highlight a longing that, in its push to call onto the other, falls into silence.

Kinship is created by the letter's ability to transcend space and time, by mode of calling upon the other, over the page. The letters also work as a space to address the limits of speech and the working-through traumas of the past. Their mode of exposing feeling outside of the realms of Western norms of the "legible" speak to the feminist politics of considering the epistemology of emotion. Emotions function as a form of knowing, which have the ability to *resound*. That is, they occupy an amorphous space that cannot be delimited. The emotional residues permeate the text as a way of unsettling imagined lines of recounted experience. Ahead, I look at the ways in which they function in relation to practices of record-keeping. I address the importance of tracing Chicana experiences in the cultural imaginary, a space where they are often absent. Yet, through Castillo's epistolary novel, we gather emotive evidence of stories untold.

Scenes of travel make up a great number of Teresa's letters to Alicia. Interestingly, the syntactical form of these letters consciously builds a memorial to events, and their emotional resonance across time. In this way, Teresa's narration performs an archive—one which dutifully and with detail lays claim to their personal histories and shared events. In some instances, we see meticulous constructions of the setting, alongside the recollection of feeling inscribed over the page. Letter 3 demonstrates this mode of record:

> My sister, companion, my friend.
> Our first letters were addressed and signed with the greatest affirmation of allegiance in good faith
> passion bound
> by uterine comprehension. In sisterhood. In solidarity. A strong embrace. Always. We were not to be separated. A fine-edged blade couldn't have been wedged between our shared consciousness, like two huge slabs of stone placed adjacent with inexplicable precision by the Incas.[42]

Similarly, Teresa enters the canvas of the page to record not only her history of travel with Alicia, her own past, but interestingly, she also recounts experiences that belong solely to Alicia. In this way, we come to see the different moments that individually mark their lives and personal formation, moments that linger in the paths of both women, as they relate to an interwoven kinship.

TO PERFORM AN ARCHIVE

In her studies on the colonial specters that haunt the postcolonial subject, Ranjana Khanna interrogates states of melancholia across geopolitical terrains. Khanna addresses the postcolonial intellectual as being "haunted by a call of justice for the future."[43] I call attention to this articulation as it amplifies a figurative understanding of the kind of work I see Castillo performing through her epistolary novel. The letters in this text create a bond of (a)filiation that extends beyond its literary representation.

Letter 5, for example, becomes a record of Alicia's racial and cultural education. Teresa's language in this letter operates as a kind of descriptive memory-scene that withholds any form of personal judgement. It simply records the moment wherein Alicia shared this recollection, while they were both "on a palm strewn beach in Puerto Rico."[44] Teresa thus builds a scene within a scene. Shifting chronologies, she proceeds by signaling to Alicia's Gypsy roots:

> Your grandmother, on your father's side was from Andalucía and part gypsy. She sang, with a spine-tingling guttural voice, lyrics you never understood but felt just the same. There was one melody, a lullaby, that your mother learned and sang to you on nights when the demons that search for children hid under your bed.
>
> [. . .]
>
> Your parents had never wanted anything to do with that mongrel race, the lost tribe, and fought in America for American ideals and the American way of life.[45]

The closing lines produce a shifting movement between time and the discomfort of racist values (as demonstrated by Alicia's family). Without including any farewell line, Teresa concludes the letter stating: "We flipped the sand that rippled between our toes and looked around at the mimosa of Puerto Rican faces, making a mental note to ask your parents what those ideas had been. Teresa."[46] Teresa includes Alicia's history as an act of political solidarity. By addressing the harms of personal experience that also form part of Alicia's personal trajectory, Teresa demonstrates how these pasts also belong to her being. They run through her, like what we might envision as bloodlines, yet here they operate through a model of affiliation. This, I contend, functions as a practice of transnational feminism. In conceptualizing the expression of colonial wounds in transnational women's experience Khanna posits how: "Women carry with them incorporated traumas swallowed whole, traumas that manifest themselves as continuing symptoms and traces where the anticolonial struggle is still so new and relevant. Political failures have brought about a disidentification with the nation that failed to represent women."[47] Repeatedly, we come to see the ways in which the nation fails both Teresa and Alicia, thereby resulting in Khanna's notion of disidentification: "It is this disidentification, of the melancholic recognition of the suffering of another as one's own 'unjustifiable violation' that . . . allows for coalitions between women internationally where a concept of justice is forged in the full knowledge of the thorniness of the specters of colonial relations and local abuses of women."[48] Khanna's theoretical framing is useful for understanding how Teresa reproduces Alicia's "unjustifiable violation" over the page, therein marking its own residual reverberation over her being. This episode portends a perverse turn of events for Alicia, who, at age seventeen, is sterilized at the hands of medical staff while posing as a "Puerto Rican woman who had already borne five children."[49] When the romantic idea of bearing a child with her boyfriend Rodney turns dim, as he "stop[s] coming around," Alicia borrows a friend of a friend's welfare card to undergo a legal abortion. The ethnoracial demarcation of this borrowed card determines Alicia's reproductive future. During the 1960s, the United States would partake in forced sterilization of Puerto Rican women on the island as part of its population control program developed by the eugenics board.[50] In the decade that followed, these practices would continue across the mainland, mainly targeting poor women of color.[51] Latinas would bear the brunt of this abuse most notably in states like New York and California.[52] The racist legacies of empire become the deciding rule over Alicia's body and her possibilities for procreation. As Teresa notes in letter 35, "There would be no babes to caress and coo, none to worry and fuss over, no bittersweet reflections in your twilight years of how they had grown up so quickly and gone off on their own."[53] Instead, the mark of (re)production emerges outside of the biopolitical state and sphere. The letter closes highlighting Alicia's opening art show, where "your strangeness had at last manifested itself in genius."[54] "There were traces of Frida Kahlo," she continues, and thereon establishes a transnational web of comradery, linked by womanhood and art production.[55]

The questions of lineage and reproduction also become grounds of interrogation and reimagining in the case of Teresa. As already noted, she eventually leaves the husband she married as young woman. In recalling a visit to him in letter 39, she mentions how "i'd left him because i thought i was fighting a society in which men and women entangled their relationships with untruths."[56] Teresa's break from marriage constitutes an ideological act that symbolically destabilizes the heteropatriarchal regime, and its quest for national reproduction. In fact, in the very composition of letter 39, we also learn how Teresa becomes a mother. Her visit to her ex-husband leads to her pregnancy, but following this engagement, she never contacts the father to share the news. Instead, she mentions how "when i was pregnant, i went to an exhibition of prints by an Italian artist. They were sardonic, comical, erotic, melancholy. i didn't meet him or ever see him, but the work touched a certain cord in those months. His name was Vittorio somebody."[57] Teresa names her son Vittorio. This christening signifies a purposeful break with patrilineal practices in naming. In noting the very absence of the artist Vittorio's last name, not to mention his complete unknowability to her, outside of his work of art—Teresa furthermore dislodges the patrilineal rituals of family formation.

Emma Pérez's foundational text on what she termed the "decolonial imaginary" functions through the lens and practice of *his*tory.[58] That is, it works to challenge the hegemonic narratives that have dominated the

field, reproducing a cis, male, heteronormative, able-bodied, and teleological gaze, while actively working to suppress non-Western "rules of order."
Pérez's intention lies in "taking the "his" out of the "story," the story that
often becomes the universalist narrative in which women's experience is
negated."[59] In examining the Chicana's entry into the oppositional grounds
that time and again have rejected her being, she traces non-Western epistemologies and actively engages with theories of epistemological and ontological difference. Although at times Teresa reproduces colonial readings of
the Mexican nation-state and her ancestral heritage, these visions work to
problematize the contradictions embodied by a transcultural subject. They
reveal the ways in which occidental thinking practices permeate all structures of living.

As already noted by scholars like Norma Alarcón and Sandra Soto, Castillo's cultural understanding of Mexican culture and what seems to be
Latinidad overall, often suffers from orientalist misconceptions, or what
Norma Alarcón deems to be "Castillo's Anglo-American political and sexual angle of vision."[60] The romance of the land of Mixquiahuala, figured in
Teresa's words as a "pre-Conquest village of obscurity, neglectful of progress, electricity notwithstanding," speaks to the Orientalist gaze that speaks
to the West as an emblem of progress.[61] Nevertheless, and as other critics
have noted, Mixquiahuala also "appears in this text as an unstable sign
for the search of origins, rather than an origin in itself."[62] In this way, we
can locate a transnational feminism invigorated by a memorialization of
histories of coloniality that have worked across time, space, gender, and
sexuality. The illusion of monolithic origins speaks to a rejection of a unitary homeland. The very nomadism that characterizes Alicia's Gypsy roots
also works to challenge conceptions of national filiation. As such, Teresa
builds a model of transnational kinship with Alicia by incorporating their
divergent struggles across trans-generational lines and histories.

Castillo asserts a politics of transnational feminism most acutely
through Teresa's interweaving of what we might cast as colonial specters
that haunt a woman's emotional life. Teresa relates story upon story of her
and Alicia's romantic experiences with men, most of which are negative.
Letter 32 expresses: "Love? In the classic sense, it describes in one syllable
all the humiliation that one is born to and pressed upon to surrender to a
man."[63]

Through an economy of accumulation, we come to witness the weight
of the oft objectifying gaze of men, their tactics of conquest and subjugation. Important to note here, is the way these experiences work in relation
to the histories of colonial power and domination over geographic regions
of colonial rule. From these archives of experience, Teresa marks a return
to the body, a return to *the land*, that like Georgia O'Keeffe once fittingly

noted can be understood as "the skin of the earth."[64] A skin *feels*. Histories of affect continue to perplex the arbiters of Western indices of knowledge production and its assumed sciences of quantification. Yet, it is precisely in the inarticulate form of the *feeling* that we come to engage with sites of ruin. Emotions spill. They hurry through the under-skin and differentially claim space. Their habitus is one of movement, as the etymological frame of emotion suggests. From *emovere*, as in "the feeling of bodily change."[65]

As other scholars have noted, Castillo's letters "resist [a] totalizing interpretation."[66] Larkin points to the theoretical contributions posited by critics like María Lugones, who makes sure to point to the ways in which the "liberatory possibilities" opened up by "Latina writers who emphasize mestizaje and multiplicity."[67] Thus, Castillo's work plays with various modes of embodied multiplicity, wherein the letter-form amplifies the possibilities of engagement for the Chicana writer, whose textual performance and identity are in constant re-signification and spilling.

Castillo strategically chooses the epistolary mode as a way through which to illuminate the experience of the Chicana woman, who is subject to continual ways of being and feeling undone. These instances emerge narratively, as seen through Teresa's discursive shifts, temporal movements, and stylistic and embodied retelling of a shared past. Thus, the letter as medium of exchange opens a generative space through which to create the self. Teresa's letters to Alicia produce an ally-ship, a commitment to self-creation and self-exploration, persisting in the edge of multiplicity instead of inhabiting a sense of wholeness.

Castillo writes the body through the epistle as a means through which to construct a knowledge system that in its genre realm of "epistolary fiction" mirrors the lived experience of gendered subjectivity. That is, it ebbs and flows, and it cuts through lines of space and time so as to construct something akin to what Ann Cvetkovich powerfully labels "an archive of feelings."[68] Under this title, Cvetkovich builds a repository of memory[69] that speaks to Castillo's fictional epistolary. Teresa's letters can be read as fragments that unveil practices of bordered formation. They record scenes of experience that render visible the wounds of coloniality—through its lines of racialization, codes of gendered and sexed behavior, cultural "failings," and quests for belonging. Castillo's use of the letter-form works to dissolve expected lines of formation. It aims to cross, as crossing forms, and space, and time, constitutes its very basis of production. In coming to see this mode of self-scattering, we come to understand identities that lie (in) between interstices: identities that spill, like the unconscious memory over the page, over human-made boundaries.

CHAPTER 2

FOR THE PLEASURE OF THE CHICANX POET

Spatialized Embodied Poetics in Ana Castillo's *My Father Was a Toltec*

SHANNA M. SALINAS

In the first stanza of Ana Castillo's poem "A Christmas Gift for the President of the United States, Chicano Poets, and a Marxist or Two I've Known in My Time," she centers the Western canon and literary tradition, evoking the image of the male philosopher-poet:

> i've left philosophy to men,
> heirs to their classics,
> lovers of silk-laden
> self-aggrandizing perceptions.
> Poetry, too, belongs to them,
> which is attributed to their feminine side,
> mystification of nature, and
> relentless desire to be divine.[1]

As the poem continues, Castillo draws a definitive line between those poets who write "verses" and the "not poems" her poetic speaker creates: "i grapple with nonexistence, / making scratches with stolen pen."[2] Throughout the poem, Castillo emphasizes the speaker's inability to attain poetic "legitimacy" on the following criteria: content, "Rape is not a poem. / Incest does not rhyme"; ethnic identity, "my Nahua eyes / and Spanish surname"; and language, "English syntax / makes its way to my mouth / with the grace of a clubbed foot."[3] By the poem's culmination, the speaker no longer seeks or desires this denied legitimacy; instead, she asserts a new motivation: "i shall read for pleasure, / write for pleasure."[4]

I begin with a synopsis of this poem in order to establish my chapter's primary undertaking: to highlight Castillo's interrogation of institutionalized racism and sexism within academic spaces, particularly how they impact the production of knowledge, inform the canonization of certain types of literature, and result in the exclusion of non-Western perspectives, narratives, and poetic forms. In this essay, I use "A Christmas Gift" not only to introduce this foundational terrain, but as a guiding mechanism to interpret Castillo's poetry collection, *My Father Was a Toltec*. I examine Castillo's positioning of poetic legacy and inheritance alongside the socio-historical construction of race and gender, wherein the foreclosure of academic spaces for the queer Chicanx female poet is concurrently informed by other gender-coded spaces.[5] I contend that Castillo infiltrates these academic spaces that would otherwise delegitimize her poetry through use of conventional poetic language and imagery; however, she utilizes these conventions in order to reimagine poetic representation, subvert traditional form, and carve out new space for Chicanx poetics. This contestation allows Castillo to refute the conventional poetic and gender markers operational within a Western framework. In turn, she not only reconstitutes the role of the poet, but she remakes the Chicanx body as a *poetic* body on her own terms, as informed by pleasure and desire, or what Castillo describes in her introduction to *Toltec* as writing "in a state of ecstasy."[6] I argue that, by reconstituting poetry as a site of pleasure, Castillo creates a Chicanx poetics that not only imagines but seeks to represent new literary possibilities within racialized gender paradigms of sexuality.

Mary Pat Brady's *Extinct Lands, Temporal Geographies* provides insight into how we can demarcate academia as both a physical site—the academic institution itself—and a discursive space, through the knowledges produced at, by, and about it.[7] As Brady contends, the "production of space" is not simply the physicality of the academic building itself or even the larger institutional network of higher education, but the "processes that shape how these places are understood, envisioned, defined, and variously experienced."[8] Paramount to these processes is the manner in which colleges and universities have been, and continue to be, entrenched within capitalist white supremacy and heteropatriarchy. In *Ebony and Ivy*, Craig Steven Wilder traces the academic institution's roots in and dependency on slavery and workers of color in tandem with a knowledge production steeped in biological racism.[9] Chris Newfield's *Unmaking the Public University* interrogates the mythos of equal access to education by highlighting the corporatization of institutions of higher learning and the "economic war" waged against the college-educated middle class.[10] Furthermore, Peter McLaren's *Life in Schools* centers pedagogical practices that negatively impact lower working class students and students of color from advancing through the system, applicable across varying levels of education.[11] The edited collection *Presumed Incompetent* highlights the inequalities women of color faculty experience, including disproportionate teaching or service requirements, the foreclosure of pathways that could secure tenure advancement, and uncompensated labor expectations (e.g., mentoring students of color).[12] For Brady, spatial production and maintenance depend on "narrative," or the "tradition, myths, and meanings ascribed to space, including how places are discussed or named and the grammatical structures that regulate their production."[13] The historical legacy of academia as an elite white male space structures and determines its navigation accordingly. Within academia, Brady's "productive narrative" encompasses both the foundational myths told about the purpose and utility of academic study, as well as the literature used to advance this study.

Literary tradition and mastery of the canon, while an important foundation for literary knowledge, centers and privileges white male authors at the expense of women, people of color, and LGTBQIA+ writers. Therefore, the insistence on literary tradition for tradition's sake ensures the continual reproduction of academic exclusion. Ana Castillo, a self-described bisexual Xicana writer, describes her experiences in academia, both as a student and an educator, noting that she was "timid" and "wary" and frequently felt "overlooked or ignored outright."[14] Sandra Cisneros, a poetic contemporary of Castillo's, speaks to her own hesitancy about her place within academia: "I was too afraid to apply for a teaching job at an institution of higher learning even though I had an MFA from the Iowa Writers' Workshop. . . . [It] might confirm my worst fears—that I didn't belong in the world of letters, that I wasn't smart enough, good enough."[15] Cisneros's and Castillo's reflections about feeling silenced, unseen, or as if they were unqualified interlopers in academia, while individual testimony, highlight larger systemic patterns affecting the Latinx community more broadly, specifically women, women-identified, and queer writers, who do not see themselves reflected in or entitled to academic spaces.

The era during which both Castillo and Cisneros were pursuing their degrees, writing, and attempting to publish their work is of particular importance because, as Castillo attests, there was a paucity of Latinx representation within academia and publishing in the 1970s and 1980s: "US Latinos and Latinas were not being published in the mainstream. A few men—Piri Thomas in the sixties and, at the other extreme of thought and consciousness much later, the essayist Richard Rodriguez—became prominent. But Latinas were not yet considered."[16] Not only were Castillo and Cisneros writing poetry without Latinx mentors and models, but without other Latinas, much less Chicanas, whose literary output would help make their literary work legible to readers. Cisneros recalls the feedback she received on her poetry collection *My Wicked Wicked Ways*, noting that "one male friend found [it] disappointingly unwicked, but he was looking for wicked as defined by a man, or perhaps a white woman."[17] In this example, Cisneros's reader brings frameworks and definitions informed by a white male gaze, not only because this reader is a white man, but because he was trained to read and interpret in accordance with a Western canon. Without any mainstream Latinx writers, particularly any writing about subject matters concerning Chicanx gender and sexuality, writing like Cisneros's won't be legible or accessible because it can only be evaluated by and through the existing literary field. Thus, Cisneros not only needed to "invent herself," but also invent a poetics that would insist on its own legitimacy.[18] As Castillo remarks, the "road ahead," or the creation and emergence of her spatialized embodied Chicanx poetics, had to be "paved with sheer force of will."[19]

While Cisneros attended what is considered to be the most prestigious MFA program, the Iowa Writers Workshop, Castillo opted to forego writing training altogether: "Having no models that spoke to my experience and my languages, I decided that I would never ever take—and have never taken—a workshop or writing class at any time anywhere. I was afraid I'd be told I had no right to poetry."[20] Castillo attests that she was "intent on being a good poet" but "had to carve out for [herself] the definition of 'good.'"[21] There is, of course, a tension inherent in "good" as a descriptor, further noted by Cisneros's reflection about what she learned in her graduate poetry workshops at Iowa: "It was assumed that if you wrote poems you had to publish them, or you weren't a real poet."[22] While "good" can be seen as a subjective valuation, it takes on a different connotation with the evaluation of literature. In this case, "good" poets get published, and published poets are seen as the only "real poets." Publishing one's work grants legitimacy and bestows recognition within literary circles and academia. The embedded logic of this equation presumes that unpublished poets simply haven't met the evaluation standard that determines "good"; it likewise contributes to a constructed fallacy that continues to justify the exclusion of women poets, poets of color, and queer poets.

This dynamic can account for why Cisneros would describe her developing voice in the academy as "unpoetic" and the writing she produced in her program as "trying as best as I could to write the kind of book I'd never seen in a library or in a school."[23] In fact, Cisneros claims she actively worked *against* the academy to form her poetics: "Each week I ingested the class readings, and then went off and did the opposite. . . . It was out of this negative experience that I found something positive: my own voice."[24] This oppositional approach functions almost like reverse modeling, in place largely to account for the absence of Latinx poets in her program, as well as for the gaps in her academic training as a poet: "I'd been trained to think about where a line ended or how best to work a metaphor. It was always the 'how' and not the 'what' we talked about in class."[25] In this instance, the "how" and "what" are presented as incompatible or, at the very least, distinctly unrelated. The elevation of the "how"—style and form—at the expense of the "what"—content and subject matter—can likely explain why Castillo didn't initially consider herself a poet, but instead identified as a member of a larger constituency of artists: "For a long time, I considered myself not-first-a-poet but a component of the growing Latino artists' community that had begun cutting across borders with machete-like vigor throughout the Americas and Caribbean."[26] The metaphoric action of cutting across borders, and therefore through barriers, can be likened to the way in which poets like Castillo and Cisneros had to contend with the rigidity of academia, the essentializing of poetry, and evaluation procedures that determine what constitutes poetry.

The development from "not-first-a-poet" and "unpoetic" to the creation of a Chicanx poetics can be better understood through José Limón's historicizing of a "Chicano poetics," which emerged during the Chicano movement in the late 1960s and early 1970s and was formed in response to textual predecessors and the social climate of the era. Limón contends the Mexican *corrido*, the social protest form for writers like Américo Paredes, served as a catalyst for *el movimiento* poets' "own strong social poems."[27] *Corridos* serve as the "master poems" that must be recontextualized, or *re-textualized*, in order to represent current political concerns.[28] In this way, Limón substantiates the Chicano poetic canon with male poets, thereby showcasing how a poetic tradition replicates itself. In *Chicano Poetics*, Alfred Arteaga similarly formulates a "poetics of Aztlán," but this poetics is "grounded in the body" and is comprised of Chicano and Chicana poets.[29] Arteaga coins the term *heterotext* to account for the way "sex and text" demarcate "textual difference"; however, notably, heterotext poetics relies on heterosexual reproduction as his primary qualifier, a legacy he originates with the colonial union of Hernán Cortés and Malinche.[30] Such theorizations of Chicano poetics promote a heterosexist and masculinist tradition created from a selfsame literary and cultural paradigm. This framework for Chicano poetics effectively functions as a "master poetics" that requires re-textualization by Chicana poets. While Elizabeth Ordóñez acknowledges that the Chicana poet likewise emerged from struggles within *el movimiento*, she argues that the theme of sexuality became a "poetic vehicle" to explore racialized gendered positionality.[31] As such, "sex and text" must consider textual bodies concurrently alongside actual bodies. In this regard, the reconsideration of La Malinche, at once a historical figure and a cultural byproduct, by Chicana scholars and artists beginning in the 1970s served as a resistance to "women-gendered forms of ethnonationalism."[32] Above all else, Chicanas sought to wrest poetry from the grasp of patriarchal, masculinist representational modes.

Norma Alarcón examines how Castillo confronted the "textual politics" of this period by using desire as a tactical force in *The Invitation*, the poetic precursor to *Toltec*.[33] Alarcón argues that Castillo stages a textual intervention with Octavio Paz's *Labyrinth of Solitude*, in addition to other prominent texts, to rescript and reinscribe Chicana desire: "It is as if the relative absence of any sociopolitical debate of the Chicana/Mexicana's sexuality had made it imperative that Castillo explore instead her speaker's desire in the light of a textual milieu," which thereby underscores Castillo's "struggle to place her erotic thematics and voices in the interstice of both her sociopolitical and textual experiences."[34] This intertwining of sociopolitical and textual experience is informed by the "Three Marias," or what 1990s-era Chicana feminists have termed the "Tres Marías Syndrome."[35] The trinity of mothers—La Virgen de Guadalupe, La Llorona, and La Malinche—serve as metaphoric virgin/whore archetypes, through which Chicana sexuality is mediated. Paz, whose text was published in the 1950s, is largely credited with the academic canonizing of already existing sociocultural metaphors that regulated women's sexuality; however, the scholarly and artistic output by Chicana feminists sought to historicize and interrogate these constructs.

Castillo's spatialized embodied Chicanx poetics, then, theorizes from the interstices of the body writ large; it must account for the spaces within and between constructed narratives and essentialized categories. It reimagines poetry and the poet in conjunction with space and embodiment, directly confronting the conscripted spatialized practices and literary tradition, as outlined by Juana Rodríguez: "Places afford preexisting narratives of former encounters; they offer a means of symbolically decoding practices"; however, the "subject brings to the encounter her own set of decoding practices that are mediated by the regulatory power of a particular discursive space, but not wholly determined by them."[36] Rodríguez posits that these decoding practices will always be conditioned by and through this regulatory space; however, simultaneously, the poet is afforded "infinite" possibilities to create and interpret. The key is offering forth "alternative methods of conceptualizing space not only by noting how social change must be spatialized but also by seeing and feeling space as performative and participatory.[37] Castillo's poem "In My Country" performs such spatialization through a contrasting poetic refrain: "In my country" versus "This is not my country." The speaker's evaluative critiques in "this is not my country" serve as a point of contrast to emphasize the alternative world in which her poet aspires to reside. Castillo builds a "performative and participatory" world for her poet, initially in the speaker's interrogation of the way her body and her contribution to academia are evaluated and attended: "In my world, I do not attend / conferences with academicians / who anthropologize my existence."[38] The speaker's representation of an academic space that doesn't malign her is generated through negative construction—what the poetic speaker does *not* do—in order to emphasize and denounce what is currently in place.

The poem's negative construction continues throughout, particularly to draw out distinctions between the world the poet occupies and that of poetic creation, a move Rafael Pérez-Torres contends is contingent upon spatiality: "The speaker stands at the interstices between an imagined world, a world that ostensibly once existed, and the world as it is actually lived. The poem bespeaks a weariness with the brutalities of this present world by negating its violence through an incantation of all an other world is not."[39] Pérez-Torres contends that this "other world," the world of poetic creation, was supplanted by the present, socially unjust world. In turn, the speaker's "weary negation" of violence emphasizes "the necessity of alternate spaces for Chicana self-affirmation and points to the impossibility of that dream."[40] However, I challenge Pérez-Torres's contention that the poem's "move[ment] between worlds of affirmation and desperation" forecloses all generative possibilities, thereby leaving the poet to toggle between these two worlds, seemingly unable to create this alternative "dream."[41] Rather, Castillo's use of the refrain "in my world" or "in my country"—or its negative construction, "this is not my country" or "this is not my world"—creates possibility through and within its repetition: "This is not my country. / In my country, men / do not play at leaders";[42] "In my country / i don't hesitate to sit / alone in the park";[43] "In my country, i am not exotic";[44] "This is not my world. / In my world, Mesoamerica / was a magnificent Quetzal."[45] As evidenced by these examples, Castillo offers variations within the refrain she deploys: some lines are end-stopped while others contain the defining reference in the same line; sometimes there is a direct interplay between the definitive and negative constructions within the same stanza. Castillo embeds possibility and flexibility in her negative construction to build internal dynamism and therefore forces the poetic line to disrupt continuity, even as it relies on repetitive patterns. These poetic variations underscore the prevailing continuity of the academic "world" that marginalizes her existence and art, while simultaneously foregrounding a Chicanx embodiment that demands to be accounted for in her published poetry collection.

Furthermore, through the flexibility of her poetic line, Castillo suffuses the refrain with continuous and dynamic alternatives, including in the final stanza, wherein she reimagines the poet:

> In my world the poet sang loud
> and clear and everyone heard
> without recoiling. It was sweet
> as harvest, sharp as tin, strong
> as the northern wind, and all had
> a coat warm enough to bear it.[46]

The poet's song, described as "sweet," sharp," and "strong," relies on a sonic alliterative movement not contained in a singular line. These adjectives are paired with both natural and forged elements—harvest, tin, and wind—made similarly cooperative through the internal rhyme. Additionally, this cooperation is echoed in the way "all"—the poet *and* the audience—are equipped to withstand the force of the poet's song. The poem does not simply contrast and juxtapose, but instead performs cooperative fusion and, in turn, instantiates the possibility for this world, one that doesn't quite exist and yet has *always* existed. While the poet "sang" of a past world in past tense, she sings now, in this poem, and will sing again, once an audience is ready to "bear" her song. Castillo invokes a contrasting spatiotemporal continuum between a Mesoamerican poetical past, a dissatisfying sociopoetical present, and a not-as-yet created future poetics.

For Castillo, poetics must be anchored in language and structure that reflect the urgency of her community, or what she calls a "Conscienticized Poetics": "We are creating not only a new poetics with our own language but a new conscientizacíon."[47] This consciousness, or the "social concerns that have given rise to my poems," structure Castillo's poetics; in other words, they produce and dictate her poems' content, language, and form accordingly.[48] Hers is a poetics that emerges from need: the poet's need and desire, as well as the community's. Such a sentiment is reflected in Castillo's statement about her writing process: "For me, writing has always been done in a state of ecstasy."[49] Writing in "ecstasy" instills Castillo's poetics with both a heightened and transcendent consciousness. The blueprint for her poetic vision, one where social concerns and ecstasy merge, is comprised of a consciousness through and for an underrepresented community: "The construction of poetics and prose, the development of ideas, is not the achievement of any one individual writer of her generation. Together, we create a tapestry."[50] As a participant in this tapestry, Castillo uses the lowercase "i" throughout *My Father Was a Toltec*, since, as she notes, "mine was a collective identity."[51] So while Castillo is a bisexual Chicana writer whose collection speaks to the localized Chicago cityscape, neighborhoods, and domestic spaces, her Chicanx poetics is a tapestry comprised of and derived from the Chicanx collective body. Thus, Castillo's "stolen pen" in "A Christmas Gift," I argue, represents the Chicanx poet's attentiveness to a poetics that strives to account for the spatialized embodiment of the queer and woman-identified members of her community.

The poetic speaker's "stolen pen" allows her to write words, likened to a "splinter of steel"[52] that ultimately unites her father ("flings from the drill press / into my father's eye"[53]) and her grandmother ("Another word, also steel, / the rolling pin / my grandmother used for the / last tortillas of her life"[54]), encapsulating the tension between and within the binary of domestic and non-domestic spaces Castillo presents in the first section of the collection. In the collection's opening poem, "The Toltec," the speaker's father, a member of a Chicago neighborhood gang, has his "emblemed jacket split in half" by a rival gang member's "blade," an image that is used in this context as synonymous with power and masculinity.[55] However, Castillo actively upsets the traditional coding of space according to gender in the final stanza of "Toltec": "Next morning, Mami / threw it away."[56] This poem is comprised of two stanzas; the first is a nine-line stanza focused on the speaker's father and his domain on the streets, while the second stanza is comprised solely by these two lines. The space between stanzas performs the spatial demarcation between the domestic and non-domestic: the speaker's father has power outside the house—"Everyone knows he was *bad*"—whereas Mami has the ability to dispose of the father's power at home.[57]

In "Saturdays," Castillo constructs the domestic space as distinctly female and sustained through women's labor:

> Because she worked all week
> away from home, gone from 5 to 5,
> Saturdays she did the laundry,
> pulled the wringer machine
> to the kitchen sink, and hung
> the clothes on the line.
> At night, we took it down and ironed.[58]

Mami spends her day off from work engaging in domestic labor, and the speaker performs this labor alongside her mother, charged with ironing her father's "handkerchiefs and / boxer shorts."[59] The speaker's father has domain outside the house only because of Mami, a direct result of what her domestic and non-domestic labor affords him: he wears a freshly ironed "tailor-made silk suit / bought on her credit, had her / adjust the tie."[60] Mami continues to iron as her husband leaves the house to meet his mistress, a woman "not like" his wife, a "Mexican woman" in the vein of his mother (20; 19). This construction seemingly delineates the gendered options for women: a traditional Mexican woman in the domestic space or a nontraditional woman outside the domestic sphere.

However, Castillo further troubles this gendered spatialization in "Daddy with Chesterfields in a Rolled Up Sleeve," when Mami confronts her daughter after making enchiladas for her husband's birthday:

> Mami takes her place now,
> tells his daughter to her face:
> "You're like your father,

> don't like to work,
> a daydreamer,
> think someday you'll be rich and famous,
> an artist, who wastes her time
> travelling,
> wearing finery she can't afford,
> neglecting her children and her home!"
> The father lowers his eyes.[61]

The third-person perspective serves as a mediating voice of condemnation, in stark contrast to the use of first person in the majority of the poem. Reinforced by the space of the kitchen, the third-person heightens Mami's chastisement of her daughter for not operating appropriately within its confines. In this stanza, there is no space for the poet, literally or figuratively. Poetry and art—described as nebulous, intangible "daydreaming"—won't feed a family or sustain a home. While Mami's "place" is clear and definitive in the kitchen, the daughter's is ungrounded, both in this space and in this stanza. Castillo will need to go outside the bounds of the domestic space and structure in order to locate her.

Castillo does so, later in the poem, with her depiction of the speaker's artistry; the daughter's storytelling abilities coincide with the expansive space of her imaginative capacities and sexuality:

> Men try to catch my eye. i talk to them
> of politics, religion, the ghosts i've seen,
> the king of timbales, México and Chicago,
> And they go away.
> But women stay. Women like stories.
> They like thin arms around their shoulders,
> the smell of perfumed hair,
> a flamboyant scarf around the neck,
> the reassuring voice that confirms their
> cynicism about politics, religion, and the glorious
> history that slaughtered thousands of slaves.[62]

The poetic speaker's storytelling is boundless; it covers myriad spaces and subjects. Yet, what her imagination produces is concrete and tactile, as seen by the appreciative receptiveness of touch: arms meeting shoulders and a scarf encircling a neck. The emphasis on touch lends the amorphous concepts like politics, religion, and history a solid, corporeal quality they would otherwise not possess. The poem emphasizes art and artistry as aligned with the artist's sexuality, something the poetic speaker uses to seduce potential lovers. Her listeners, comprised of pursuing men and pursued women, serve as contrasting audiences the speaker must please. The speaker's bisexuality aligns her artistry with queerness and recalls Sandra K. Soto's theorization of what it means "to queer" a literary text, derived in part from Elizabeth Freeman's definition "to make its most pleasurable aspects gorgeously excessive."[63] Soto's focus on "de-mastery" and the necessity of "expansiveness" is a response to the term "intersectionality," which Soto considers "too *spatially rigid* and exacting a metaphor" to capture the experience of enmeshed identity categories that inform racialized and sexualized bodies.[64] Soto contends that race, sexuality, and gender are "too spatially and temporally contingent, *ever* (even if only for an instant) to travel independently of one another" and argues that the term itself spatializes these identity categories as separate entities that "eventually [meet] each other here and there."[65] Queering, in this sense, serves to encapsulate the internally complicated intertwining of race, gender, and sexuality within and across structural and sociocultural spaces. In this regard, by rendering these entanglements visible and legible on the page, Castillo not only queers poetics, but creates a Chicanx poetics that represents the "expansiveness" of a spatialized embodiment and performs that expansiveness accordingly.

This technique can be seen in "Alternatives," wherein Castillo returns to the blade imagery from "Toltec," repeatedly playing with the word, as well as the imagery associated with it. Castillo's use of a visually expansive form imbues the word's meaning and application with a similar expansiveness:

yes—yes
we—no
so
maybe i can be
an "exotic" version
of Pati Smith/strike
lewd poses for Fan-Belt
Mag/make heavy comments to
Time like "i'm into Razor Blades,
mon, double-edged, of *coarse*"/my shaved
head back up could call itself Los Razor
Blaides and wear shark skinned suits without
collars and very pointed high heeled boots/my
poems would emit musk—and would NEVER be repeated
except by electronic sound and to make it that much
more heavy, mon, i'd muffle the mike with pantyhose so
nobody would know how heavy i really was and up would go
the acoustic guitar to accent the poetry of my ever so heavy
mammary glands.[66]

This section of the collection, titled "Heredera," invokes what it means to be an heiress. While the male poets in "A Christmas Gift" are "heirs to classics," Chicanas are heiresses who inherit a gendered positionality within the Chicanx community. "Alternatives" takes the masculine "blade" and reconstitutes it to extend power to the feminine: "blades" becomes "Blaides" and suits are paired with "very pointed high heeled boots." The poetry the speaker produces is unapologetically and insistently female: it "emits musk," is delivered through a pantyhose covered microphone, and is set to the strumming of an acoustic guitar that "accents" the poet's poetic "mammary glands." The poet's body *is* poetry as she *creates* poetry, and the poetry produced creates her in return. The poetic line is erratic; it stretches—at one point extending to the brink of the page margin—then gradually recedes again. Castillo takes up as much space as possible on the page, allowing her poem to perform a spatial reclamation. Furthermore, the poem is one long sentence, the cumulative effect emphasizing a rush of feeling and breath that defies conventional grammatical structure and rules. Toward the end of the poem, the speaker reveals the extent of her performative posturing: "and all this happened shortly before i was taken to a hospital with my wrists intact / since I wasn't really into razor blades."[67] This admission likewise reveals that the poetic speaker has stretched her male inheritance as far as she possibly can and created all she could from it. Since she "really [isn't] into razor blades" the speaker announces the necessity of creating a poetics more reflective of her racially gendered body.

In "Women Are Not Roses," Castillo furthers her direct engagement with poetic tradition, in particular its use of nature metaphors for women and/or the female body: "Women are not / roses / they are not oceans / or stars."[68] In these lines, Castillo refutes the way images in nature—roses, oceans, stars—have been used literarily to expand upon the beauty of women. In declaring "women are not roses," Castillo contests the traditional male poet's gaze and redirects our attention away from his desire. Obviously, on a very literal level, women are, in fact, not roses, oceans, or stars; however, within literary tradition, women have more frequently served as metaphors for beauty or male desire more than they have as women. By challenging the prevailing literary tradition, Castillo demands poetry about real women and their lives beyond metaphor. In turn, Castillo's poetic undertaking not only recovers women trapped within the metaphor, but allows for different modes of sexuality to be accessed and represented. Given this context, it is crucial that Castillo's recovery project entails repeated representations of women as agents of their own desires. Emma Pérez's *The Decolonial Imaginary: Writing Chicanas into History* presents a "genealogical exposition of specific cultural bodies, pleasures, and desires" in order to "[thematize] the body, power, and social institutions where fictive truths and values are enacted upon the body."[69] In short, Pérez theorizes how the decolonial imaginary can move the Chicana from being strictly a colonial object of desire to a decolonial subject who desires. No longer inscribed by and with "fictive truths," the desiring Chicana decodes herself and her body as a cultural text, as seen in "Wyoming Crossing Thoughts," when the poetic speaker proclaims in the first stanza: "i will never / in my life / marry / a Mexican man."[70] The poem rejects the image of devotion and service, particularly how domestic responsibilities and sex are conscripted within marriage as wifely duties:

> i won't serve him
> a plate of beans
> stand by warming
> the tortillas
> on the comal.
>
> Not i.
> Not i.
>
> i will desire him
> my own way
> give him
> what i please
> meet him when
> and where
> no one else sees,
> drive an obsidian blade
> though his heart,
> lick up the blood.[71]

In this poem, Castillo revisits both the kitchen space and blade imagery from the first section in her collection. The poetic speaker emphatically refuses the role she is supposed to play, reinforced by the repetition in the short stanza, "Not i. / Not i." The certainty with which the speaker makes this declaration is further emphasized by the short, end-stopped line; this structure denies any and all room for questioning, or additional clauses. It is precise in its brevity and eliminates any possibility for explanation because no explanation is required. The poetic voice is assertive, using "i will" paired with verbs that elicit strong action, in order to connote definitive control. The speaker chooses what, how, and who she "desires" and vows to do so her "own way" and how she "pleases." Thus, instead of serving her husband tortillas she heats on the comal, the speaker ingests his spilled blood to serve herself and her pleasure.

Castillo furthers her exploration of pleasure, desire, and control over her own body in "An Idyll," a poem that focuses on a toxic relationship. The title immediately references poetic tradition and sets up reader expectations to encounter a narrative poem depicting rustic life or the pastoral; however, Castillo not only disrupts reader expectation, but the idyll as well. The poem is, in fact, not a pastoral in the traditional sense of the term, or even a pastoral romance; instead, it is a first-person account of love, or lust, gone awry. The first stanza immerses us in the physical beauty of the speaker's lover:

```
now
i    can         tell
of   being       swept b
y    a god       a Michael
angelo's         david      a
man  of          such       phys
ical  perfection,
one could        not        be
lieve  him       human.⁷²
```

From the outset, Castillo uses poetic form, in this case unconventional enjambment in the poetic line, to highlight the distortion at the center of her subject matter. The form is center-justified to create a column on the right side of the page, evocative of the structural integrity of Greek and Roman columns, or the slabs of marble artists would use as material for their sculpture. The "man of such phys / ical perfection," an allusion to Michelangelo's *David*, highlights of the romanticization of the ideal male form. The speaker's attraction to this unnamed man is countered by the enjambment in "phys / ical perfection" and "one could not be / lieve him human"; by splitting the words "physical" and "believe," Castillo ruptures the corresponding relationship to what follows: "perfection" and "him." With it, the speaker's "pleasu / re" becomes synonymously broken as the poem continues.⁷³ Thus, Castillo's poetic form performs its denunciation of literary tradition and its requisite subject matter. Since it also relies on additional spacing between words to maintain the right and left margins of the poem, Castillo's form gestures to the accommodations, poetic and otherwise, that must be made in order to maintain this structure.

"An Idyll" gains greater formal coherence—in this case, the enjambed line relies less on split words—as its content devolves from initial attraction into domestic abuse and violence. Carl Gutiérrez-Jones considers the way the poem "leads us to fundamental questions about gender itself and the way it appears to be socially constructed through the actual or impending transgression of women's 'supposed' consent."⁷⁴ Castillo figures this lover through the imagery of a statue, whose heavy "weight" the speaker must bear. The "cruel" aspect of the man's perfection is equated with the "fa / lseness" of his body.[75] The poetic speaker's control over her body wavers with her lover's "fa / lseness," or his increasing abuse of her. Yet, as the poem builds, the form becomes more phrasal; ideas and statements are completed within the poetic line: "We stood, / before him in awe / of such 'beautiful / useless beauty.'"[76] The final stanza only has one separated word: "until one of us c / ould not stand it / any longer and / shot him."[77] The resolution, wherein the poetic speaker regains control over her body once her abusive lover is shot, coincides with the formal accessibility and clarity that emerge in the last few lines.

In comparison, "The Invitation" also utilizes columns, but Castillo "invites" her readers to help construct the meaning of poetry, as well as the desired and desiring bodies it depicts. The opening lines of the first stanza gesture back to the tension between the "verses" poets write and the "not poems" the speaker creates in "A Christmas Gift": "On a certain night / I will compose a verse."[78] Read in relation to "A Christmas Gift," this statement shows the evolution of the poet, one who now claims a rightful space for her own poetics. However, the multiple possibilities within the verse emerge in the next stanzas:

> On a certain night
> I will compose a verse:
>   Long and Winding
>   from your mouth
>   to just below
>   the thighs
> A rhyme of
> Quiet sunbursts
>   Fingers
>   finding their way
>   to a subtle rhythm[79]

This composed verse can be read different ways: it is either "Long and Winding / from your mouth" or "A rhyme of quiet sunbursts." Both are applicable, but neither is prescribed because, while Castillo supplies the form, the reader chooses the order in which the stanzas should be read. Additionally, the only punctuation in the poem is the semicolon that follows "verse" in the second line and the ellipses that occur after the final line of the last stanza: "two bodies blending / into a poem / that never ends. . . ." This choice not only underscores the spatial mobility within and between columns, since the stanzas are not restricted by end-stopped lines, but also serves to introduce everything following the semicolon as a modifier. The concluding line, "that never ends . . ." is, in fact, the only option for the last line given the spatial placement of the columns; however, the ellipses ensure that the poem will do exactly what the line says: never end.

More than that, the form beckons readers to return, implores them to explore the poem once again, and compels them to interpret the poem continuously within and through differing structures and contexts. This construction works to reinforce a spatialized and embodied Chicanx poetics by aligning poetry—both its composition and interpretation—with the physical bodies for which it speaks. The spatial mobility between the columns enhances this alignment, wherein a pleasure-inflected poetic body emerges. The "[f]ingers / finding their way / to a subtle rhythm" at once speak to the writing of poetry—the poetic "rhythm" borne from the elements of poetic creation—and of a sexual encounter that produces a "rhythm" between two bodies. Bodily pleasure is mapped onto poetics and vice versa, thereby merging the two into a single cooperative entity: "lines will run along / the curve of your spine / on and on." Poetic lines are indistinguishable from the curvature of the lover's spine. Notably, here, the lover, and therefore the poem, is not gendered or racialized; instead, Castillo opts to use the gender neutral pronoun "you" to denote the poem/lover's body. Additionally, the poem/lover's body parts are likewise not gendered: mouth, thighs, hips, spine, fingers, legs, rather than genitalia. These body parts appear almost entirely in the third column, which focuses on what and how the poetic body is produced: "in perfect coordination / from hips to hips."

Castillo's decision to mark the poem/lover's body by and through poetry itself, ultimately, confronts racialized gender paradigms of sexuality as the focus of her poetics: the manner in which textual bodies represent actual bodies. However, she refuses to allow either the poetic or textual body to be trapped within the textual confines of spatial structures; instead, she enlivens them through many possible permutations that don't restrict or delimit the Chicanx body or Chicanx poetics. Castillo's poetics perform the pleasure of writer in ecstasy, one committed to centering the concerns, needs, and desires of the Chicanx community. By writing for herself and her community, Castillo demands that publishers and the academy recognize and validate her poetry on her own terms. In doing so, Castillo, and other writers and poets of Castillo's generation, altered the literary tradition and the Western canon by shifting perspectives, voices, form, frameworks, and reading practices to account for their bodies and the bodies of their literature.

CHAPTER 3

UNBOUNDED AND LIMITLESS

Ana Castillo's Poetics of Place and the Body

OLGA L. HERRERA

An arm stretches into midair; another reaches up to join it as notes from a guitar drift through the air. Palms clap, and the flamenco dance begins. In the 1999 novel *Peel My Love like an Onion*, Ana Castillo's unforgettable protagonist, Carmen la Coja, remembers her transformation as a dancer: "I put my hands up the way Miss Dorotea had hers. I focused on the guitar music coming from the record player. I didn't know anything about the music or about what she wanted to teach us. . . . I tried harder at that moment than at anything I had ever tried before. I could not walk right and I was being asked to dance. But I would dance. . . . Why not? Why not?"[1] As a metaphor for the artistic process, the power of flamenco comes from the tension between the intensity and passion of the dancer and their expression in formal movements. In this scene, in which we witness Carmen's sheer desire wrestling with the formal aspects of a dance she had no experience with, we might think of Ana Castillo's own emergence as a writer: an act of self-invention, creating a new poetics born of the struggle to write against literary conventions.

I can't help but think of flamenco and Ana Castillo's own interest in it as I contemplate the contours of a poetics suggested by her body of work. Castillo's written text often stretches across the page, testing and pressing against the boundaries of margin and formal convention, whether it be poetry, fiction, essay, or play. Likewise, a passionate interest in the world and an unflagging dissatisfaction with the status quo animates her exploration of social and cultural conventions and an insistence on breaking with expectations. The essays in this section, "The Chicanx Letters: Transnational Poetics, Language, and Form," invite us to consider Castillo's innovations in form that stretch, and at times break with, the genres she works in to more adequately express racialized, classed, gendered, and queer subjectivities. In "Lettered Encounters: Ana Castillo's Poetics of Spilling in *The Mixquiahuala Letters*," Ximena Keogh Serrano traces through Castillo's 1986 epistolary novel the emergence of a poetics that refuses formal boundaries in order to gesture toward a "transcultural, *fronteriza* state of being." Shanna M. Salinas likewise finds in Castillo's earlier poetry, from 1973–1988, the invention of a poetics against convention in her essay "For the Pleasure of the Chicanx Poet: Spatialized Embodied Poetics in Ana Castillo's *My Father Was a Toltec*." In rich, nuanced readings of Castillo's earlier work, Keogh Serrano and Salinas offer us frameworks for understanding Castillo's experiments with form as a young poet, and provoke us to consider what new readings and discoveries may emerge from a rereading of her wider body of work in light of these poetics. In this response, I suggest that Keogh Serrano and Salinas provoke us to think about boundaries and borders (both those embodied and of the nation) in such a way as to appreciate their dissolution in Castillo's poetics and her visions of an anti-national space of belonging.

Simply stated, poetics has been understood as the tradition of analyzing the mechanics of a work of art: "The term poetics has been interpreted as an inquiry into the laws and principles that underlie a verbal work of art and has often carried normative and prescriptive connotations."[2] As poets and writers traditionally left on the margins of literary and knowledge production, Chicanx authors devised methods and created art that fell outside of precisely these normative and prescriptive connotations. Critics, then, have worked to name new poetics engendered by these conditions on the margins, seeking the singular features that might characterize the emergence of Latino/a poetry, for example. Urayoán Noel, in surveying Latinx poetry from 2000 to 2009, identifies a significant feature of the Chicano/a movement and Nuyorican poetry of the 1960s and 1970s, writing that "Latinidad matters as a performative identity, attuned to the struggles that have shaped and continue to shape the Latino/a experience," and points to the work of Juan Bruce-Novoa and Lázaro Lima who have similarly characterized Chicano and Latino poetry as a response to chaos and crisis. With Lima, Noel writes, "it is not just that Latinidad becomes crucial in moments of crisis, but that (from the earliest colonial encounters) it has been defined by crisis, by violence and resistance played out on the body."[3] Chicana feminist poets emerged from the movement, critiquing the same social, racial, and economic injustices as Chicano writers, but foregrounding gender as a concern and writing against the movement's masculinist politics. Noel notes that "what is perhaps most noteworthy about Chicana feminist poetics . . . is its nuanced, self-reflexive exploration of writing and the body as they relate to social movements."[4] In this anthology, Salinas and Keogh Serrano pay particular attention to this connection between Castillo's experiments with form and the elaboration of the Chicana body and sexuality.

Salinas writes of Castillo's struggle to define herself and her art against traditional notions of what constitutes poetry, noting that her feelings of exclusion in academia led her to decide to never take any formal writing training, afraid that she would be told she "had no right to poetry." Rather, she set out to define for herself what qualified as "good" poetry, and Salinas notes that regardless of inherent quality, publication also establishes what is considered "good" and bestows legitimacy and recognition.[5] Castillo, then, liberates herself to write what she wants and how she wants to write it, and produces collections of poetry that explore resistance to political and social injustice, as well as to cultural and gendered expectations for women, including those for romantic and sexual relationships. Salinas finds in Castillo's collection *My Father Was a Toltec* a potent articulation of a poetics anchored in *conscientizacion*, motivated by social concerns as well as need and desire, and written "in a state of ecstasy."[6] If desire here connotes both a desire for social action and the physical desire of the body, then we find that Castillo's poetry brings them together, and as Salinas asserts, "creates a Chicanx poetics that not only imagines but seeks to represent new literary possibilities within racialized gender paradigms of sexuality."[7] Salinas's fine close readings of selected poems in *My Father Was a Toltec* uncover Castillo's persistent interest in breaking with Mexican American cultural gender norms, and underscore the spatial experiments in form that mirror the poet's insistence on rejecting conventions. This analysis prompts us to look toward later work in *I Ask the Impossible*, written between 1989 and 2000. In the introduction to that collection, Castillo notes the connection between the collections: "When I started writing in verse seriously nearly three decades ago, I wrote as a witness to my generation. . . . Here you have the seeds and soughed-off snakeskins of some new stories."[8] Castillo's articulation of the poetic body remains here, but the desire has shifted to that of the body's role in motherhood, and the body's breakdown whether through disease (as in "Nothing But This at the End") or state violence (as in "'Like the People of Guatemala, I want to be free of these memories . . .' —Sister Diana Ortiz").

Keogh Serrano shares Salinas's interest in the spatial quality of Castillo's textual production. In *The Mixquiahuala Letters*, she finds that the epistolary form of the novel offers a space for the contestation of borders, leading to what Keogh Serrano calls a "poetics of spilling": "A poetics of spilling points to what emerges outside of the confines of recorded speech. Emotion, resonance, and silence are but some of the few ungraspable elements that emerge in acts of 'spilling.' Here, 'spilling' points to that which cannot be contained. It registers the quality of both fluidity and mess, as it evidences a form of excess."[9] The "poetics of spilling" is invested in pushing, expanding, and breaking borders through its engagement with the physical page, with formal literary conventions, and with social, cultural, and gender norms in the narrative. One form of "spilling," then, includes the novel's possible reading trajectories, in which a reader may opt for different reading paths, which dovetails with Salinas's analysis of the poem "The Invitation," which offers columns of verse that a reader may organize in several ways to produce different readings.[10] Keogh Serrano also investigates the epistolary form for its capacity to allow the writer to produce (re)constructions of the self, suggesting that through letter-writing, Teresa accesses a "method of writing and history-making [that] makes claim[s] to feminist models of knowledge production that aim to locate intersectional struggles, and work to account for embodied subjectivities."[11] Following Gloria Anzaldúa's and Cherríe Moraga's delineation of "theory in the flesh," Keogh Serrano ascribes to Teresa's letters a corporeal registry in which "her personal subjectivity permeates the text."[12] Spilling here then occurs when Teresa's thoughts "spill" across the page in a disjointed fashion; Keogh Serrano observes that "access to a complete and unified vision of . . . Teresa, is purposefully made null."[13]

Through Keogh Serrano's and Salinas's essays, we see the body emerging as a potent site for negotiating subjectivity, knowledge production, gender roles, and literary conventions, whether as a poetic body capable of desiring pleasure, or as embodied subjectivity through the epistolary genre. In Castillo's literary texts, the Chicana figure contains multitudes, as another poet once said—a *mestiza* both racially and culturally, a bisexual woman, a *transfronteriza* subject. A border-crosser fluent in multiple languages and cultures at once, la Chicana represents ambiguity and contradiction productive of new ways of being and seeing. Again, I am reminded of Carmen la Coja from *Peel My Love like an Onion*, the cynical and wise Chicana who pursues flamenco dance despite a leg debilitated by polio, and finds she must return to service work on the economy's margins to make a living. The body here establishes primacy as the medium through which traditional forms of subjectivity must be completely revised; in the necessity and desire for dance established by the disabled body, a new means of dance must be born. Carmen shows us that not only through sheer *ganas* may we achieve our desire, but that the mestiza's tolerance for ambiguity is also necessary for achieving it.

If the poetic body exhibits through formal innovation an unbounded desire, whether for the pursuit of art or for sexual expression, Castillo's texts also express a longing for connection with the land. Keogh Serrano notes that in *The Mixquiahuala Letters*, the novel demonstrates a cartographical impulse, pointing to critic Anne Bower's observation that the letters serve as a "'site of remapping' wherein 'remapping' serves to respond 'to the historic link between conquest of land and conquest of the female body that has characterized patriarchal societies.'"[14] This key insight into the operation of the textual body as a site of connection between recovering the female body and recovering the land opens the way to thinking about how spatialization and borders in the text are materially linked to the subjectivity of Castillo's poetic speakers or narrative protagonists as either *transfronteriza* or transnational. Keogh Serrano further suggests that through the accumulation of letters into an archive of experience, "Teresa marks a return to the body, a return to *the land*,"[15] foregrounding the primacy of emotion and feeling as a way of knowing, the theory in the flesh.

Castillo's emphasis on the mestiza subject, then, the one with a tolerance for ambiguity and multiplicity, leads us toward inquiring into the way the subject inhabits space, as both Salinas and Keogh Serrano have both suggested. Salinas observes that as Castillo plays with formal poetic boundaries "she refuses to allow either the poetic or textual body to be trapped within the textual confines of spatial structures; instead, she enlivens them through many possible permutations that don't restrict or delimit."[16] Returning to Urayoán Noel's insight about the link between social movements and the Chicana writer's self-exploration of the body, what might these points help us to understand about Castillo's vision of the Chicana subject's occupation of geopolitical location and its production of an ontological perspective generative of a particular poetics? If Castillo's response to physical borders and boundaries is to create a poetics of excess, of spilling, then envisioning her fictional and poetic Chicana subjects as transnational seems likely. In *The Mixquiahuala Letters*, Teresa's travels across the United States and Mexico produce a facility with crossing borders and an engagement with multiple languages, cultures, and gender expectations. Regina, the protagonist in the novel *The Guardians* (2007), resides in the borderlands but lives a transnational life with family on either side of the border; the story centers around her brother's attempt to cross into the United States and his disappearance. However, I want to press further to suggest the limitations of the term *transnational* for an author like Castillo, whose work is deeply invested in notions of unbounded place, nation, and belonging. If a woman doesn't feel grounded in any one country, then to suggest a transnational sensibility seems to address only the surface of her border-crossing experience. Indeed, Keogh Serrano recalls critic Linda Margarita Greenberg's observation that in *The Mixquiahuala Letters*, Teresa and Alicia's "erotic friendship and national ties are performative endeavors, continually and strategically reimagined. The lack of a fixed authentic homeland pains the characters, who can neither lay easy claim to the United States nor nostalgically yearn for Mexico."[17] The Chicano movement, of course, posited the symbolic homeland of Aztlán in response to this feeling of deterritorialization. However, the representations of Aztlán in the former Mexican lands in the US Southwest have been exclusionary of those not sharing a Chicano/a identity, particularly one forged in movement politics.

What concept of home and land can we imagine instead that expands to include others and establishes affinities?

In *Massacre of the Dreamers*, Castillo proposes the concept of "A Countryless Woman" in the title of her first essay, in which she argues that as a Brown Chicana born to the lower class, she is "commonly perceived as a foreigner everywhere I go, including in the United States and Mexico."[18] Responding from a Chicana feminist position, she writes that "until we are all represented, respected, and protected by society and the laws that govern it, the status of the Chicana will be that of a countryless woman."[19] As she issues a call for recognition and representation by the state, in her art Castillo envisions kinships with a diversity of women and cultures, dissolving borders to better connect with other perspectives.[20] This is the expression of Xicanisma, which she defines as "an ever present consciousness of our interdependency specifically rooted in our culture and history."[21] In *Peel My Love like an Onion*, Carmen recognizes that her own labor falls into a global system of industrial work benefiting from the precarious position of women of color. She walks into a sweatshop with her mother to pick up piecework, and is shocked to see conditions recalling the nineteenth century: "These weren't British waifs or Jewish immigrants like in my schoolbooks either but chinas and indias—meaning they could be women from anywhere— reedy and dark, thin-limbed younger copies of myself, sewing in mausoleum silence, quick-fingered and agile-eyed, like indentured servants toiling in exchange for their freedom."[22] We recognize with Carmen her first-world privilege as she cries in outrage, "You can't do this to people, you just can't! Slavery was abolished a long time ago. Wasn't it?"[23]

Castillo's affiliations with women of color, regardless of nationality, run persistently through her work. Notably in her poetry collection *I Ask the Impossible*, she evokes the experience of women in places throughout the Americas, including the United States, Mexico, Guatemala, and Peru, often to draw attention to the injustices of patriarchal oppression. In writing about Sister Dianna Ortiz, a New Mexican who worked as a missionary in Guatemala in 1989 and was abducted, tortured, and raped by members of the Guatemalan military, Castillo highlights Ortiz's commitment to the people of Guatemala while expressing the horror of her experience through multiple genres. In the poem "Like the people of Guatemala, I want to be free of these memories . . ." Castillo jolts us out of our complacency in our citizenship and our material comforts to inhabit Ortiz's experience of violation both at the hands of the Guatemalan military, and those of US State Department officials and federal investigators as they actively worked to dismiss her story and distract attention from US funding of the Guatemalan military. Castillo dramatizes the poem in her play adaptations titled *Psst . . . I Have Something to Tell You, Mi Amor* (2005), writing a one-act play to be performed at the Goodman Theatre's Latino Theatre Festival in Chicago in the summer of 2003, and a two-act play performed in Mexico City in December 2002. Sister Dianna Ortiz's story, told by Castillo in multiple genres and to international audiences, recalls Keogh Serrano's assertion of the connection between colonial violence to the land and to the female body, but here we witness a decentralized state power enacting physical and sexual violence on Ortiz's body. Ortiz is Castillo's "countryless woman" during her ordeal, and Castillo's intent here is not to establish artificial feelings of sisterhood, but to shake us out of our self-satisfaction and return us to the call to action of her essay, crying at the end of her poem: "It is real, the nightmare, / and without end. / How can we sleep? / How can we sleep?"[24]

I look to Castillo's articulation of an embodied Chicana subjectivity with attention to place, land, and nation, and her attempts to draw connections between women's experiences across national boundaries, not to gloss over specific material and sited differences but rather to highlight how these differences find room in Castillo's vision of a Latina or global women of color shared experience. Castillo reminds us that "nationalism throughout the history of civilization excludes certain groups that will inevitably feel intimidated and react in like manner . . . nationalism always finds justification for manipulation for power."[25] If Castillo's challenges to nationalism and borders leaves us grasping to name her textual Chicana poetics as something other than transnational, these challenges give way to a vision of unbounded belonging, imagined as but not limited to place. In her 1990 novel *Sapogonia*, Castillo describes a country located in the Americas "where all mestizos reside, regardless of nationality, individual racial composition, or legal residential status—or, perhaps, because of all of these."[26] Despite the markers identifying this fictional country as a "real" place, its symbolic significance emerges toward the end of the prologue when she writes that "Sapogonia (like the Sapogón/a) is not identified by modern boundaries. . . . Due to present political conditions decreed by the powers that be, the Sapogón pueblo finds itself continuously divided and reunited with the certainty of the Northern winds that sweep across its continents to leave evershifting results."[27] Described as a diaspora, then, the Sapogón pueblo can be imagined as the literary representation of a Latino/a/x people, displaced by history and politics, laying claim to a broad swath of the Americas but often not residing in their birthplaces. Perhaps in response to the concept of Aztlán as a homeland, *Sapogonia* gestures to the difficulties and contradictions of establishing place as the origin of identity. In that sense, it is both everywhere and nowhere, and indeed, Castillo says as much in an epigraph to the novel, writing that "this is the story of make-believe people in a real world; or, if you like, the story of real people in a make-believe world." This insistence on the intersection between reality and make-believe returns us to Salinas's engagement with the poem "In My Country," which she argues "instantiates the possibility for this world, one that doesn't quite exist and yet has *always* existed."[28] Rafael Pérez-Torres writes that the speaker of "In My Country," in constructing an "anti-country of imagined beauty and harmony—recasts a vision of the historical world from which the poet speaks."[29] Salinas differs from Pérez-Torres's contention that the poem suggests the impossibility of the dream for an alternate country; I agree and suggest further that rather than read the poem as a deferral of an ideal place, we see instead a vision of a Latina subjectivity in process, made real through the metaphor of place. That the dream is in process does not suggest its impossibility, but rather encompasses at once the existence of the "Mesoamerican poetical past, a dissatisfying socio-poetical present, and a not-as-yet created future poetics."[30] Rather than calling this a transnational poetics, which suggests circuits of crossing, to me this suggests an occupation of multiple locations and subjectivities at once. Here, I wish to adopt Pérez-Torres's suggestion of an "anti-country" as a way to describe Castillo's Chicana poetics, embodied and unbounded, stretching across national borders to create a Latina sensibility imagined through place and belonging, inclusive and boundless.

PART II

SO FAR FROM NATION

Borders and Immigration

CHAPTER 4

"¿A'CA'O QUÉ, COMADRE?"

Border Languages and Xicanisma in Ana Castillo's
So Far from God

AYENDY BONIFACIO

Until I am free to write bilingually and to switch codes without having always to translate, while I still have to speak English or Spanish when I would rather speak Spanglish, and as long as I have to accommodate the English speakers rather than having them accommodate me, my tongue will be illegitimate.

I will no longer be made to feel ashamed of existing. I will have my voice: Indian, Spanish, white. I will have my serpent's tongue—my woman's voice, my sexual voice, my poet's voice. I will overcome the tradition of silence.

Gloria Anzaldúa, "How to Tame a Wild Tongue," *Borderlands / La Frontera*

To apologize for our bilingualism is to be illegitimate. It is to always accommodate an anglophone culture that does not accommodate you. The Chicanx poet Alfred Arteaga argues that "the articulation of languages (e.g., English or Spanish) and that of social discourses (anything from regional dialect to legalese) participate in the push-and-pull struggle to define some version of 'self' over and against some 'other'."[1] Such discursive relationships actively shape power relations, social hierarchy, and cultural hegemony. In Ana Castillo's 1993 novel *So Far from God*, border languages, particularly Spanglish and fragmented English, participate in this "push and pull struggle" for self-creation, particularly in the lives of women who are marginalized and traditionally excluded from white heteropatriarchal anglophone society.[2] In this chapter, I argue that in Castillo's novel, border languages are acts of decolonial thinking and doing, shaping the ways in which the postcolonial woman discursively maneuvers the public and private spheres.

I define border languages as languages that are spoken within and beyond the Mexico-US border. Border languages are tongues and discourses that border Western conceptions of modernity.[3] As such, they complicate the linguistic homogenization of the modern nation-state, that is, the de facto / de jure colonial bond a language has within a nation and its borders. Because border languages often stand in contrast to national identity, they can function as instruments of resistance and defamiliarization. At the same time, however, border languages are often stigmatized as foreign, as nonnormative, and, most dangerously, as the defining identity category of the other.

Border languages are points of linguistic difference and sameness emphasizing the emerging local, regional, and transnational conceptions of collective identity. These languages encompass what Walter Mignolo calls "border thinking," that is, a type of thinking and doing "decolonially" which creates the "necessary condition for the existence of dewesternizing and decolonial projects."[4] Mignolo famously states that "we should perhaps begin to think from border languages instead of from national languages" in order to combat imperialist and hegemonic epistemologies.[5] Such an effort would give rise to new epistemes, new centers, and new ways of seeing. This chapter takes up Mignolo's suggestion. I place border languages at the center of my analysis to resist white heteropatriarchal society and recognize border languages and the people who practice these forms of communication.

When the self and other collapse in a moment of identification, there always remains a dangerous difference of power. This power difference is best conceptualized in Castillo's use of border languages. Although *So Far from God* is written mostly in English, the novel features two important types of border languages: Spanglish and fragmented English. Spanglish and fragmented English may be respectively defined as an open-border language that allows characters like Sofi and "la comadre," one of her neighbors, cultural access and exchange, and a closed-border language that limits Fe's cultural access and exchange and perpetuates a discriminating racial hierarchy. Ultimately, in *So Far from God*, Spanglish is a language of political consciousness and power, while fragmented English, on the other hand, is labeled a "disability" at times equated with the progressive deterioration of Fe's physical body.[6] As Anzaldúa makes clear, the tradition of illegitimacy is also the "tradition of silence" that makes us feel ashamed of existing. Overcoming this "tradition of silence," illegitimacy, and shame is, in part, the plot of *So Far from God*.

Briefly summarized, *So Far from God* primarily chronicles the lives of Sofia (Sofi) and her four doomed daughters, allegorically named La Loca, Caridad, Esperanza, and Fe. They live on land that Sofi inherited from her father in Tomé, New Mexico. At a young age, Sofi elopes with a forbidding love interest, an infamous gambler named el Domingo. Sofi separates from Domingo after she notices that he is gambling away their land and belongings. She raises her daughters independently, becoming a leader in her private and public life. Her leadership doesn't come easy, however. Time after time, Sofi and her daughters suffer financial and health-related hardships. The third-person omniscient narrator details these hardships in flashbacks depicting the progressive demise of Sofi's four daughters and the changing cultural and social landscape of Tomé.

The deaths of Sofi's daughters catalyze the novel's plot. The first one to die is Sofi's fourth and youngest daughter, La Loca (the crazy woman), who suffers from epileptic fits. Shortly after La Loca's funeral, she miraculously resurrects and, "within the limited ability of a three-year-old's vocabulary, in Spanish and English" describes the afterlife to Toméseños.[7] From this moment on, some of the Tomé townspeople consider La Loca a divine being. Sofi's third daughter, Caridad (charity), is horrifically raped and severely abused. One day, she is left for dead on the side of the road after being stabbed in the throat and "branded like cattle."[8] After her injuries magically heal, Caridad becomes a *curandera* (healer). She later falls in love with a woman, Esmeralda. Both of them end up leaping off a mountaintop in Acoma Pueblo and disappearing into the earth. Throughout the novel, La Loca and Caridad are considered saintlier than the older daughters, Fe (faith) and Esperanza (hope), whose lives seem to be partially based on assimilation and acculturation and not religion or *espiritualidad* (spirituality). Fe, Sofi's second daughter, is invested in the American dream, which leads her in and out of odd jobs and relationships. Fe ends up working for a company called Acme International, "which was in the business of subcontracting [dangerous] jobs from larger companies that had direct contract with the Pentagon."[9] At her work, Fe is exposed to dangerous glow-in-the-dark chemicals that stimulate a lethal cancer which causes her death. Lastly, Sofi's oldest daughter, Esperanza, is a news reporter who considers herself a politically active Chicana. She dedicates her college years to the Chicano movement and lives her life as a shining example of La Raza politics. However, her life is cut short when she is kidnapped and killed while covering the Gulf crisis in Saudi Arabia. Throughout the novel, Esperanza's spirit, like the spirit of Mexican folk characters, occasionally presents itself to La Loca. From the progressive and grotesque deaths of her daughters, Sofi gains political and spiritual strength and insight. She becomes politically active and, after some initial resistance from her neighbors, runs and is elected mayor of Tomé.

In the years following the deaths of Fe, La Loca, Esperanza, and Caridad, Sofi founds Mothers of Martyrs and Saints (M.O.M.A.S.), an organization dedicated to the mothers of "*santos y martires*" (saints and martyrs).[10] M.O.M.A.S. draws thousands of visitors and spectators from around the world seeking cures from ailments and vendors selling souvenirs. M.O.M.A.S. is a political, social, cultural, and transnational space for retelling and rewriting old and new Chicanx folk traditions that redefine Chicanx feminist archetypes. In many ways, M.O.M.A.S. is a site of resistance, or what bell hooks would call a "homeplace," a "site where one could freely confront the issue of humanization, where one could resist."[11] One can also think of M.O.M.A.S. as a "contact zone" or, as Américo Paredes defines it, "a place shaped by the confluence—and conflict—of cultures and struggle of identities."[12] The narrator says, members of the group "brought all kinds of news and advice [to the meetings] that was, as part of the bylaws, generously passed on to relatives . . . as well as to relevant local or federal governments. In the case of the . . . [latter], however, although accepted graciously, it was never done without some obvious skepticism on the part of officials, which, I guess, is the nature of politics."[13] As both a Chicanx homeplace and a contact zone, M.O.M.A.S. is a radical space for scrutinizing and challenging cultural, social, and linguistic norms that shape women's lives. As *la mayor* of Tomé and founder of M.O.M.A.S., Sofi builds a movement and organization that celebrates Chicanx rituals and beliefs and communicates the political needs and desires of her four daughters and Toméseños.

In *So Far from God*, Spanglish is part of the cultural repertoire of Toméseños. It is a fusion language that gives voice to political, spiritual, and familial concerns. Before the novel formally begins, Castillo introduces *So Far from God* as a story that embraces a bilingual crossroads that both stimulates and challenges the anglophone reader. Castillo dedicates *So Far from God* "[t]o all the trees that gave their life to / the telling of these stories / y / A m'jito, Marcel, y a las siguientes siete / generanacios" (and for my son, Marcel, and the next seven generations).[14] Castillo's dedication suggests that her novel is a type of inheritance that, starting with her son, passes down to the next seven generations. Castillo's Spanglish dedication is in the authorial first-person voice. This is the only part in the novel where the author's life—Castillo's relationship with her son, the land, and the future—intersects with the story that the trees tell. This dedication is a liminal space, a type of extradiegetic border, or contact zone between the author and the novel's characters, particularly Sofi, who like Castillo uses Spanglish to transcend the white heteropatriarchal confines of the world that surrounds her. Ed Morales claims that to be "Spanglish is to live in multisubjectivity; that is, in a space where race is indeterminate, and where class is slipperier than ever."[15] As we will see in the following pages, Spanglish gives voice to the multisubjectivity of mothers, who are activists and curanderas.

Sofi uses Spanglish to categorize and declare the needs and desires of her daughters and farming families in Tomé. Spanglish is also the language of spiritual matters, as in the phrase "giving a person a limpia" (a spiritual cleaning), as well as the language of community activism addressing land rights and agricultural gentrification.[16] In other words, Spanglish facilitates what Castillo calls "Xicanisma," that is, a feminism of self-awareness and not of self-recognition. In *The Massacre of the Dreamers* (1994), Castillo argues that "on a pragmatic level, the basic premise of Xicanisma is to reconsider behavior long seen as inherent in the Mexic Amerindian woman's character, such as, patience, perseverance, industriousness, loyalty to one clan, and commitment to our children. . . . Simultaneously, as we redefine (not categorically reject) our roles within our families, communities at large, and dominant society, our conscientización helps us to be self-confident and assertive regarding the pursuing of our needs and desires."[17] In a white heteropatriarchal society, stereotypes about Spanglish language, limited education, socioeconomic status, and women's roles often marginalize Chicanxs. This marginality, Castillo posits, makes her a "second class citizen," a "non-citizen," a "countryless woman," and, I would add, an overly politicized body.[18] Because they are women, nonwhite, and their language is hybrid, they stand in opposition to the white anglophone patriarchy and to white feminists norms.

Chicanxs are always already politicized. Yet the anglophone patriarchy does not always see them as engaging the political—at least not in conventional and legible ways. There is an inherent cultural contradiction in the Western perception of the nonwhite ethnic woman who is visibly political but whose views don't align with the white feminist paradigm. In *Voicing Chicana Feminisms* (2003), Aída Hurtado argues that oftentimes hardworking and uneducated Chicanas and Mexican women do not identify as feminists but exhibit Xicanista (Chicanx feminist) virtues. These women are foundational to the family and community structure.[19] In Hurtado's words, "they wear the pants in the house."[20] It is also important to note that Xicanisma in part depends on *conscientización*. In Paulo Freire's seminal study of critical pedagogies, he defines conscientización as critical awareness that allows one "to perceive social, political, and economic contradictions and to take action against the oppressive elements of reality."[21] With regard to Xicanisma, conscientización namely addresses a Chicanx's place within a white heteropatriarchal world and the linguistic, societal, and cultural transformative moves that will aid a more inclusive and complete future for Chicanxs.

In *So Far from God*, Sofi is the clearest example of a Xicanista with conscientización. After La Loca's resurrection and while Caridad recovers from her injuries, Sofi decides to run for mayor of Tomé. She tells la comadre (a neighbor who lives down the road) that she wishes to enact "community improvement" in her town.[22] Before la comadre's reply, the narrator interjects and poses to the reader several rhetorical questions in Spanglish that challenge Sofi's credibility: "Then why stop at mayor? Why not elect herself la juez de paz or la comandante of Tomé as they had in the old days? Why not be Queen of Tomé for that matter?"[23] In this scene, the narrator performs the rhetoric of the Toméseño comadres from Sofi's neighborhood, that is, the neighborhood gossips who see and relate all the information they know. The narrator satirizes Sofi's political endeavors. "La juez de la paz" translates to "the judge of peace," which speaks of both the law of the land but also of a spiritual law.[24] The reference to "la comandante of Tomé as they had in the old days" implicitly connects Sofi to the Mexican-American War (1846–1848) and the Mexican Revolution (1910–1920), while the phrase "Queen of Tomé" associates her with a colonial history of Spanish invasion and consequent Spanish sovereignty.[25] Like the narrator, la comadre doubts Sofi's ability to become mayor of Tomé. La comadre maintains that Sofi has "always had a lot of . . . imagination."[26] For la comadre, Sofi's mayoral pursuits are delusional because they have no precedence in Tomé. In the eyes of la comadre, dreams of becoming a mayor belong to members of a white heteropatriarchal society and not to Toméseño farmers. La comadre's ridiculing comeback suggests that even if Tomé elected a mayor, it could never be Sofi, who does not fit the conventional image of one. Sofi responds:

> "Imagination? I don't know what that means, but I can tell you this. I have been living in Tomé all my life and I have only seen it get worse and worse off and it's about time somebody goes out and tries to do something about it! And maybe I don't know nothing about those kinds of things but I'm sure willing to work for community improvement." [La comadre replies:] "'Community improvement'? And what does that mean? You are starting to sound like your daughter, the revolutionary! . . . Anyway, there has never been no mayor in Tomé!"
>
> "¿A'ca'o qué, comadre?" Sofi said, hands on her hips, ready to take anyone on.[27]

Sofi's experience as a mother and a native Toméseña motivates her desire for bringing about "community improvement."[28] As a Toméseña, Sofi expresses her legal right to run for office in order to make a difference in her community. Her lack of formal knowledge about how to become mayor does not stop her aspirations. Furthermore, Sofi's "¿A'ca'o qué, comadre?" ("right here or what, comadre?") is a revolutionary call for political action, which la comadre initially reads as arrogance.[29] Sofi expects la comadre to "be excited about her news, ready to help out, considering [la comadre] hasn't had a decent crop in three years."[30] Instead of supporting Sofi's mayoral plans, la comadre returns: "¿A'ca'o qué?, ¿A'ca'o qué? What d'you mean, comadre? You can't just decide one day, like today, that you are going to be mayor of a place and that's that, and everyone's gonna listen to you, 'Yes, Mayor Sofi, just command us'!"[31]

Sofi and la comadre's heated debate begins in English and shifts to Spanglish when discussing "community improvement" and "the things they need to do to keep their land."[32] Appalled by her neighbor's response, Sofi calls la comadre a "conformist."[33] Appearing "like she was about to hyperventilate" over Sofi's remark, la comadre returns, "A conformist? A conformist? And what does *that* mean?" Sofi replies: "That's what my 'jita la Esperanza used to call people who just didn't give a damn about nothing! And that's why, she said we all go on living so poor and forgotten!"[34] Seeming to understand Sofi's definition of "conformist" and not wanting to appear as one, la comadre conveys to Sofi that she indeed cares about her community and that her farm has suffered diminishment in recent years:

> "Well, what ARE we supposed to do, comadre? All we have ever known is this life, living off our land, that just gets más smaller y smaller. You know that my familia once had three hundred acres to farm and now all I got left of my father's hard work—and his father's and his father's—is casi nada, just a measly ten acres, nomás, comadre! Barely enough for my family to live on. . . . And now we have los gringos coming here and breeding peacocks. . . . Now, I ask you, what can you do with peacocks? Do these New Yorkers eat them, like in fancy restaurants or something?"[35]

Sofi and la comadre's Spanglish dialogue is a type of call and response for "community improvement." In a few sentences, la comadre shows Sofi that she isn't a conformist. In fact, la comadre is *conciente* (conscious) of the gradual loss of her family farm and the recent agricultural gentrification of peacock farmers.[36]

Sofi's and la comadre's Spanglish dialogue is an act of decolonial thinking and doing that confronts and resists the dominant discourse. In Sofi and la comadre's dialogue, the synthesis of English and Spanish demonstrates two crucial aspects of decolonial thinking and doing. First, Spanglish is a representative language, reflecting the cultural, social, and linguistic hybridity of Toméseños. Second, Spanglish is the language of concientización. It is the language that Sofi and la comadre use to articulate and debate pertinent issues of land rights and land development. B. J. Manríquez argues that *So Far from God* is "about the aesthetics of confrontation as it ignores the ideological . . . and rebels against essentialist beliefs of both traditional culture and literature."[37] Sofi's Spanglish confrontation of la comadre's fixed views shows us that confrontations can lead consciousness raising.

Spanglish showcases their political consciousness as Xicanistas resisting white heteropatriarchal forms of political discourse and activism. Sofi raises la comadre's political consciousness, allowing la comadre to see their shared losses and political strife. For example, in order to show la comadre that "community improvement" is an achievable prospect that is important for Toméseño farmers, Sofi builds la comadre's self-confidence and as-sertiveness. In the above dialogue, Sofi shifts the topic and tone of their conversation from civic responsibilities to personal accountability, that is, to the problem of Tóméseños "who don't give a damn about nothing."[38] This topical and tonal shift takes place in a Spanglish conversation about land rights. As a result, la comadre responds to Sofi in Spanglish, revealing her own geopolitical complaints and concerns about generational land is-sues. La comadre claims "now all I got left of my father's hard work—and his father's and his father's—casi nada, just a measly ten acres, nomás, co-madre!"[39] Spanish terms like "casi nada" and "nomás" become integrated into la comadre's political discourse. These words and phrases are discursive signs of solidarity among Tóméseños, who for generations have been losing their land. This is the point in the narrative when Sofi is able to "win the conformist [la comadre] over: (And if she had this one on her side, the rest would be easy . . .)."[40]

Sofi goes on to become "La Mayor Sofia," and in town hall meetings speaks to her constituents in Spanglish. Just as she intended with la co-madre, Sofi's political purpose as la mayor of Tomé is to raise conscien-tización among Tóméseños and all those who can no longer "live off their lands."[41] The narrator states, "As time went on, the morale of Tomé had gone up and most of Sofi's neighbors were interested in contributing in some way to their community's improvement."[42] Sofi's breakthrough with la comadre and her neighbors reveals the political potential of Spanglish for articulating their needs, desires, and the steps they need to take to enact community improvement.

Sofi's desire to become mayor of Tomé in order to enact "communi-ty improvement" is not a product of her imagination. Instead, Sofi's faith motivates her political actions: "It's not 'imagination' that I've always had, comadre, it's faith. Faith has kept me going."[43] In the context of the novel, the word "faith" has a dual meaning. On the one hand, "faith" has a spiri-tual and religious implication; it is a type of *espiritualidad*, which according to Castillo can be both religious and political. In an interview with María Ángeles Toda Iglesia, published in *Critical Essays on Chicano Studies* (2004), Castillo states the following about the relationship between "espirituali-dad" and *la política*:

> "Yo estaba pensando desde hace diez años cómo se puede hacer la mezcla de la espiritualidad que hemos heredado como chicanas, como mejicanas, como Latinas en los Estados Unidos, de nuestras abuelas; y es igual con la política, porque de todas manera la mayoría de las chicanas y latinas que trabajan en los Estados Unidos con una concienciación política son curanderas a su mane-ra, porque hay mucho trabajo que hacer en las comunidades. . . . No necesar-

iamente estamos ahí haciendo brujerías, ni haciendo eso, pero compartimos muchas cosas, e incluso pues son doctoras, médicas, social workers, todo eso como digo es healing; pero estamos buscando la manera de mezclar nuestra espiritualida feminista chicana latina.[44]

In the novel, curanderos (traditional healers) like Doña Felicia, Caridad, and to some extent La Loca—who have spiritual faith—are not mainly concerned with fixing the economy and education system in Tomé. Sofi, however, is concerned with "community improvement," which is a type of community healing that makes her a curandera in her own right. The word "faith" also implicates Sofi's daughter's name, "Fe," the Spanish word for faith. As both spiritual belief and Sofi's daughter's name, "Fe" is a source of inspiration for Sofi's political endeavors.

Up this point, I have discussed how for Sofi, Spanglish is a tool for "community improvement" and conscientización. In contradistinction to Sofi's border language and consequential epistemic reclamation of decolonial thinking and doing, the rest of the chapter shows how Fe's fragmented English determines the series of unfortunate events that plague her life. Unlike Sofi, who claimed and deployed Spanglish, Fe did not claim her language. Fe's fragmented English is the consequence of oppressive social conditions outside of her control. The narrator depicts Fe as an assimilationist who "couldn't wait until she got out—of her mother's home as well as Tomé—but she would get out properly, with a little more style and class than the woman in her life had."[45] Fe aspires to get away not just from Tomé, New Mexico, but from her Chicanx identity as well. Her fate, however, takes a different course. In the novel, Fe becomes a part of the industrial apparatus and is worked to death.

Fe's fragmented English limits her from acculturating into white heteropatriarchal society, turning her into an allegory for the voiceless Chicanx. As a disenfranchised Chicanx, Fe represents what Castillo calls a "countryless woman," a woman of color who is not represented by her country or any country for that matter.[46] Castillo examines how white heteropatriarchal capitalist systems of power rely on women of color. In many cases, this capitalist machine turns ethnic women ("Latin American and Southern Asian women") into industrial commodities, that is, into dispensable resources that multinational interest groups own.[47] Fe's character shows us that linguistic difference must also be factored into the equation of oppression. Fe represents the nonwhite women workers in the United States, who become the instruments and resources of industry and have little to no control over the dominant language of English.

Fe's inability to communicate in normative English speech is a metaphor for Hispanophone monolingual Latinxs working in alienating workplaces in the United States. The life of the working-class Chicanx is mapped on to Fe's unfortunate series of events. In the novel, Fe permanently damages her vocal cords after months of crying over her broken engagement with Tom, her high school sweetheart. From this moment on in the story, Fe's speech becomes fragmented and incomplete. She is unable to complete sentences with prepositions and articles. Fe's fragmented language causes her to lose her "steady job at the bank."[48] Her employer at the bank labels her English "irregular," a "disability" and a "handicap."[49] She is told that her language makes her unfit to engage with the "public."[50] In this scene, the "public" is synonymous with white and anglophone heteropatriarchal society and its institutions. The bank that Fe works for caters to an anglophone public. Thus, when Fe loses her ability to formally engage with this public, she is fired and replaced. The narrator says, "What she was finally told [by her employers at the bank] was that although the company did not want to discriminate against her new 'handicap' [her nonnormative English], her irregular speech really did not lend itself to working with the *public*. Fe replies, 'what do __ mean, handi__?'" She never gets an answer. Instead, Fe is instructed to visit a speech therapist.[51]

After Fe is fired from bank, she becomes a stand-in for what Castillo calls the "ideal worker of the semi-legal, exploitative operations of multinational factory production."[52] Fe finds employment as an assembler at a chemical company called Acme International. At Acme, Fe works under inhumane working conditions. She is assigned to only the "bigger jobs" like lifting heavy containers full of "Ether."[53] The odors of those chemicals in "Ether Hell," as Fe calls Acme, give her excruciating headaches and "breath that smelled suspiciously like glue."[54] However, as a self-described "utilizing and efficient worker," she never complains about her work conditions.[55] As a working-class Toméseña, Fe's life solely advances the "survival of the profit-based system of the U.S."[56] Eventually, the hazardous environment at Acme induces a cancer that kills Fe.

Mignolo's call to action of thinking "from border languages instead of from national languages" invites us to read Castillo's *So Far from God* from the perspectives of Toméseños maneuvering white heteropatriarchal society with border languages.[57] In a novel that confronts white heteropatriarchal society in a historically geopoliticized region in the United States, one is compelled to think about how border languages shape identity and politics. The examples of Spanglish and fragmented English in this study lead to a couple of preliminary conclusions about *So Far from God*'s use of border languages. First, Spanglish is the novel's most representative border language for promoting and enacting concientización. As Sofi's political discourse, Spanglish allows Sofi to articulate her subject position as a Toméseña Xicanista and to raise concientización among Toméseños like la comadre. Second, Fe's fragmented English is a type of border language that is deemed "irregular" when measured against the needs of white patriarchy. Fragmented English does not allow Fe social, cultural, or political mobility. Instead, Fe's fragmented language makes her a type of "countryless woman" in the face of a white heteropatriarchal society. Thinking through the use and deployment of border languages in Castillo's novel will help us better understand understudied and undervalued methods of communication of peoples who are marginalized and traditionally excluded from Western conceptions of modernity.

IDENTITY FORMATION AND DISLOCATION

Transnationalism in *The Mixquiahuala Letters* and *The Guardians*

TEREZA M. SZEGHI

I think that the whole process of becoming a human being and living in a democracy is still a work in progress for us all, and I never give an easy answer because I don't think that there is ever an easy answer in a society.

Electra Gamón Fielding, "Crossing Borders, Boundaries, and Identities—A Conversation with Ana Castillo"

To those working for a world without borders, and to all who dare to cross them.

Epigraph to *The Guardians*

The above quotation from Ana Castillo taken from a 2016 interview conducted with her by Electra Gamón Fielding cuts to the core of her career of literary activism. Castillo's oeuvre is baldly and unapologetically political, as she puts her art to the service of social change without apparent concern about restrictive and ahistorical views of literature that might suggest its literary qualities will be undercut by overt politics. And yet, as much as she forefronts political concerns—particularly the ways that sexism, racism, and nationalism variously undermine the basic human rights of Chicanxs and Mexicanxs—she does not offer simple solutions to the problems she poses, but pushes the imperative upon readers to take action against the injustices she exposes.[1] One of the recurring arguments Castillo advances is the right to transnational movement as essential to the identity formation and/or quest for material survival of her (primarily Chicanx and Mexicanx) characters.

Transnationalism is a highly significant area of concern in academia, politics, and the everyday lives of many people. However, exactly what is meant by transnationalism is not always clearly defined or sufficiently interrogated and developed. In this chapter I place two of Ana Castillo's novels, *The Mixquiahuala Letters* (1992) and *The Guardians* (2007), in conversation, with an eye toward developing a robust conception of how Castillo frames the importance of transnational migration and its many components. This analysis will not only yield a deeper understanding of Castillo's work but also serve to advance some of Castillo's larger aims with her writing: to make a compelling argument for the fluidity of borders and the rights of all peoples to cross them (an idea crystalized in the epigraph to *The Guardians*, quoted above). Importantly, her advocacy for the transversal and ultimate erasure of national borders does not participate in the championing of transnational mobility as a panacea for economic and cultural challenges associated with diaspora—particularly given, as Silvio Torres-Saillant and Dalia Kandiyoti note, the fact that the sort of fluid and seemingly effortless movement such glamorized notions imply is inaccessible for most.[2] Castillo, however, refuses to idealize transnationalism as a means of promoting easier access to it.

On their face, the types of migration that take place in *The Mixquiahuala Letters* versus *The Guardians* may appear of too different a character to invite productive comparison. However, I argue that by illustrating the importance of repeated travel to Mexico for Teresa's identity formation in *The Mixquiahuala Letters*, as well as the many ways barriers to migration across this same border stilt the identity formation of multiple characters in *The Guardians*, Castillo makes a powerful case for the importance of cross-border migration for peoples on both sides of the US-Mexico border. *The Mixquiahuala Letters* is an epistolary novel comprised of letters from Teresa to her friend and frequent travel companion, Alicia. One of the novel's consistent themes is Teresa's desire to visit and revisit Mexico as part of her negotiation of her cultural identity, which she feels is deeply rooted there. Notably, Teresa is a US-born Chicana who is able to travel freely across the border, without the need to seek out dangerous routes off the radar of border patrol agents or to pay coyotes to aid her passage. Her right to cross goes unquestioned and she therefore is free to travel as part of her coming of age experience as a US citizen of Mexican descent who feels compelled to grapple with her cultural connections to Mexico. This does not mean that her travel is free of difficulty, as she repeatedly struggles with the sexism she finds throughout Mexican society. Yet she experiences this struggle as necessary to negotiating her autonomy in relation to and apart from various men in her life.

The Guardians' Regina and Gabo, by contrast, do not experience transnational migration as socially sanctioned, but rather as transgressive, secretive, and largely destructive. Although Regina gains US citizenship through marriage and thus is able to live openly in the United States, having first come to the country as an undocumented migrant worker continues to undermine her confidence and ability to pursue her ambitions. She continues to think of herself as a nobody even decades after her childhood experiences of undocumented migration—illustrating how significant and enduring those early experiences are for her.[3] Like *The Mixquiahuala Letters*'s Teresa, Regina confronts sexism within Mexican and Chicanx cultures, but she lacks the confidence to directly confront or find ways to overcome it. At the same time, she raises her nephew Gabriel (Gabo), who lives in the United States without documentation due to his parents' financial needs and desire to see him gain a quality education. But the lasting trauma of his mother's murder while crossing the border and anxiety about the status of his missing father take a significant toll. These events move him from a life of piety to dangerous negotiations with members of a local gang he hopes can help him find his father while authorities on either side of the border fail. Through Gabo, Castillo illustrates how the intergenerational trauma inflicted through borderlands' violence stunts his emergent identity and ultimately destroys him.

With these two novels, Castillo suggests that transnational migration is an essential human right that, when freely permitted, is a formative element of Mexicanx and Chicanx coming of age experiences in a manner, I argue, that is consistent with the 1948 United Nations Declaration of Human Rights' (UDHR) advocacy for the "free and full development of the human personality." However, when that migration is restricted and policed, it yields damaging and even devastating consequences. *The Guardians*'s characters are denied this essential element of identity formation and the right to cross borders for basic survival, whereas Teresa's US origins allow her an entirely different transnational experience. Read together, the novels illustrate how human rights are unequally accessed along national lines and thus, I contend, shed light on gaps between the promise of the UDHR and the realities many face. For instance, article thirteen of the UDHR protects all individuals' right to leave and return to their country of origin and article twenty two prescribes that "everyone, as a member of society, has the right to social security and is entitled to realization, through national effort and international co-operation and in accordance with the organization and resources of each State, of the economic, social and cultural rights indispensable for his dignity and the free development of his personality." *The Mixquiahuala Letters* and *The Guardians* collectively offer a stark portrait of how unevenly borders are experienced, depending on one's nation of origin, while also arguing that such inequity is ingrained in border formation itself. The novels thus suggest that borders should be reconceptualized as necessarily porous, rather than as fixed, if the human rights of all are to be achieved.

Insistence on belonging to one nation and excluding all who reside outside of the nation enacts an extreme form of nationalism that runs counter to the lived experiences of many. As other critics, such as Monica Kaup, have observed, many Chicana writers have distinguished their work from that of Chicano writers by refusing nationalism and articulating an identity that draws upon the varied cultures formed throughout the US-Mexico borderlands.[4] What a comparative analysis of Ana Castillo's *The Mixquiahuala Letters* and *The Guardians* can add to this conversation is a more complex and variable understanding of the forms of travel and related identity formation at work in her novels, which comprise her view of transnationalism as a broadly based right. It would be easy to argue that, strictly speaking, *The Mixquiahuala Letters*'s Teresa does not *need* to travel. And yet this very assertion invites us to think more critically about what comprises *need* with respect to travel—particularly in the context of diaspora. Teresa does not migrate between the United States and Mexico because she is fleeing violence or because she needs to find work in order to survive; she would not meet the standards for asylum in either nation. Rather, her casual and routine crossing of the US-Mexico border undercuts the border's role in keeping individuals in their nations of origin. At the same time, her experience of starkly divergent—though frequently stifling—gender norms in the two countries pushes back against facile conclusions about travel serving to undermine the border as a marker of notable differences that bear upon the lives and well-being of individuals.

THE MIXQUIAHUALA LETTERS

There is considerable scholarship about the frustrations Teresa faces in Mexico as a function of her female identity and her refusal to conform to traditional Mexican norms around appropriate behavior for women. She wears jeans, travels without a male chaperone, and is perceived as sexually promiscuous due to being from the United States. Teresa and Alicia face a barrage of unwanted sexual advances and harassment, and even fear for their safety at times (as when Alicia is threatened with sexual violence at gunpoint[5]). And yet, notably, Teresa's attraction to Mexico and sense of connection to it persist in the face of its patriarchal norms and the behavior of men she meets there. Regarding a trip she takes to Mérida, she writes to Alicia, "You may wonder why, of all places to vacation, i chose that one. It wouldn't let me rest. In all honesty, the men, the bitter resignation, hold no significance and didn't hinder the beauty of the place. There are recollections everywhere we turn, the cafe down the blvd., the movie house on Clark St., mutual friends. Why hold a grudge against a place, a country?"[6] Here the appeal of Mexico is geographic and sentimental (given the memories and connections she has forged to people there through her repeated visits to the city). Although elsewhere Teresa seems much more troubled by the patriarchy and harassment she encounters in Mexico, in this passage she downplays it and separates men's behavior from the place itself—a point she amplifies later in the same letter by noting that Alicia does not seem to resent Italy or Cuba despite being treated badly by the men of these countries.

Further, we see that it is not her ancestral roots that Teresa cherishes in Mérida, but its function as a scrapbook of her time there, particularly with Alicia. Earlier in this letter she writes of Mérida, "Yes, something of us remained, solidified by the potent sun and engraved with the memory of travelers."[7] And yet as much as Teresa's overall tone in her discussion of this city is lighthearted—it is a vacation site, a place of white beaches and happy memories where friendships were forged—the idea that "It wouldn't let me rest" is notable as well. This sentence contains a suggestion, echoed throughout the letters, that Mexico continues to pull her to it, that her work there is unfinished and repeated trips are required to heed its ambiguous call. Indeed, it would be a misreading of the novel to overlook how and why Teresa's urgent imperative to return to Mexico—which she persists in calling home—threads through the letters, even as she grapples with her disappointments and frustrations.

Juxtaposed with the toxic elements of Mexican machismo the novel exposes is Teresa's location of a matrilineal inheritance in Mexico that she longs to access and heal herself through. She writes,

> Mexico City, revisited time and again
> since childhood, over and again as a woman. i sometimes saw the
> ancient Tenochtitlán, home of my mother, grandmothers, and
> grandmother, as an embracing bosom, to welcome me back and
> rock my weary body and mind to sleep in its tumultuous, over
> populated, throbbing, ever pulsating heart.[8]

Teresa returns to Mexico City to cut through to its heart, to her maternal center, ancient Tenochtitlán. Even as the busyness and movement of contemporary Mexico City soothe her, it is the city's Indigenous roots she identifies as home and as remedies to the challenges she faces navigating gender expectations on either side of the border. And yet there is an equivocation in this vision for healing in a maternal, Indigenous bosom: she "sometimes" sees Tenochtitlán this way. Indeed, the majority of the passage begins primarily details feeling unwelcome in the family home where Teresa and Alicia are staying, and Teresa's wealthy fiancé from the Yucatán calling off their engagement. Further, any notion of maternal shelter from the caprices of men is shattered in this letter. For instance, when she returns to the United States brokenhearted, her mother says, "'You were married, divorced, been around, a veteran of wars. . . . How could you have expected him to take you seriously? Men like that, with status, money, use women like you for playthings!'"[9] These words then "sowed themselves into [Teresa's] depleted spirit."[10] Not only does Mexico and the mother Teresa identifies as her line to its Indigenous heart fail to succor, but Teresa also is reminded once more of the patriarchal norms operating within her family on the US side of the border that she has always found stifling—particularly the expectation to marry and forge her sense of self-worth through her relationship with a man. Teresa's travels to and from Mexico are a critical part of negotiating and fleeing from these norms (as well as US racism),[11] while working to forge a sense of self through access to the cultural roots she locates there.

As I alluded to above, paired with Teresa's desire to locate her cultural, specifically maternal, roots in Mexico, is the value she places on the country as a site of forging an intimate connection with Alicia—and both of these imperatives spur her travel. In fact, these two elements of her attraction to Mexico overlap in several letters as Teresa characterizes Indigenous Mexico as a space of exceptional connection between Teresa and Alicia. Referencing instances when the women's connection with one another is framed with Indigenous iconography, thus interconnecting the two,[12] Lesley Larkin notes, "In these passages, Teresa articulates female identity in the idiom of Indigeneity, reimagining her body outside of the United States and separate from the cultural matrix of Euro-American feminism. Associating transcendent, biological femininity with pre-Colombian civilization, Teresa claims universal womanhood for Indigenous and mestiza women."[13] Whereas in the United States Teresa's mother suggests that a woman should give up her female friendships upon marriage and "keep her emptiness to herself" if her husband cannot satisfy all her needs,[14] Teresa routinely leaves her husband to travel with Alicia in part to flee "patriarchal traditions" and "the husband's guiding hand."[15] Although the sight of two women traveling alone together is the perceived infraction that invites the most pervasive censure in Mexico, it is there that the women create most space for one another—even as they sometimes clash and are estranged over their differential relationships with men.[16]

Scholars, including myself,[17] also have addressed the ways that Teresa's views of what she regards as authentic Mexico perpetuate a form of *Indigenismo*[18] that appropriates romanticized and anachronistic views of Indigenous peoples—and, by extension, keep her at a distance from it. Lourdes Alberto views Teresa's romanticizing of Indigenous Mexico and related failure to reconnect with it as an illustration of the limitations of mestizaje that, when tested, reveal the relative privilege of the Chicanx subject, expose her fallacious claims to Indigenous identity, and give lie to idyllic notions of transnationalism that allow individuals a seamless bridge across time and place. I take exception with Alberto's argument that mestizas are not Indigenous[19] and that mestizas do not have a legitimate claim to Indigeneity, as well as with her related argument that *The Mixquiahuala Letters* exposes these alleged truths. As Larkin notes, beginning with *Massacre of the Dreamers*, Castillo has made the strong and consistent argument that Indigeneity is a foundational element of Xicanisma (Castillo's term for Chicana feminism) and Chicana inheritance while also cautioning against a romantic view of Mexican Indigenous tribes that might gloss over the patriarchal structures of some, such as the Aztecs.[20] I contend Teresa's claim to Indigeneity is not fallacious, but that her conception of it is. By positing Mexican Indians largely in the past (as with Mixquiahuala itself, which she describes as a "Pre-Conquest village of obscurity, neglectful of progress"[21] rather than seeing Indigeneity in new and vital forms within contemporary Mexico, Teresa undermines her efforts to recognize and reconnect with Indigenous Mexico—an argument I have developed in detail elsewhere.[22]

Although I am more sympathetic to Alberto's claim that Teresa's inability to find the home she seeks in Mexico illustrates the limitations of transnationalism—that is, that reconnecting with an ancestral country is not always clear or easy—I argue that the novel does not suggest that Teresa's travels are unproductive or ill-advised, as frustrating and even alarming as they sometimes are. Teresa does not reconnect with Indigenous Mexico as she conceives it but does cultivate a feeling of belonging, at times, simply by spending sufficient time in particular locations to develop memories and friendships there (as discussed above). Were she not free to travel routinely between the United States and Mexico, Teresa would not have the opportunity to separate her dreams of Mexico from lived experience there or negotiate between overlapping patriarchies that constrain her aspirational sense of self in various ways on either side of the border. The novel suggests that it is a birthright for a diasporic Chicana to move freely across this border to negotiate ancestral and cultural ties that straddle it, to sort myth from reality, even when no easy answers are provided. *The Mixquiahuala Letters* confirms Alberto's view that transnational connections are not always easily maintained or recovered but, at the same time, attests forcefully to the right to transnational travel, particularly for diasporic peoples.

THE GUARDIANS

For all of Teresa's frustrations with Mexican patriarchy and the structures of sexism and racism in the United States that prompt her travel, the act of crossing the border itself is relatively uncomplicated. The book contains no mention of legal barriers, problems with authorities at official ports of entry, or significant financial obstacles. She does work odd jobs to save money for her trips and once has to have money wired to her for a flight home, but she is able to finance her travels relatively easily. By contrast, *The Guardians*'s central migratory characters enter the United States without documentation in ways and with consequences that come with lifelong trauma. After Gabo's mother is killed by coyotes in the desert and her organs are harvested, his father, Rafa, eventually concedes to allowing him to stay with Regina in order to obtain an education. However, as noted above, Rafa soon goes missing, and the combined trauma inflicted on Gabo by his mother's murder and his father's disappearance gradually eat away at him and ultimately place him on a path that leads to his own death. According to Regina, Gabo's "mind sort of got stuck in that time when his mother didn't make it," and as time passes with no word from Rafa, Regina witnesses her nephew's innocence "oozing out of him a little every day."[23]

Both Regina and Gabo recall their experiences of undocumented migration as children in ways that signal the lasting effects of these experiences on them, particularly in their sense of identity formation. Regina recalls,

> When I was a girl and came up to work in the fields, I'd see humongous swirls of smoke coming up from the smelter. I'd feel like the way immigrants must've felt seeing the Statue of Liberty. Those puffing chimneys were a pair of lamps, calling the huddled masses. I didn't know no better. Now the American Smelting and Refining Company that had reigned over the region might open again. The company officials have been trying to renew their air-quality permit. That's where my "honey" comes in. Not just him, but all kinds of gente must do a whole lot of huffing and puffing to prevent the waking of the sleeping giant. Miguel My Honey takes it personally. "The personal is political," he says all the time. Not only did the smelter take his great-grandfather's life, but Miguel believes pollution affected his own son.[24]

Only as an adult does Regina come to understand that the large monument of welcoming that came into view as she entered the United States from Mexico actually is responsible for polluting the area and causing various forms of illness for the people living there. She now has the perspective to compare her early experience of feeling awed in the face of the smelter and beckoned to enter into this country for economic opportunity to the experiences of so many European Americans able to come to the United States with the official sanction of the government. Of course, linking the smelter to the Statue of Liberty draws readers' attention to the critical difference between these two sets of migration experience (migrants' countries of origin) and underscores racism that has driven and continues to drive much of US policy surrounding immigration and policing of its borders. The passage above concludes with discussion of citizen activism in the face of environmental racism and the particular role Regina's romantic interest, Miguel, plays in fighting the company he identifies as responsible for health problems within his family. Notably, Regina sees herself as too much of a "nobody" to be listened to by the government, though she does write letters to politicians. Although Regina engages in activism—with her letter writing and in joining Miguel in community gardening to avoid contaminants in the local soil—she downplays it as such and sees Miguel as the champion who can rally the people "to prevent the waking of sleeping giant"—thus figuring him as the hero of a revolutionary children's tale of sorts.

Regina's political collaboration with Miguel, along with its rupturing, develops in a way that signals how Chicanxs and Mexicanxs share certain challenges and have the potential to forge meaningful, transnational political movements. As Regina notes, "We didn't forget that what brought us together in the first place was searching for my Gabo's papa. But I will be the first to say, being a teacher's aide and seeing what I see at school every day, that me and my sobrino are not the only ones with problems."[25] She then elaborates on the contaminants that plague their (primarily Latinx) area. At the same time, Regina's and Miguel's relationship ultimately illustrate how relationships can be fragmented by the traumas associated with borderlands violence. The idea that Regina and Miguel share common cause comes full circle when his ex-wife, Crucita, is abducted while doing missionary work in Mexico. Ultimately Rafa and Crucita are victims of local gangs and their criminal enterprises, and Regina and Miguel share the frustration of feeling powerless to locate their loved ones when authorities appear to be failing. And yet, despite, or maybe because of, being thrown so closely together in this trauma, their relationship falls apart as they continue their searches. Speaking of himself and Regina, Miguel reflects, "So, for now, we're a pair of U.S. Mexicans living in parallel universes. People we care about go AWOL."[26] In this way Castillo illustrates that the violence of the borderlands affects not only those born in Mexico, but those born in the United States as well. And, without widespread government recognition that all people targeted by this violence should benefit from assistance and proactive efforts addressing the root causes of that violence, US citizens will suffer. The novel multiply illustrates how the border is, and always has been, a fluid space and that the peoples, cultures, and challenges of the region permeate the international border. Thus, nationalist immigration and border policies should be replaced by transnational approaches to shared issues that recognize the essential human rights of all, regardless of national origin.

As much as *The Guardians* exposes the dangers peoples on both sides of the border face due to the drug trade, human smuggling, and the power of gangs—all of which Castillo links to US border and immigration policy[27]—she makes clear that women suffer most. Regina notes after a long list of deadly threats migrants face, "Whatever happens to men, in my opinion, is worse for women."[28] Ximena's execution and dismemberment in the desert is the most violent and disturbing illustration of women's unique challenges—notably she and other women are separated from the men in a group of migrants being smuggled across the border—but Castillo also offers more mundane but nonetheless significant examples of convergences between gender identity and legal status along the US-Mexico border. In fact, directly following her assertion about undocumented migration being worse for women, Regina recalls menstruating during her first crossing of the US-Mexico border: "When they [her future husband's family] drove out to the desert, to the designated meeting point and picked us up, my slacks were caked with dried blood. I wanted to die of embarrassment. I cried so much, Mamá kept saying 'Shut up already—don't be such an escandalosa.' We were safe. That was all that mattered. Embarrassment is nothing when you're at the mercy of not just 'your' coyote but all coyotes, all traffickers prowling out there for the victims of poverty and laws against nature."[29] Because Regina's first period occurs in the context of a life or death situation away from home, she does not have access to the sanitary supplies she likely otherwise would. Moreover, her mother minimizes the embarrassment Regina suffers, as it seems insignificant in comparison to having survived the journey. This female rite of passage is not marked as a substantive transition in Regina's movement from girlhood to womanhood, complete with guidance one might expect from her mother. Instead, what Regina recalls is her mortification due to her blood-encrusted pants and her mother's admonition not to be an embarrassment with her cries.

The mother's behavior in this moment is not entirely unsympathetic, as it is understandable that when so many disappear and are killed in the effort to cross back and forth across the border, having survived the journey with the only mishap being her daughter's menstrual blood soaking through her pants would seem like a triumph. Instead, the passage is written in such a way as to call attention to collective human experiences that are minimized and go unacknowledged in the context of being forced to cross the border illegally for work.[30] Although properly recognizing and being prepared for a girl's first menstruation may not be as important as surviving the undocumented crossing of the border, certainly outside of this context, a girl might justifiably hope for more and expect some sympathy in feeling mortified by her bloody pants—particularly in front of her future husband's family. The fact that these concessions are not afforded her due to her legal status and the need for her and her mother to find work points to basic inequities created and perpetuated through unjust immigration policies and inhumane border patrol methods.

Although Regina ultimately secures her status as a legal citizen of the United States—and elsewhere links having papers to officially becoming a person[31]—*The Guardians* dramatizes how her early experiences of dehumanization (including, as a child migrant farm worker, being expected to be a robot without feelings or thoughts),[32] continue to influence her self-image as an adult. She participates in US democracy through such essential acts as writing to the White House and voting, yet she quickly undercuts the power of citizenship these acts might give her: "I know I am a nobody; no one has to tell me that. But I still vote like everyone else."[33] Regina's struggle with a positive self-image is further reflected within the passage quoted earlier about being greeted by the smelter when crossing the border, as she tries out referring to Miguel as her "honey," first in quotation marks, and then more assertively in capital letters. Whereas Miguel sees her as a goddess, Regina regards herself as too old and unattractive for a man whom she must build up the courage to refer to with affectionate nicknames, albeit just in her head.

Ultimately Regina emerges as a powerful force for change in the borderlands, though without a self-aware identification as an activist. Instead, her activism emerges through family loyalty and need, as she repeatedly appeals to the US police to find Rafa, consults with Grupo Beto (the arm of the Mexican government dedicated to assisting migrants), and enlists Miguel's help as well. On a similar note, she recognizes Gabo's need for a steady home and an education and prevails upon Rafa to allow her to offer these things to his son. She disregards immigration policies that forbid this care for her nephew in a manner that calls attention the unethical nature of those policies. Regina simply wants her nephew to finish high school; "I don't care what the authorities say about his legal status."[34] Regina prioritizes Gabo's right to an education over laws that run counter to ensuring this basic human right for all. Her activism becomes broader in scope throughout the novel as well, as with the community gardening mentioned above, and, in the end, mothering the child of Tiny Tears (the young gang member Gabo had hoped to save for Christ but who ultimately stabbed Gabo fatally with a shard of glass). Taken as a whole, these various and sometimes unbelievably virtuous actions (particularly the mothering of Tiny Tears's daughter) comprise a broader argument the novel makes about what it means to mother in the borderlands, and how mothering in this context can be an essential and transformative form of activism. Regina does not save Gabo, and there is no end to borderlands violence projected in the novel, but Regina's final act of mothering arguably will prevent the various forms of trauma that shaped Tiny Tears from being passed down to her daughter.

This theme of parenting in the borderlands also emerges through Gabo's telling of his childhood as an undocumented migrant who traveled between Mexico and the United States with his parents repeatedly. He recalls crying when his parents left him with Regina early on, when he was too young to work in the fields. He remembers his mother, Ximena, saying, "This is why you have to go to school, mi'jito. So you don't end up living the life of a burra, like your mamá."[35] Ximena suffers the physical tolls of back-breaking labor while being forced to be without her child so as to spare him that same labor. She has no direct access to providing the education she sees as ensuring a different future for him, but here, again, Regina steps in to carry forward and realize this hope. Further, undocumented migration involves parenting about how to cross through territory where fear of coyotes and Border Patrol runs high, as Gabo recalls his father pushing his head down "when we were crossing el desierto and helicopters were hovering over us."[36]

Importantly, a key part of the impetus for the repeated migrations Gabo and his family go through, despite the dangers, is the need to retain a robust sense of cultural identity. Gabo's parents travel to the United States because they need the work, but they return in large measure because of Rafa's sense of connection to his homeland. As Gabo writes in a missive to Padre Pio, "How many times had mi tía Regina begged my father not to return to México, to take his chances and stay, Santo querido? But México had a pull on my papa. It was his country. 'No soy un gringo,' he'd say. He came up to el Norte only for the sake of supporting his familia."[37] With this passage Castillo counters the mythology of American exceptionalism and the America dream that generates popular views that everyone wants to come to the United States and US borders must be protected fiercely to avoid being overrun. As Rafa makes clear, his home is Mexico, and his sense of identity is located there. Although Regina refutes Rafa's geographically-rooted sense of identity by noting the prior Indigenous and Mexican claims to the US Southwest,[38] the novel itself nonetheless provides powerful illustrations of the ways routine migration is so often a function of the imperative to fulfill multiple human rights—as with Rafa's need to do what it takes to support his family and to return to the nation that validates his sense of cultural identity.

Rafa's competing impulses prompting cyclical transnational migration invite haunting parallels with Teresa's experiences. Rafa pays, with his life, for responding to the call for both economic and cultural survival. He refuses to make the choice that begins the iconic poem of the Chicano movement, "Yo Soy Joaquin": "My fathers / have lost the economic battle / and won / the struggle of cultural survival./ And now! / I must choose / Between the paradox of / Victory of the spirit, / despite physical hunger / Or / to exist in the grasp / of American social neurosis, / sterilization of the soul / and a full stomach."[39] By contrast, Teresa does not share Rafa's financial constraints and is free to respond to the "pull" from Mexico she likewise feels without fearing she may not survive border crossing. However, like Rafa, Teresa rejects the paradoxical choice Joaquin articulates—only from a position of comparative privilege to repeatedly and openly visit Mexico in an effort to nourish her cultural identity. In sum, *The Guardians* offers transnationalism as a human right on the basis of its necessity for material survival *and* a whole sense of self (or at least the authorized attempt to forge one).

With these two novels, and through her larger oeuvre, Castillo makes a powerful and multifaceted argument for the right to migration—not just on the basis of economic need (which, no doubt, plays a significant role in her larger argument), but also on the basis of identity formation. Seen in the light of *The Mixquiahuala Letters*, *The Guardians*'s illustrations of the ways undocumented migration stifles and distorts identity formation are even more visible. Although the reason Gabo and Regina migrate is economic need—and the fact that both of their parents travel with their children through dangerous territory and for low-paying, often inhumane work, speaks to just how strong their economic need is—the effects of being forced to do so outside of official view, without basic essentials for travel, and even while fearing for their lives, has a lasting impact on their senses of self. The relative ease of Teresa's border crossing experiences in her (albeit frustrating and sometimes even terrifying) quest to understand the Mexican roots of her identity and the varied forms of patriarchy on both sides of the border, underscores the extremely divergent, nationally-based access to transnational movement individuals encounter.

Although *The Mixquiahuala Letters* was first published in 1986 and *The Guardians* in 2007, their arguments remain timely in the wake of President Donald Trump and his administration's seemingly relentless assault on the rights of migrants and campaign of fear against US citizens and residents of Latinx descent. While these assaults are too numerous to address here, and seemingly made headlines daily throughout Trump's presidency, some of those that resonate most with the novels under consideration in this chapter include: the Trump administration's routine efforts to overturn the Deferred Action for Childhood Arrivals (which protects undocumented immigrants brought to the United States as children from deportation), a "zero-tolerance" border security program that included the separation of migrant children from their families at the border and the protracted housing of these children at US Immigration and Customs facilities, efforts to restrict the number of people who could apply for asylum through such means as denying requests from individuals who did not arrive at an official port of entry,[40] and even using tear gas on migrants who tried to enter the United States.[41] Moreover, it has been reported that US citizens of Latinx descent who live near the US-Mexico have faced steeper challenges renewing their passports, thus undermining their citizenship and ability to travel freely.[42]

Despite the fact that even before the end of Trump's presidency, several of his most prominent immigration-related policies had been terminated or undermined repeatedly through US courts, their impacts are longer lasting. DACA recipients and other immigrant youth eligible for the program, for example, endured years of uncertainty about their legal status and ability to remain in the United States, and while DACA has been upheld by the US Supreme Court and multiple federal judges, the program continues to face legal challenges.[43] Moreover, countless migrants and asylum seekers have been returned to countries where they continue to endure the poverty and violence from which they fled. In the case of family separation, although the practice was ended by executive order in June 2018,[44] as of December 2020 hundreds of children still had not been reunited with their parents.[45] In the end, the anti-immigrant sentiment of the Trump administration and its exclusionary practices targeted toward Latinx peoples generally and peoples trying to cross the US-Mexican border specifically are manifestations of what Castillo exposes as a toxic nationalism that rests on the violation of Latinx lives, bodies, and identities.

Ana Castillo does not allow readers to think in abstractions about the costs of anti-immigrant policies but humanizes the individuals whose lives are materially and profoundly affected by them. Moreover, Castillo's transnationalism positions her in a broader Chicanx literary tradition, as Marissa López argues, of "a progressive politics of global humanism"—a vision López terms "transamerica."[46] Castillo's transnationalism is not merely about being able to cross national borders fluidly, but rather about living and bringing about the borderless world suggested by the epigraph to *The Guardians*. And yet, as I have argued throughout this chapter, her call for this borderless world does not rest on idealizations, but rather on dramatizations of the deep-seated need to return to the lands associated with individuals' sense of cultural identity and home (as with Teresa and Rafa) and the violence done to individuals' self-conceptions (Regina and Gabo) and bodies (Ximena, Rafa, and Gabo) when the human right to migration is not honored. It is not just a transcendence of national borders that Castillo demands, but a transcendence of the very concept of nation that so often is used to justify systemic inequality.

CHAPTER 6

SELLING THE "AUTHENTIC"

Performance and Hybridity in Carlos Saura's *Carmen* and Ana Castillo's *Peel My Love like an Onion*

ELECTRA GAMÓN FIELDING

El cante hondo. Flamenco. Carmen: expressions of culture that build and reinforce the stereotype of an entire nation, a nation perceived and consumed by the outsider as the land of bullfighting, passion, and fire. Sold as the emblem of Spain itself during the Franco years, flamenco becomes the motive, in both Carlos Saura's *Carmen* and Ana Castillo's *Peel My Love like an Onion*, to search for authenticity and identity. *Carmen* uses the visual beauty and power of the dance to seek the authentic, while *Peel My Love like an Onion* employs the constant back and forth of a stream-of-consciousness-like narrative, creating its own dance on paper, exploring the essence of the authentic in order to create a new identity. Although Castillo's work has been widely researched and studied, there has been scarce criticism written on *Peel My Love like an Onion* as a search for authenticity from the point of view of hybridity. Saura's film *Carmen* serves as an effective counterpoint to Castillo's work in order to analyze the performance of the so-called authentic from the perspective of those supposedly represented by flamenco. Both works converge to provide insight on, for instance, the nature of the identity of the hybrid subject, flamenco as either a true representation of Spain as a nation, or an inclusive art form accessible to all.

By analyzing these works within the context of hybridity and performance, this chapter will demonstrate that the authentic cannot endure in a postcolonial, hybridized world. Instead, it is hybridity that becomes the means of survival in today's globalized society. Anthony Giddens sees globalization as "the intensification of worldwide social relations which link distant localities in such a way that local happenings are shaped by events occurring many miles away and vice versa."[1] This phenomenon is a defining point of our era. Never before have different cultures been as intersected as they are at this point in time to create a new globalized society. Migratory movements are constantly changing the face of the world we live in, and with every passing year the global community becomes more interconnected through travel, international markets, social media, and many other means. Borders are porous and cultures live both within and outside of the physical boundaries of the nation. In the process, cultures become exposed to each other, and consequently there is a preoccupation with a loss of authenticity. Vincent Cheng explains that "the pressure to define a unique and authentic national character and identity, one that is distinct from all others . . . may indeed be growing more urgent with the globalization of our own postmodern era."[2] This anxiety to define "national identity" stems from the fact that with the constant mixture of cultures and interchanges between peoples, cultural traits may be lost or intermixed with others deemed "non-authentic" or different. Because of this constant interchange, there is a perceived loss of the authentic: "Cultures all grow increasingly to resemble . . . millennial inauthenticity."[3] It would be logical, then, to assume that there is a preoccupation with losing authenticity, an anxiety over losing one's roots in the constant flux of multiculturalism, because becoming inauthentic would mean relinquishing part of one's identity as a member of any given culture. As the global community continues to develop and evolve, the authentic loses its grip, cultures intermix, peoples connect, and hybridity in the end becomes the means to thrive in the postmodern world. *Carmen* and *Peel My Love like an Onion* exemplify this particular conundrum of modern times.

AUTHENTICITY AND THE STEREOTYPE IN THE CASE OF FLAMENCO

Flamenco has been considered representative of Spain since the nineteenth century, when dancers performed for foreigners and tourists who were in search of the "romantic" Spain.[4] The consumption of flamenco reached its peak during the 1950s, when, under Francisco Franco's regime, the Andalusian dance was used to sell Spain to the world, to make it more appealing and attractive to European and American tourists who visited the country in search of the exotic. Even today the most common representation of Spain in image is that of the flamenco dancer. A product like Maja Soap, for instance, widely found in global markets, needs no introduction or explanation as to where it comes from: the woman used as its emblem is dressed in red and black attire. She wears a hair comb and mantilla, and carries a fan in her right hand while her left provocatively lifts her ruffled skirts. Flamenco, however, is not representative of the nation as a whole, but rather is a general representation of a localized community in southern Spain: Andalusia. Furthermore, flamenco is often identified with Spain's most prominent ethnic minority, the Gypsy. Enrique Baltanás explains that "from the moment of its birth, *flamenco*—in its music, song, dance, literature, mentality—assumes the role of a creator of a new set of identities; moreover, it proposes a new archetype of dissidence: gitanismo."[5] "Gitanismo," the

Gypsy lifestyle, is at the same time rejected and glorified by the dominant culture: rejected because of its marginality, but glorified in the aspects related to specific cultural expressions, such as song and dance. By emphasizing the exotic, alluring aspects of Gypsy culture rather than its marginality, the dominant culture turns what is Gypsy into commodified objects in the global market precisely because they are perceived or deemed as "authentic"—without outside influence. Thus flamenco, a localized expression of a marginalized culture, is valued by the hegemony as a representation of the national spirit of Spain. It is undeniable that the dance, the cante hondo, and Andalusia itself have been immortalized by numerous authors, from Lord Byron to García Lorca. These aspects that make Spain "different" from other European nations imbue the idea of Spain with "authenticity" and exoticism.

Homi Bhabha's theories on historicity and localization of culture suggest that when flamenco was chosen as the image to market the nation, an imposition of nation over culture was created. Bhabha explains that "the narrative and psychological force that nationness brings to bear on cultural production and political projection is the effect of the ambivalence of the 'nation' as a narrative strategy."[6] During the Franco dictatorship the Gypsy was elevated through flamenco as a true representation of the nation. However, the Gypsy was an ethnic minority marginalized and persecuted by the dominant culture.[7] The fact that a totalitarian regime would choose to be symbolized as a nation by a minority group is a representation of that "ambivalence" of which Bhabha speaks. The nation tries to maintain its homogeneity and its monolithic status, but in order to do so and to define itself, the nation needs to highlight cultural difference because the cultural is what gives the nation a sense of historicity. As Bhabha argues: "The language of culture and community is poised on the fissures of the present becoming the rhetorical figures of a national past."[8] Without cultural difference, the nation cannot create its own myth, its own "national past." Flamenco aids in the construct of Spain as myth, as a utopian space, and gives the community a false sense of cohesion.

This mythical Spain is none other than a stereotype of the nation. Bhabha argues that by creating this "myth of historical origination,"[9] the different aspects of culture, society, and the subject are normalized. This normalization seemingly forms a homogenous nation with a common origin, but what of cultural idiosyncrasies? In a country such a Spain, one finds a variety of languages and cultural groups, such as the Catalans and the Basques. This multiplicity of cultures problematizes defining a nation based on only one paradigm. Regardless of the fact that the figure of the Gypsy was used as a symbol of freedom and rebellion by the opposition during the years of the Franco dictatorship,[10] it is because of the otherness of flamenco that it was utilized to construct the identity of Spain as nation. After the Spanish Civil War, the Franco regime cut all ties to the exterior, striving to become a self-sufficient nation. When this approach didn't work, Franco opened the country to tourism, and in order to sell and market the idea of Spain, the regime resorted to the myth and the stereotype: flamenco and bullfighting. This idea of Spain had been previously disseminated in Europe by the French, through a "colonial vision, where Spain represented a kind of exotic world in Europe."[11] This exotic world was specifically embodied by the Gypsy. If Spain was perceived as exotic by the rest of Europe, then the Gypsy, Spain's ethnic minority, was doubly exoticized as "non-European, non-white and non-Christian,"[12] turning the Gypsy into an alluring object for the European gaze. The Franco regime utilized this fascination to its advantage and marketed a whole touristic image of the country based on stereotypes and generalizations.

This idea of Spain has remained embedded and repeated as a true and authentic representation of "Spanishness" for almost two hundred years. According to Bhabha, the subject will always be seduced by the "primal fantasy" in the form of a "pure origin that is always threatened by its division."[13] By claiming that flamenco is in effect representative of the nation, the outsider is drawn to it in order to find within it the essence of the authentic. This primal fantasy, the performance of flamenco and the achievement of the authentic, become the central motif in both *Carmen* and *Peel My Love like an Onion*. Saura's *Carmen* was filmed in 1983, only a few years after Franco's death and right in the midst of "La Movida," the post-Franco period during which Spaniards were reinventing their identity within the framework of democracy.[14] Gerhard Steingress explains that flamenco musicians were "able to use the musical expression of flamenco to echo the new and dramatic challenges of life in the suburbs of big cities like Madrid or Barcelona."[15] The film questions whether or not flamenco is a valid representation of the nation, as the struggle for achieving authenticity takes the central role in the film.

Ana Castillo's *Peel My Love like an Onion* is framed within a different scenario, yet the marginal construction of flamenco due to its Gypsy influence allows it to serve as the theme that brings together issues of concern to US Latina writers such as *mestizaje*, decentralization, identity, and the empowerment of women of color. Fatima Mujčinović explains how US Latina writing creates an effect of destabilization through the representation of diverse cultures in opposition to a uniform nation.[16] Ana Castillo exemplifies this characteristic of US Latina writing through *Peel My Love like an Onion*, in which boundaries between nations and cultures become porous and movable as hybridity permeates the lines of the text, creating a mixed community that is anything but homogenous. This hybridity is represented most obviously by the constant code-switching between English and Spanish: "*Corazón de melón de melón melón melón corazón . . . de melón* is the jumpy chachachá my jefitos danced to when they were still young and in love."[17] This hybridity is also represented in the novel's three main characters, who, to one degree or another, are caught between worlds and are in the process of defining their identity: Manolío has "five passports";[18] Agustín, "a calorro born in Cleveland" who attended college,[19] lives between two worlds—the Gypsy world and that of mainstream society; and Carmen is of Mexican parentage, was raised in Chicago, and earns a living by performing a dance from southern Europe. Manolío, Agustín, and Carmen's predicaments will be analyzed in the subsequent sections of this chapter.

AUTHENTICITY AND DEATH IN *CARMEN*

In Saura's 1983 film *Carmen*, the search for the authentic dominates the plot from the very beginning: Antonio needs to find not just any talented dancer, but "la Carmen," the authentic Carmen. His dance company is putting together a flamenco version of Bizet's 1875 opera *Carmen*, and finding a woman who can truthfully portray the main character is essential. Bizet's opera is based on Prosper Mérimée's novella *Carmen*, in which the author builds a vision of Spain based on stereotypes and folklore. Carmen, a Gypsy woman, becomes the representation of Spain's character in her wildness, passion, and promiscuity. Saura's movie reinvents the myth of Carmen by not doing a "straightforward adaptation of the story, because the story embodies a colonial gaze that they intend to question."[20] The puzzle, however, is whether or not they succeed in their efforts to move away from stereotypes and generalizations through performance.

The search for the right woman to represent Carmen develops in a meta-cinematic context. This context allows for a vision of the process to bring Bizet's *Carmen* to more faithfully represent the culture surrounding flamenco, which results in a space where diverse perspectives on Spanishness collide. Flamenco's *taconeo* (foot-tapping) and guitar playing mixes with the music of Bizet's opera, resulting in a hybrid sound that permeates the whole of the film. In one of the opening scenes, the character played by Antonio Gades listens carefully to the French opera while his companions, accompanied at the guitar by Paco de Lucía, sing *bulerías* (fast-paced flamenco). During this scene, Antonio's colleagues comment that he would enjoy himself more by playing and singing flamenco than by listening to the opera. This attitude implies that a hybrid performance, caught between Andalusian folklore and the formal French operatic structure, cannot represent the authentic. Saura emphasizes a stylized vision of flamenco, away from the expected complex dresses and dance moves.[21] In order to play flamenco, all that is needed is a Spanish guitar, while the rhythm is carried with the *palmas* (clapping), and the *taconeo* of both the singers and the dancers. The castanets also help give dimension to the music. The essence of the flamenco portrayed in this film version of *Carmen* lies in its simplicity: guitar and body are all that are needed to produce the music and the dance. Bizet's opera, on the other hand, is anything but simplistic; violins, trumpets, flutes, drums—the instruments of an entire orchestra—work together to produce a formal musical piece. There is no spontaneity and improvisation in Bizet's *Carmen*. Thus, the two kinds of performance clash in this scene. From the relaxed mood and demeanor of the singers, it is obvious that Paco de Lucía's character and his acquaintances rather quickly improvise a performance. Bizet's opera, however, takes planning and the coordination of countless musicians and performers in order to be brought to life. The organic nature of Antonio's dance and Paco's music is the counterpoint to Bizet's artifice and exaggeration. This contrast exemplifies the conflict between what is "authentic" and what is exoticized/stereotyped, between the organic and improvised and the artificial and rehearsed. This is the differentiation between authentic performance and cliché that Gades and Saura attempt to demonstrate in the movie. In *Peel My Love like an Onion*, Castillo's Carmen echoes the idea of the organic nature of flamenco when she says, "But flamenco is not Broadway. It is not just a dance. It is how you sleep, dream, think."[22]

The search for the right woman, "La Carmen," ends when a woman named Carmen arrives late to a dance class and catches Antonio's attention. Her rebellious nature and disregard for constraints of any type are obvious from the very beginning. She is deemed perfect to perform the role of Bizet's heroine. The discovery of this "authentic" Carmen is rendered more poignant because the film is set during the years of "La Movida," when Spaniards were searching for a new identity within the frame of democracy after the death of Franco.[23] As Geraldine Heng argues: "Throughout global history, with few exceptions, women, the feminine, and figures of gender, have traditionally anchored the nationalist imaginary. . . . At some point of their historical emergence, nations and nationalisms inevitably posit and naturalize a strategic set of relationships linking land, language, history, and people."[24] Heng then explains how this situation brings about terms such as "motherland," "mother tongue," and "mother culture."[25] Antonio is not only looking for Carmen, he is looking for the authentic nation. It is ironic, however, that Antonio chooses the woman who best fits the French stereotype of the Spanish woman as developed by Mérimée and Bizet. It is apparent that he cannot escape the already established vision of Spanishness; he is just as enamored with the concept of Carmen as the outsider and the embodiment of Spain in her. Bhabha defines the stereotype as being an ambivalent concept since it is both unchangeable and disorganized, rigid and corrupt.[26] This ambivalence can be observed in the relationship that develops between Antonio and Carmen. There is a need for rigidity as Antonio repeatedly shows Carmen the way she should dance: there is no room for variation in her dancing; she must conform within the specific aesthetic of the dance developed by Antonio. In this way, Antonio turns the improvised and organic nature of flamenco into a Bizet-like opera of a dance that thrives in structure and repetition.

When it is time to rehearse *La tabacalera*, Carmen dominates the scene, demonstrating in the process her status as the best dancer and the true Carmen. This is probably one of the most powerful scenes of the movie, as a mixed group of singers and dancers perform together in the rehearsal. The rhythm is carried with the body as instrument, through *taconeo* and *palmas*. The *cante* (song) of the singers rises powerfully over the clapping. There is nothing French or operatic about the music: Gypsies and *payos* (non-Gypsies), minority and hegemony, together bring to life the construction of the authentic in a hybridized manner. In Spain, during the years previous to democracy there had been a clear division between "the authentic and pure '*cante gitano*' . . . on the one hand, and the folkloristic flamenco of the *payos* . . . on the other."[27] With the arrival of democracy, however, this division came to an end, with the following result: "This reconsideration of [Spain's] own traditional cultural values not only stimulated the burgeoning Spanish tourist-industry, it also responded to a growing cultural sensibility."[28] Therefore, the *La tabacalera* scene can be interpreted on two levels: The first level has to do with the selling of the nation to the viewer who is looking for the mythical Spain. Although the scene does not include the typical flamenco elements (shawls, hair combs, and ruffled skirts), it does echo a stylized version of the myth, giving the viewer a glimpse into the essence of this art form without being distracted by superfluous elements. The same aesthetic appears in Castillo's work, when Carmen readies herself to go to a party and puts on her "best black leotard, [her] brightest long skirt, all [her] costume bangles and [her] favorite earrings."[29] She would fit in the movie scene seamlessly. On the second level, this performance is a representation of the search for a new identity as a nation without the constraints of a totalitarian government, a nation with the potential to be inclusive of both the hegemonic and the minority.

In a different scene, Antonio stares at himself in the mirror after spending the night with Carmen, and he mutters, "Con el abanico, la peineta, la flor, la mantilla . . . con todo, el tópico" (With the fan, the hair comb, the flower, the shawl . . . with everything, the cliché), to which he himself replies: "¿Y qué más me da? ¿Por qué no?" (And so what? Why not?). At that very moment the reflection of Carmen appears in the mirror, dressed in full nineteenth-century Goyaesque garb. From the curls framing her ears and her black-lined eyes to the ruffles of her black dress and a rose, Carmen is the vivid image of the representation of the Spanish woman in the minds of millions of people. Antonio recognizes that fact, and he knows that they are putting together a performance that only heightens stereotypes—a performance meant to be consumed by the public. However, at the imagined sight of Carmen, he cannot help but admire her because he is attracted to "that 'otherness' which is at once an object of desire and derision, an articulation of difference contained within the fantasy of origin and identity."[30] Antonio recognizes that he is attracted to that portrayal of Spain that he himself deems false when he describes it as a "cliché."

Carmen represents the excess of the stereotype both in appearance and in behavior: in appearance she is the vivid image of the flamenco dancer; in behavior, she follows in her namesake's footsteps, taking lover after lover and claiming, when Antonio asks for a clarification, "I am free." Carmen's excess, however, drives Antonio to stab her in the last scene. The penetration of the knife inside Carmen's body is a representation of the need for conquest and control. Whether the stabbing is part of the intra-fictional plot of Bizet's play or whether Antonio really does kill her in the first layer of fiction (the movie the viewer is watching) is inconsequential. The true significance remains in the fact that he stops her. He needs to control the excess that she, the stereotype, the "authentic," possesses. The very aspect of Mérimée and Bizet's colonial gaze that Antonio had been striving to avoid at all costs as he prepared this new adaptation of *Carmen* has wormed its way into his mind, becoming the fantasy of the nation, clad in "authenticity." However, Carmen, that embodiment of the authentic, dies, leaving only a memory, bringing to question the place of the unchangeable authentic in the context of a fluid globalized society.

HYBRIDITY AND SURVIVAL IN *PEEL MY LOVE LIKE AN ONION*

The problem of performing the authentic in a context of hybridity also appears in *Peel My Love like an Onion*. The protagonist, Carmen la Coja, embodies the operatic Carmen and has a life similar to the cigar maker, needing to make a choice between her two lovers. The conclusion to her story is not as tragic as Mérimée's Carmen, since this New World Carmen does not self-destruct and, in fact, fulfills the American dream, achieving a seemingly happy ending. Identity becomes a central theme in Castillo's work, since it is the need of Carmen la Coja to belong somewhere that drives her to become a flamenco dancer regardless of her physical limitations: "The idea of being one hundred percent anything appealed to me so I didn't argue."[31] She dresses as a flamenco dancer; she speaks as a Gypsy. She makes the world of flamenco her own, appropriating the Gypsy culture in order to define her own identity:[32] "Hay un deseo constante de saber más sobre la otredad para señalar la propia identidad."[33] Carmen's involvement in the Gypsy world gives her a sense of belonging and identity, regardless of the fact that she recognizes that she will always be a Chicago Latina, neither fitting in here nor there, but rather an *atravesada*. Introduced by Gloria Anzaldúa, the term defines those pertaining to a border culture: "The squint-eyed, the perverse, the queer, the troublesome, the mongrel, the mulatto, the half-breed, the half dead; in short, those who cross over, pass over, or go through the confines of the normal."[34] Carmen la Coja falls within this definition, and multiple times speaks to her place of belonging within border culture: "I don't think that most Americans end up doing piecework like my amacita and I did, or find themselves in an illegal sweatshop having to produce a passport or risk deportation. . . . I'm not [a Mexican], I said. Yes you are. If you look like a Mexican, walk like a Mexican, talk . . ."[35] Carmen feels out of place in mainstream US culture, even though she was born and raised in Chicago, yet she also does not fully identify with Mexican culture, the culture of her parents. She exists between worlds: "You try like no one else on earth tries to be in two places at once. Being pocha means you try here and there, this way and that, and still you don't fit. Not here and not there."[36] Carmen's world would fit into the decentralized view of nation that Bhabha describes, a place based on temporality rather than on historicity.[37] Castillo provides Carmen with the tools to rewrite the nation, as she does when she tells her story in the first person. As Carmen's story unravels, she constructs her own identity, which consequently empowers her as a woman of Amerindian descent.

Language is another aspect by which hybridity is represented in the novel. Carmen tells of her struggles as a bilingual member of US society, and her need for belonging to a specific culture leads her to learn Romany, the language of the Gypsies. As Ella Shohat and Robert Stam point out, "People do not enter simply into language as a master code; they participate in it as socially constituted subjects whose linguistic exchange is shaped by power relations."[38] Carmen's life is flamenco—she lives it and she breathes it. But she is also aware of her own linguistic hybridity: "My first language was Spanish but I am not really Mexican. . . . But when Agustín became part of my life there was his language too . . . and his language brought me into a world nobody but nobody from the outside knows about."[39] She had already lived at the margins of hegemonic society; entering this new world opens the door for her to become part of an even more marginalized world, as her father's warnings against the usage of Romany, "the language of thieves,"[40] demonstrate. However, she is fully aware that she is an outsider still, among the Gypsies: "Calorro is what he calls himself. Calorro is what 'the people' are. The rest of the populace consists of payos, gajes. It not only means someone who isn't a gypsy, it is equivalent to idiot. . . . Gajo. Gaji. That probably means you. And in the end, it meant me, too."[41] She is accepted within Gypsy culture because she has *duende*, "something you are born with, soul to the blues. You can't buy it."[42] She can feel the music and perform the dance in a way that can be read as authentic, regardless of her physical limitations, but her identity as an atravesada warns her that she is not really a part of that culture. Being an atravesada has taught Carmen that identity is, in reality, performance. She is keenly aware of her own non-fixity and her ability to perform different aspects of herself in different contexts. She may speak their language, she may feel their music, but in the end, she knows that she is not *calorra*.

Just as language plays an important role in the emphasizing of hybridity, so does *mestizaje*. Agustín claims to be Gypsy, but he is a Gypsy born in Cleveland, red-haired and blue-eyed, far removed from the stereotype Manolío fulfills with his dark hair, Don Juan attitude, and dark eyes. Agustín, a Gypsy who has gone to college, however, relies on performance of his Gypsy identity to appear even "more gypsy." He follows the Gypsy culture, their concept of honor, and their attitude toward women to the point of exaggeration: Agustín is more of a Gypsy than a traditional one. He compensates for those aspects of himself that deviate from the "authentic" through exaggerated performance, building in the process an identity that is perceived as authentically Gypsy. Manolío is described as a product of the mixture of cultures: "that Byzantine finger-snapping boy. My Muslim-Christian-Jewish saint of sacrilegious yearnings, Indo-Pakistani with at least one line of maybe Otomí American blood going through his throbbing veins."[43] The Gypsies' multicultural aspect explains why Carmen feels most comfortable when she is with them, since she herself is a mixture of various ethnicities. This *mestizaje* is representative of Castillo's writing, which "demonstrates that in conditions of oppression and subjugation hybrid identity becomes a politicized mode of existence at the intersection of distinct cultures and values."[44] Carmen la Coja recognizes her hybridity, and because of it, she is stronger. She can survive in an age of globalization, taking qualities from all three cultures, Mexican, US mainstream, and Spanish, that allow her to dance regardless of her maimed body, permit her to survive in the most severe of circumstances, and in the end, empower her to be free from male/societal control due to her newfound talent and eventual fame. This last characteristic of Carmen's journey through life is a common factor in US Latina writing: "Latina authors have brought to light the specificity of female subjectivity by exposing multiple forms of women's subjugation and providing feminist perspectives on the issues of self-definition and emancipation."[45] Carmen thrives once she defines herself, once she acknowledges that she is part of a border culture, and accepts it. One of the most illustrative examples occurs when a young woman asks Carmen about her nickname, "La Coja." Carmen responds by explaining she is crippled. At the fan's bewildered reaction, Carmen reiterates: "Maybe it's a cultural misunderstanding, I say. In my culture people get called by their most evident characteristic. . . . She really looks bewildered since it isn't clear what culture I'm talking about. . . . It won't help clarify things if I say I'm from Chicago."[46] Carmen is able to define herself and even to try to explain to another her identity. She is articulating her own identity and coming to terms with various aspects of herself that are marginalized in mainstream society: her disability, her gender, and her ethnicity. There is no regret or embarrassment on Carmen's part, only acceptance of who she is. Emancipation is the other means by which empowerment occurs. Once Carmen becomes successful and defines herself, she is able to become independent from the men who had manipulated and then abandoned her when she most needed help: "When I don't want to see anyone I don't answer the telephone at all, pull the shades down tight, put on my CD on the new stereo with six speakers around the apartment and just dance."[47] Both Agustín and Manolío are back in her life, but with her success, her acceptance of her identity as atravesada, and her emancipation, she is empowered to do as she wishes. Saura's Carmen voices this situation when she states: "I am free." The same sentiment is applicable to Carmen la Coja.

The cohesive factor that unites the three main hybrid characters, Carmen la Coja, Agustín, and Manolío, is the dance. As Silvia Lorente-Murphy points out: "El flamenco borra sus diferencias y los incorpora a un mundo exclusivo, una especie de utopía donde las convenciones, las restricciones y los prejuicios no los alcanzan."[48] This exclusive world is the space where the authentic can be performed and parallels Malefyt's observations that the flamenco performed for the public in Spain is not the one that flamenco artists deem "authentic," as authenticity only happens in an intimate setting.[49] The same argument is made in *Peel My Love like an Onion* when Carmen la Coja states, "The real thing is not only too raw but too much of everything."[50] The flamenco performed for the public commodifies culture; there exists a hierarchy of various levels of authenticity and purity, and only those who are deemed worthy can participate within the highest levels of this hierarchy. The public performance is to be consumed by an audience who is not worthy of feeling and understanding the authentic. This raises an important problematic. While the artists struggle not to give away the "flamenco puro," they are at the same time willing to sell it for public consumption. Why this preoccupation with not giving the outsider a glimpse of the real? I maintain that the artist strives to preserve the real as removed as possible from outside influences because in reality there is an anxiety of loss. Graham Huggan explains that "if authenticity conveys the idea of self-discovery through experience . . . this desire may often betray its opposite—the fear of loss or alienation, of being or having become somehow inauthentic."[51] The nation needs to be defined through the performance of the authentic, restating in the process why a specific nation is different from others. Flamenco is what makes Spain "different," is what identifies Spain as a nation apart from the rest of the world. In order for authenticity to reiterate itself, it needs to be repeated and performed, and it needs the reaffirmation from those who are deemed "authentic," as well. Cheng argues that "the concept of authenticity implies and mandates the existence of its opposite, the inauthentic, the fake, the nonauthorized."[52] This would explain the need to perform something deemed inauthentic for the outsider. By performing the inauthentic, the flamenco puro is, first of all, protected from the eyes of outsiders who would not be able to understand this art form. But secondly, the performance of the inauthentic serves the purpose of defining and reiterating the existence of the authentic.

The approach to flamenco in the novel is quite different from the approach taken in the film. In the novel there is an understanding of the fluidity of flamenco, and a recognition that anyone can be born with the "soul" to perform it. In the film, flamenco is based on technique and imitation. Talent is important, as well, but there is significant emphasis put on a technical approach to the dance,[53] as is implied when students imitate the more experienced dancers over and over in front of the mirror. When Carmen la Coja takes it upon herself to teach a group of American women, she worries that she will not be talented enough to teach them the spirit of the dance. Agustín replies: "Even with a bad leg you are better than any of those rhythmless creatures!"[54] Once she decides she can teach, she is exasperated by the looks of disbelief and mistrust on the women's faces. She vents her frustration by yelling: "Don't watch me! . . . Don't worry about my brace!"[55] Carmen believes that the dance must be felt and not imitated. She conceives flamenco as a product of one's individuality: "Listen to the music . . . the guitar is trying to tell you what to do! When you actually know the steps, you can tell the guitar!"[56] Carmen la Coja's recognition of flamenco as a subjective art form contrasts sharply with Antonio's conception of flamenco in the film *Carmen*, where rather than letting Carmen perform her own interpretation of the dance, he yells at her "*¡Pero mírame!*" (But look at me!). Carmen la Coja searches for authenticity through personal experience and interpretation, while Antonio expects Carmen to observe and mimic that which he deems to be the authentic. A parallel between colonized and colonizer may be established. Antonio, the Spaniard, the colonizer, expects to be obeyed and imitated by the woman: he is the model to be followed. Carmen la Coja, the colonized, rewrites the discourse of the colonizer to make it her own and triumphs in the end. Castillo offers an interpretation of what happens to the idea of nation in an age of globalization when many cultures coexist and cross over, adapting and turning borders into flexible, porous entities. The nation develops into a transnational entity when the authentic becomes available to those who wish to claim it and have the sensibility and affinity to do so. Castillo offers a peek into a community in which all are, in one way or another, atravesados.

Both in the film and the novel, there exists a preoccupation with performing the authentic within the context of hybridity. Is flamenco a true representation of Spain? The repetition of the stereotype has become so commodified that it is impossible to see a flamenco dancer and not think of Spain; the performance of flamenco does sell the nation under the guise of the authentic. However, because the image of the flamenco dancer as the essence of Spain is nothing but a stereotype, flamenco is not symbolic of Spain as a whole. *Sardanas, jotas, muñeiras*—traditional dances of Spain—and other forms of cultural representation are forgotten and swallowed by the globalized phenomenon flamenco has become. The dance has reached beyond the borders of the nation to become a transnational product to be consumed and even appropriated. After all, who is to say that this Romany-speaking Mexican American *bailaora* from Chicago does not have as much *duende* and *gracia* as any dancer born and bred in the very heart of Sevilla?

CHAPTER 7

SO FAR FROM NATION

Borders and Immigration

AMELIA MARÍA DE LA LUZ MONTES

All three essays in this section question the complex constructions of nationhood by examining distinct aspects of what it means to live at the confluence of personal and political identities. By placing a lens on Ana Castillo's novels *So Far from God*, *The Mixquiahuala Letters*, *The Guardians*, and *Peel My Love like an Onion*, these essays offer a panoramic view of Castillo's lifework, which continually seeks to unravel draconian frameworks of *nation* while also complicating how *nation* culturally, politically, and sexually impacts the individual, specifically *la mujer*, the marginalized, on both sides of the border. The title of this section is "So Far from Nation," but perhaps it may be that Castillo's work is proposing, as does Gloria Anzaldúa, to remain "far" and on the margins of nation as a way to survive, and as a way to observe and analyze oppressive structures of power. The writers in this section work toward steering readers outside of national barriers and into ways of considering Castillo's characters as they successfully or unsuccessfully achieve an Anzaldúan "new consciousness." To undertake such a study, Ayendy Bonifacio focuses on border languages and Xicanisma, while Tereza M. Szeghi investigates identity formation across US and Mexico borders. Electra Gamón Fielding takes the reader to transnational/colonial aspects of nationhood by including Carlos Saura's film *Carmen* as a way "in" to further push the boundaries of the personal and political. All three work to offer readers various challenges these characters must navigate as they move within familial, societal, and political arenas.

In his essay, "'¿A'ca'o qué, comadre?': Border Languages and Xicanisma in Ana Castillo's *So Far from God*," Bonifacio focuses on language and what it means to be a Xicana (with an "X") from the town of Tomé. He begins his essay with a defense of speaking Spanglish, quoting from Anzaldúa's *Borderlands / La Frontera:* "I will no longer be made to feel ashamed of existing. I will have my voice: Indian, Spanish, white. I will have my serpent's tongue—my woman's voice, my sexual voice, my poet's voice. I will overcome the tradition of silence."[1] It is this quotation that allows for his investigation of the journey the mother (Sofi) and her daughters (La Loca, Caridad, Esperanza, and Fe) make toward self-creation or silence and the circumstances that challenge them.

Bonifacio's introductory page also brings to mind the *Borderlands / La Frontera* chapter "How to Tame a Wild Tongue." Anzaldúa takes the earlier declaration further, ascribing to multiple languages or a "rasquache" aesthetic, by then confronting those structures of power that have silenced her.[2] She writes: "*Deslenguadas. Somos los del español deficient.* We are your linguistic nightmare, your linguistic aberration, your linguistic *mestizaje*, the subject of your *burla.*"[3] The characters' presence and actions in Ana Castillo's works, then, are the embodiment of this confrontation Anzaldúa describes. We learn, through Bonifacio's analysis, the many ways Castillo develops what it means to have *conscientización* through these characters, particularly Sofi, the mother. Bonifacio is looking particularly at how Sofi has "entered the serpent," and she becomes the conduit for survival and going forward after her children have died. By becoming mayor, she brings working class concerns to this position of power in order to create a new societal order. He points out that the structure of the novel includes a narrator who questions Sofi, who speaks in Spanglish to remind the reader of the multiple linguistic strands within the novel. In this way, the reader viscerally journeys within the spaces of code-switching. When the novel was published in 1993, I spoke to Castillo about the Spanglish. One of the reasons she included whole paragraphs in Spanish was to have monolingual English readers struggle. She wanted them to feel what immigrants to this country feel, struggling to learn a language. When I first taught the novel, I observed the effects of Castillo's intent. My students who were unfamiliar with Spanish were indeed struggling and they complained (some bitterly), which then led us to important conversations about what migrants must experience. By not knowing Spanglish, they were experiencing being "deficient" or marginalized, an "other" outside of the text. Bonifacio underlines this fact when he writes, "Sofi's and la comadre's Spanglish dialogue is an act of defamiliarization." He also points out that it "reflects the cultural hybridity of Toméseños."[4] In this way, readers are placed within a "new" linguistic normative structure that leads to various movements within the novel: a solidarity among the townspeople. They feel comfortable to participate, which leads to discussions and mobilizing around various issues affecting the town, culminating in community improvements.

As Bonifacio also points out, the relationship between the comadre (narrator) and Sofi works much like that between the reader and text. Their dialogue is "a confrontation that exemplifies the political consciousness of Xicanistas rebelling against white heteropatriarchal forms of political discourse and activism."[5] He also describes their hybrid Spanglish conversation as a "call and response," and as readers, we are invited to observe and consider this philosophical dialogue while also experiencing how the daughters navigate patriarchal structures. Bonifacio, then, is able to tease out how the dialogue becomes the scaffolding around the lives of the daughters: Fe (Faith), Esperanza (Hope), Caridad (Charity), and La Loca (the Crazy Woman).

The names of these characters are no accident. Sofia, whose namesake is the Greek goddess of wisdom, must contend with what is happening symbolically to Faith, Hope, and Charity on a global level. La Loca, similar to the Shakespearean clown or fool, becomes the divine one, the seer, the healer. Hope (Esperanza) becomes the international journalist who is killed while reporting in the Middle East. Faith (Fe) falls victim to toxic poisoning from the weapons factory where she worked, while Charity (Caridad) is raped and mauled, her voice silenced for a good part of the novel. Outside of and within Tomé where these daughters tread, the reader is led to global patriarchal structures set to destroy Faith, Hope, and Charity. Bonifacio points out how Fe's "broken English limits her from acculturating into white heteropatriarchal society, turning her into an allegory for the voiceless Chicana."[6] She is caught within a normative English-speaking world that stands ready to exploit her. Yet, it is Sofi, according to Bonifacio, who is at the center of the novel, who emerges from the serpent (Coatlicue), bringing her dead children symbolically with her to form Mothers of Martyrs and Saints, or M.O.M.A.S. Bonifacio writes: "Sofi's legacy as *la mayor* of Tomé and founder of M.O.M.A.S. made possible a political movement for celebrating rituals and beliefs and communicating the political needs and desires of her four daughters and Toméseños."[7] "Communicating" is key here.

By returning to Anzaldúa and her study of the snake goddess Coatlicue (fertility) and Coatlicue's daughter Coyolxauhqui, one can merge the Greek myth of the goddess Sofia with that of the Nahua goddess. The moon goddess, dismembered, and a symbol of conquered enemies (a warning against those who cross the Aztecs), becomes a powerful omen here, too. One can then view a more complex hybrid symbol Castillo creates. Bonifacio's focus on the characters of Faith (Fe) and Sofi, then, places an important lens on Castillo's choice to present the novel as a border language text. I return again to Anzaldúa and her second chapter of *Borderlands / La Frontera*. It is here, under the section "Cultural Tyranny," where she writes: "Culture is made by those in power—men. Males make the rules and laws; women transmit them."[8] Bonifacio analyzes how Castillo places her characters within a rich linguistic space in order to dismantle patriarchal structures, and because he begins his chapter using a quotation from Anzaldúa, I underline his argument by returning to Anzaldúa, especially the sections on "Overcoming the Tradition of Silence" and "Linguistic Terrorism" in the "How to Tame a Wild Tongue" chapter. It is here where Anzaldúa declares that "for a people who live in a country in which English is the reigning tongue . . . what recourse is left to them but to create their own language?"[9] Bonifacio's analysis carefully unpacks those crucial sections in Castillo's novel where each character suffers and negotiates (in varying ways) language barriers, ultimately pointing to Sofi who creates (via M.O.M.A.S.) a communal, supportive space, its strong scaffolding built on dialogues of broken English.

The back and forth of language and culture is also important within coming of age narratives, and Tereza M. Szeghi deftly investigates how Castillo uses the border as a site for the possibility of becoming a bridge between a more nuanced view of cultures and language. In her essay, "Identity Formation and Dislocation: Transnationalism in *The Mixquiahuala Letters* and *The Guardians*," Szeghi investigates the ways that Castillo situates the border as a frame to locate the complexities inherent within markedly different kinds of migrations. Szeghi writes that Castillo "refuses to idealize transnationalism as a means of promoting easier access to it."[10] In *The Mixquiahuala Letters*, the epistolary form brings together the personal experiences of Teresa and Alicia. It is Teresa who is the most naïve, who does not critically think about the fact that she can move easily between borders due to her privilege, her class standing. The film *El Jardín del Edén* (2005) by Maria Novaro comes to mind because Castillo's Teresa is a mix between Novaro's characters Jane and Elizabeth. Jane is white and blond, upbeat, and ready for adventure, not thinking twice about her comings and goings across the border. When she is on the Mexican side of the border, interacting with locals, specifically the Indigenous individuals she meets, Jane is all about exploiting them by constantly photographing them (without their permission) for her portrait portfolio. Elizabeth, her Chicana friend, has come to Mexico to set up an installation of her artwork that includes a performance video (and we see a short excerpt) of Guillermo Gómez-Peña questioning what it means to be Chicanx; Elizabeth is visibly emotional watching it. She also faces a language barrier because she cannot speak Spanish. The scenes where Elizabeth attempts to speak Spanish are awkward, her embarrassment obvious. Later in the film, Elizabeth's daughter plays with neighbor kids who also make fun of her limited knowledge of Spanish. Elizabeth's hesitancy to speak, her visceral pain over not having grown up within a strong Mexican cultural and linguistic heritage, work to emphasize Jane's privileged, contented ignorance. Castillo's Teresa features aspects of Elizabeth and Jane. Teresa seeks, like Elizabeth, to recover an identity lost to her, but unlike Elizabeth, Teresa's efforts become more an appropriation of culture. The kind of "recovery" she seeks, as Szeghi points out, is a romanticized idea of the Mexican Indigenous people, which is why she then enacts a "Jane" mentality. Yet, unlike in Novaro's film, a major theme in Castillo's novels that figures prominently here is gender. In addition to navigating issues of identity and despite her privilege, Teresa must contend with patriarchal structures that define her as a loose woman because she is traveling without a man, is a divorcée, and has had multiple relationships. Castillo makes clear to the reader that misogyny exists on both sides of the border.

Ana Castillo continues to place a lens on the border with *The Guardians*, but this time, as Szeghi notes, the emphasis is on the dangers and trauma surrounding the actual crossing. Here, the characters do not easily move between checkpoints. They are the undocumented and the children of those who have died trying to cross. In addition, characters like Crucita who do cross are subject to kidnapping and other acts of violence, victims of the drug and gang wars. Szeghi writes: "As much as *The Guardians* exposes the dangers people on both sides of the border face due to the drug trade, human smuggling, and the power of gangs—all of which Castillo links to US border and immigration policy . . . she makes clear that women suffer most."[11] To prove this statement, Szeghi points to Ximena's violent death, and to Regina's first menstrual period during the days they are crossing. Castillo has readers follow Regina as she matures and becomes documented, but then even into adulthood she must contend with the trauma of crossing the border in childhood.

The Guardians was first published in 2007, three years after Roberto Bolaño's novel *2666*, which also includes horrific descriptions of the abduction, rape, and murder of women along the Juarez border. I mention Bolaño's novel because both authors place us within fictional spaces in order to more viscerally portray the reality of the border, the reality of a woman's place in multiple societies. Critical theorist Homi Bhabha writes, "The importance of hybridity is not to be able to trace two original moments from which the third emerges, rather hybridity . . . is the 'third space' which enables other positions to emerge."[12] Castillo and Bolaño, then, create a third space in which the reader can inhabit multiple and intersecting discourses; this space is like a prism—the viewer may take in all of the many surfaces while also considering each spectrum of color. Castillo goes further than Bolaño, however, by humanizing these victims, allowing us to get to know them. In *2666*, the victims are not characters but police reports. With Bolaño there is a distancing, whereas Castillo places the reader in the midst of conflict. She empowers the characters while also empowering the reader in this joining of a borderless third space. Castillo, as Szeghi argues, is positing "the human right to migration" in order for one to become a self-actualized individual, to become whole.[13] This cannot happen without establishing a "borderless world."

A similar argument is made with Castillo's *Peel My Love like an Onion*. Electra Gamón Fielding, in her essay "Selling the 'Authentic': Performance and Hybridity in Carlos Saura's *Carmen* and Ana Castillo's *Peel My Love like an Onion*," continues the conversation that Szeghi and Bonifacio posit, but with transnational, Spanish colonial perspectives. While Bonifacio works to locate identity within border languages and Szeghi illustrates Castillo's advocacy for borderless worlds to achieve a dynamic and fully idealized *gente*, Fielding beautifully investigates hybridity in terms of authenticity by setting her focus on Spain and the culture of flamenco. She gives a superb explanation of how flamenco has been commodified for economic and political, nationalist concerns. This is rasquache in reverse: the nation appropriates that which is at the cultural center of a people, reshapes it, and then packages it into their narrative for consumption: "By claiming that flamenco is in effect representative of the nation, the outsider is drawn to it in order to find within it the essence of the authentic. This primal fantasy, the performance of flamenco and the achievement of the authentic, become the central motif in both *Carmen* and *Peel My Love like an Onion*."[14] Carlos Saura's 1983 film in dialogue with Castillo's 1999 novel work well to analyze each historical moment side by side. As Fielding points out, Saura's film arrives fifteen years after Francisco Franco dies and ten years after Spain votes to ratify the 1978 Spanish constitution, repealing many of Franco's constitutional laws. This ushered in the era of a reconsideration of Spain's identity, also known as "La Movida Madrileña." The Carmen who appears in Saura's film symbolizes the energy of La Movida while confronting the rigid moves that Antonio (a character situated still within Franco's Spain) forces upon her.

Castillo takes this image of the "atravesada" and delves further into otherness creating a Carmen who is "*coja*" (lame) but more than determined to dance despite a relapse of childhood polio. Castillo sets the novel in her home city of Chicago, where she often felt on the margins of belonging. Disability, gender, and ethnicity are points of contention within the hegemonic society that Carmen la Coja inhabits. Although this novel was published in 1999, it deserves Fielding's smart analysis at this moment in history. Fielding writes: "The approach to flamenco in the novel is quite different from the approach taken in the film. In the novel there is an understanding of the fluidity of flamenco, and a recognition that anyone can be born with the 'soul' to perform it. In the film, flamenco is based on technique and imitation."[15] Given this statement, it is fitting to consider the twenty-seven-year-old singer and dancer Rosalía Vila Tobella, who has experienced a meteoric rise in the international music industry of late. Not only has she made it big in Spain, she has also crossed into the rest of Europe, Latin America, and the United States. In 2017, she won Best New

Artist at the Latin Grammy Awards. In 2019, she received the BBC "Sound of 2019," the Billboard Latin Music Award, Latin Pop Album of the Year, and the Latin Grammy Award for Record of the Year.

Much like Saura and Castillo, Rosalía creates a third space, in this case with her feminist lyrics, her inclusion of R & B and reggaeton, and her electric sound, which has come to be called a "hypnotic flamenco fusion."[16] And yet, she has been met with controversy. Despite her many years of training in dance and flamenco singing at Barcelona's La Escola Superior de Música de Catalunya (ESMUC), where she studied under José Miguel Vizcaya, a famous flamenco *cantaor*, she has been labeled a fake. Critics call her an appropriator of Roma culture and music mainly because she was born and raised in Catalunya, an area of Spain that is considered privileged and "white." In an open letter, members of the Roma community in Barrio de La Mina write: "Flamenco means everything for Gypsy practitioners. It is not an entertaining sound; it is a broken throat with its blood-taste. . . . We are expressing the huge pain of the Holocaust, of the Gran Redada, of people like [Matteo] Salvini getting to have power, the pain of outcasts. Flamenco hurts. Flamenco is being policed because Capitalism is taking cultural features, which are the resistance of historically disadvantaged people, and using them like someone who puts on fake eyelashes."[17] The Roma letter specifically illustrates what Castillo investigates in almost all of her writings: the attempts, the failures, and the successes of working toward self-actualization while also questioning the idea of authenticity.

Like Anzaldúa, Castillo seeks to explore the complexity inherent in identity. For example, the letter written by Roma community members offers examples of who they believe are "authentic" Flamenco aficionados. On their list is Paco de Lucía, with whom Vizcaya worked, and who was not Andalusian at all. Because of this, supporters of Rosalía question the Roma complaints and posit that Rosalía is being targeted because she is a woman. They also have declared that Flamenco belongs to no one. And yet, perhaps this controversy could be allayed by simply acknowledging the Roma's long, painful, and rich Andalusian flamenco history. Their efforts to resist the commodification of flamenco align with Castillo's work.

The work of Mexican artist Frida Kahlo is a perfect example of material consumption and appropriation. The mass marketing of Kahlo's paintings does not give any indication of Kahlo's relevancy within the context of other female surrealist artists of her time. Mainstream consumers of Kahlo's work are unaware of, for example, Mexican artist María Izquierdo, and how she figured into Kahlo's maturity as an artist. Fellow artists such as the photographer Lola Álvarez Bravo and painters Remedios Varo and Leonora Carrington were all part of a vibrant community of women artists. But in US museums and bookstores, these women go unmentioned, and what the consumer is offered are Frida Kahlo T-shirts, mugs, and dolls. Journalist Jenny Valentish writes that "Kahlo's face has become shorthand for modern feminism. Typing her name into Etsy's search engine brings up 15,456 results of non-licensed merchandise. . . . In the UK, Theresa May wore a bracelet made up of miniature panels of the artist's paintings at the Conservative party's 2017 conference."[18] Imagine: a right-wing Conservative leader wearing, for all to see, the paintings of a Mexican Communist painter, who, toward the end of her life, was a Stalinist. But again, all the complex particulars of Kahlo's personal, political identity have been watered down, shaped and packaged to mean whatever one wants her to mean. Since May has experienced much adversity in her position as prime minister, I would not be surprised if she was identifying with Kahlo as a woman having to negotiate her right to paint and be acknowledged in a male-dominated world, just as May continually had to spar and insist on her right to lead. So much is left wanting in May's choice of adornment. That said, Fielding, Szeghi, and Bonifacio's arguments, braided together, illustrate the mastery of Ana Castillo's work, her insistence upon a nuanced and borderless world, an Anzaldúan third space.

PART III

GIVE IT TO THE GLOBE

Considering Gender and Sexuality

CHAPTER 8

QUEERING SPACE IN ANA CASTILLO'S *GIVE IT TO ME*

DANIEL SHANK CRUZ

As its title suggests, sex is everywhere in Ana Castillo's 2014 novel *Give It to Me*. The protagonist Palma has sex with many of the people she meets from Chicago to New Mexico to California regardless of their gender or sexual preference. While the high number of sex scenes (there are at least twenty-five, about one every ten pages on average) cause the novel to resemble bad pornography at times in that the plot seems repetitive and the non-sex scenes seem to be there simply to act as conduits to the next coupling, the sex scenes' function is not as banal and boring as this comparison might suggest. Instead, like good pornography, they play an educational role for readers because they celebrate Palma's bisexuality and create a conceptual space that is both politically and sexually queer.[1] This space is moveable, which allows Palma to manifest a transnational queer Latinx solidarity as she travels from the United States to Colombia, Mexico, and Brazil. Ed Morales argues for the liberating possibility of "a pan-Latinx . . . identity," and claims that this liberation manifests itself in "Latinx art forms" because they "defy categorization."[2] In other words, the concept of Latinx is a queer one because of its openness. It refuses to fit nicely into prescribed societal categories, instead opting for belief in the possibility of a radically trans-formed society just as queer theory does.

Give It to Me is an example of how the queerness of Latinx intersects with the queerness in the sexual and political realms enumerated by queer theory in art. This queer Latinx intersection is what draws me to the novel as a reader. As a bisexual Latinx I was thrilled to encounter Palma as a character when I first read the book because depictions of us in literature are so rare. The book became for me what Sara Ahmed calls "an archive of rebellion" because of how Palma lives according to her own queer terms.[3] Ahmed contends that living out an "archive" of queerness "derive[s] as much from our struggle to write ourselves into existence as from who appears in what we write. This intimacy of standing against and creativity can take the form of a book."[4] This is what Castillo, another bisexual Latinx,[5] does in writing Palma's story, and I value the novel because of how it archives queer Latinx experience. Since at least the publication of Ann Cvetkovich's *An Archive of Feelings* and Juana María Rodríguez's *Queer Latinidad* in 2003, a strain of queer theory has been interested in how queer experience gets archived in material culture.[6] This work emphasizes the importance of paying attention to lived queer lives for queer theory in order to make it more accessible to non-academics. In the way it does this by delineating queer space and offering a model for how to successfully live queerly, thus advocating for a transformed society, *Give It to Me* functions as what Alison Reed calls "literature as theory."[7] The novel uses Palma's experiences to theorize what a queer way of living for all might look like rather than beginning with theory. I use this backwards-seeming approach, which dates back at least as far as Jane Gallop's 2002 book *Anecdotal Theory*, and which Rodríguez champions as one tool for theorizing queer Latinx experience,[8] in my reading of the novel. Such a model is especially necessary in these troubled times when Latinxs, queers, and women, among others, have been under attack by the recent US regimes.

In modelling queer life as a form of theory, *Give It to Me* extends what Fiona Mills calls "Castillo's queering project" in her earlier fiction throughout Castillo's oeuvre,[9] establishing her as an important queer author, not only an important Latinx one. Although there are bits and pieces of LGBTQIA+ plot in Castillo's earlier books *So Far from God*, *Loverboys*, and *Watercolor Women, Opaque Men* that critics such as Mills, Ibis Gómez-Vega, and Alicia Gaspar de Alba examine, *Give It to Me* is Castillo's queerest book in both plot and message because of how it uses its sex-saturated narrative to educate readers.

Alongside its depiction of Palma's sex life, *Give It to Me* illustrates queer space via at least three elements. First, it critiques mainstream American values. This critique, which begins on the novel's first page in its naming of consumeristic Americans as "Mulch,"[10] immediately sets the tone for Palma's search for new, queer, radical ways of living that are more fulfilling than those offered her by conventional mores. Second, the book places itself into the queer Latinx literary tradition via its mention of John Rechy's work. Although fleeting, Palma's discussion of her friendship with Rechy is an important act of queer archiving, signifying more than it might first suggest. It reminds readers that queer Latinxs have existed long before there was space to write openly about our experiences as Castillo does, that the queer tradition has not been as white as queer theory has often portrayed it to be. Palma's joyful claiming of her sexuality is reminiscent of the stories in Rechy's account of gay life in the 1970s, *The Sexual Outlaw*, and both books share an episodic form. Third, the novel claims the importance of an intersectional selfhood through Palma's explorations of spirituality, especially her encounter with the Buddhist teacher Thich Nhat Hanh. Palma's interaction with Hanh toward the end of the novel, which is given its own chapter to show its importance, is significant because it illustrates the possibility of queer spirituality, an intersection that is marginalized in much of queer theory and queer literature. This spirituality is an open, accepting one rather than a dogmatic one, just like the Buddhist canon. In exploring queer spirituality, the novel critiques the queer tradition—itself a quintessentially queer act—even as it claims its rightful place in it. *Give It to Me*'s exploration of spirituality, a subject that remains prominent in Latinx life in the United States and elsewhere, is an essential element of its role as Latinx queer theory.

Palma begins mapping out *Give It to Me*'s queer conceptual space early on in the narrative. She names the necessity for this nonphysical location, noting that "if you had a job or relationship, a place made some sense" (34), but because she does not have either of these things keeping her anchored in New Mexico she needs to travel in order to find happiness. Palma's journeys throughout the book reference the American road trip genre while simultaneously queering it because her travels do not have a single destination. They are circular rather than linear, jumping back and forth between the Midwest, the Southwest, and international locales. Similarly, Palma's itinerant work as a freelance translator, which is itself a transnational occupation as well as a job she can take with her on the road, is significant because it is a difficult intellectual occupation that emphasizes that Palma is a whole person rather than just a body interested in sex.[11] She wants a balanced, healthy life, and realizes that she must use unconventional means to find it.

Palma's first sexual relationship, one that ebbs and flows throughout the novel unlike the others, is with her "cousin" Pepito. Although it is between a woman and a man, the relationship is a queer one because it is portrayed as incestuous (although Pepito is not Palma's cousin, she, and therefore readers, believes he is until the final chapter).[12] Palma displays no shame in lusting after Pepito, whom she has wanted to have sex with since she was a teenager and whom she would want to be her "co-star" if she acted in "porn" (8, 12). The novel thus signifies immediately that it will explore non-heteronormative sexual desires without judgment, affirming that any act between consenting adults is acceptable. It is also significant that Palma highlights pornography here because it signals to readers that the rest of her narrative will resemble the pornographic trope of a series of sex scenes loosely tied together by a throwaway plot. Unlike in pornography, where the plot does not really matter even though it is there to add some sort of perceived legitimacy to the work, the sex in *Give It to Me* is the plot; it is the action that readers are supposed to pay attention to, not for sexual gratification (it is not erotica, and almost none of the sex scenes are detailed), but because of the argument it makes about what a queered society might look like.

Part of this argument comes via the conclusion of Palma and Pepito's relationship at the end of the novel. As part of their on-again, off-again rhythm, they sometimes engage in intercourse and sometimes only foreplay (e.g., 15, 57, 87, 90, 159), and the question of whether they will ever want each other at the same time hangs over the entire narrative. When Palma discovers that Pepito is not her cousin, it seems as though a fairy-tale ending with them living happily ever after is imminent, but instead Palma definitively ends the relationship and decides she will move to Brazil for her next adventure (254–55). The novel teases readers with a conventional straight ending and then rejects it in favor of its queer trajectory, broadening Palma's queer reach even further. She chooses the freedom of her queer space rather than the bonds a relationship with Pepito would put on her despite having been besotted with Pepito for much of the book. As I discuss further below, Castillo's decision to have Palma reject a permanent relationship with a man negatively affected *Give It to Me*'s publication. Such a reaction shows the revolutionary nature of Palma's choice.

Ursula, who works as an erotic dancer, is Palma's next partner, and they date for a short while before Ursula moves away from Albuquerque. Their relationship, which has a three-page chapter devoted to it (24–26), is significant because it firmly establishes Palma's attraction to all genders. While Palma names her bisexuality early in the novel (6), and while one can certainly be bisexual without being in relationships with multiple genders, bisexuals still face discrimination from both the heterosexual and queer communities, so *Give It to Me* fights against this biphobia by having Palma embrace the openness that bisexuality epitomizes.[13] Shiri Eisner asserts that bisexuality's openness encompasses more than the sexual, instead functioning as an "epistemology" through "its ideology of inclusion, diversity, and political awareness."[14] Palma lives out these values. Her bisexuality is not a phase before she fully commits to a man, nor, as her lifelong crush on Pepito illustrates, is it a cover for lesbianism that she might fear fully revealing. Gómez-Vega accuses Castillo of this kind of unwillingness to admit her supposed lesbianism in her early work. Gómez-Vega fails to consider the possibility that Castillo is bisexual and thus of course would refuse to acknowledge her actually nonexistent lesbianism.[15] It is thus no surprise that *Give It to Me* takes pains to make Palma's bisexuality evident early in its narrative. As the novel amply shows, she is attracted to specific individuals rather than to specific genders. Palma's open bisexuality along with her refusal to judge Ursula's sex work, which both indicate her desire for a new, sex-positive society, show that she is both politically and sexually queer.

Soon after Ursula leaves, Palma has two sexual encounters that again serve as sly nods to readers, acknowledging the novel's porn-like structure. In the first, Palma sunbathes topless in her backyard to entice a day laborer, whom her neighbor has hired to do some gardening, to have sex with her. His attempts to actually trim her house's bushes—an activity that the novel obviously means as a double entendre—"annoy her but there were some things one had to put up with to get certain things [i.e., herself] done" (45). They have mediocre sex and then he emphasizes the pornographic reference by pulling out and giving readers a cum shot, ejaculating onto Palma's "butt" (47). In the second, Palma invites a worker from the computer store home. They have sex standing up with him "thump[ing . . . her . . .] against the wall" as she laments that his facial expression makes it clear that he is only interested in his pleasure, not hers (65). Both scenes replicate the "horny lonely woman seduces an unsuspecting service worker" pornographic trope, but queer it because Palma controls each scene, living out her own fantasies rather than a male viewer's. Her willingness to assert herself in this manner is radical in light of society's continual policing of female and queer sexualities even though the resulting sex is unsatisfying. Here *Give It to Me* is realistic in its acknowledgment that sometimes sex does not live up to one's expectations. Palma does not live a fairy-tale sexual existence where every encounter is wonderful. It is her willingness to continue to seek pleasure despite her occasional bad experiences that make her sexual experiences important rather than their end results.

Palma also engages in several queer liaisons with unconventional combinations of bodies and practices. Early in the book, she showers with her gay friend Randall as they prepare to go out drinking, and after drying off they masturbate together and Palma fellates him (38). Although this scene seemingly performs heterosexuality, as with all of Palma's encounters with men it is queer because of her polyamory, which is nonnormative because it goes against society's expectations for women's sexual behavior. It is also queer because it is solely about the participants' orgasms rather than the possibility of "couplehood," as symbolized by their choice of non-procreative acts. Likewise, because the encounter is about desire and gratification, their seemingly mismatched genders and orientations fall away, epitomizing Eisner's bisexual epistemology. In the moment, they do not worry about the labels they put on themselves.

The two threesomes that Palma participates in also emphasize queer desire. The first involves her gay friend Mishu fucking their mutual acquaintance Austin while he fucks Palma (80). While being another example of unsatisfying sex for Palma—she feels squished under the two men despite being initially excited to join in—the formation of the threesome (a man fucking a man while a man and a woman fuck) is important because it symbolizes the possibility of a new society where queers and straights can live harmoniously. In the words of Lauren Berlant and Michael Warner, the threesome's form is a "world-making project," an act that helps sustain "queer culture."[16] Viewed in this light, the attempt is more important than the success of the act, which is interrupted by a hotel maid before any of the three orgasm.

The second threesome includes Palma's ex-girlfriend Dani, whom she had met in Mexico after fleeing her bad marriage in Colombia (170). The two hook up with Dani's current girlfriend after running into each other at a hotel (162). The all-female roster of the encounter combined with the international resonances of Palma and Dani's relationship acts as a metaphor for the necessity of a global queer feminism of the kind Castillo explains affects her thinking on gender because of its examination of the gender/race/class intersection, something that she finds missing in white US feminism.[17] The conceptual space of this worldview is illustrated by the scene's anonymous context because the hotel setting for each threesome deemphasizes their physical locations in favor of the transferable queer spaces they create. They happen to take place in New Mexico and Florida, respectively, but they could occur anywhere queer bodies are.

I have attempted to examine these scenes, which represent a mere sampling of the sexual encounters in the novel, in a way that replicates the way they are written. They are short, without much commentary, and then the narrative moves onto the next one, a structure that is, again, reminiscent of pornographic films, especially from the 1970s. Michael Perkins calls this form in erotica and pornography "assaultive eroticism" because of how it overwhelms the reader or viewer, thereby having "a liberating effect" because of the way it breaks down its audience's inhibitions.[18] *Give It to Me* causes this effect through its insistence on allowing Palma to experience all kinds of sexual encounters. Readers may be shocked at the beginning of the book when Palma lusts after her cousin, but by the end we have been trained to appreciate her sexual explorations and to look forward to what will happen next. Therefore, these short scenes are what give *Give It to Me* its weight as a piece of theory because Palma gives us an example for how to live a queer life in both the sexual and the political sense. The best pornography is a celebration of sexuality rather than a degradation of it, and likewise the novel espouses a sex-positive message that is desperately needed in these repressive times. Palma rejects the patriarchal restrictions society attempts to place on women's bodies and uses hers for her own pleasure. Although Castillo laments that many queer women still feel pressure to conform to heterosexual standards,[19] Palma is able to break free of these expectations. Her active sex life functions as a path toward finding herself as a person, not merely as a means to achieving sexual gratification.

Palma's sex life is only one example of how she maintains a politically queer existence. She insists on a cosmopolitan lifestyle, engaging in intellectually rewarding work, traveling whenever she can, freely celebrating her sexuality, and eating well-made food when she can get it. Although she appreciates fine things, she does so out of a sense of curation rather than crass "mulch" materialism. As someone who has been destitute, she understands the importance of quality objects. But at the same time, she is not willing to settle for the kind of economic security that would be available with a steady job in one place and with a traditional middle-class relationship. She does not want to be one of the "Little Mulch mice in a maze, rushing toward parenthood, taking care of aging parents, obtaining mortgages" (205). She tried that once with her ex-husband Rodrigo and it did not work out. Similarly, she does not have a good relationship with her biological family. When she tracks down her parents, who abandoned her as a baby, she finds that they are homophobic and not interested in including her in their lives (233–34). Instead, Palma creates a queer family with her friends and commits to living her itinerant queer life. There is no guarantee that her new business venture at the end of the novel will succeed, but Palma understands that it is what she needs to make her happy, so she pursues it. The company will sell everything "from handbags to fuzzy handcuffs—a brand without borders" (243). Palma is queer in her business philosophy both in the sex-themed items she sells and the openness the company embraces in its refusal to be easily categorized. This double-edged queerness exemplifies what Rodríguez calls the Latinx "disturb[ance of] the numbing monotony of straight middle-class whiteness" in her theorizing of the intersection between queer and Latinx, which she views as a symbiotic combination because Latinx "racialized excess is already read as queer" by mainstream society.[20] Palma's rejection of mulchdom is therefore both a queer and a Latinx move.

Palma's decision to sell handcuffs is also significant. One glaring, and, in light of the rest of the book, rather surprising omission is the lack of a sex scene involving BDSM, although the Marquis de Sade gets mentioned favorably once (60). Rodríguez claims BDSM as a queer Latinx practice in both *Queer Latinidad* and *Sexual Futures*.[21] Although Palma's mention of "handcuffs" is fleeting, it is important to highlight it because she also affirms kinkiness as valid even though she does not engage in it herself. *Give It to Me* thus adds BDSM to the queer Latinx archive.

While Palma's narrative exemplifies queer activism, *Give It to Me*'s existence is itself an act of activism in light of the publication difficulties it encountered. Castillo notes in an essay from 1989 that Chicana writing about sexuality has only been able to find a publishing home in "the small press and self-published chapbooks."[22] Similarly, in an essay from 1991 she observes that women's erotic writing is not seen "as serious intellectual discourse."[23] It may seem anachronistic to cite these early works, but unfortunately their sentiments remain relevant, as the publishing world has changed little enough in the subsequent quarter century that *Give It to Me* was not viewed as marketable by Castillo's then-publisher, Random House. Random House refused to publish the novel because it does not include a more traditional love story, so Castillo was forced to break her contract with them in order to have it published elsewhere.[24] Castillo writes that it took "the relentlessness of a holy mission" to get her early books printed,[25] and despite her successful career since then she still had to struggle in this way to find a publisher for *Give It to Me* even though it is just as aesthetically accomplished as her more well-known books. This institutional silencing of queer narratives shows why the novel's celebration of queer life remains necessary. The novel's publication by a small press epitomizes how this oppression is present even in the seemingly liberal world of publishing. Castillo's willingness to break her contract for the book shows that she is willing to stand up to censorship in the publishing industry so that she can create the art she wants to create.

Give It to Me acknowledges its place within the queer literary tradition that has flourished despite such institutional opposition via its mention of queer authors such as Anaïs Nin (herself a queer Latina), Gore Vidal, and Colette (180), and, most notably, of Palma's friendship with John Rechy (185). T. Jackie Cuevas writes that "contemporary queer Chicana texts" often converse with "texts of the previous generation."[26] Although Castillo is of the older generation of writers that Cuevas claims has influenced younger writers, *Give It to Me* enacts the intergenerational communication that Cuevas names through its citation of Rechy, a member of the generation of queer Latinx writers before Castillo's. Although Palma is not a writer, the novel's inclusion of Rechy affirms that the queer literary community is another kind of queer family akin to that which Palma creates with her friends. When Palma visits Austin and Mishu in Los Angeles, Rechy comes to her mind because some of his books are set there. She muses that "he was beautiful when he wrote his [1967] novel *Numbers*" (185).[27] *Numbers* is about a man who tries to have as many sexual encounters with men as possible during a trip to Los Angeles. Its form is episodic like *Give It to Me*'s, emphasizing the sex scenes rather than what comes in between them. So one can read Castillo's book as a feminist rewriting of Rechy's.

But Rechy himself also does a queer—in the radical queer theory sense—rewriting of *Numbers* in his 1977 book *The Sexual Outlaw: A Documentary; A Non-Fiction Account, with Commentaries, of Three Days and Nights in the Sexual Underground*, a book that is also relevant when exploring *Give It to Me*'s highlighting of his legacy. *The Sexual Outlaw* includes the same kind of sex scenes found in *Numbers* with even less filler in between as its protagonist again tries to have as many sexual encounters as he can during a weekend. Cuevas notes the importance of these scenes because of the queer "nonreproductive time of [the] erotic subcultures" in Rechy's work.[28] Just as time is used for the pursuit of pleasure rather than for seemingly respectable conformist, capitalist activities in *Numbers* and *The Sexual Outlaw*, so, too, is it used by Palma throughout Castillo's novel.

The Sexual Outlaw also includes "Voice Overs" interjected into the narrative that provide commentary about the societal importance of queer sex. For instance, Rechy asserts that "the promiscuous homosexual is a sexual revolutionary," and that queer sex questions the foundations of monogamy and thus of society.[29] Through these statements he argues that the sex in his books (and, by extension, in *Give It to Me*) is not just about sex in the moment and the bodily pleasure it provides, which is itself revolutionary in our body-hating society. It is also about creating a completely transformed society, one that embraces those on the margins rather than insisting on the conformist "mulchdom" that Palma despises.

Aside from its subject matter, *The Sexual Outlaw*'s form is also queer. It calls itself a "documentary," which is a genre of film rather than literature, so the book names itself ambiguously. Although its second subtitle (which is only printed on the title page, and is thus easy to miss) classifies it as "Non-Fiction," and although its "Foreword" describes it as what today we would call a memoir or creative nonfiction, with the narrative based in actual experience but some details changed, Rechy writes all of the sex scenes—two-thirds of the book—in third person and the main character is named "Jim" rather than "John."[30] These characteristics lead to a reading experience that falls into an amorphous area between fiction and nonfiction. The ways the book thus plays with genre epitomize queer principles, which are interested in the in-between and the previously unnamed.

Rechy's doubling of the same narrative in *Numbers* and *The Sexual Outlaw*, which he acknowledges in the latter,[31] emphasizes its importance as a new queer model for being, one that unabashedly claims bodily pleasure as good without worrying about standards of conventional sexual propriety. *Give It to Me* furthers this message by replicating it in a female transnational context, making it accessible to everyone, not just men from the United States. Castillo's novel also does a better job of showing how sex may be healthily integrated into a queer life whereas the men in Rechy's books actively seek it out as a form of self-validation; it succeeds as a revolutionary act by the men when they are able to find sexual partners, but fails when they are not, whereas Palma views the attempt as the important thing, another example of her bisexual epistemology.

In an interview with Alicia Cole, Castillo names the importance of the revolutionary fervor of the 1960s as an inspiration for her work.[32] Rechy's early work is a precursor to this activism, as his seminal 1963 novel *City of Night* was published before both the gay liberation movement and the Chicano movement became widely visible,[33] thus it is understandable that *Give It to Me* pays homage to him. Christopher Castiglia and Christopher Reed laud *The Sexual Outlaw* as an important radical ancestor of queer theory, and lament that queer scholarship now embodies "an academic depressiveness" that no longer contains "the rage, amusement, passion, defiance, pride" that characterizes the writing of Rechy and his queer contemporaries.[34] In contrast, *Give It to Me*'s narrative works as an exuberant piece of queer literature as theory in the same way Rechy's work does.

Castillo's novel also works to broaden queer thinking in its treatment of religion. Patrick S. Cheng posits that "it is difficult to be . . . out" as religious in many queer settings, and Ann Pellegrini also claims that queer theory is built around a "religious/secular divide," which assumes that the religious has nothing to offer the queer.[35] Although Mills argues that there are "queer" religious expressions in Castillo's 1993 novel *So Far from God*, and Cynthia R. Wallace also examines the importance of religion in Castillo's earlier works,[36] *Give It to Me*'s investigations of spirituality are more positive than these previous instances because they abandon queerphobic Christianity in favor of other practices. Palma offers Castillo's clearest example for how to integrate religion into a queer life even when one's religious experiences are not always liberating. Again, *Give It to Me* acts as an example of literature as theory, offering a way for queer theory to ease away from its utter suspicion of religion. Palma acknowledges her difficult experiences with religion, noting that the Christian God she was raised with has been cruel to her (6), so in this way her experience matches the all too common North American queer religious experience. However, Palma does not give up on her spiritual life, seeking after spiritual succor throughout the novel, a journey that is intertwined with her queer sexual one because, as Castillo argues elsewhere, "the violent repression of our spirits and sexuality" is completely unnatural.[37] In discussing the two together, Castillo, and by extension *Give It to Me* via Palma, claims spirituality and sexuality must be viewed as complementary to one another rather than as the opposites that many religions and many queer theorists assume them to be.

Palma needs to find a way to be present in her life because she does not have geographical roots to center her, and her spiritual journey is one way she tries to accomplish this. The importance of her journey is acknowledged by how *Give It to Me* bookends her story, as the book is dedicated to a saint and the last word is "ALELUYA" (255), so it is ensconced in the spiritual. The story's spirituality is an open one, drawing from many traditions including Native American practices, Catholicism, and Buddhism. Palma's interactions with Buddhism are especially important symbolically because of the Buddhist tradition's openness. As Donald S. Lopez Jr. observes, Buddhism does not have a set canon of sacred texts like religions such as Christianity and Islam do, which means that the religion's theology and practices are much less dogmatic than in other religions.[38] The acceptance of people no matter where they are spiritually that results from this philosophy is evident in Palma's interaction with Thich Nhat Hanh. She gets an audience with him when he sees her crying in a crowd, and in their conversation he tells her that to "heal" herself of the anger she has with her biological family she must work to heal others (220–21). His advice is politically queer because of its emphasis on ethics and its belief that it is possible to radically transform society through one's actions. It also emphasizes the importance of queer community whether that community includes one's relatives or not. Hanh's last words to Palma before they meditate together, which are the only ones from the novel in bold, are "everyone has the right to achieve happiness" (222). This chance for happiness depends on an end to the oppressions Palma combats intersectionally as a queer woman of color. Palma's interaction with Hanh gives her hope for inner peace in the future and helps to make *Give It to Me* a hopeful book despite the various difficulties she encounters.

Aside from other previously mentioned similarities to Palma, Castillo writes that, just as Palma finds it best for herself to move from partner to partner, she has never been able to have a "relationship" of more than a few years.[39] Thus the novel is based in part on lived experience, which is where the best theory originates. As Cuevas posits, we need to "allow queer brown texts and lives to theorize themselves" rather than just relying on mostly white academic theory.[40] *Give It to Me* does this by letting Palma find a way of living that works for her without judging her. The narrative does not force her to "settle down" or to "find the answer." Instead, she keeps living her itinerant, exuberant life, moving to Brazil to begin yet another queer transnational adventure, open to whatever she may find. In doing so, Palma embraces the openness that being Latinx and queer each entail.

Palma's risky yet hopeful choice rejects the conformity of US mulchdom, offering an example of the kind of radical act necessary for creating a queered society. *Give It to Me*'s archiving of Palma's queer Latinx actions across a transnational landscape teaches readers how to live intersectional lives. Through Palma's bisexual epistemology, the novel argues for the importance of learning from the queer Latinx tradition, and shows how to queer the tradition itself by making space for spirituality within it. Whether through our sex lives or in other ways, it urges us to work for a radically transformed society.

CHAPTER 9

QUEER(ING) MOTHERHOOD IN ANA CASTILLO'S *BLACK DOVE: MAMÁ, MI'JO, AND ME*

ELENA AVILÉS

> The woman in the United States who is politically self-described as Chicana,
> mestiza in terms of race, Latina or Hispanic in regards to her Spanish-speaking
> heritage, and who numbers in the millions in the United States, cannot be summa-
> rized nor neatly categorized.
>
> Ana Castillo, *Massacre of the Dreamers* (1995)

Castillo's latest publication, *Black Dove: Mamá, Mi'jo, and Me* (2016), focuses on bringing visibility to the modern and urban concerns of gender,
sex, and sexuality for mothers in Chicanx culture. This chapter centers a
critical discussion of motherhood in *Black Dove* and more specifically, the
ways in which Castillo paves inroads for conversations of queer motherhood, queer mothering, and queering motherhood, as describes Shelley M.
Park in *Mothering Queerly, Queering Motherhood: Resisting Monomaternalism in Adoptive, Lesbian, Blended, and Polygamous Families* (2013). Castillo
transgresses recent motherhood scholarship such as Park's by contesting the
lens of whiteness in the interpretation, study, and analysis of the category
queer. She instead shows its evolution from a derogatory term or substitute
for homosexual, broadening its connotations as solely affixed to sexual orientation and gender identity by detaching the term from binary Western
colonial neoliberal constructs. Castillo's interpretation of queer contests the
ways dominant forms of writing privilege colonial ideas of whiteness by
modifying what queer may signify.

Correspondingly, Castillo's memoir, *Black Dove*, offers a voice of empowerment and demonstrates the pliability of the concept of *madre*—
mother—by "queering" the way the term has been constructed. She uses
her own lived experience as a bisexual Chicana mother to challenge estab-

lished ideas of sexuality and gender, especially within heterosexual norms affixed in Chicanx culture. Castillo's narrative maps out lesser-known representations of queer motherhood: what it means to be queer while being a mother and what it means to be a mother while being queer within people of color contexts in the United States. As such, she questions the means and ends of motherhood studies—meaning the underrepresentation of women of color voices—by using Chicanx theory to interrogate the frontiers of queerness and the implications of queerness upon the maternal body in representations of women of color across the western hemisphere.

Moving beyond strict definitions of motherhood, in her memoir Castillo emphasizes the absence of absolutes relating to the experiences of mothers in Chicanx/Latinx communities. This move forces her readers to reimagine borderlands and transnational mothers who subvert the patriarchal sacrifice of self for the betterment of their children and society at large. The memoir unveils intergenerational epistemologies of queer motherhood, queering motherhood, and queer mothering; it also brings visibility to the emerging concept of Chicana m(other)work as layered women of color feminist affirmations unfolding in the era of globalization.

Through a Pérezian lens of third space feminist consciousness that nurtures a decolonial imaginary, I analyze Castillo's historical re-visioning of sex, gender, and sexuality for border-crossing women through the lens of desire. In "Beyond the Nation's Maternal Bodies: Technologies of Decolonial Desire," in *The Decolonial Imaginary: Writing Chicanas into History* (1999), Emma Pérez examines "the power of sexuality and how its discourse circumscribes historical studies," to show how family values have a steadfast hold on power relations and therefore relations dealing with desire because "the normal and normative was and has been considered heterosexuality in Europe and in the Americas since the sixteenth century.[1] Pérez shows how the maternal body has been marked by colonial desires and illustrates how women can only be seen as objects of and metaphors for the patriarchal nationalism that defines Aztlán—itself an imaginary construct.[2] Pérez's critical contributions to Chicana studies demonstrates the need to decolonize gender, sex, and sexuality, which is crucial in understanding the myriad ways Castillo asks readers to question the contours of normative traditions, images, and expectations of mother and motherhood. And yet, to move against the loop of the patriarchal image of mothers, mothering, and motherhood serves, as Pérez names it, as "a modernist trapping" that inhibits mothers from thinking and therefore acting upon better worlds within which to exist.[3]

I argue that Castillo's presentation of female subjectivity, specifically that surrounding motherhood, engages in the complexity of the interstitial spaces and modes of difference that exist for women of color along the US southwestern borderlands and its diaspora across both sides of the border. Pérez names the hidden, opaque, and silenced utterances of "the maternal body of the nation" that fall outside the limits of hegemonic thought as the decolonial imaginary. *Black Dove* advances a decolonial imaginary of the "unnamed, sexual power relations [that] are present, often hidden and unspoken yet performed between and among people" through a new poetics of Chicana m(other)work that not only amplifies our cognition of mothers and queers, but also creates dialogue about it, and therefore protects it from erasure.[4]

Castillo's memoir also voices another layer of empowerment and pliability toward the concept of *madre* by pushing on transnational ideas of motherhood of minoritized populations. Sandra Soto's queer analysis of the discursive relationship between racialization and sexuality in *Reading Chican@ like a Queer: The De-Mastery of Desire* (2010) is useful for demonstrating Castillo's own critique of dominant/hetero conceptions of queer subjectivity in relation to desire within Chicanx culture. While Park stresses that "the family is a point at which the axes of feminism, postcolonialism and queer theory frequently diverge,"[5] and she uses family as the category under which to examine how queerness manifests in mothering and families, a nuanced reading of *Black Dove* posits a different reality for queer *madres* of color. Castillo moves beyond the limits of white-centered interpretations of queer(ing) motherhood through a queer of color critique of heteronormative legacies that permeate US thought on queerness, as well as white-centered colonial legacies embedded in Latin American thought that define Chicanx communities. Soto allows us to see how Castillo de-masters Chicana desire to "se[x] the colonial," to use Pérez's words, and to reinterpret constructions of gender, sex, and sexuality that explore the experiences of immigrant working-class women of color in her family. Her account validates intimate yet public gendered genealogies tied to collective decolonial identity for women across experiences.

In this regard, Castillo's latest publication serves as a transnational bridge between US Chicanx/Latinx queer and decolonial contemporary scholarship in locating what José Esteban Muñoz terms "a sense of brownness in the world," "queerness on horizon," "futurity," and "disidentifications via revolutionary thinking," as she forges a new logos of Chicana m(other)work. Castillo's Chicana m(other)work emphasizes the relevance of bisexual subjects who add to the discourse on queer motherhood by contesting "Latinx bisexual erasure" and by the "other ways of being Latina," or "Latina longing" as conceived by Juana María Rodríguez.[6]

Mothers, motherhood, and mothering in Chicana/o studies have always been a topic of scholarly and personal interrogation for women. Revisioning, historicizing, and reexamining the role of a Mexican American woman at the intersections of identity (as daughters, mothers, sisters, lovers, etc.) has been at the forefront of Chicana feminist thought.[7] For example, Sylvia Morales's documentary *Chicana* (1979) is an early illustration of the interest to interrogate representations of the figure of mothers in early Chicano movement rhetoric. Morales offers a revisionist analysis of the cultural image, historical representation, and social understanding of the mother figure shaping the perspective of emerging Chicana feminists that Castillo features in her own writings: the binary of the good versus bad mother.[8] Whether through the author's early works such as *Otro Canto* (1977) and *My Father Was a Toltec* (1988), or her later works *So Far from God* (1993) and *The Guardians* (2007), Castillo focuses on maternal and divine figures in relation to women in quotidian life in similar fashion to Chicana writers such as Gloria Anzaldúa, Cherríe Moraga, and Sandra Cisneros, to name a few.

In *Black Dove*, Castillo continues to demonstrate a woman-centered vision of the maternal and divine that decolonizes the notion of "madre no hay más que una" (mother there is only but one) and shows that the power and possibility of Chicanas rests in not being neatly categorized. In *Black Dove*, Castillo's cultural heritage and logos articulate a Chicana body reclaimed through the real, lived experiences of motherhood across generations. This is captured in her son's learned lesson. In "What's in a Nombre," Marcello notes, "As a writer, I have a chance to name myself. In honor of my mother (a living legend in Latino Literature), I take the surname Castillo. It is my way of thanking my mother for putting me through college and encouraging me to write."[9] Marcello conveys the interconnectedness of his mother to her Chicana feminist politics when he states:

> As far back as I can reach into my culturally rich memory banks, I have memories of my mom giving talks, signing her books for readers and colleagues, and carrying herself with grace. In my eyes, she was a powerful woman, like a lioness hunting stealthily among the grasslands for a juicy antelope to take down to feed her cubs. I saw how many hours she spent on the computer revising and proofreading her work, giving birth to the bravest metaphors and capturing ideas that most perfectly represented her people. I witnessed how she was inspired by Mexico and the Southwest, and her impact on Xicana culture.[10]

In the quote above Marcello defines the ways Castillo amplifies definitions about motherhood, especially working-class women of color. Castillo demonstrates her understanding of the weight of being a speaking mother in Chicanx cultural heritage and channels her unique queer logos on the importance of theorizing Chicana motherhood when she states:

> Perhaps some of you may come away from this book feeling like my stories have nothing to do with your lives. You may find the interest I've had in my

> ancestors as they were shaped by the politics of their times irrelevant to your own history. My story, as a brown, bisexual, strapped writer and mother, constantly scrambling to take care of my work and my child, might be similarly inconsequential. However, I beg your indulgence and a bit of faith to believe that maybe on the big Scrabble board of life we will eventually cross ways and make sense of each other.[11]

Castillo's direct message to the reader demonstrates a decolonial act; she resists erasure at the same time she enacts resistance through an unnegotiable respect and love for her role as a mother and at the same time as an individual.

The Chicana feminist lens of the study "Mejor Sola Que Mal Acompañada: Strengths and Challenges of Mexican-Origin Mothers Parenting Alone" (2011), conducted by J. Maria Bermúdez, Morgan A. Stinson, Lisa Zak-Hunter, and Bertranna Abrams, is particularly useful for understanding Castillo's amplification of single parenthood and complicating parenting as a whole through a nuanced telling of the significance of her bisexuality within a parenting framework. The study's aim was to "extend previous research in understanding the strengths and challenges of single motherhood by highlighting the unique circumstances Latina mothers face [as well as in examining] support systems, or lack thereof.[12] Similar to findings from the study, *Black Dove* illustrates "the importance of disentangling both constructs: family form and relationship status," that is, the idea of what family means in Chicanx/Latinx culture.[13] Definitions of family as seen through the tales of women in Castillo's text feminize familism through a heuristic approach to motherhood. We see the real "hands-on" logics of women in the roles of mothers making choices from a desire to be able to choose what motherhood means in a case by case and circumstantial context. Castillo educates readers that one thing is to be a mother and another thing is to be a woman having to make choices independent of her position as a mother. In not making woman and mother mutually exclusive, she helps readers begin to understand that Chicanas and Latinas have always struggled to unpack family from relationship status. Whether it is the desire to be themselves outside of the historical scripts assigned to the mother role, in choosing different partners than what is status quo, or in deciding to be single as a parent, these women demonstrate the complex world of motherhood. In *Black Dove*, Castillo shares her experience of motherhood to an only male child as an openly bisexual Chicana, while at the same time explicitly distinguishing her mother's voice and articulating a desire to be understood as a racialized and sexualized subject.

Castillo's push to extend social constructions of identity respective of a mother's sex, gender, and sexuality challenges readers to rethink existing conceptual maps about mothers, which she concludes when she affirms: "In the end it was left to me. By age forty, a woman took higher risks with a pregnancy. [*sic*] What compromises or sacrifices would an aspiring writer have to make as a mother? I could only imagine." While she admits thinking that marrying a "hardworking Latino" would satisfy her parents because he was like them, she became a single mother. And yet she interrupts the stereotypes of images of women of color and the historical record built on the misconception of women of Mexican American descent as strains to social, cultural, and economic structures that circulate in the United States by stating, "While my life was unfolding in ways I hadn't planned, working mothers were familiar to me."[14] Thus, *Black Dove* functions as an homage to all the working women in her life and to the lessons of survival and resistance she has learned across time that serve as "benchmarks in [her] spiritual journey" as a single mother.[15]

A not so apparent mapping of queering motherhood relates to *Black Dove*'s release date. While the United States celebrates Mother's Day on the second Sunday during the month of May, Castillo released her book on May 10th, or Mexico's celebration of Mother's Day. In this act, she uses history to forge her story. The celebration of women centered on women's desire for self-celebration edifies a return to feminist transnational motherhood practices and consciousness. She privileges transnational cultural traditions by paying homage to the feminist roots of one of the holiest days in the western hemisphere; that too is a critique of the apparatus of capitalist desires in the overly commercialized mother's day practices of US Mother's Day. Her release date, May 10, 2016, counters heteronormative custom of celebrating motherhood, as the memoir serves as a gift—a tool for decolonizing women's histories, bodies, and desires.

Castillo honors a border-crossing holiday to educate readers about the need to understand the hidden transcripts of feminist contributions to history: the first official Mother's Day celebration in Mexico was held on May 10, 1922, and in the month of May to venerate the Virgin of Guadalupe (with some oral history linking it to Oaxaca, her family roots).[16] The history of this particular date connects and reifies the transnational links of Mexican and Chicano culture: Mother's Day. An online article on the history of Mother's Day in *El Periódico* details how Castillo's release date is significant because of the ways it resists US imperial establishments of celebrating Mother's Day and elevates the radical feminist history of the origins of Mother's Day:

> A principios del siglo XX emergió un movimiento feminista, alentado por la Revolución Mexicana, que discutía sobre la maternidad, los métodos anticonceptivos y defendía la emancipación y los derechos de la mujer. Como respuesta

a este movimiento, según recoge el libro "El diez de mayo" de Marta Acevedo, en 1922, el periódico "Excélsior," el Arzobispado, el entonces secretario de Educación Pública y otras entidades empezaron a celebrar el Día de la Madre el 10 de mayo. El periódico pidió la participación de los lectores para que propusieran un día de fiesta para las mamás y, de esta manera, quedó instaurado el 10 de mayo. El medio comunicó que lo hacía para "rendir un homenaje de afecto y respeto a la madre."[17]

Castillo's use of Mexican Mother's Day as a historical legacy in order to stress the need to celebrate the subjective meaning-making processes of the maternal with a coming of age tale that contests understandings of the logics of gender, sex, and sexuality enacts a decolonial imaginary. By disrupting romanticized, boxed, and singular representations on motherhood, Castillo switches the position of the need for historical celebration all the while making gestures toward her own transnational queer motherhood and the possibilities of queer(ing) motherhood under the auspice of Chicana cultural heritage.

Queer motherhood also develops through the physical presence of a narrative in homage to the contributions of mothers—from Castillo's biological mother to the tales of her two grandmothers on the one hand, and the centering of diverse gradations of maternal contributions by women who carried out what today is termed m(other)work,[18] from her aunt to her friends and close acquaintances, on the other hand. Following the introduction, in "My Mother's Mexico," "Remembering Las Cartoneras," and "Her Last Tortillas," Castillo focuses on the women in her family to challenge the invisibility of women's history, particularly the history of frontier, pioneer, and working-class women. To detail the lives of females left outside the historical record is to decolonize historiography and enrich the terrain of Chicana history. To detail the lives of divorced, remarried, and widowed women or women's experiences with sans fairy-tale lives and in imperfect realties is to queer motherhood.

Through her memoir, Castillo gives exposure to borderlands and transnational motherhood from a unique lens—a queer lens that offers a nuanced vision of women with fluid identities. It is from the acknowledgment of this density, of Castillo's own lived experience reckoning with the intersections of the coloniality, that gives the writer authority to present what Pérez terms a decolonial imaginary, by writing herself and her maternal lineage into history. Developing a collective language of resistance across time, discourse, and borders, Castillo has "given it to the globe,"[19] by affirming what Pérez points out in writing about gendered history that "Chicanos are also women, Chicanas,"[20] and she extends vision about her own family history into what Cathy J. Cohen[21] terms "The Radical Potential of Queer Politics."[22]

Castillo's narration shatters absolutes related to the experiences of mothers in Chicana studies since the Chicano movement because it defies the heteronormative, mono-maternal, nuclear, and holy family narrative, which opens the first few chapters of the memoir. Following Pérez's assertion that "To en(gender) history . . . means to transfigure questions that have been assumed to be universal," Castillo creates agency for herself and women like her who take on the roles of mother or mothering.

The introduction brings honor to migrant mothers through a historical overview of the push and factors of US-Mexico politics that explain why she was born in Chicago. In "My Mother's Mexico," "Remembering Las Cartoneras," and "Her Last Tortilla," Castillo brings a queer interpretation to the role of women to recount the life of her mother, her aunt, her grandmothers, and other women who survived despite linguistic barriers, undocumented statuses, domestic violence, and poverty. At the same time, she manages to illustrate the ways women practiced their own forms of queering motherhood, whether by defying family expectation or subverting masculine domination. However, "Peel Me a Girl" speaks to the importance of telling stories of women for the next generation specifically for the examination of the predatory practices young women face in society. Castillo expands the limits of queerness and motherhood by speaking about her inability to speak to her parents, the silence that damages families, which often leads to complicity in reinforcing perverse forms of masculine fantasies. From smoking to partying to writing about her dad's drinking problem and an adult male relative who tried to take advantage of her, Castillo speaks about the layers of social violence that are meant to exploit the female body. In this particular chapter, Castillo's elaboration of the mechanisms of repression and oppression that target women becomes a way she coalesces queerness and motherhood; her voice is a strategic intervention to stop the continuation of the cycle of violence women face. In addition, Castillo generates individual agency by linking her own experience as a single mother to transnational experiences because too often, as we have seen in our modern times, women are abandoned or are left to toil in the labor of child rearing as single mothers due to violence across the US-Mexico border that systemically rips families apart.

The expression of queer motherhood and queer mothering in *Black Dove* also illustrates the empowerment Castillo enacts in her interest to bring language to self-identity vis-à-vis having to generate a politics of bisexual motherhood. Soto's study on racialized sexuality in *Reading Chican@ like a Queer: The De-Mastery of Desire* (2010) is particularly useful for understanding Castillo's queer motherhood and queer mothering praxis as it relates to Marcello, her son.[23] Castillo is blunt about the ways her sexualized and racialized body has worked against her as a minoritized woman, and at the same time, her critique serves as a way to contest the very systems that not only have oppressed her, but which will negatively work to oppress her *mestizo* son.[24]

A nuanced application of the author's Xicanisma politics as a writer and activist to her politics about motherhood begs the question from the locus of racialized sexuality: Can Castillo ever really be an overprotective mother? Can parents of color ever be accused of overprotection? I ask, can an educated, working-class, urban-raised, woman of color feminist be overprotective when we consider the historical and contemporary treatment of young males of color in US society? "I raised my son much the same way that I would have raised a daughter, conscious not to fall into gender stereotypes," she declares in the essay "Are Hunters Born or Made." She wrote the essay as a cognitive-emotional response to the influential power of patriarchal dominance in respect to male socialization and its effects on her son.[25] When her son refers to himself as a "hunter" in respect to relationships to women, Castillo admits the shock of the impact of his words: "The blood left my brain. Would I faint or grab the nearest blunt instrument at this news that was in such opposition to all the principles I have ever tried to instill in him."[26] With temples pulsing, her struggle to consciously raise a male outside American heteronormative gender constructions shows its limits. She intricately identifies the forces shaping her son's affirmation of gender, sex, and identity in the public realm through a Xicanisma reading of male superiority, privilege and machismo in US culture.

We come to understand how Castillo challenges heteronormative standards of masculinity through a queer mothering politics, while she also disrupts the perpetuation of patriarchal norms. In respect to his relationship with a young woman in which he is romantically involved, Castillo subverts male-privileging behaviors in the socialization of mothers and sons by urging her son to dialogue with the young woman in question. A moment of queer motherhood is documented when she instructs: "Ask her to meet you somewhere for a cup of coffee so that you can explain things. More than anything, women want to be respected as people. Don't pillage."[27] While Castillo struggles to teach her son how to challenge his own gender conformity of what it means to be a male and to encounter his own machismo, she queers the politics of Chicanx culture in order to raise consciousness. Her concern and concentration on Marcello through a queer mothering lens reveal Castillo's Xicana politics at work: expanding gender norms and working toward gender nonconforming ideologies. To ask him to explain himself reframes male social norms and expectations and makes men accountable and responsible not only for their actions but also their words. In a culture that has historically permitted men to act without explanation, "to explain things" queers heteronormative standards of masculinity.

Other instances where Castillo showcases queer motherhood in similar contexts are noted in her attempt to understand hip-hop and graffiti culture through Marcello's eyes. Despite a descriptive in which Castillo admits to her reservations, internal challenges, and disagreement with his cultural heroes and role models, she takes an unconventional approach of learning about hip-hop culture to ameliorate her disapproval. After all, it is her disapproval not his. She faces her own limits. Mothering from a queer lens helps Castillo come to terms with a mother-son Chicanx intergenerational *différance*: she is able to teach readers about a mother's concern for her child in a world that is set up to discriminate against people of color. She understands that just like her parents did not understand her, she too may not be able to fully understand the experiences her son faces as an urban man of color. Her writing showcases a queer mother's concern over society's inherent power to influence Marcello to consecrate gender roles as a fatherless boy with limited positive male role models.

All the while, Castillo refuses to acquiesce to the stereotype of the single mother akin to women of color—single motherhood is an accident (and therefore, so too is the offspring), single mothers raise criminals, single mothers are on welfare, single mothers are loose women, single mothers are unstable, and so forth. Even when her worst-case scenario about what her son could become manifests and Marcello ends up in prison, she debunks the mother-shaming and mother-blaming discourse of colonial paradigms and contests patriarchal assumptions. She remarks, "Single mothers are held to a special standard since they have 'failed' to have a positive male role model in the home."[28] Her dedication to maintaining a strong "straight-son-bisexual-mother" relationship illustrates a queer sense of love and compassion through an oppositional stance.[29] The following words, "You could be unmarried, as opposed to divorced, but you could not stop being a mother. Or maybe you could. Not me,"[30] is an articulation of what Chela Sandoval refers to as "differential consciousness" that promotes a hermeneutic of love for the oppressed. In this case the oppressed is Marcello.[31]

In *The Chicana M(other)work Anthology* (2019) Castillo reminds readers that working mothers who support each other to navigate through the hostile waters of racism, patriarchy, institutional misogyny, daily microaggressions, and the many ways in which an educated woman may nonetheless experience economic hardship trying to support her family isn't a revolutionary concept in the strict sense.[32] However, Castillo makes a powerful intervention in favor of new approaches to Chicana scholarship on motherhood by acknowledging "Chicana M(other)work" as a strategy and concept helping women to bring voice to the array of experiences about the signifier "mother" that transgress neat categorizations of Chicanas.[33]

Castillo's Chicana interpretation of Descartes's "cogito, ergo sum" (I think, therefore I am) in the foreword of *Chicana M(other)work* situates "the immediate urgency of being a thinking mother," what she later terms as "mother awareness."[34] Castillo defines "mother awareness" as a mothering-specific form of consciousness that functions as a radical act of knowledge and power stemming from the author's lived experience as a queer mother. *Black Dove* pioneers a queer "mother awareness" in the field of gender, sex, and sexuality by transgressing visions of Chicanx/Latinx LGBTQ+ motherhood via her bisexual narrative.[35] Hence, *Black Dove* is a guidebook through which to build consciousness about the inherent ways language use reaffirms heteronormativity across identities. By challenging mores of what motherhood is and is not, Castillo brings voice to mother identity outside heterosexual-homosexual binaries within domestic spaces, or what Parks defines as "domestinormativity."

Here I propose how Castillo's queer politics align with Chicana feminist writings on *domesticana*, and through such analysis, honors and extends Amalia Mesa Bains's contributions in her essay "Domesticana: The Sensibility of Chicana Rasquache" (2003). For example, Castillo speaks of cooking and cleaning, and of doing domestic work, but it does not shackle her female identity. In the essay "Her Last Tortillas," Castillo states: "As I grew into a young teen, some of the chores were passed on to me. Tortilla making was only one responsibility to be accomplished before we moved onto the next thing. . . . Tradition would have held the role of Mamá's helper for the first-born daughter but, since she was gone, I became the daughter who learned to clean, iron and, yes, make tortillas. In the long run, this training served me well. Whatever image one has of a feminist at home, I've always taken pride in the upkeep of my house and kitchen."[36] The *domesticana* elements in the passage transcends traditional representations of mothers as nonfeminist and naturalize feminists as mothers. Such *domesticana* moments reference a radical form of feminist praxis based on seeing a power in motherhood akin to the feminine divine.[37] Castillo speaks of her grandmother's and mother's ability to manage the home with great respect and the role of tortilla making as a tool for survival on two levels: knowing how to make tortillas for nutritive substance and also knowing how to make tortillas as a tool of cultural empowerment. The transmission of grandmother-mother-daughter knowledge takes new terrain when Castillo teaches her son about tortillas' transnational force and as a revolutionary act of love that decolonizes gendered practices and social roles.

In "Her Last Tortillas," Castillo acknowledges that while her sister and mother shared an intimate and personal connection, it was she whom her mom requested to make her tortillas on her deathbed. She came to value the empowerment women generate in the kitchen across transnational lines and of her participating in the cultural heritage of Chicana foodways. Furthermore, when she states, "Mi'jo was waiting for the first waft of tortillas on the comal. Soon he too would be put to roll out the masa. Soon, she, like my abuelita, would only live in a memory,"[38] we see Castillo enter into a *domesticana* understanding of mothering, but she also advances such understandings from a queer lens and a queer politics. Tortilla making becomes a praxis as she writes, "The tradition of la tortilla linking us, past to present, living on and on."[39] Finally, Castillo elevates her queer identity as a bisexual mother in "Her Last Tortillas" when we consider the moniker of "tortilleras"[40] to refer to Chicana and US Latina lesbians as written in *Tortilleras: Hispanic and U.S. Latina Lesbian Expression*.[41] To teach her son how to make tortillas *is* queer mothering.

The memoir's multilayered rumination on being a single mother is further met by the mapping of a lifetime struggle of feminizing traditional concepts of familism by focusing on child-rearing practices that expand the definitions of motherhood to be inclusive of Castillo's own identity as a queer subject. *Black Dove* is a queer expression of *rasquachismo* because it articulates how Castillo through her queer perspective allows her to make do with what she had. And yet, there is an invaluable lesson to learn from Castillo's literary imprint of *rasquachismo* in respect to motherhood: the affirmation that her queer subjectivity does not reflect an instability, a lack or impoverished understanding of motherhood. It is, actually, quite the opposite. In queer(ing) motherhood politics, Castillo advances *domesticana* arguments to the Chicano sensibility of *rasquachismo* by recording elements and associations of feminine and domestic life from Chicana queer feminist visions. Seen through *rasquache* aesthetics, Castillo's experiences as a queer mother combat the tradition of negative logics associated with queer bodies and show the creativity and innovations of queer mothering. If we think about Cherríe Moraga's reflections on family from her lesbian experiences in *Giving Up the Ghost: Teatro in Two Acts* (1986)[42] and *Woman Waiting in the Wings: Portrait of a Queer Motherhood* (1997), we come to understand the power of "making *familia* from scratch"[43] in the same way we see the empowerment of making tortillas from scratch.

If Castillo's narrative challenges cultural specificities of Mexican-origin mother identity and heterosexual frameworks, she also confronts intergenerational biphobia and discrimination against bisexual parenthood and domestinormativity in child rearing. For instance, while there are many inroads to understanding the complexity of gender, sex, and sexuality, Castillo reminds readers about the difficulty of promoting an unrepentant bisexual politic since the 1970s. In "On Mothers, Lovers, and Other Rivals," she reminds readers that the 1980s "was an era when sexual identity was black and white. There were two genders. There were two sexualities.

You were either gay or lesbian or you were straight. You chose one camp or the other. Queer meant being gay and not what it currently refers to now—anything in between gay and hetero."[44] By critiquing a reference to her femme identity during youth as a "costume" and voicing the opinion that she believes men never really saw who she was (queer)—rather their own projections of her—she "sexes the colonial imaginary" to expose the perversions of fantasy within heteropatriarchal desire that objectify women. Such forms of desire she wishes not to play, engage, or reproduce. Simultaneously, it is precisely through her critique of others' limitations on gender, sex, and sexuality where she manifests a political identity where queerness can vacillate across spectrums. Through such reworkings she creates openings and pathways for amplifying the borderlands of queer politics, which resonate with emerging ideas of Chicanx/Latinx in the twenty-first century such as those of José Esteban Muñoz and Juana María Rodríguez.

Likewise, Castillo's text challenges the parameters of LGBTQ+ notions of queer motherhood in relation to family. Her confessions in the essay "On Mothers, Lovers, and Other Rivals" challenge the heteropatriarchal impression in LGBTQ+ family dynamics during two decades of the Chicano movement (1970s–1980s), a decisive time for her adult identity formation and her son's first years of life. She calls attention to being displaced as a mother and as an individual with a sexuality while in a relationship with another woman via domestinormativity. Although she honors the regard this lover demonstrated for her son, she writes about re-creating heteronormative family roles within an LGBTQ+ context when it comes to parental roles.

The receptive language of *Black Dove* enacts Chicana feminist progenitrices for theorizing queer(ing) motherhood. Castillo compiles diasporic and transnational accounts of the lived experiences of women purposefully filtered through the lens of motherhood to illustrate the agency of scholarship on Chicana m(other)work. She brings attention to the effects of transnational experiences of migrating mothers and the shifting terrains of their identities vis-à-vis their labor to wage new definitions of their true gender nonconforming identities because of their transnational perspectives and through their roles as day laborers, factory workers, domestics, artists, and more. The presentation of maternal myriads—biological mothers, foster mothers, step-mothers, motherhood as by-product of social tradition, or a person who serves in the role of parent out of will or circumstance such as in the case of grandmothers, aunts, sisters, lovers, and friends—pushes readers to think of the truly undetected acts, performances, and behaviors women carry out in their lives for survival, self-preservation, and cultural continuity. Be it Castillo's grandmother crossing borders, her mother going out to dance alone, or Castillo enjoying Black popular culture and music despite her mother's objections, the author shows how each woman theorizes and contributes to queer(ing) motherhood, each subject changing and creating shifts in the meaning-making process of motherhood. In sum, *Black Dove* creates a rupture in the classical coming of age narratives that define the canon of Chicanx studies by queering the trans-American cultural adage "sin mujeres, no hay revolución" (without women, there is no revolution).

CHAPTER 10

NOSTALGIA FOR A FUTURE

Queer Longings and Lesbian Desire in Ana Castillo's
The Mixquiahuala Letters

LILIANA C. GONZÁLEZ

Ana Castillo's epistolary novel *The Mixquiahuala Letters* (1986) stands as an exemplary Chicana text that confronts patriarchy within the Chicana/o community. The letters detail the story of two friends—Teresa, a Chicana writer, and Alicia, an American artist of Spanish descent—and their many travels through Mexico. Told exclusively from Teresa's perspective, the novel recounts her nostalgic reminiscence over her travels to Mexico and her close friendship with Alicia. A stylistic ode to novelists Julio Cortázar and, as various scholars have observed, Miguel de Cervantes to a certain extent, *The Mixquiahuala Letters* underlines the difficulties of traveling as women, solidarity in friendships between women, and above all else, love and desire. While some authors including Anne Bower have suggested that the two friends are more than "just friends," others like Irene Campos Carr have instead explicitly left it for readers to decide. Despite this ambiguity, any reading of *The Mixquiahuala Letters* presents considerable homoerotic undertones. Whether the text presents a lesbian relationship as such is not as crucial as the actual suggestion of queer longing and lesbian erotic desire interweaved with the text's social reality.

The use of nostalgia in my title suggests a simultaneous look to the past and to the future. That is, I'm interested in nostalgia as generative rather than limiting, as an affective and discursive site for sensing past potentialities as possible realities for the present and future. I am here thinking of Mexican gay poet Xavier Villaurrutia's 1946 collection *Nostalgia de la muerte* ("Nostalgia for Death") and critic José Quiroga's consideration of absence, nostalgia, and sex in Villaurrutia's work. I play off both Villaurrutia and Quiroga because nostalgia and absence are themselves inextricable from one another and intimately linked to queer longing and desire. I read *The Mixquiahuala Letters* not as portraying a lesbian relationship in a concrete sense but instead as mapping out specific queer longings and lesbian desires evoked through the novel's plot, its main characters, and

Castillo's candid writing style. By queer longings, I mean to signal the ways in which letter-writer Teresa imagines otherwise, longing for new worlds of social justice and alternative gender and sexual futures. By lesbian desire, I'm referring to the way in which Teresa loves and eroticizes Alicia and their intimate friendship.

I use queer in all its breadth and in all its specificity. Queerness eludes simplistic definitions and suggests sexual subjectivities that diverge from expected norms. Yet as Chicana literary critic Sandra K. Soto notes, queerness is more complex than simply indicating a difference from the mainstream. Soto writes: "While one cannot utter 'queer' without evoking the sexual, it should also be noted that, for better or worse, the term has, over time, become capacious enough to be used loosely to describe any arrangement, object, or event that differs from the mainstream. But to reduce 'queer' or 'queerness' to mere difference is to miss the impact of its politics, and, for many, it does have a specific politics and sensibility."[1] I am interested precisely in the politics and sensibilities of queerness that Soto suggests as specifically concerned with sexuality and the ways in which they are integrally shaped by race. Castillo's novel, while clearly questioning Chicano and Mexican patriarchal structures, embodies a simultaneous cognizance about and yearning for queerness as desire between women in the context of racialized sexuality in the United States. The letters, conceptually and politically informed by Chicana feminism, gesture toward Chicana sexual liberation's desire to be outside of heteronormativity, something Castillo explores more explicitly in her later works.

Within a Chicana literary genealogy and concurrent to *The Mixquiahuala Letters*'s publication, Chicana lesbian writers like Gloria Anzaldúa, Carla Trujillo, and Cherríe Moraga were at the forefront of the Chicana feminist movement in the 1980s and early 1990s, problematizing sexism, homophobia, and racism in a US context. Gloria Anzaldúa's *Borderlands / La Frontera: The New Mestiza* was instrumental in thinking queer in relation to Chicana/os. While primarily thought of as a Chicana lesbian and feminist theorist, Anzaldúa's engaging of queer in *Borderlands* expands beyond lesbian identity politics. Anzaldúa asserts that for her, queer was a choice: "For the lesbian of color, the ultimate rebellion she can make against her native culture is through her sexual behavior. She goes against two moral prohibitions: sexuality and homosexuality. Being lesbian and raised Catholic, indoctrinated as straight, I *made the choice to be queer* (for some it is genetically inherent)."[2] By stating that for some, queerness is inherent and for others including herself, it is a choice, Anzaldúa asserts political differences between sexual subjectivities. Anzaldúa's words denote a consciousness and politics of queerness against the dominant institutions and power structures of Catholicism and patriarchy within Chicano/a and

US white culture. Similarly, Cherríe Moraga's "Queer Aztlán: The Re-Formation of Chicano Tribe" engages queer as a Chicano/a site. Moraga asks for a "Chicano homeland that could embrace all its people, including its jotería."[3] Moraga imagines and summons a queer Aztlán understood as a political and symbolic space attached to a geopolitical site. Moraga adds, "If women's bodies and those of men and women who transgress their gender roles have been historically regarded as territories to be conquered, they are also territories to be liberated. Feminism has taught us that."[4] Both Anzaldúa and Moraga expressly consider queer to be deeply about gender and sexual political liberation.

While I'm interested in the radical politics that queer invokes, I'm also concerned with more nuanced political aspects of queerness related to nostalgia, desire, and pleasure as tied to notions of futurity. Futurity more specifically conveys the possibilities of sexual futures. In the next section, I take cues from queer Latinx scholars José E. Muñoz, Juana María Rodríguez, and José Quiroga, who have extended the work of Chicana lesbian writers by theorizing queerness in relation to Latinx sensibilities and expressions. Queer nostalgia, longing, and desire are constructed by Castillo as invested in a politics of transformation. To look at Castillo's work as emerging alongside Chicana feminist and Chicana lesbian writers of the 1980s, and to view it through the lens of queerness, is to access a range of possibilities in the present. Queerness in *The Mixquiahuala Letters* thus signals toward radical Chicana possibilities that mobilize heterogeneous interventions against normative sexuality. In other words, queer longing and lesbian desire bolster sexuality as the focal point and organizing axis of Chicana experience expressing bisexuality, same-sex desire, and other homoerotic pleasures.

NOSTALGIA FOR A FUTURE

On the heel of the civil rights, Chicano/a, and feminist movements, Castillo's narrative can be read as a nostalgic love letter to the hopeful and radical possibilities of these social movements but also to the potential of human connection across geopolitical and societal boundaries. I situate my reading of *The Mixquiahuala Letters* thirty-three years after its publication, against the backdrop of our current moment, when transnational ties are heightened virtually and economically but human ties are challenged. Latin American and Latina/o/x communities in the United States are increasingly subject to racist policies of removal and extermination manifested in deportations, detentions, family separations, and a rhetoric that purports the building of a wall on the US-Mexico border. This violent trauma is coupled with the effects of global economic deregulation and the "War on Drugs" across the hemisphere that have meant devastating violence especially against women and those who transgress gender and sexual norms. In this context, *The Mixquiahuala Letters*'s publication in the eve of NAFTA (North American Free Trade Agreement), even if not knowing how it would profoundly transform the United States and Mexico, is more relevant than ever. A threshold for rethinking and remembering futures, *The Mixquiahuala Letters* expresses a longing for queerness and reveals a desire for love, closeness, and community within a capitalist, sexist, and heteronormative world. Expressed through Teresa's affection for Alicia and her narration of her and Alicia's love affairs across racial and transnational borders, Teresa in many respects desires a queer socially just world of sexual freedoms and free love clearly beyond the parameters of mainstream white feminism and the Chicano movement.

Castillo expresses a similar notion to what scholars such as Kara Keeling, David Scott, and Gary Wilder have deemed as "futures past." Keeling writes, "Persistent anti-Black racism continues to delimit otherwise visionary movements and possibilities, shaping existing geopolitics and other present realities."[5] Keeling's summoning of "futures past," while concerned in Black existence, serves to understand queerness as a potentiality "that might be accessed now, in these queer times."[6] Teresa's "queer" longings and lesbian desire embody the yearning in the present for something that was, or at least was possible at some point but never quite crystalized. While many of the imagined and pursued possibilities of the civil rights, feminist, and Chicana/o movements came to be, even if only to a certain point, many others did not precisely because of persistent racism, sexism, and homophobia. *The Mixquiahuala Letters* thus provides a textual basis for recovering those futures past, exploring past possibilities by situating them within and against the material realities of the present. For instance, in letter 8 Teresa writes about a memory with Alicia: "We wrapped up all our thoughts we had ground over the summer like Colombian Coffee beans, hoping to come up with a resolution that would make future tolerable. On the bureau in the guest room of your parents' home lay a plane ticket to California. Again, i was the deserter, giving up Woman's Quest for Freedom and Self Determination. i was on my way to my husband, stopping off in New York to spend just a few days with you——as if postponing a sentence to Siberia."[7] Teresa recalls being with Alicia, plotting their futures, desiring to be liberated from her married life, but feeling pressured to give in at certain moments. Hence, *The Mixquiahuala Letters* doubly embodies Chicana liberation and specifically sexual liberation as an ongoing process that must continue. As literary critic Raymond Williams argues, literature as a work of art is not necessarily in the past, "[but] it is not only that, to complete their inherent process, we have to make them present, in specifically active 'readings.' It is also that the making of art is never itself in the past tense. It is always a formative process, within a specific present."[8] Indeed, it is through an active reading and critique of nostalgia, queerness, and desire within *The Mixquiahuala Letters* that those specific "futures past" are activated.

This way of reading is especially important considering that the possibility of futures for queers of color and other marginalized communities, as José E. Muñoz and Juana María Rodríguez have argued, have often been framed as nonexistent and as limited in the best-case scenario. Rodríguez writes; "Futurity has never been given to queers of color, children of color, and other marginalized communities that live under the violence of state and social erasure, a violence whose daily injustices exceed the register of a politics organized solely around sexuality, even as they are enmeshed within a logic of sexuality that is always already racialized through an imagine ideal citizen-subject."[9] For Rodríguez, futurity is tied to specific notions of racialized sexuality and sex more specifically. Futurity in this sense goes beyond reproductive rights, but is inextricable from the exercise of power over one's body. For instance, Teresa retells the story of Alicia's sterilization after posing as a Puerto Rican teen. This scene calls attention to the systematic sterilization of Puerto Rican women without their consent and echoes Rodríguez's assertion of the violent denial of a certain kind of sexual future for racialized populations. Rodriguez adds, "The utopian desire Muñoz articulates activates a politics of refusal as a productive gesture that aims to conjure the potential of new horizons. A politics of refusal has a long history in feminist of color scholarship, and should not be equated with the rejection of futurity, much less sociality."[10] For Rodriguez and Muñoz, the politics of refusal highlights that despite this physical and rhetorical violence, queers of color, women, and children of color refuse to give up on futurity. In other words, refusal "demands rather than forecloses futurity."[11] In a similar move, I argue that *nostalgia for a future* in Castillo's *The Mixquiahuala Letters* is in fact the longing for queer futures. Nostalgia is both the memory and desire for something that is not quite present, possibly past or possibly future. I echo Quiroga's use of nostalgia in "Nostalgia for Sex" to signal the absence and at the same time to activate it. Discussing the poet Villaurrutia mentioned above, Quiroga argues, "Villaurrutia writes poetry from the point of view of absence. This absence is what turns *Nostalgia for Death* into a book about sex, about the absence of the person and the presence of bodies, about the questioning of identity and affirmation of flesh. Its sense of uniqueness is not necessarily predicated on individuality but rather on the lack of personhood."[12] Although the absence of the body in Quiroga's analysis of Villaurrutia differs from Rodriguez's emphasis on the presence of the body, Quiroga, nevertheless understands Villaurrutia's collection as embodying a sex-positive progressive stance where the absence of the body stimulates desire recalling the possibility of a future. Quiroga admits, "I realize the contradictory position at play here: rescuing Villaurrutia as homosexual in order to let him recall, for us, the difficulty of homosexuality; allowing Villaurrutia to dissolve the subject for the sake of its future constitution, its eternal return."[13] Paradoxically, nostalgia and absence are what produce futurity. But it is Quiroga's concluding observations on Villaurrutia that seem the most relevant to a reading of Castillo's work. I, like Quiroga, am interested in the "melancholic subject who refuses the confession, the subject who chooses to mask it, while at the same time showing us the mask."[14] Through Teresa, Castillo shows us the mask, narrating and gesturing toward possible queer readings but refusing to show us clearly without foreclosing the presence of queer desire and love. Nostalgia thus comes into focus both politically and erotically to suggest that the political realities that were truncated and the intimacies that once existed between Teresa and Alicia remain active through the text for an "eternal return."

QUEER LONGINGS AND LESBIAN DESIRE

Teresa, who some critics have contended is a semiautobiographical representation of Castillo, can be viewed as writing unrequited love letters to Mexico (the country her ancestors left) and of course to Alicia (her best friend). Through Teresa's character and her recollection of events, *The Mixquiahuala Letters* determinedly extends past white feminisms of the time, affirming Chicana sexual openness and suggesting the setting for lesbian desire. They are unrequited love letters in a symbolic and literal sense because Teresa longs to connect with Mexico, yet Mexico doesn't necessarily treat her as she would have hoped. After being treated as a second-class citizen in the United States, Teresa longs to belong and be recognized. She yearns for an imagined space of racial justice. While she is confronted with Mexican reality, Teresa's travels through Mexico hold other promises, specifically understanding that social problems of racial and gendered inequities are not unique to the United States but instead exist across the continent. In letter 2, Teresa writes about her experience when she first arrived in Mexico: "Didn't they tell anything by my Indian-marked face, fluent use of the language, undeniably Spanish name? Nothing blurred their vision of another gringa come to stay as i nodded and shook hands during introductions and took my seat."[15] Teresa's letters manifest a nostalgia for a Mexico she imagines and desires and a nostalgia for Alicia's love and affection. Teresa writes: "Mexico. Melancholy, profoundly right and wrong, it embraces as it strangulates."[16] For Teresa, Mexico is a place full of contradictions that represent her freedom and at the same time asphyxiating social parameters. Teresa communicates a narrative where she yearns for a home and chosen family and feminist community to share with Alicia. In letter 3, Teresa details how they sent each other gifts and longed for each other's company; "i'd receive a copy of Neruda's poetry, you, a ten-page letter of self-recrimination, you, a long-distance call in the dead of night, i, hand-painted postcard, you, a copy of the Diary of Anais Nin, i, pair of copper earrings from your recent collection, you, seven poems fresh out of the typewriter, I, a ceramic brooch. We begged for the other's visit and again the battle resumed. We needled, stabbed, manipulated, cut, and through it all we loved, driven to see the other improved in her own reflection."[17] Teresa's memories as told her in letters suggest that Alicia longed to have a family (but knew she could not in traditional terms) and was never as committed as Teresa was to living a free-spirited life. However, since the story is told from Teresa's perspective, Alicia's feelings are not known. Teresa, nevertheless, consistently refers to their friendship as a "love affair," a phrase that indeed suggests a simultaneous pleasurable reality and longing for "queerness."[18]

Moreover, *The Mixquiahuala Letters* underscores the complexities of travel that some like Teresa as a Chicana might experience while traveling in Mexico. Even if somewhat familiar, it is a still foreign place. Teresa's letters in a sense narrate the realities of navigating Mexican social and cultural aspects, particularly in relation to popular views on gender, sexuality, and race. Being a traditionally patriarchal and predominantly Catholic country that also privileges whiteness even as brown skin is the norm, Mexico presents different challenges and a whole new set of insecurities compared to the problems of racism and sexism Teresa experiences in the United States. As Anna Nieto-Gómez writes, "The roots of the psyche of la Chicana lies deep within the colonial period in Mexico. The conquest, the encomienda system and the colonial Catholic Church were to play a major role in forming the sexual-social roles of the Mexican woman."[19] As a Chicana, Teresa is doubly confronted with US sexual and racial hierarchies and a legacy of colonial structures upon her travels through Mexico. Often labeled as a "liberal" woman, Teresa also details the colorism she experiences being of a darker complexion than her travel companion Alicia: "i, with dark hair and Asian eyes, must've appeared like the daughter of a migrant worker or laborer in the North (which of course, i was)."[20] Chicanas with sexual agency deemed as liberal or loose women is a common motif taken up by Chicana feminist scholars and writers. For instance, Sandra Cisneros questions the virgin/whore dichotomy by ironizing the Virgen de Guadalupe as the model of Chicana femininity. Cisneros argues, "She was damn dangerous, an ideal so lofty and unrealistic it was laughable. Did boys have to aspire to be Jesus? I never saw any evidence of it. They were fornicating like rabbits while the Church ignored them and pointed us women toward our destiny—marriage and motherhood. The other alternative was putahood."[21] One of the primary difficulties of Chicana sexuality as Cisneros affirms has been unrealistic expectations, where anything short of being virginal was considered whorish. Similarly, what becomes increasingly evident for Teresa is the paradox of being hyper-visible and sexualized as a Brown woman and at the same time invisible as a human with ideas: "How revolting we were susceptible to ridicule, abuse, disrespect. We would have hoped for respect as human beings, but the only respect granted a woman is that which a gentleman bestows upon the lady. Clearly we were no ladies."[22] Teresa here acknowledges that they are not viewed as ladies regarding expectations of proper social and sexual behavior. Her awareness and recognition of society's rampant sexism unfortunately didn't always translate into decisions and actions. However, Teresa's reflections on these disheartening experiences are in fact what trigger the retrieval of "futures past," unleashing the potentiality of her defiant will in that moment and thus creating ripple effects in posterity.

The novel, on the one hand, stresses the possibility of travel as a macronarrative of the Chicano/a movement (a narrative that would certainly encounter problems today), where travel to Mexico and other Latin American countries became the soul-searching and radicalizing process for activism in the United States. On the other hand, the novel also permeates significant political and social themes of love and desire for intimacies that have been restricted. Teresa's memories of her intimate friendship with Alicia and the very idea of Alicia are what give Teresa hope and keep her desires alive. Teresa narrates how such an intimate friendship among unmarried women or those separated from their husbands was shunned: "Stones of silent condemnation were thrown from every direction, relatives and friends who believed 'bad wives' were bad people."[23] Even as *comadrazgo* (a term derived from "godmotherhood" that can also indicate close friendship) is common and well documented within the Chicana community, there are instances when friendship between women is censured: "My mother had only been close to female companions during her adolescence. My older sisters never maintained close relationships with women after marriage. When a woman entered the threshold of intimacy with a man, she left the companions of her sex without looking back. Her needs had to be sustained by him. If not, she was to keep her emptiness to herself."[24] Through Teresa's reflection on her family's disapproval of her friendship with Alicia, Castillo is explicit and direct in her criticism of how patriarchy is sustained through impeding meaningful solidarity in women. The fact that friendship between women is frowned upon after marriage highlights the threat of homoerotic desire to heteronormativity. As Catrióna Rueda Esquibel has argued, lesbian desire happens quite often within *comadrazgo* and spaces of feminist solidarity.[25] While not always exhibiting homoerotic lesbian desire, examples of *comadrazgo* in Chicana literature exist in Sandra Cisneros's *The House on Mango Street* (1991), Denise Chávez's *Loving Pedro Infante* (2001), and Terri de La Peña's *The Last of the Menu Girls* (1987), among others. As

Esquibel notes, these texts offer material from which to explore friendship between women including those that challenge patriarchal codes and heteronormative interpretations precisely because they are "less valued than heterosexual relationships."[26] Nevertheless, though *The Mixquiahuala Letters* is not an isolated case in showing the value of solidarity and friendship between women, it does take *comadrazgo*'s power one step farther into the realm of lesbian desire in further strengthening radical solidarity against the everyday effects of patriarchy. The need for friendship between women that Castillo narrates can be traced and understood through the feminist of color genealogy of a "politics of refusal" discussed above. The key importance of Teresa's "refusal" lies in the fact that Teresa leaves her husband indefinitely to travel within the United States and to Mexico with another woman. In other words, even though he was considered a "good" husband, Teresa chooses to leave him.

While some scholars have interpreted *The Mixquiahuala Letters* as a Chicana feminist text with queer elements, others have also read it more specifically as a queer text. Citing Mary Gossy's claim of *Don Quixote*'s characters of Aldonza/Dulcinea as butch/femme, Barbara F. Weissberger proposes a butch/femme Quixotic reading of Teresa's and Alicia's relationship. Weissberger writes, "Teresa echoes the butch Aldonza Lorenzo, while Alicia fulfills the role of the femme Dulcinea. Like Dulcinea, Alicia never 'appears.'"[27] Weissberger then adds, "She is the focus of Teresa's reexamination of her past, so much so that the all-consuming relationships with men of a decade earlier are finally revealed to be distractions from the real story: 'This isn't a tale of our experiences, but of two women.'"[28] Certainly, there are queer parallels and Quixotic influences in Castillo's work; I am not necessarily concerned with ascribing a butch/femme framework to Teresa and Alicia's relationship. Nevertheless, in offering a queer interpretation to Teresa and Alicia's friendship, Weissberger further highlights how according to Teresa, men in the end were mere distractions from what truly mattered—the telling of the story that connected both friends.

Men in many respects were vehicles of misplaced emotion and frustrated love between the friends, especially in the case of Teresa as the narrator and sole letter-writer. For instance, Teresa often disapproves of Alicia's love interests, displaying jealous behavior through satirical descriptions of Alicia's suitors while simultaneously undermining Alicia's interest in them. In one biting remark, Teresa says, "You told yourself that he was interested in you, the woman, Alicia, the person."[29] Indeed, Teresa describes how both she and Alicia are objectified by men, yet paradoxically, she also depicts how she and Alicia use men as instruments for other means—to be closer to each other, to incite jealousy in each other, and/or for sexual pleasure. Teresa writes in explicit detail about how men became the answer to everything including their pain: "[We] licked our wounds with the underside of penises and applied semen to our tender bellies and breasts like Tiger's balm."[30] This moment in *The Mixquiahuala Letters* exhibits a candid awareness of the relationship between pain, pleasure, and heterosexuality, and of the pain caused by patriarchy. In letter 28, the reader finds out that Teresa takes Alexis as a lover; he is a Gypsy flamenco guitar player and, coincidently, Alicia's distant cousin. Alexis embodies the allure that attracted Teresa to Alicia in the first place, and while Teresa hints that Alexis was queer, she notes that he preferred to be with women: "He preferred the intimacy with woman [*sic*]to that with a man."[31] The suggestion of Alexis's bisexuality emphasizes the presence of sexual openness and the continued desire for sexual freedom that permeates the world represented by *The Mixquiahuala Letters*. Castillo, as I discuss earlier, invokes queerness in different ways, where bisexuality is but one manifestation of queer possibility and potential. Queer longing thus gestures towards the possibilities of sexual freedom across identities and social relations. More significantly, it indicates the reclaiming of women's sexuality and pleasure, within Teresa's relationship with Alexis, but most notably outside of heterosexual parameters, as in Teresa's relationship with Alicia. In Teresa's eyes, Alexis's masculinity and sexuality are nonnormative, different from the male masculinity and sexuality that she had encountered all her life. The fact that the representation of lesbian desire within *The Mixquiahuala Letters* is not perceived as absolute but as another possibility of sexuality's indefiniteness and flexibility is exactly the point. Bisexuality as sexual subjectivity both in the case of Alexis and Teresa marks an important thread on sexual openness within Castillo's work. Her desire for Alexis is both a desire for Alicia and for Alexis's perceived socially progressive masculinity; "he professed sincere humanitarianism and took avid interest in our community undertakings."[32] Teresa's words here show how the fact that a man not solely interested in women who was sympathetic to the social causes about which Teresa cared was perhaps an attempt to realize her longing for alternative futures across social, national, and sexual borders. For Teresa, being with Alexis was perhaps also a way to be with Alicia and to remain connected to her. Although men are continuously regarded by Alicia and Teresa as a medium to remain linked to one another, Teresa and Alicia's relationships with men signal Castillo's recognition of patriarchy as a determinant in women's decisions. *The Mixquiahuala Letters* is thus a direct and literal representation of patriarchy getting in the way of women's fulfillment. Despite their feminist politics, Alicia and Teresa cannot escape patriarchy's dominant grasp. Castillo, for instance, wastes no time in making this point by quoting Anaïs Nin from *Under a Glass Bell* in an epigraph: "I stopped loving my father a long time ago. What remained was the slavery to a pattern."[33] The quote foregrounds the difficulty of breaking patriarchal patterns in spite of being aware of their detrimental effects, but more importantly tells the reader how to interpret Teresa's story as a statement of defiance against this reality and its barriers.

LESBIAN TEXTUALITIES AND QUEER FUTURES

Plenty of moments within *The Mixquiahuala Letters* suggest lesbian textualities, but more significantly there are also moments that articulate a politics of queer possibility and refusal. One moment that impeccably exemplifies Teresa's queer longing and lesbian desire in the face of Mexican patriarchal codes happens upon Teresa's second visit to Mexico, while she waits for Alicia's arrival. While Teresa eagerly waits in the town's plaza, she describes the scene: "As dusk fell, the ritual that echoed and haunted young romances for centuries began. The male, usually accompanied by friends, went around the square in one direction, the female, usually accompanied by chaperones, walked in the opposite."[34] Castillo in this passage describes a ritual that is classically representative of Mexican and mestizo heteronormative customs, especially in small Mexican towns in the countryside. As one of the most well-crafted parts of the book, it masterfully details Teresa and Alicia's anxiously awaited reunion: "I'll never forget the laugh I had when finally i spotted you, going 'round and 'round and no less in the same direction as the men, towing your knapsack over your shoulders. But we were joyous to see each other, weren't we? Then and there in the face of prim pretense we hugged and jumped about in each other's embrace."[35] Castillo's strategy to have Teresa and Alicia meet and reunite in that precise moment and place paired with its detailed description is significant on multiple levels. Teresa notes how Alicia is fortuitously walking in the same direction as the men when she finally spotted her in the crowd. Teresa's mention of this detail suggests that regardless of whether she knew it or not, Alicia was literally walking through gendered divisions. Instead of participating directly in the ritual, both Teresa and Alicia are uninterested in the men who are strategically positioned to draw women's attention. This scene exhibits how their intimate friendship and embrace in the middle of the plaza at least momentarily loosens the grasp that patriarchal customs and expectations have on both women.

While the content of Teresa's letters provides the material and context of their friendship, Castillo's specific style offers an added erotic element. The way in which Teresa physically describes Alicia in her letters goes beyond mere admiration for a friend. This is especially perceptible in letter 14: "Why do you shun the plum breasts, the raisin nipples that stand perpendicular to your torso."[36] Teresa describes Alicia's physical beauty with no pretense in objectivity: "Hermana, i wish I could have convinced you how beautiful you are, then perhaps you might not've gone through so much personal agony during the second journey to Mexico, or at other romantic times."[37] Teresa begins the letter by addressing Alicia as "Hermana" and, as the only time she does so in Spanish, self-evinces her intention to suppress the homoeroticism of the passage to anticipate moral judgments from Alicia or any other potential letter readers. Teresa continues her affective description and narrative of veneration: "I, the poet, never praised you lyrically, instead scolded to put an end to your timid inhibitions; i've imagined it's done no good. They were only the words of another woman."[38] Teresa indeed recognizes and laments that her words, even if out of love and desire, do not bear enough weight in Alicia's balance of things as they come from a woman. The passage above highlights one constant throughout *The Mixquiahuala Letters*—the way in which Teresa alternates between expressing what can be interpreted as a nostalgic love and desire for Alicia, and downplaying the eroticism by attempting to make it appear as simple admiration for a friend. A possible interpretation would imply that Teresa's ambiguous recollection of moments with Alicia are contingent on the social limits of normative gender and sexual expectations, restricting what could happen between the friends, or at least what could be retold in the letters. Conversely, another reading would suggest that rather than being limited by the social parameters of the time, Castillo wagers between suggesting explicit homosexual relationships and insinuating queerness, "showing us the mask" to lay emphasis on the possibilities of alternative gender and sexual futures beyond conventional romantic relationships.

REMEMBERING FUTURES

Teresa's revisiting of her experiences with Alicia taps into the potential of those precise moments to be remembered and actualized now through the letters' writing and rereadings. The lesbian erotics and desire of the letters are catalysts for the lingering queer promise in the text's past and present. Although it remains arguable that Alicia saw Teresa as more than a friend even in absence (regardless of whether they ever had sexual intimacy), it seems clear that Teresa did indeed have a profound emotional and sexual attraction for Alicia. Castillo's *The Mixquiahuala Letters* at first glance might be interpreted as a dated narrative considering the increasingly harsher border and immigration laws where many do not have access to mobility and travel in the same way. Yet, in an age of restricted access for some and encouraged travel for others, *The Mixquiahuala Letters* with its Chicana travel storyline stands as a nostalgic and hopeful tale of the possibilities of connection and closeness across time and distance. *The Mixquiahuala Letters* is unmistakably still relevant, but more than anything, its message of desire for meaningful intimacy despite dominant and alienating structures of capitalist patriarchy and whiteness is undeniably urgent.

GIVING IT TO THE GLOBE

EMMA PÉREZ

With more than twenty books published, Ana Castillo is one of the most prolific writers of our generation. She began her career with poetry books and the award-winning novel *The Mixquiahuala Letters*, which uses stylistic devices from Julio Cortázar's *Rayuela (Hopscotch)*. That first novel received the prestigious American Book Award from the Before Columbus Foundation in 1987. In a sense, its innovative approach set the tone for what was to come from Castillo, who is consistently prepared to experiment with genres to offer fresh ways of reading. For example, she plays with verse and wrote a novel entirely in poetic passages in *Watercolor Women, Opaque Men: A Novel in Verse*, and to illustrate additional range, she also wrote the sci-fi *Sapogonia: An Anti-Romance in 3/8 Meter*. One of the many qualities I admire so much about Castillo is that she consistently flourishes as she experiments with genre, characters, voices, rhythm, structure, and plot. Additionally, she is not intimidated by controversial topics like gender and sexuality in her essays, poetry, novels, and memoir.

When I spoke with her in Salamanca, Spain, in May 2018, I was captivated with her keynote address in which she delivered a poem on number forty-five, never mentioning Trump's name while enumerating in stanza the damage he and his administration inflict upon the United States and the world while targeting Brown and Black bodies, along with women, queers, and transwomen/transmen. What struck me when we talked after her keynote is how unassuming she was when I told her how much I appreciated the poem she had read. I had met Ana years prior and I promptly became a fan of her fiction, poetry, and essays while continuing to be awestruck by her productivity. We proceeded to discuss writing and its process as we walked through the narrow cobblestone streets of the city accompanying a large group of Chicanx/Latinx on our way to lunch. As we sauntered, we landed on the topic of gender/sex/sexuality, the theme of the section I am addressing in the essays by three Chicanx/Latinx scholars. It seems fitting to mention the conversation Ana and I had about how to write sex scenes, how audiences respond to sex scenes, and the purpose they serve along with for whom we write.

I had not read *Give It to Me* (Lambda Literary Award, 2015) when we spoke that day in Salamanca, but I appreciated her perspective on how the novel was received by her audience. We agreed that most readers and critics seemingly shy away from tackling explicit sex in prose even when written with a purpose. In *Give It to Me*, the protagonist, a Chicanx bisexual woman, has sex when she wants, with whom she wants and how she wants, demonstrating explicitly that her agency propels her sexuality in behaviors often reserved for men in a patriarchal, "machista" world of double standards. We also reflected on readers who claim to want sensuous writing yet appear bashful when confronted with explicit sexual writing or perhaps enjoy reading the scenes but prefer not to engage the uninhibited episodes with their book clubs. After all, the publication of *Fifty Shades of Grey* gave many women permission to participate in promiscuous topics and discuss desire in ways formerly considered taboo. Many other women's passionate desires enacted and expressed remain a taboo within the current era. In any case, I was fortunate that this meeting with Ana Castillo launched many more conversations about writing and its method, the frustrations, the bliss, and the merit of bringing to light topics like sex and sexuality despite criticism and/or distaste.

The three essays in my rejoinder center on two Castillo novels, her first one—*The Mixquiahuala Letters*—and *Give It to Me*, published a few decades later. I'll begin by working backward to discuss her recently published memoir, *Black Dove: Mamá, Mi'jo, and Me* (Lambda Literary Award, 2017), which is the focus of the essay by Elena Avilés. The literary critic scrutinizes the manner in which "queer motherhood, queer mothering, and queering motherhood" are all encompassed in Castillo's memoir. Avilés argues that "Castillo's memoir, *Black Dove*, offers a voice of empowerment and demonstrates the pliability of the concept of *madre*—mother—by 'queering' the way the term has been constructed. She uses her own lived experience as a bisexual Chicana mother to challenge established ideas of sexuality and gender, especially within heterosexual norms affixed in Chicanx culture."[1] For Avilés, Castillo explores the often neglected voices of queer of color mothers who must negotiate cultures that do not support or acknowledge anything other than heteronormative motherhood. It's difficult enough to be a single mother in a patriarchal, capitalist economy that places women of color at the bottom of wage-earning hierarchies as well as social status. The ongoing social stigma attached to being a single mother persistently accuses single mothers as lacking and irresponsible because they do not have a male head of household to grant them patriarchal privileges. Add to that queerness and bisexuality, as in

Castillo's circumstance, and you find a mix of defiance with an onslaught of ongoing critique from a traditional Chicano community that can be quite homophobic and unrelenting when it comes to feminism and formidable, courageous women. However, Avilés promptly explains that the Chicanx/Latinx community is far more complex than the customary stereotypes. One does not have to venture too far to witness activist mothers who have been subverting stereotypes in their own struggle for agency. In her essay, she relies upon Sandra K. Soto's "de-mastery of desire,"[2] my own "decolonial imaginary,"[3] José Esteban Muñoz's "queer futurity,"[4] and "disidentifications via revolutionary thinking,"[5] along with Juana María Rodríguez's "Latinx bisexual erasure" and "Latina longing"[6] to illustrate Castillo's memoir as a transnational bridge between and among Chicanx and Latinx scholars. Avilés uncovers the manner in which Castillo consistently interrogates the role of motherhood, not only in her recent memoir, but also in her novels and poetry while "de-master[ing] Chicana desire," and "revolution[izing] thinking." Castillo's memoir particularly advances through and with these theoretical moves as she addresses her own "bisexual erasure" and "sense of brownness in the world."[7]

Moreover, the writer Castillo implements her idea of feminist brownness through "Xicanisma," a Chicana feminist perspective that she coined in 1994 with the publication of her book of essays, *Massacre of the Dreamers*. The term itself has been taken up by a younger generation that often neglects to cite Castillo, but erasure is often a part of inhabiting Xicanisma in US politics that flings women of color on the back burner permanently; however, the author enacts an ardent racialized queer/bi sexuality that cannot be snubbed. Through daily practices, Castillo provides examples of Xicanisma. For example, because she must raise her Brown son in patriarchal, heteronormative spaces, she teaches him to "challenge his own gender conformity of what it means to be a male and to encounter his own machismo."[8] In this way, argues Avilés, Castillo "queers the politics of Chicanx culture in order to raise consciousness."[9] Again, her enacted Xicanisma while "mothering from a queer lens"[10] is vital to note. Avilés reiterates the importance of Castillo's contributions as someone who has unswervingly intervened through her political essays, fiction, poetry, and this vibrant memoir that creates an aperture for a diasporic and transnational reading of what motherhood is outside visions of straight-gay paradigms.

In her most recent novel, *Give It to Me*, published twenty-eight years after her first, for scholar Daniel Shank Cruz, "sex is everywhere"[11] as suggested by the title. Cruz notes that Castillo offers up twenty-five sex scenes, which average approximately one in every ten pages. Elsewhere, I've asked the question that I take from Michel Foucault: What does it mean to "put sex into language"? Here, Castillo shows us precisely how to put sex into language in a way that acts like an "educational role for readers because they celebrate Palma's bisexuality and create a conceptual space that is both politically and sexually queer."[12] By choosing to write realistic sex scenes, Castillo also elects to impart complex relationships that are feminist, queer, bisexual, Chicanx, and transgender. She honors the many identities while traversing the plight of sexual pleasures, sexual inhibitions, and excruciating societal judgments. Cruz points out that Castillo dares to venture into sexual and sexed territory that many avoid because they risk being deemed pornographers. In our current time of Trumpian far-right religion that praises white supremacy, celebratory queer-bisexual sex scenes are even more imperative. Cruz addresses further how Ana Castillo is not one to allow any type of censuring or inhibition that robs her of a creative process that intervenes and contributes to Xicanisma and overall feminist queer of color politics. He posits, "Unlike in pornography, where the plot does not really matter even though it is there to add some sort of perceived legitimacy to the work, the sex in *Give It to Me* is the plot; it is the action that readers are supposed to pay attention to, not for sexual gratification (it is not erotica, and almost none of the sex scenes are detailed), but because of the argument it makes about what a queered society might look like."[13] Unwittingly steering toward queer futurity, Cruz also confirms the overtone of bisexuality and the manner in which Castillo's chosen sexuality has been habitually erased by literary critics who often mark her as "lesbian" instead of bisexual. He adamantly declares that bisexuality is often left out of queer politics, which perhaps remains part of a future not yet here. While reaffirming the import of bisexuality as queer, he also asks us to consider John Rechy's pioneering books, *The City of Night* and *Numbers*, to show the genealogy of Chicanx/Latinx queer writing. In other words, he makes the claim that Rechy's early works have influenced contemporary queer writers, including Castillo. The documentary *The Sexual Outlaw* is also appraised because it illustrates, in Rechy's own words, "the promiscuous homosexual is a sexual revolutionary."[14] Cruz reviews Rechy's seminal texts and documentary, based upon *Numbers*, precisely because Castillo references him in *Give It to Me* as reverence to the first Chicanx queer writer who consciously penned brazen sex to liberate an entire queer generation of the 1960s and 1970s. In her protagonist Palma, the novelist esteems Rechy by replicating unabashedly bodily pleasure for women, not only men. Cruz further argues, "Castillo's novel also does a better job of showing how sex may be healthily integrated into a queer life whereas the men in Rechy's books actively seek it out as a form of self-validation; it succeeds as a revolutionary act by the men when they are able to find sexual partners, but fails when they are not, whereas Palma views the attempt as the important thing, another example of her bisexual epistemology."[15]

Both Elena Avilés and Daniel Shank Cruz acknowledge Castillo's unequivocal bisexual politics while queering her memoir and fiction. Liliana González expands the queering of Castillo's fiction and exposes the homoeroticism and seemingly "lesbian desire"[16] between two female friends in Castillo's epistolary novel, *The Mixquiahuala Letters*. González's is a refreshing take that explores nostalgia as a critical maneuver to entertain what José Esteban Muñoz challenges us as Brown queers to do: to queer futurity as we cruise queer utopias of our own making. The literary critic González also points out that "whether the text presents a lesbian relationship as such is not as crucial as the actual suggestion of queer longing and lesbian erotic desire interweaved with the text's social reality."[17] The social reality to which González refers comprises "the difficulties of traveling as women" (through Mexico), "solidarity in friendships between women, and above all else, love and desire."[18] Along with citing queer of color theorists Muñoz, Sandra K. Soto, Gloria Anzaldúa, Cherríe Moraga, and Juana Maria Rodríguez, González also refers to José Quiroga's "consideration of absence, nostalgia, and sex"[19] through Mexican gay poet Xavier Villaurrutia's *Nostalgia for Death* (1946) to argue that "nostalgia and absence are themselves inextricable from one another and intimately linked to queer longing and desire."[20] Ultimately, González invites us to contemplate the magnitude of "nostalgia for a future." Borrowing from Muñozian utopian desire and Rodríguez's politics of refusal, that is, refusing to repudiate the future for queers of color, González maintains that nostalgia itself is at once an impossible yet possible memory that may have been or could be. In essence, she provokes us to think about Castillo's letter-writing Teresa, who constructs desire through a longing for what may have been as well as what could be in a future not yet here. The melancholic tone of the novel is itself a treatise to nostalgic desire as aching, craving, wanting that which one feels that cannot be in the present but that perhaps in a future will be for others if not for the main characters of the novel, Teresa and Alicia. Teresa is perhaps Castillo herself, although this is a work of fiction, and Alicia is the paramour who carefully chooses her words of longing. Both women couple with men, often deliberately making each other jealous. In fact, Teresa leaves her husband at home in the United States to travel through Mexico with Alicia, something that is frowned upon by the patriarchal heteronormative Chicana/o family. González also reminds us that the point of view in the novel is predominantly Teresa's, denoting we are never sure of Alicia's desires although they are routinely implied in the text. It is that longing, that nostalgic, melancholic pitch that drives the plot and makes the desiring women insatiable perhaps. Or perhaps they are not necessarily insatiable but they seem to have a limitless passion for a queer futurity that is not yet here, compelling a powerful, deep nostalgia that overwhelms the tenor of the women's relationship, which itself remains ambiguous in its fundamental yearning. González has definitely offered us a paradigm for exploring a text such as this. The literary critic ventures into Latinx queer theories and expands upon them with the notion of "nostalgic futurity."[21]

There is a way in which all three of the literary critics here are venturing into queer futurity, whether about mothers and queering motherhood, or about sex and queering sexualities, or friendships that are seemingly queer in their desire for a distinct, tender, affective intimacy. For each of the essays, the literary scholars are hopeful for a future that no longer restricts and restrains Chicanx/Latinx generations who want to live outside of patriarchal, traditional constraints placed upon women, mothers, queers (bisexuals included), and transwomen/transmen. The promise and desire for difference can finally be freeing. In Ana Castillo's writing, the scholars each point to the promise and desire for difference and sexual freedom. Castillo herself has committed to a writing life that exposes injustices for those living on the margins, the Chicanas ignored, the Brown mothers neglected, the queers brushed aside, the bisexuals and transwomen/transmen erased. The prolific, award-winning writer challenges her readers to consider the pleasures and bliss of being Chicanx, of living in the now while visualizing another future: kind, just, and compassionate. At a moment when chaos overwhelms world politics, she asks us to harness Xicanisma and undo gendered roles that have only inhibited sex and sexuality. In other words, Castillo's writings continue to demand that we practice a more principled way of being.

MAMÁ, MIJXS, AND ME

*Connecting Chicana Feminism and Transnational
Feminism in the Era of Globalization*

CHAPTER 12

PRIESTESS *Y PASTORA*

Chicana Feminist Representations of Transnational Female Spiritual Leadership in Ana Castillo's *So Far from God* and María Amparo Escandón's *Esperanza's Box of Saints*

LAURA ELENA BELMONTE

Pero es difícil *differentiating between*
lo heredado, lo adquirido, lo impuesto.
She puts history through a sieve, winnows out the lies,
looks at the forces that we as a race, as women, have been a part of.
Luego bota lo que no vale,
los desmientos, los desencuentros, el embrutecimiento.
Aguarda el juicio, hondo y enraízado, de la gente antigua.
This step is a conscious rupture with all
oppressive traditions of all cultures and religions.

Gloria Anzaldúa, *Borderlands / La Frontera: The New Mestiza*

Anzaldúa's epigraph above poignantly applies to the consciousness of the protagonist characters in Ana Castillo's *So Far from God* (1993) and María Amparo Escandón's *Esperanza's Box of Saints* (1999); these characters break with traditions that oppress Chicanas and Chicanos by "[botando] lo que no vale," or "throwing away," what does not have value, as Anzaldúa explains that the new mestiza must do when embracing her culture. These novels present protagonists who continue participating in a Christian faith through a patriarchal institution such as the Catholic church, yet "throw away" the patriarchal aspect in their embrace of their own spiritual authority. The protagonist women in both novels gain spiritual authority through their role as mothers, and actively utilize their motherhood to transgress into roles and spaces deemed only for men, both religiously and culturally. These protagonists subvert the dominant and patriarchal structures of the church and the heteronormative nuclear family by claiming the roles of priestess and *pastora* (a female pastor)—what I read as enactments of their agency and Chicana feminist praxis. These actions, in turn, reposition *la madre* from being an idealized figure of submission to a powerful figure of spiritual authority in her home and community, which she uses to determine the religiosity and spiritual expression that dignifies her children through decolonial love. By examining the literary work of Ana Castillo, a Chicana writer, and María Amparo Escandón, a feminist writer who was born in Mexico City and moved to the United States in adulthood, this essay argues that representations of the mother through the protagonist Sofia/Sofi of *So Far from God* and Esperanza in *Esperanza's Box of Saints* emphasize spiritual authority in her home and community. These mothers determine the religiosity and spiritual expression that dignifies their children rather than abide by patriarchal religious institutions for guidance on spiritual matters. Sofia and Esperanza take hold of their spiritual authority through their motherhood as women of color who face global issues harming their children. Thus, the term *"la madre"*—the Spanish translation of "the mother," and thus a linguistic border-crossing that decenters hegemonic notions of the English language—will be used because this essay has a transnational Chicana feminist approach (which will be further developed) to Sofia and Esperanza's feminist spiritual authority.

The novels written by Castillo and Escandón reveal how the figure of *la madre* challenges any notion of borders by crossing national boundaries; she's a transnational subject, defying hegemonic notions of citizenship. Sofi, a Nuevomexicana, and Esperanza, a Mexicana, are women of color and *las madres* who face global issues that harm their children. In other words, their subjectivities and struggles are the same despite the physical border that separates them. These transnational maternal representations "throw away" and break with oppressive traditions, and demonstrate that mothers are the spiritual leaders of the home space and the community. This chapter establishes that the *la madre* figure is portrayed as a leader who: 1) protects and guides her children as well as members of her community; 2) serves as an intermediary between that which is secular and that which is sacred; and 3) transcends borders that are represented in both novels.

Sofia and Esperanza's spiritual authority manifests in a variety of ways; however, the literal decentering of male religious authority occurs in two specific scenes. These are parallel scenes of each other, as Sofia and Esperanza gain authority in different ways that result in recentering Brown mothers who theologize with male Catholic priests about the nature of the miraculous reappearances of their daughters after death.[1] In *So Far from God*, Sofia's youngest daughter dies and resurrects during the funeral. When the child awakens, she flies from her coffin to the top of the church roof. Father Jerome inserts himself in the scene by attempting to decipher the nature of this supernatural occurrence, asking the child: "Is this an act of God or of Satan that brings you back to us, that has flown you up to the roof like a bird? Are you the devil's messenger or a winged angel?"[2] Sofia, a grieving mother who is done with her role of a palatable self-sacrificing mother, confronts Father Jerome:

> "Don't you dare!" she screamed at Father Jerome, charging at him and beating him with her fists. "Don't you dare start this about *my* baby! If our Lord in His heaven has sent my child back to me, don't you dare start this backward thinking against her; the devil does not produce miracles! And *this* is a miracle, an answer to the prayers of a brokenhearted mother, ¡hombre necio, pendejo . . . !"[3]

Sofia confronts Father Jerome's theology of miracles and articulates her own theology that declares La Loca's resurrection a miracle. This declaration is an act that defies patriarchal norms because it is usually Vatican officials who can declare miracles. Sofia theologizes to dignify her daughter's supernatural resurrection by confronting the priest; she defends the well-being of her daughter against "backward thinking" that will inevitably harm her daughter, even as she was nicknamed "La Loca" after this supernatural occurrence by the community as she refused human contact with anyone other than her mother.

Similarly, Esperanza confronts Father Salvador's imposition on her search for her missing daughter Blanca after an apparition of Saint Judas Thaddeus, or San Judás Tadeo as he is known in Mexico, on Esperanza's dirty stove tells her Blanca is not dead. Esperanza goes on to exhume Blanca's coffin to find that it is indeed empty. She commences a search that takes her from brothels in Tlacotalpán, her hometown in Veracruz, and the US-Mexico border town of Tijuana to an illegal border crossing and on to Los Angeles. Esperanza's transnational search to the United States borderlands leads her back home to Tlacotalpán. While taking a bath, she hears Blanca's voice and sees her in a rusty stain: "In that stain, I saw Blanca's face. She was wearing a beautiful Jarocha costume. She said, 'Mommy, you and me, we'll always be together.'"[4] Anticipating Father Salvador's disbelief, Esperanza goes on to theologize the nature of this miraculous apparition, even when he asks if she will notify the Vatican:

> Father, do you understand? I finally know what San Judás Tadeo meant. Blanca is not dead. Blanca is not alive. She is that little space in between. That's where I was supposed to look for her. . . . Blanca's apparitions are not important to the rest of the world. Why do you think she's appearing before me on my bathroom wall and not before the whole town on the bridge wall moss, like San Juan Nepomuceno did six years ago? This is just between the two of us. She's my own little saint, my little *santita*. So, please don't start paperwork.[5]

Esperanza experiences the sanctification of her daughter Blanca, whom she interprets as neither dead nor alive. The miracle of Blanca's sanctification could have only happened with Esperanza's fierce search for her daughter in the face of the mystery of Blanca's empty coffin. Instead of going to the priest to ask for an interpretation of the miracle, Blanca gives the priest her theological interpretation, and declares that Blanca's apparition is between herself and Blanca. Sofia and Esperanza experience the death of their young daughters, as well as the miraculous apparitions of these daughters after death. As the spiritual authorities of their homes, Sofia and Esperanza are the protectors of their daughter's souls, and thus assert their authority by theologizing with the priests regarding the nature of the miracles of their daughters' coming back from the dead. Their spiritual authority is a transgressive crossing of gender roles that serves as a vehicle for social change, and this is possible through their roles as mothers dignifying their children's existence.

TRANSNATIONAL CHICANA FEMINISM IN THE SPIRITUAL AUTHORITY OF *LA MADRE*

Transgressive crossings such as crossing the US-Mexico border (whether undocumented or by seeking asylum), crossing into the workforce as a woman, or crossing the patriarchal parameters of religious authority are all feminist acts subverting the nation-state parameters of citizenship. Norma Alarcón, Caren Kaplan, and Minoo Moallem discuss how "the nation-state sharpens the defining lines of citizenship for women, racialized ethnicities, and sexualities in the construction of a socially stratified society."[6] To continue the project of nation-building, the nuclear family is thus crucial for the reproduction of more citizens, but within parameters of the ideal citizen in accordance to how hegemonic groups define citizenship. The creation of borders and a continued rhetoric for borders is thus necessary as well, as both determine the other, the foreigner, the noncitizen. Alarcón, Kaplan, and Moallem present a "communal identity crisis" in which the parameters of citizenship are disrupted by racial and sexual determinants: "At the core of the modern nation-state, a contradiction is set in motion insofar as there is denial of sexual or racial difference or both, and simultaneous universalization of difference."[7] The significance of religion comes into play as it creates a universalization of what a nuclear family ought to look like: that which is based on patriarchal Christian tradition with parameters around the composition of the family as a husband, wife, and children. This structure in turn leads into defining borders of women's bodies as being determined by male presence. Chandra Mohanty describes this bordering of women's bodies: "Borders suggest both containment and safety, and women often pay the price for daring to claim integrity, security, and safety of our bodies and living spaces."[8] Indeed, when women do not subscribe to heteronormative notions of family structures, or their circumstances have brought them to existing on their own without a male presence, they become the leaders and authorities of their nuclear family, which disrupts and causes a "communal identity crisis" that shakes the established borders and parameters as defined by hegemonic institutions. An act of defiance against patriarchal Christian notions of family is an act of defiance toward parameters of citizenship. Chicana feminist praxis, as represented by Sofia and Esperanza's mothering, decenters male headship of the family structure and challenges these parameters of citizenship at the nuclear level.

Laura E. Pérez manifests that "for Chicanas/os, 'nation' is made to signify differently, and symbolic language is made to course through alternative venues than the ones imagined, colonized, legitimized by the order that denies oppressed peoples access to its center of articulation."[9] The transnational nature of the identity of Chicanas/os thus allows them to imagine citizenship in a transgressive light: *ni de aquí, ni de allá*. Chicanas/os, as well as other racialized groups, experience systemic oppression through racial and gendered violence manifested at the nuclear level through the family. However, these are microcosms of global issues that reach beyond the nation-state borders, as these demonstrate capitalist transnational power structures. This point is echoed by Leigh Johnson's discussion of how Chicana literary characters in the novels *Black Widow's Wardrobe* (1999) by Lucha Corpi and *Mother Tongue* (1994) by Demetria Martínez are "global citizens." Johnson argues that the nature of the characters' narrative arc is transnational because there exists an "inability of any novel to so stay contained within the hemisphere."[10] As transnational and Chicana feminist texts, Ana Castillo and María Amparo Escandón's novels feature characters who defy notions of citizenship as dictated by American, as well as Mexican, patriarchal power structures; the women also decenter white male power—those who are typically the "actors"—and in turn, recenter Brown mothers to determine family structures. Castillo and Escandón's protagonists achieve this through religious authority as *las madres* within their home and family structure, particularly when racist, sexist, and homophobic violence affects their daughters.

The importance of social change by mothers of color for their children is one of the main points of Johnson's analysis of transnational Chicana feminist representations in Chicana literature: "Motherwork can be concentrated on one family, one community, but more frequently, it reverberates through communities to produce social change."[11] Building on Johnson's argument, I employ Chela Sandoval's concept of the "oppositional consciousness," which she develops in her influential work *Methodology of the Oppressed* (2000), as the method through which Chicana feminism brings about social transformation; it is a consciousness that results in actual change. The oppositional consciousness locates the Chicana/o according to their social position within the United States while at the same time uses the "tactical subjectivity" to deconstruct the cultural norms that oppress them; it is an awareness and theoretical understanding of oppression.[12] While oppositional consciousness is necessary, it is only a starting point. The actual application of dismantling systems and institutions of white supremacy and gender inequality has to move forward through what Chela Sandoval calls "de-colonial love." This concept of decolonial love encompasses the *concientización*, taking action on this *concientización* through deconstructing sexist, racist, and homophobic language, policies, and power structures, and finally establishing equalizing structures that allow for the oppressed to live a dignified existence. Decolonial love destroys oppressive norms against people of color because it is a rupture against the normalization of accepting oppression. Having an oppositional consciousness means that the oppressed are no longer able to find comfort in the status quo, and alternatively the oppressed have ways to function through decolonial love. One method of decolonial love is "differential consciousness": "[It] represents a strategy of oppositional ideology that functions on an altogether different register . . . [it] is the expression of the new subject position . . . it permits functioning within, yet beyond, the demands of dominant ideology."[13] Sofia and Esperanza embraced differential consciousness as *las madres*, which ultimately provides a freeing and safe space for themselves as well as their children.

TRANSNATIONAL VIOLENCE PRESENTED IN *SO FAR FROM GOD* AND *ESPERANZA'S BOX OF SAINTS*

In the world outside of Sofia and Esperanza's homes, hegemonic forces represented through neoliberal ideologies, as well as racist and homophobic politics, enforce a patriarchy that rejects the woman. These forces are represented in the novels as responsible for harming and destroying these women's daughters. The policing of the maintenance of the ideal citizen is a form of policing the borders of a body politic. Identities that are queer, nonwhite, poor, and non-evangelical are deemed causes to the previously mentioned "communal identity crisis." The violence perpetuated against those who are deemed other is thus targeted in a variety of ways. In *So Far from God*, while Sofi's daughter Caridad, who was initially characterized as an overly sexual hetero woman, finds true love with a woman named Esmeralda, she commits suicide after a *penitente*, who was in love with Caridad, rapes Esmeralda in a jealous rage.[14] While she ultimately falls in love with a woman, Caridad's sexuality was transgressive from the beginning of the novel, because even though she had sexual relations with men, she was still seen as a *puta* for her embrace of her sexuality. A second daughter of Sofi's, Fe, develops cancer while working in the Acme International factory in her attempts to assimilate to US dominant culture. Seeking career success as a journalist brought another of Sofi's daughters, Esperanza, an untimely death, as she was assigned to cover the war in the Middle East and killed in a conflict zone. And even Sofi's baby, La Loca, the daughter who never left home, inexplicably contracts AIDS and, at the end of the novel, also dies.

Each of the daughters' deaths are stark reminders of the ways capitalist systems that monetize all things and do so at a global scale also target the other. In her 1999 essay "Chicana Feminism: In the Tracks of 'the' Native Woman," Norma Alarcón discusses the notion of how women of color, in this case Mexican and Chicana women with Indigenous roots, are seen as wild or "'non-civilized' dark" women.[15] She argues that while the brownness of women includes them in Mexico under the national identity of mestizaje, in the United States the Brown woman is othered in the face of white supremacy and therefore deemed wild; Alarcón concludes that Brown women are then "often compelled to acquiesce with the 'civilizing' new order in male terms."[16] Attachment to men therefore allows Brown women to enter within the acceptable terms of belonging in the body politic as a member of society. Being an independent Brown woman, on the other hand, is deemed taboo: an independent Brown woman is a target for the perceived vulnerability.

In *Esperanza's Box of Saints*, Esperanza is precisely this independent Brown woman: she is a young widow who lives with her only daughter, Blanca, and her friend, Soledad. After the apparition of San Judás Tadeo, Esperanza traversed dangerous spaces in search of her daughter. Among them is the cemetery where she exhumed Blanca's coffin to confirm that she had, in fact, died. She finds that Blanca may have possibly been kidnapped and is now being sex trafficked.[17] A 2016 United Nations report on human trafficking worldwide reports that between 2012 and 2014, 63,251 victims were identified in 106 countries. The same report states that in 2014, 28 percent of reported victims of human trafficking are children and 54 percent of all victims are forced into sexual slavery. Esperanza, while being in a small town in Veracruz, is well aware of the world's sexual depravity and how her daughter could have become a victim of its utter violence. Father Salvador describes her drive to find her daughter as "unstoppable": "She's on a mission. It's [God's] will. All I can do is pray for her. Am I wrong to believe her?"[18] The targeting of women deemed vulnerable due to lack of male presence is not by accident. Justifications for sex that include women "being in the wrong place at the wrong time" perpetuate ideal citizenry parameters determined for women by male presence, sponsorship, and protection. Thus, the motherwork, and in this case, spiritual authority, is powerful as it takes an idealized notion of womanhood—motherhood—and is utilized to counter the bordering and policing of women's bodies. *La madre* goes into the dark and dangerous places and brings her child home to heal, regardless of the expectations of what a society, nation-state and its borders, and policing deem illegitimate about her and her child.

DEFIANCE AND TRANSGRESSION OF *LA MADRE*'S SPIRITUAL AUTHORITY AND LEADERSHIP

This essay conceptualizes *la madre* as a literary representation of religious authority—a controversial idea within Chicano/a culture. In Mexico and the southwestern United States, religious teachings mainly derive from the Catholic church. This religious institution has influenced acceptable gendered behaviors, with strong foundations in Catholic theology.[19] Culturally speaking, women have only been able to take on the role of the teacher when it comes to religious instruction of the children. The irony is that, while teaching children religious doctrine is expected, women are not permitted to have any kind of leadership role within the church. For example, the Catholic church still does not allow women to become priests.[20] The Vatican has justified women's exclusion from these leadership roles with the dogma of "complementarity"—the theological teaching that women and men were created as complements to one another, each given a different role by God. In *When Women Become Priests: The Catholic Women's Ordination Debate*, Kelley A. Raab explains: "Complementarity refers to the idea that men and women have different roles to perform within church and society, originating from innate, predetermined functions. In this 'two nature' vision of humanity, men and women are ordained to complement one another, leading to a division of male and female roles, which are not interchangeable."[21] One of the "roles that [is]not interchangeable" is leadership within the church or the home. While the woman complements the man in her procreative capacity and thus aids in augmenting the number of Catholics in the "Reign of God," according to doctrine, she will never be able to become a priest, nor have the headship of the home, which is a supposed role of the man.

Raab's research includes an investigation of official Vatican documents, which she utilizes to clarify the theological explanations preventing women from becoming priests.[22] She divides her findings into three justifications: 1) tradition; 2) the male biological or "natural" resemblance to Jesus Christ; and 3) the biblical allegory depicting Christ as the bridegroom and the church as the bride. The first justification of tradition is not insignificant; in the Roman Catholic church, tradition carries the same doctrinal weight as scripture. A 1976 Vatican declaration directly addressing the "Question of Admission of Women to the Ministerial Priesthood" indicates that traditionally, a woman has never been named to the priesthood. Additionally, explanations regarding men's natural resemblance to Jesus Christ and the image of the bridegroom and bride demonstrate a direct intention of subjugating women according to the doctrine of complementarity. Considering the 1976 declaration, Raab asserts: "The document states that the incarnation took place in the form of the male sex and that this fact cannot be disassociated from the doctrine of salvation. Fundamentally, the argument runs, Christ cannot be symbolized as a woman because the historical Jesus was not a woman."[23]

The Vatican emphasizes Jesus's sex to justify preventing women from entering the priesthood. Raab defines this reason as "biological determinism," a concept established by Thomas Aquinas in *Summa Theologica* (1485).[24] Aquinas declared, "Because the female sex cannot signify eminence of rank—women being in a state of subjection—it follows that she cannot receive the sacrament of orders."[25] (This Thomist belief has had repercussions affecting women's participation in the Catholic church to this day.) Sofia and Esperanza directly transgress this biological determinism by the simple fact that they *are* female and they establish their religious authority over Father Jerome and Father Salvador.

The influence of Catholicism and its dogma of complementarity within Chicana and Chicano culture affected relationships between Chicanas and Chicanos during the Chicano Movement in the 1960s and 1970s. Tenets of cultural nationalism at the center of the movement emphasized a romanticized notion of "the family" because Chicanos wanted to embrace Mexican culture and reject the dominant culture of the United States. Denise Segura and Beatriz Pesquera explain that this idealization of "the family" is an empowering tool for activists who support Chicano cultural nationalism: "Politically, cultural nationalism called for self-determination including the maintenance of Mexican cultural patterns, culturally relevant education, and community control of social institutions."[26] However, the maintenance of "Mexican cultural patterns" turned "the family" into a romanticized concept, which had consequences for the ways that male activists treated women. Many Chicanos had no interest in listening to Chicana activists who denounced sexism and sexual harassment, and effectively marginalized them within the movement. As Segura and Pesquera explain: "Chicanas who deviated from a nationalist political stance were subjected to many negative sanctions including being labeled *vendidas* (sell-outs), or *agabachadas* (white identified). Once labeled thus, they became subject to marginalization within Chicano Movement organizations."[27] Calling these Chicanas *vendidas* and *agabachadas* was a way to control them and maintain traditional notions of family that were both patriarchal and sexist. One of these traditions was women's submission to male authority, designed to maintain complementarity within "the family." Due to these conflicts, feminist Chicanas started their own liberation movement with art, literature, intellectualism, and queer sexuality that subverted the notion that women must submit to men.

One way that Chicana feminists attempted to undermine such ideas in the 1970s was to appropriate the concept of *la madre* (the Mother)—to decolonize her and rid her of patriarchal ties. Chicana feminists have written, painted, and represented the mother figure in ways that continue to decolonize *la madre* as well as all Chicanas. Artists' and writers' creativity throughout the 1970s and 1980s has allowed future Chicanas to create religious representations of the mother figure that include different religious expressions—artistic production that continues to this day. Gloria Anzaldúa discusses the importance of *la madre* in relation to Chicana/o identity in articulating the three mothers of Chicanas/os: Malinche, La Llorona, and Guadalupe. According to Anzaldúa, "'The *virgen*/whore dichotomy' pits Guadalupe against Malinche and La Llorona: Guadalupe as *virgen*, that is, the ideal example of Chicana/*mexicana* womanhood and fits well within the borders of the ideal woman citizen, and Malinche and La Llorona as the whores."[28] However, like Anzaldúa, other Chicana feminists have reappropriated the figure of Malinche and La Llorona to demonstrate transgressive Chicana motherhood that embraces sexuality and agency, and breaks barriers.[29] Ana Castillo and María Amparo Escandón depict the Chicana/*mexicana* mother as the practitioner of "de-colonial love," which is the vehicle by which the mother is or becomes a spiritual authority, therefore providing a sacred place for her children to heal and transcend systems of patriarchy, racism, and capitalist globalism that are so damaging and violent toward people of color.

Ana Castillo deliberately writes the mother character of Sofia to go against these Chicano nationalist ideals of Chicana motherhood. Melissa Schoeffel explains: "Rather than focusing on how motherhood threatens an woman's individual autonomy, her [Castillo's] focus is on how the cultural idealization of motherhood is always paired with the denigration of actual mothers, and that such a paradox is the patriarchy's response to the (re)creative power of women evidenced in the physical and cultural work of mothers. . . . Reclaiming motherhood—which means recognizing the political effects of its ideologies—is for Castillo an essential step in imagining 'truly nurturing society' (125), one that does not idealize or denigrate mothers but, rather uses maternal practices as models for ethical social relations."[30] It is through this reclaiming of motherhood that Castillo and Escandón explore how *la madre* is a source of social transformation through their transgressive roles as spiritual authority figures. Sofia functions as a priestess of her temple, which is her home, and Esperanza functions as a *pastora* and journeys across the US-Mexico borderlands. These roles are distinctly to dignify the existence of their children while at the same time legitimizing their leadership in the face of hardship, and their agency in matters of sexuality and political identity.

As priestess in her home/temple, Sofia evokes animal sacrifices for the good of the congregation (her children)—a motif that most vividly encapsulates her role as a priestess. In the novel, "Sofi single-handedly ran the Carne Buena Carnecería she inherited from her parents. She raised most of the livestock that she herself (with the help of La Loca) butchered for the store, managed all its finances, and ran the house on her own to boot."[31] The blood and sacrifice of the animals sold in Sofia's butcher shop support her home/temple, mirroring temples in other religions that ritualized the sacrifice of animals. Throughout the novel, La Loca manifests supernatural healing powers, but, as she is inseparable from her mother, La Loca also manifests the spiritual power of the home. Even so, Sofia is the one with the authority to allow others to enter into this sacred space. Only Sofia can touch La Loca because she is the priestess; she is the intermediary between the divine power, the community, and most importantly her daughters who are in need of healing and protection.

Castillo's differential consciousness is represented throughout the novel in the miracles that occur in Sofia's home/temple because they impact the lives of Sofia's daughters and the community that surrounds them. Her decolonial love creates a social change in the community of Tomé, when she runs as a candidate for mayor even though the town does not offer such a position. Nevertheless, with her candidacy, Sofia gains the trust and respect of the community. This is empowering for women of color, and is precisely what Chela Sandoval indicates happens when decolonial love causes a social transformation.

However, Sofia and her daughters suffered long before this transformation took place. Each daughter (with the exception of La Loca) goes out into the world and comes back damaged to Sofia's home/temple. While the example of Caridad depicts physical violence, the other daughters face emotional harm and literal violence, as well. Out of all of Sofia's daughters, Fe is the one who most desires to assimilate into American society. She seeks the American dream—getting married, having children, and buying a house— and seems to be on the path to achieve it. However, everything changes when Tom, her fiancé, breaks off their engagement. Fe reacts very strangely, as she begins to scream and does not stop. This incident happens around the same time that Caridad is brutally attacked by *la Malogra*, an evil monster that originated in New Mexican folktales, and as a result both sisters are home, hurt, and recovering while La Loca prays for them and Sofia looks after the well-being of the home.[32] This goes on for several months. Then one day, all of the sudden, Caridad's mauled body is miraculously restored to its original state from before being destroyed by *la Malogra*, and Fe stops screaming. The differential consciousness is manifested in this miracle, as the older sister, Esperanza, perceives it: "Caridad's and Fe's spontaneous recoveries were beyond all rhyme and reason for anyone."[33] Moreover, this differential consciousness of the miracle in Sofia's home results in decolonial love and is the rupture in Esperanza's logic, as the intellectual daughter of the family.

By studying at the university, Esperanza became an atheist and developed a cynical attitude toward religion. However, her sisters' tragic experiences motivated Esperanza to search for understanding of what was happening in her mother's home: "She read everything she could find on dysfunctional families, certain now that some of her personal sense of displacement in society had to do with her upbringing. But nowhere did she find anything near to the description of her family."[34] Esperanza was unable to find logic in her sisters' healing. Her intellectualism prevented her from seeing that her home, the temple of Sofia the priestess, was a sacred place that activated Caridad and Fe's recovery. La Loca, being the healing power, prayed for her sisters: "She also prayed for [Fe], since that was La Loca's principal reason for being alive, as both her mother and she well knew."[35] But although La Loca represents the healing power of the home, the healing could not occur without Sofia, the priestess. Sofia, flustered by her two daughters' precarious conditions, suffers a nervous breakdown in the presence of Esperanza. Even with her lack of faith—which reflects Western society's emphasis on logic, scientific thought, and scorn for human strength and the supernatural—Esperanza begs Sofia to not be overcome by her circumstances. It is precisely in these inexplicable cases that rupture exists, encouraging those present to consider a third space, a spiritual world, where everything is possible.

On the surface, the ultimate deaths of her children may be a blow to Sofia's decolonial love. However, Castillo writes into the narrative several border-crossings that are miraculous and an act of differential consciousness: these are the border-crossings from death to life, from despair to healing and remembrance. These border-crossings are La Loca's resurrection when she was a child, and Esperanza's spirit coming back to visit Sofia's home. At both of these events, Sofia, along with the Tomé community, witnessed the transcendence of women of color despite what patriarchal and hegemonic systems dictate are the destinies of people of color and, especially, women of color. The paradox of these miraculous events is that they are tragic yet produce hope, because it is transcendence over the border that ultimately separates families. Death is the miracle through which Sofia's daughters overcome racial and sexual violence, while at the same time Sofia's temple and priesthood—those spaces and roles not established in religious institutions—provide the place where this transcendence takes place. Castillo beautifully weaves this narrative of unfettering faith and love of the *la madre* that burst through the very terminal concept of death, and in the following section María Amparo Escandón similarly takes the transcendence of decolonial love to create a transnational narrative in *Esperanza's Box of Saints*.

In *Esperanza's Box of Saints*, Esperanza leaves home to look for her daughter, Blanca, thus performing the role of the *pastora*. Biblical narratives represent this figure as someone who tends a flock of sheep, which includes going out in search of those who are lost. The mother-*pastora's* transgression also conflicts with the Catholic dogma of complementarity. With her call to go out into the world to care for the flock and search for lost sheep, she challenges the designation of the man as shepherd, or pastor. Miguel de Cervantes's most famous novel, *El Ingenioso Hidalgo Don Quijote de la Mancha* (1605), provides an example of a woman vilified for being a *pastora*. The character of Marcela is a young woman who wishes to be a *pastora* and to enjoy the solitude of the land. She is blamed for the death of Grisóstomo, a shepherd who fell madly in love with her. Don Quijote and Sancho Panza encounter the procession of mourning for Grisóstomo, and, by inquiring about the deceased, are informed that an "endiablada moza" (a young woman possessed by a demon) rejected him, thus causing his tragic death. Regardless, Marcela appears during the funeral to defend herself, saying, "No todas las hermosas enamoran. . . . Yo nací libre, y para poder vivir libre escogí la soledad de los campos. . . . Tengo libre condie ción y no gusto de sujetarme. Ni quiero ni aborrezco a nadie" (Cervantes, *Don Quijote de La Mancha*, 101–2). Because Marcela is a *pastora*, the men around her feel justified in dehumanizing her, as she has entered into "male space." In this way, Marcela's transgression, in addition to not reciprocating Grisóstomo's love, was to be bold enough to step outside the home space and find her calling as a *pastora*. As this example demonstrates, going out into the world, as Marcela did, constitutes subverting the virgin/whore dichotomy, and is thus the most transgressive role discussed in this essay.

Esperanza's faith is so strong that she believes the apparition, and throughout the novel does everything in her power to find Blanca. She believes that her daughter is not dead, but rather has been kidnapped and made a victim of sex trafficking, leading her investigation to brothels in Tijuana and Los Angeles. Esperanza is not afraid to enter these incredibly dangerous places in order to find her daughter, mirroring the proverbial shepherd, or pastor, in search of their lost sheep. The mother-*pastora* as a figure of spiritual leadership is the more transgressive of the two representations because of her calling to leave the home space. According to patriarchal customs, the home is the designated space for a woman, and in leaving it she may be considered a "public woman," that is, a woman who is sexually immoral. As a mother in search of her children, the mother-*pastora* can be a representation of the multifaceted figure of *La Llorona*—a woman who, depending on the differing versions of the legend, drowns her children in a fit of rage after being betrayed by her beloved or because she was protecting her children from violence, and endlessly wanders bodies of water weeping.[36] Significantly, both *La Llorona* and the mother-*pastora* can be characterized as transgressors for rejecting the submission and abnegation expected of a mother in mourning; instead, they look for their children that society has determined are dead.

SACRED PLACES AND SPACES THROUGH CHICANA TRANSNATIONAL FEMINIST MOTHERWORK

La madre has to carve out sacred places and spaces for her children in light of the violence perpetuated against them. Sofia's home and Esperanza's holy journey are spaces and places that are a sanctuary that dignify the existence of their children. The representation of the home as a refuge is a leitmotif in literature as well as art. However, this leitmotif resonates more profoundly with people of color due to the violence and oppression of the world outside the home. This idea is reflected in the way that African American feminist author bell hooks describes her grandmother's home in *Yearning: Race, Gender, and Cultural Politics* (1990): "I speak of this journey as leading to my grandmother's house, even though our grandfather lived there too. In our young minds houses belonged to women, were their special domain, not as property, but as places where all that truly mattered in life took place; the warmth and comfort of shelter, the feeding of our bodies, the nurturing of our souls. There we learned dignity, integrity of being; there we learned to have faith."[37]

This understanding of the home as a refuge is crucial in considering Ana Castillo's novel, *So Far from God*, as Castillo similarly emphasizes the home space as fundamental for the well-being, development, and survival of people of color.

Sofia's home is a manifestation of Ana Castillo's differential consciousness: this little house is a space in which a *mestiza* has the power to decolonize her daughters. Sofia functions as a mother-priestess in her domestic space to maintain, as hooks states, the characters' dignity. In his article "Priests and Priestesses in Prehistoric Europe," Johannes Maringer discusses the characteristics and functions of a male (or female) priest. According to Maringer, institutionalized religions define the priest as the person in charge of the spiritual affairs of the community. The priest spreads religious teachings and looks after the physical structure of the temple or church, while the institution he represents assures his well-being. In addition to religious institutional authority, a sense of divine authority is also bestowed upon the priest. As Maringer clarifies, "Their specific character consists of being invested by a community as supernaturally authorized mediators to the transcendental world for the performance of the public cult."[38] Thus, the role of priesthood is assigned by a supernatural entity.

This home, Sofia's temple, is important to her daughters' welfare and serves as a refuge and sacred place. The decolonial love that Sofia manifests in her home represents a parting and entering point, as is the state of Coatlicue, in which the Chicana experiences a transformation as a result from colonial trauma and gendered violence. It is where the physical, emotional, and psychological violence toward the *mestiza* woman has no power. In addition, the home's healing and refuge is an example of the rupture of "whatever controls in order to find 'understanding and community.'"[39] Kathryn A. Rabuzzi explores this theme in *The Sacred and the Feminine: Toward a Theology of Housework* (1982), arguing that the home, like the church, provides a refuge from the world and thus can be described as a sacred place.[40] Considering the etymology of the word "home," Rabuzzi determines that in ancient texts written in Hebrew or Greek no such word exists. She only finds the word for "house," the physical structure.[41]

Rabuzzi also touches on the designation of a place as sacred. She explains that a "space" transforms into a "place" when it holds emotional significance. A "place" representing emotional connections requires a transformation from its inhabitants, which is to say that "place," whether it be religious building, home, or landmark, becomes a "place" rather than "space" because of the value, emotional experience, and history the devout give it.[42] When a "place"—the home in this case—is appointed as sacred, the transformation of the inhabitants reaches an even more intense level. It is important to observe two things in this process: 1) the purpose of this "place," and 2) the experience of those who enter into this "place." Sofia's home in *So Far from God* is a literary expression of a sacred place. As Doña Felicia declares after a demonic animal, *la Malogra*, ferociously attacks Caridad, "All they did at the hospital was patch you up and send you home, more dead than alive. It was with the help of God, heaven knows how He watches over that house where you come from . . . but *you* healed yourself by pure will."[43] Because Sofia's home is a "place" of sanctuary, it is a temple, and Sofia is its priestess, given the task to sanctify this place for the refuge and healing of her community: her daughters. Those who enter into this home are astonished by the miracles that occur there.

Another function of Sofia as a priestess in her home is her rejection of those who disturb the sacredness of the place. Sofia's husband, Domingo, is a gambler, and due to his addiction, he abandoned his family and home. Sofia did not see him again for years, until he unexpectedly appeared one day. Although she was still angry, Sofia forgave Domingo and allowed him to come back home. There are moments when it seems that they have reconciled, but Domingo soon goes back to his old gambling ways, and ultimately bets the house and loses. It is when Domingo loses the house that Sofia finally divorces him. She forgave him for abandoning and neglecting his daughters, but she could not forgive his losing the sacred place that served as their refuge.

Taking control of her home while caring for her daughters provided Sofia with empowerment as a leader. However, when she could not protect her daughters, she decides to take her leadership beyond her home and into her community. She and a friend plan a campaign to elect Sofia as mayor of Tomé. Her friend, resisting the idea at first, tells Sofia that her imagination is too big, but Sofia responds, "It's not 'imagination' that I've always had, comadre, it's faith! Faith has kept me going."[44] Although their campaign did not result in Sofia's election to office, she and her friend initiated community meetings and debates to determine how to turn Tomé into an economically self-sufficient district. They formed "Los Ganados y Lana Cooperative," a cooperative that collects wool from community members' sheep. Although Sofia could not heal Esperanza or La Loca in her home/temple and their death caused Sofia unbearable pain, losing Esperanza brought forth an oppositional consciousness in the community that allowed them to conceive of a collective effort for self-sufficiency.

The sacred space in *Esperanza's Box of Saints* ventures outside the home and across the US-Mexico borderlands. Esperanza's investigation into Blanca's disappearance also leads her to the brothels of Tijuana. After Esperanza discovers her daughter's empty coffin, San Judás Tadeo appears to Esperanza two more times, insisting that she continue to search for Blanca. At the suggestion of Father Salvador, Esperanza begins her journey at La Curva, a well-known hotel where sex workers and their patrons meet. It is there that Esperanza determines that her daughter has become a victim of sex trafficking: "I've heard there are people who kidnap girls and sell them to houses of sin."[45] In the novel, Escandón depicts the mother's differential consciousness through acts of entering and leaving these transgressive spaces. Chela Sandoval explains that decolonial love also manifests in what Roland Barthes calls "drifting": "The movement of meanings that will not be governed; it is the intractable itself as it permeates through, in, and outside of power."[46] In addition to entering these transgressive spaces of prostitution and sex trafficking, Esperanza poses as a sex worker—a transgressive act "outside of power"—in order to find her daughter. Moreover, Escandón emphasizes that Esperanza never has sexual relations with her clients, adding to the miraculous nature of her journey to find her daughter. Her encounters with sexual predators like Cacomixtle demonstrate her unyielding will to enter immoral and dangerous spaces in her quest. In one of the brothels, Esperanza meets Mr. Scott Haynes, a judge from San Diego, California, with whom she has an intimate relationship, but never penetrative sex. This relationship enables her to enter the United States, as Haynes signs her visa, and thus allows Esperanza to continue her search.

Along this journey, Esperanza is steadfast in her spirituality. In the moments when she steps outside of her sex worker pretense, she prays continuously and looks for opportunities for San Judás Tadeo to appear to her again, as he did at the beginning of the novel. In addition, because of entering transgressive spaces, Esperanza frequently feels compelled to confess, which she does over the phone with Father Salvador, the priest in the church back in Veracruz. Although she has committed no sin, her descriptions of her journey awaken an intense lust in the priest, as Esperanza reminds him of a sexual relationship he had when he was young. Father Salvador's lust represents the subversion, or recentering, of another binary: male confessor / female confessant. In this case, the person who listens to the confession, Father Salvador, is the one who sins, rather than the person who confesses, Esperanza. The recentering of Esperanza as pure and free of sin leads Father Salvador, as well as Scott Haynes, to acknowledge their own male power and privilege, as they take advantage of Esperanza's innocence to satisfy their sexual and egotistical desires.

Interestingly, as a mother-*pastora*, Esperanza also subverts the virgin/whore dichotomy. She is a mother who goes out into the world in search of her lost daughter, staying true to her spiritual convictions despite posing as a sex worker. Ironically, she impersonates a sex worker although she has not had intercourse with the clients, but she is not a virgin in the literal sense, because she is a widow and a mother, or in the figurative sense, because she does not stay at home and accept the supposed death of her daughter. This intermediate space that Esperanza inhabits evokes a parallel with the biblical image of Christ. Jesus Christ himself declares, "I am the good shepherd. The good shepherd lays down his life for the sheep."[47] Just as Christ "gives his life for his sheep," Esperanza is a mother-*pastora* because of her intense belief that Blanca is alive, and her incredible willingness to enter dangerous places to find her. When the depravity of those who want to sexually exploit her becomes clear, this parallel with Christ reveals a differential consciousness in Esperanza's search for her daughter and the rupture it causes.

Esperanza's suspicion that her daughter has been kidnapped and sold as a sex slave is a double-edged sword. On the one hand, the kidnapping is a horrible possibility, but on the other, it allows for hope that Blanca may still be alive. Esperanza draws on her spirituality to navigate dangerous spaces in search for her daughter, and it is this spirituality that helps her to survive these experiences. The *limpia* that Esperanza performs in the Pink Palace is an example of using folkloric religiosity as a tool against sexual slavery.[48] Even in a brothel, the prostitutes and the woman in charge, Doña Trini, wish for Esperanza's *limpia* to rid themselves of bad spirits. Esperanza takes advantage of the *limpia* to inquire about what Doña Trini is hiding in the "Scarlet Room." Convinced that the room contains young women as prisoners, including Blanca, Esperanza gives a *limpia* performance to make all of the women believe that they are being purified. The paradox of pureness in a transgressive space like a brothel demonstrates the power of folkloric religious expression. As Laura E. Pérez explains in *Chicana Art : The Politics of Spiritual and Aesthetic Altarities*: "The 'spirit work' of Chicana visual, performing, and literary artists studied here counters the trivialization of the spiritual, particularly of beliefs and practices from non-Western traditions, as 'folk religion,' 'superstitious,' or 'primitive.' It attempts to derail Eurocentric cultural evolutionary arguments in the sphere of religious belief or disbelief that demean that which is culturally different as inferior."[49]

Pérez determines that it is the spirit work of the Chicana novel that challenges the degradation of folklore as an expression of third-world people with "primitive" religiosities. Through her *limpia*, Esperanza discovers that, in fact, there are not kidnapped girls in the Scarlet Room, but rather Doña Trini's hidden sexual fetish: a cow called Felicitas, the Sixth. This discovery enables Esperanza to continue her search in other spaces, and in this way, fulfill her role as a mother-*pastora*. Entering transgressive spaces, she finally "finds" her daughter, ironically, back in her own home. Esperanza represents a spiritual leader because of her astonishing faith incited by apparitions of San Judás Tadeo. Her belief gave her the conviction to directly confront sex trafficking. In the process, the novel offers a message about human trafficking and sex slavery as a result of the neoliberalism embraced by first-world countries, such as the United States, as well as the detrimental policies enacted by the US government against migrants crossing the border.

The literal border-crossing of Esperanza is one representation that signifies the leadership of Latin American women to provide a better life for their children. Tragically, in 2018 the Trump administration's Department of Homeland Security separated thousands of children from their parents as they were apprehended by Border Patrol or simply seeking asylum at port entries. The heart-wrenching endeavors of reuniting the children with their parents has been at the forefront of discussion of violent racism manifesting along the US-Mexico border, and it is this narrative of looking for a child by a mother across borders that is also the main plot of Escandón's *Esperanza's Box of Saints*. After searching for her lost child in dangerous and taboo spaces, she finds and places her in the sacred "place": returned to the care and healing of the mother. Spiritual female headship recentered in Castillo and Escandón's novels is a relevant conversation of the transnational experience of women of color and their children living through circumstances of racism and sexual violence and their survival of such violence.

THE DECOLONIZING LOVE OF *LA MADRE*

Toward the end of the twentieth century and the beginning of the twenty-first, women are becoming more involved in leadership, even within the Catholic church.[50] The Chicana cultural production presented in this essay demonstrates the rising spiritual expression of women practicing leadership roles. These works reveal that the mother does not have the same iconographic meaning as she has in the past within Chicana culture. Yolanda López, the first Chicana artist to depict the Virgin of Guadalupe in non-traditional ways, argues that the holy mother, the Virgin of Guadalupe, is not the only image representing the Chicana woman. Now, the woman is represented as an active mother, ready to show her love for her children. The love of *la madre* has the goal of decolonizing her children to achieve social equality. In this way, the Chicana, by being a mother, draws on her leadership to mobilize her community.

This rings true regarding the migratory experience for many young mothers from Central America and Mexico, in which they turn to the option of crossing the US-Mexico border for the survival of their children. Ana Castillo and María Amparo Escandón approach the topic of border crossing in literal as well as metaphysical and spiritual ways, lending to the discussion of the treatment of those who cross borders, what their prior and subsequent circumstances are after border crossing, and finally the exalting of these women by the acts of *la madre*. The empowerment of people of color does indeed lie in the decolonial love of *las madres* who crossed borders, whether they are patriarchal, racial, gendered, or spiritual, to give their children a dignified existence and remembrance. Border crossing, as Anzaldúa has written, is what the mainstream and hegemonic power structures deem where the queer, the "sexually deviant," the poor, the unacceptable human beings commit their grand sin, while it is writers like Ana Castillo and María Amparo Escandón who take border crossing and turn it into the ultimate form of rising above these power structures in a way that is dignifying and brave.

CHAPTER 13

THE UNBREAKABLE LINK

Ancestral Memory in Xicanista and African Diasporic Women's Poetry

REBECCA KENNEDY DE LORENZINI

The poetry of a people comes from the deep recesses of the unconscious, the irrational and the collective body of our ancestral memories.

Margaret Walker

In a recent interview for a radio program, Ana Castillo expressed her sense of place and belonging as being deeply tied to ancestry and an expansive understanding of geography: "Living in New Mexico, I feel a profound connection to my ancestors and an awareness of location as a continuum."[1] She calls New Mexico home, but the Chicana activist and author grew up in Chicago during a tumultuous time in US history. She was sixteen years old when Martin Luther King Jr. was assassinated in April of 1969. Her teenage years were marked by the multiple freedom movements of the era related to the civil rights of African Americans, Native Americans, and Mexican Americans, to women's liberation and second-wave feminism, and to environmental protection. Each of these movements was part of a radical upheaval of the Anglo-European power structures that have dominated US culture since the nation's founding.

The legacies of both the Chicano and Black freedom movements have traditionally been understood as addressing separate issues, closely linked to particular experiences of ethnicity, race, and labor. Yet when we focus on Chicana feminist and female authors of African descent, similarities emerge in their approach to poetic expression of their liberation movements. Ana Castillo's *Xicanisma* presents understandings of ancestral memory that are especially relevant when placed in conversation with African Diasporic poetry. In fact, the poets discussed here consciously addressed both Latinx and African Diasporic populations, crossing borders and producing transnational and transcultural dialogues that blur the traditional division of nation-states, national regions, and ethnicities in the Americas.

This essay explores poetry of Gloria Anzaldúa (1942–2004), Ana Castillo (b. 1953), and their Afro-Colombian contemporary, Edelma Zapata Pérez (1954–2010), analyzed in light of Castillo's ideas of Xicanisma. Castillo explicitly traced her strong sense of urgency and social justice action to the earlier movements of the 1960s and 1970s, saying, "I was immensely shaped as a witness to those times. The memory and understanding of the significance of social activism since then sustains and directs me today."[2] In this sense, Anzaldúa, Castillo, and Zapata Pérez are linked together through their common participation in, and inspiration drawn from, the social movements of the twentieth century and their respective cultural expressions.

The poetry discussed in this essay moves away from concerns of class divides, legal rights, and participation in the democratic process and moves toward a more spiritual and chronologically expansive approach, which was used as a form of empowerment for personal and collective change. Ancestral memory, discussed explicitly and implicitly, is a common theme that emerges from Xicanista[3] and African Diasporic women's writing of this time period. Both Chicana and African Diasporic female poets invoked the transformative power of ancestral memory for three interconnected purposes: to access a deeper spiritual awareness or consciousness, to heal from generational trauma that was the result of systemic patriarchal sexism and racism, and to inform dreams of a possible future for their communities. These literary forms use language that evokes the memory of the ancestors, rooting social justice action in a non-Western cosmovision that while expressed in the imperial English and Spanish lexicons, uses Indigenous and West African language, words, and symbols to signal a decolonizing epistemology. The discussion of ancestral memory is thus a radical departure from that of the traditional Western canon, creating cultural manifestations "in their own context and on their own terms."[4]

The Chicano movement articulated much of this context. It was foundational to Castillo's understanding of social justice and traced its injustices to both the English and Spanish colonial systems, emphasizing the hemispheric nature of labor exploitation. It began with the establishment of the United Farm Workers of America, a labor union founded by Cesar Chavez, Dolores Huerta, and Philip Vera Cruz in 1962.[5] Specifically addressing the Chicano population of California, the movement had a widespread impact throughout the United States. Castillo, located in Chicago at the time, engaged with the movement through poetry as a form of protest.

Poetry as an artistic medium used for social justice action work has a long legacy throughout the late twentieth century in both Chicanx and African Diasporic communities. We can follow a burgeoning of poetic production by Chicana and Black female poets writing in response to civil rights movements.[6] The body of work they produced was not unique to the United States, nor bound by its political and geographical borders; rather, it was a hemispheric phenomenon that addresses the common legacies of slavery, racism, and labor exploitation within the Americas.[7] At the center of these experiences, as expressed in the poetry analyzed here, are specific concepts of dispersal, relationships to homeland, and ancestral memory. When understood through Castillo's Xicanisma, these poetic themes illuminate a more complete understanding of American experiences in the broadest sense.

DEFINING XICANISMA, DIASPORA, HOMELAND, AND ANCESTRAL MEMORY

Building from the legacy of the Chicano movement, Ana Castillo published her groundbreaking text *The Massacre of the Dreamers: Essays on Xicanisma* in 1994, the same year that Maya Angelou published the fourth edition of her influential collection of poetry, *Phenomenal Woman*. Castillo considered *Massacre of the Dreamers* academic, artistic, and activist in nature. The book was completed as part of a doctorate degree at the University of Bremen, Germany, yet it radically departed from the traditional scholarly forms of the monograph or critical essay. *Massacre of the Dreamers*, which Castillo has stated is "unapologetically devoted to my heart,"[8] is a text that seamlessly weaves together history, theory, personal and critical essays, poetry, and free form prose that are all necessary to express what Castillo defines as Xicanisma, a form of Chicana feminism. It differs from the latter in its departure from nationalism and narratives of patriarchy espoused by the Catholic church. While departing from Western organized religion, Xicanisma is deeply spiritual. For the Xicanista, spirituality is "the key to her strength and endurance as a female throughout all the ages."[9]

Another key aspect of Xicanisma is its rejection of dualities. Castillo explains that in Chicana culture, "women must choose between two polarized roles, that of mother as portrayed by the Virgin Mary vs. that of whore/traitor as Eve."[10] *Xicanisma* breaks free of this dyad by drawing from ancient examples that inhabit both masculine and feminine characteristics, but especially a positive femininity that is life-affirming and nurturing in a broader sense. The expansion of such previously limited ideas is in line with what fellow Chicana feminist Gloria Anzaldúa addressed in her earlier work, *Borderlands / La Frontera: The New Mestiza* (1987).[11] Castillo's rejection of polarized feminine identities is similar to Anzaldúa's concept of the "new mestiza," which works against the binaries of Mexican and Anglo-European culture: "Within us and within *la cultura chicana*, commonly held beliefs of the white culture attack commonly held beliefs of the Mexican culture, and both attack commonly held beliefs of the indigenous culture. Subconsciously, we see an attack on ourselves and our beliefs as a threat and we attempt to block with a counterstance."[12] Anzaldúa offers a third way, a new path to reconciling supposedly irreconcilable differences: "But it is not enough to stand on the opposite river bank, shouting questions, challenging patriarchal, white conventions. . . . At some point, on our way to a new consciousness, we will have to leave the opposite bank, the split between the two mortal combatants somehow healed so that we are on both shores at once and, at once, see through serpent and eagle eyes."[13] Anzaldúa's powerful suggestion breaks down the binary of perspectives between the oppressor and the oppressed, without denying either.

Xicanisma similarly breaks down binaries by drawing from female archetypes to revive the sacred feminine spirit in all people. It is a linking of feminism that bonds more than it separates. Its spiritual application can be applied fruitfully to other experiences: "It may also help others who are not necessarily of Mexican background and/or women."[14] Xicanisma, as a theoretical and practical approach to countering repressive systems in the Americas, relates directly to the wider diasporic conditions of the hemisphere. Castillo draws the link explicitly: "The repressive attitude that we have experienced is not only found in the United States but throughout the Americas and other places in the world where primal peoples reside and where white colonialism has reigned. . . . The black diaspora is a long, mournful wail reminding of [sic] us of the inhumane history of European and Euro-American greed."[15]

This inhumane history of colonialism in the Americas, while manifested differently for different populations, resulted in the diasporic dispersal of people of African and Indigenous/mestizo descent. Historian Kim Butler provides a useful theoretical approach to diaspora that differentiates it from related experiences such as migration and exile. She discusses diaspora status as a process that involves forced removal to multiple locations, relationship with the homeland and "hostlands," and interrelationships within diasporic communities.[16] She is especially interested in comparative studies of different diasporas; comparing Chicana feminist and African Diasporic women's poetry creates the opportunity for comparative study with a focus on points of convergence and exchange. Expanding our understandings of the language of ancestral memory addresses the diasporic process of cultural production. While the African Diaspora is a process rooted in forced removal that differs greatly from other diasporas, the long history of dispersal, movement, and displacement experienced by the Chicanx and Latinx populations and addressed by Chicana feminists such as Anzaldúa and Castillo sheds light on wider experiences throughout the hemisphere.

Gloria Anzaldúa summarizes the Mexican American experience of movement across borders, understood in historical terms: "We have a tradition of migration, a tradition of long walks. Today we are witnessing *la migración de los pueblos mexicanos*, the return odyssey to the historical/mythological Aztlán."[17] Anzaldúa explains that Aztlán is the homeland of the Aztec peoples, and it is located in the borderlands of the current United States and Northern Mexico. She states that her ancestors migrated from the Southwest to what is today Mexico and Central America in AD 1168. With the arrival of the Spanish in the sixteenth century, the tradition of migration continued, as *mestizo* (of Spanish and Indigenous heritage), Spanish, and Indigenous peoples continued to move throughout what is currently the US Southwest and Mexico. In a radical act of claiming her ancestral land, Anzaldúa uses poetry to express the simultaneous deep connection to a land that cannot be easily constrained by Western, European border markings. She writes,

> This is my home
> this edge of
> barbwire.
>
>
> But the skin of the earth is seamless.
> The sea cannot be fenced,
> *el mar* does not stop at borders.
> To show the white man what she thought of his arrogance,
>   *Yemayá* blew that wire fence down.
>
>
> This land was Mexican once,
> Was Indian always
>   and is.
> And   will be again.[18]

This poem excerpt ties the land and sea of the Southwest to the Indigenous population that inhabited it before European arrival and evokes the African Diasporic maternal goddess (*orisha*) of the sea, Yemayá. Yemayá is active in the poem: her domain is the ocean, yet she uses wind to destroy the wire fence that attempts to mark a landed boundary between the United States and Mexico. Barbwire is an important symbol of settler colonialism and the imagined and real boundaries that settlers of European descent established. Private land ownership and divisions of people, livestock, and wildlife shaped the trajectory of life in the American West from the nineteenth century to the present. Yet Anzaldúa draws upon energetic powers that are not Western in origin. She tells the story of Yemayá, the life-giving spiritual power of West African Ifá origins, thus linking the Chicana and African Diasporic struggles, fostering resistance to the European hegemonic colonial legacies.

Another poem by Anzaldúa refers to the African Diasporic deity of crossroads, Eshu: "A chicken is being sacrificed / at a crossroads, a simple mound of earth / a mud shrine for *Eshu* / Yoruba god of indeterminacy / who blesses her choice of path. / She begins her journey."[19] The act of drawing from other cultures to access guiding symbols and metaphors resists European cultural dominance of the Americas. This solidarity of resistance between Indigenous peoples and people of African descent illuminates common diasporic experiences. Central to those experiences is a focus on the importance of homeland in diaspora, intricately tied to ancestral memory.

IN SEARCH OF THE ANCESTORS, AWAKENING TO A NEW CONSCIOUSNESS

Xicanista understandings of belonging to home and place are closely tied to relationships with the land and the ancestors. Similar to in the West African cosmovision, there is no strict separation between the spiritual and physical.[20] Land, place, and ancestral connection are inseparable. To be geographically close to the ancestors is also to be in spiritual proximity. Castillo explains the inner calling to that ancestral-geographical-spiritual place early in her Xicanisma text: "If in search of refuge from the United States I took up residence on another continent, the core of my being would long for a return to the lands of my ancestors. My ethereal spirit and my collective memory with other indigenas and mestizo/as yearn to *claim* these territories as homeland."[21]

Moving one stop beyond simply existing in an ancestral place or homeland, Castillo emphasizes that the homeland must be actively claimed. The Chicana feminist consciously, and intentionally claims the land and the ancestral relationships. Castillo recalled her active seeking of these relationships: "I was unable to unearth the female indigenous consciousness in graduate school that I am certain is a part of my genetic collective memory and my life experience. Nevertheless I stand firm that I *am* that Mexic Amerindian woman's consciousness . . . and that I must, with others like myself, utter the thoughts and intuitions that dwell in the recesses of primal collective memories."[22] Gloria Anzaldúa echoes Castillo's reclamation of "genetic collective memory." She articulates it differently, but similarly signals the ancient connection to knowledge that she believes was held by the ancestors: "I know things older than Freud, older than gender. . . . Like the ancient Olmecs, I know Earth is a coiled serpent."[23]

Both Anzaldúa and Castillo used writing as the vehicle through which they explored and accessed their connection to the ancestors of their homeland; Castillo wrote that in "choosing to be conscious transmitters of literary expressions, we have become excavators of our common culture, mining legends, folklore, and myths for our own metaphors."[24] Poetry is an especially powerful medium through which to excavate this common culture because it allows for creative and fluid use of language and symbols that creatively break with the traditional bounds of prose. Edelma Zapata Pérez understood poetry as "la brújula que me ha conocido, desde mi más tierna edad, a acceder al camino de la reafirmación étnica, cultural, y a la comprensión del mundo."[25] The form itself thus reflects the content: the verbal expression of the poetry literally gives voice to previously silenced experiences. It expresses a way of living those silences, and pulling power directly from them.

Castillo intentionally draws from Indigenous ancestors to counteract the damage and destruction of the Spanish colonial legacy that is also part of her heritage. Her poem, "III," names specific ancestors from whom she draws personal power:

> That power is my inner self, the entity that is the sum total of
> all my incarnations, the godwoman in me I call Antigua, mi
> Diosa, the divine within, Coatlicue-Cihuacoatl-Tlazolteotl-
> Tonantzin-Coatlaopeuh-Guadalupe they are one.[26]

The results of this inner power led Castillo to her Xicanisma activism, focused on radical feminine self-love: "With this knowledge so deeply emblazoned upon my heart, / how then was I supposed to turn away from La Madre, / La Chicana?"[27] For Castillo, connection to ancestral memory and knowledge was essential to awakening to a new consciousness as a social activist.

She explains the practical results of writing poetry, that moves far beyond art, far beyond a new poetics "with our own language but a new conscientizacíon."[28] The result, as Castillo explains it, is a profound awakening into a new consciousness, what Brazilian scholar Paulo Freire and, later, Mexican and Latino activists called *conscientización*.[29] The word was traditionally used to signal class consciousness and a move toward socialism that addressed exploitative labor practices. This new awareness led to concrete political, legal, and labor activism within the Chicano movement, yet Castillo redefines the word for her own purposes. She criticizes the ways in which "efforts at socialism have not given women the kind of humanitarian restitution" that class equality seemed to promise.[30] Thus conscientización, according to Castillo, is a spiritual awakening that goes far beyond class and ethnic divides to address the full being of any individual. Conscientización accesses a knowledge of the self that transcends social identifiers, is tied to the homeland, and emerges from ancestral memory and knowledge.

As in the poetry of Castillo, Anzaldúa, and Zapata Peréz, the very act of writing poetry is an access point to ancestral memory and its incarnation in verse form. It reveals a certain knowing that then empowers the Xicanisma and African Diasporic processes of healing and creating a new future. It is at once a personal, individual experience and a collective endeavor to raise awareness within society for concrete advances, moving through and beyond the damaging colonial legacies. Indeed, "the construction of poetics and prose, the development of ideas, is not the achievement of any one individual writer of her generation. Together, we create a tapestry."[31]

HEALING FROM THE PAST, DREAMS OF THE FUTURE

Edelma Zapata Pérez came into this world on the Caribbean coast of Colombia on July 6, 1954. She shared a birthday with Mexican artist Frida Kahlo, who coincidently passed away that same year in July. This connection held great significance for Zapata Peréz, who referred to Kahlo as "diosa de la muerte y de la vida, encadenada a mí en el tiempo" and as "Creación de profunda resistencia espiritual que incendió el sufrimiento."[32] Edelma's birth was accompanied by her own tears of such suffering that "were destined, from the beginning, to become a river."[33] She cried so vehemently, so ceaselessly, that her mother often remarked: "'We did not know how to quiet you, crying night and day. There was no way to distract you and no lullaby to put you to sleep. It was as if you did not want to join the kingdom of this world.'"[34] Zapata Pérez's hesitancy to join the kingdom of this world reaffirms her strong connection to the spiritual realm, a consistent metaphorical and physical current throughout her life and writing. Access to this spirituality has been a part of her relationship to ancestral memory from three dominant cultures in her heritage: African, Indigenous, and Spanish. She actively identified with all three origins as central to her being, emphasizing Afro-Latinx experiences that have historically been less recognized in the popular imagination than divisions between the two ethnic groups.[35] Her father, Manuel Zapata Olivella, was an influential anthropologist, physician, author, and diplomat, and a leading figure in the *movimiento negro* in Colombia. While he, and Zapata Pérez, identified as Afro-Colombian, he similarly emphasized the concept of tri-ethnicity in the Americas (the African, Indigenous, and European origins of many Colombians and people of the Americas) and celebrated these rich cultural heritages together.[36]

Zapata Pérez, for her part, used poetry to address social justice and ethnic identity from a young age. Embedded in her poetry are rhythmic resonances of Afro-Colombian coastal musical forms such as *mapalé, cumbia*, and *bullerengue*.[37] Themes of healing from physical pain are also strongly present in her work, a reflection of her struggles with rheumatoid arthritis for much of her life. Poetry is both an expression and a form of healing in the physical world, and from the painful past of colonial exploitation.

Edelma Zapata Pérez echoes Castillo's and Anzaldúa's tracing of direct ancestral lineage in order to heal from the painful past of slavery in her poem "Ancestral Fears." The poem is short and direct:

> I come from ancestral fears
> metallic symbols imprison me
> in the vast solitude of daydreams,
> I listen to the voice of the drums conversing
> with the flight of the dead.
>
> I convoke you:
> Totems,
> Gods,
> the invisible and visible world!
> Come with all your thundering lightning
> to liberate my tribe![38]

Zapata Pérez's engagement with ancestral memory addresses fear and imprisonment that the narrator has inherited from the past. In order to heal from that legacy, she convokes the "Totems" and "Gods," which bring spiritual power and the possibility of liberation.

In a parallel gesture to non-Western epistemologies, Zapata Pérez signals the role of ancestry and spirituality: "When I gaze into my ancestors' mirror, I see harmony of movement and the sound of a slow plaintive saxophone that echoes the lament of a far-flung prayer."[39] The saxophone, alluding to the jazz musical form, signals to the reader that this prayerful moment with the ancestors is African Diasporic in essence, firmly placed in the hostland of the Americas.

This American hostland is at once familiar and foreign for Zapata Pérez. To be in conversation with the ancestors in the Americas is an action that requires rewriting and reliving history through multiple perspectives. Her poem "América" reflects upon the ancestral connections lived in America:

> América
> Mis entrañas
> hablan memorias antiguas.
>
> Mágicos momentos
> pueblan mis venas.
> Por mi, sangra la historia.
>
> El lazo
> vínculo irrompible

que me une a los ancestros.
Susurra:
negra, india, blanca.

¡Voces palpitan!
voces me llaman!
¡Mestiza!
¡Chaman!
¡Cristiana!

Soy
Danza enajenada en
la noche de tambores
Tristeza de una quena india
Conquistadora de coraza y arcabuz.

Voces palpitan, Voces me llaman.
Confluyen:
las aguas, las sangres, los ríos.

¡América!⁴⁰

The poetic voice is of the continent itself, personified and identified along ethnic and racial heritage that has been crucial to the history of the continent since European contact. The exclamation points serve to emphasize the calling by name of the feminized ethnic identities that include the mestiza (who for Zapata Pérez is of African descent), the Indigenous healer ("Chaman"), and the Christian, presumably Catholic.⁴¹ These identities are defined by the ancestors in the poem, who are connected by an "unbreakable" link that softly whispers three races of the continent: Black, Indigenous, and White.⁴² Thus race, including social identity defined by religion and spirituality, is the way in which the ancestors are understood as a part of the continent itself.

"América" is an exploration of a homeland felt foreign. Zapata Pérez writes, "Soy / Danza enajenada en / la noche de tambores." The "alienated" dance is from Africa, marked by drums. While it assimilates with the "Sadness of an Indian flute" and the "Conquerer of breastplate and arquebus," it embodies a home that is permanently distant. The imagined Africa is significantly mentioned first throughout the poem when the poetic voice lists elements of the tri-ethnicity of the Americas. The order consistently mentions blackness first, indigeneity second, and whiteness third. Thus, we can understand the African Diaspora as the primary process that marks

American (in the broadest sense) history, intricately tied to ancestral memory that incorporates that process with Indigenous and Spanish heritage. By
privileging the traditionally marginalized groups first, Zapata Peréz claims
Black and Indigenous identity, offering the possibility of healing from the
"bleeding" of history that runs through America.

In other works, Zapata Pérez directly addresses Mexican culture as being highly influential for her and part of her understanding of the Americas. In a poem addressed to Frida Kahlo, with whom she felt an intimate
connection, she mentions the Aztec mother goddess of fertility, the earth,
and death, Coatlicue. The narrator enters into a conversation with Kahlo,

> . . .
>
> Hoy te daré mi canto y la alegría
> no hablaremos de tu noche ni la mía.
> Bordaremos un vestido en honor a Coatlicue:
> le pondrás clavos de tu corazón de luna
> yo derramaré al viento una Lluvia de plumas.
> Miraremos volar su falda en los jardines."[43]

Both Kahlo and Zapata Pérez experienced physical limitations due to
long-term illness that influenced their artistic production of other ways of
expressing the self. Dressing Coatlicue is presented as a form of healing
from physical pain and bodily limitations, fostering a sense of fertility and
creativity that flowed directly from the ancestral memory of that goddess.
Castillo, in her poem "III" discussed above, also called upon Coatlicue,
along with other Aztec goddesses, as a means of accessing "the divine
within." Castillo explains further this tie to ancestral heritage that departs
from a dominance of Western European mythical emphasis: "Ours is not
Homer but Netzahualcoyotl, not Sappho but Sor Juana, not Athena but
Coatlicue."[44]

Ana Castillo writes of the power of healing that will inform a new future in line with Xicanisma ideals of self-love, self-affirmation, and self-
actualization that transfer to collective benefits for society: "I firmly believe, along with many women of conscientización in the Americas, that
U.S. society must eventually acculturate our mestiza vision. Our collective
memories and present analyses . . . hold the antidote to that profound sense
of alienation many experience in white dominant society."[45] She warns that
moving ahead into dreams for the future requires a vigilance and attention to which ancestral memories we embrace and embody: "We must take
heed that not all symbols that we have inherited are truly symbolic of the
life-sustaining energy we carry within ourselves as women. . . . We might if
necessary give it new meaning, so that it validates our instincts to survive
on our own terms." The ultimate goal, as Castillo states, is "to achieve joy."[46]

Ana Castillo ends her call to action by summoning dreams of the future. Dreams that, achieved through joy, will "form the vision that all dreamers share, tho' ever so briefly, as in the following pre-Conquest canto which invokes the moon goddess:

> So Coyolchiuqui left it said:
> Soon we come out of the dream,
> we only come to dream,
> it isn't true, it isn't true
> that we come to live on Earth."[47]

The reader leaves the journey through *Massacre of the Dreamers* having understood that dreams and prophesy were essential to understanding the pre-Columbian Aztec world from which Castillo draws ancestral memory and inspiration for her Xicanista writings and poetry.

Created in different spaces, though in parallel, African Diasporic female poets write of ancestral memory that also connects the past to the present in ways that awake a deeper knowledge than has been offered by the colonial European legacies of the Americas. This knowledge allows for greater possibilities of action made manifest in a future time. While dreams of the future imply that they are not yet realized, African Diasporic concepts of time must be understood in ways that are potentially nonlinear. This renders the past, present, and future as linking the ancestors to their descendants in ways that are more energetic than memorial in nature. Historian William Fagg explained in the 1970s that many African cultures "tend to conceive things as four-dimensional objects in which the fourth or time dimension is dominant and in which matter is only the vehicle, or the outward and visible expression, of energy or life force. Thus it is energy and not matter, dynamic and not static being, which is the true nature of things."[48] Conceptually, ancestral energy can be used to create something new.

Author and scholar Marta Moreno Vega emphasizes this aspect of African Diasporic lived experience, which is echoed in the poetry discussed in this essay: "Embedded in the cosmology of the different African belief systems that traveled to the Americas are the ancestors, including *Eguns* (deceased persons) and spirits, and African deities (orishas, *nkisis*, and *luas*). All of these entities possess divine intelligence and the power to create."[49] Poetry is one manifestation of this creative cultural production.

For many Xicanista and women poets of African descent, the power of ancestral memory, as expressed in poetry, offers the possibility of healing from past traumas and creating new space for dreams of a future free from the oppression of patriarchal narratives that have so long dominated historical discourses of the Americas. Zapata Pérez urged us, "Dejemos los actos piadosos para las beatas y liberemos de sus cadenas al ser intuitivo, al creador de versos, al fuego y al silencio, a las diosas de amor. Devolvámosle la vida a la noche oscura que el amanecer libera."[50] Her call to liberate the creative intuitive beings and goddesses of love in all of us resonates with Xicanista ideals. Her voice, joined with the voices of Castillo, Anzaldúa, and other poets of the twentieth century, expands the possibilities of what a more liberated future for the Americas could look like: a future informed and enriched by the diasporic movements of people, ideas, and cultural references that can empower all in society.

CHAPTER 14

FEMINIST IMAGINARIES OF JUSTICE

Ana Castillo, Sister Dianna Ortiz, and Political Violence in Guatemala

ARACELI ESPARZA

Ana Castillo's oeuvre demonstrates a commitment to social justice by representing the experiences of vulnerable and marginalized people while simultaneously challenging audiences to consider that another world is possible. Chicana/o/x, Latina/o/x, and other US populations of color are most often centered in Castillo's work through a variety of genres including poetry, short stories, novels, essays, journalism, and theater. However, there is also a palpable transnationalist focus in her publications. In this chapter, I am particularly interested in how Castillo represents questions of justice in the context of the armed conflicts that engulfed Guatemala during the post–World War II era. Castillo represents violence in Central America and against Central Americans in several texts, including the unpublished 1984 poem "Margo del Salvador," the novel *Sapogonia*, "Righteous White Boyz" in *Watercolor Women, Opaque Men*, and the texts discussed in this chapter, "Like the people of Guatemala, I want to be free of these memories" and *Psst . . . I Have Something to Tell You, Mi Amor*.[1] Both "Like the people of Guatemala, I want to be free of these memories" and *Psst . . . I Have Something to Tell You, Mi Amor* narrate the details of Sister Dianna Ortiz's 1989 disappearance and torture at the hands of Guatemalan military forces. Sister Ortiz herself recounts these unimaginable experiences of violence in her testimonio *The Blindfold's Eyes: My Journey from Torture to Truth*.[2] This essay traces Castillo's conceptualizations of justice for the disappeared in her poem and plays about Sister Ortiz's disappearance, ultimately arguing that Castillo arrives at an understanding of justice that centers the disappeared in justice-making processes.[3] Together these works are a call for justice and human rights that is evident throughout much of Castillo's body of work and in Sister Ortiz's anti-torture activism. However, as I discuss further at the end of this essay, such desires for solidarity and justice across geopolitical borders are not without contradictions, as they have the potential to marginalize and appropriate the pain of Guatemalans and other Central Americans who predominantly experienced the histories of violence Castillo represents. Nevertheless, Castillo and Ortiz are part of a genealogy of Chicana feminist authors who understand and position their writing as a form of political activism and theory.[4] Feminists of color have long asserted that creative writing is a site for theorizing and disrupting power relations, particularly for communities that have been historically marginalized.[5] In this context, literature becomes central to both theorizing and fighting for justice by providing frameworks for understanding the way that things are and for imagining the way the world can be otherwise.

LITERARY GENRE AND THE STRUGGLE FOR JUSTICE

Castillo's representations of Sister Ortiz's disappearance, torture, and reappearance can be located within a genealogy of activist literary production, including *testimonio* and Chicana/o theater. Both genres have at their core the urgency of participating in ongoing activism against social wrongs and widespread violence. Testimonio, which is largely considered a genre that is rooted in a Latin American tradition, is critically theorized as a form of writing that is driven by an urgent need to speak about an ongoing experience of violence and terror.[6] Such testimonios are typically told by a narrator who is assumed to represent an economically, politically, or racially marginalized collectivity. During and after periods of mass violence, acts of telling about survival, witness, and erasure are means through which people make sense of what has transpired while simultaneously (re)imagining different ways of being in the world. *Testimoniadoras/es* (testimony-givers) and critics anticipate that the ideal audience will take action against the ongoing violence that is represented in the testimonio narrative. The urgency with which Castillo narrates Sister Ortiz's story places her work within a testimonio tradition that aims to inform an audience about ongoing violence and to move people to action. As Castillo told Norma Cantú in a 2008 interview, "When I have a story that is very important to share, I go from one genre to the next because I'm driven by this sense of urgency that I want many people to know about it."[7] This multi-genre approach is evident in Castillo's writing about Sister Ortiz's torture, which includes a poem and two plays. Castillo elaborated on the contemporary importance of her work in a now defunct blog on November 7, 2007: "More relevant than ever is the subject of what we think about torture as a valid means to obtain information from 'enemies.'"[8] She also contemplated the topic on November 13, 2007, before a staging of *Psst . . . I Have Something to Tell You, Mi Amor* at Cornell University: "I hope [the play] will allow students, faculty, and others to [think about] the ethical, moral, and political value or lack thereof of the practice of torturing enemies or suspected enemies."[9] In these two blog posts, Castillo clearly states her political stance and grounds her work in the immediacy and relevance of the post-9/11 debates about the use of torture as a means of national defense. However, Castillo's texts also break with conventional testimonio genre development in that her plays are not presented as mediated texts wherein the testimoniadora tells her story to a Western writer/academic so that it can be edited and published. In this case, Sister Ortiz published her own testimonio and Castillo has fictionalized Sister Ortiz's experiences, allowing both writers greater agency in terms of narrative development, creativity, and expression.

Psst . . . I Have Something to Tell You, Mi Amor can also be situated within the genealogy of Chicana/o theater while simultaneously presenting a challenge to its masculinist history. From its modern inception, typically marked by the establishment of El Teatro Campesino in 1965, Chicana/o theater has been recognized as a political theater that offers a "living testament" to Chicana/o struggles against class and racial injustice.[10] As Jorge Huerta argues, "Chicano theatre groups attempt to produce works that speak to the immediate issues affecting the barrio," which in Castillo's case means dealing with questions of political violence across geopolitical borders and the lack of justice for the disappeared.[11] While Castillo's plays fit well within the political genealogy of Chicana/o theater, the genre often (re)produced gender inequalities. Yvonne Yarbro-Bejarano, Yolanda Broyles-González, Elizabeth Ramírez, and Huerta himself later noted that Chicana theater expanded during the 1970s and '80s as a critique of male-dominated Chicano theater.[12] Chicana theater underscored a commitment to political struggle through stage representations that aimed to create social change with an emphasis on intersectional concerns that centered gender and sexuality, hemispheric struggles for liberation, and the critique of racism and labor exploitation that were prominent in Chicano theatre. *Psst . . . I Have Something to Tell You, Mi Amor* can be understood as part of a tradition of Chicana theater that used actos (short theatrical skits that offer social critique) and teatropoesía (a combination of performance, poetry, and music) to deliver an intersectional political message.[13] Yarbro-Bejarano notes that Chicanas began developing teatropoesía as a way of overcoming limited resources and training by bringing prolific poetry production by Chicanas to the stage.[14] Often, actos and poetry became the script that Chicanas performed onstage as they negotiated a lack of formal theater training and scarce resources. Indicative of the professionalization trend in contemporary Chicana/o theater, Castillo's collection is more formal than most actos and teatropoesía performances: it is available in print, offers stage direction, and is not necessarily improvisational.[15] Nevertheless, Castillo's work continues to be inspired by early Chicana/o theater, particularly in its use of minimal stage production and in its desire to deliver an urgent political message in order to move people to action.

SISTER DIANNA ORTIZ'S DISAPPEARANCE AND REAPPEARANCE

Castillo's texts reimagine the details of Sister Ortiz's disappearance, to which I will now turn, drawing on Sister Ortiz's testimonio, *The Blindfold's Eyes*. On November 2, 1989, Sister Dianna Ortiz, a Chicana Ursuline nun from New Mexico, was disappeared by Guatemalan security forces from a convent named Posada de Belen in Antigua, Guatemala. Unlike more than forty-five thousand other disappeared people who have never been seen again, Sister Ortiz survived her disappearance. After her abduction, Sister Ortiz was taken to La Escuela Politécnica, a military training academy and clandestine detention center in Guatemala City, where she was questioned, tortured, raped, burned, and forced to murder another woman with a machete while standing in a mass grave—an experience that I focus on in my reading of Castillo's texts. Sister Ortiz reappeared after international pressure mounted, leading a military official, whom she describes as an American and her abductor called Alejandro, to remove her from captivity. Contradictorily, her reappearance simultaneously positioned Sister Ortiz as a person without juridical rights who could be subjected to torture as many Guatemalans were, and as someone with access to "protection" from an exceptionalist US government that responded to public demands for her reappearance by locating her and removing her from confinement. This story reveals the complicity and participation of multiple state bodies, administrators, and representatives in violence against those who were disappeared and tortured in Guatemala. Sister Ortiz's torture emphasizes that experiences of disappearance are intertwined and co-constituted, that is, that her experiences overlap with and are made possible by the violence Guatemalans and other Central Americans also endured at the hands of their own governments and with support from the United States.

Before and after her disappearance, Sister Ortiz was constructed as a threatening subject based on her volunteer work as an educator, her identity as a student and religious worker, and her perceived deviant sexuality. The positionalities these activities suggest—student, teacher, protestor, lesbian—made her a target of the Guatemalan military, which actively targeted members of these groups and cast social-justice organizations as the ultimate sites of subversion and national disintegration.[16] While Sister Ortiz was accused of aiding guerrilla fighters and having a sexual affair with a woman, her activities in Guatemala mainly consisted of teaching Maya children how to read and write. Here it is important to note that my attempt to explain Sister Ortiz's work in Guatemala is not meant to suggest that her torture would be justifiable if she were in fact engaged in revolutionary struggle or in nonnormative sexual behavior. It is critical to recognize that such dichotomies are often used to demonize victims of torture and to justify the violence perpetrated against them. As Sister Ortiz recounts, she may have been identified by Guatemalan security forces when she stopped to see what was happening at a teachers' strike during one of her trips to a Spanish class in Guatemala City. After this incident, Sister Ortiz began receiving threats warning her to stop her support for unions and revolutionaries and to leave Guatemala. While the military argued that it was fighting for freedom and democracy, the targeting of teachers and students makes clear that the dangers presented by the masses gaining literacy and knowledge were too great to be left unchallenged. Recognizing a threat to the status quo, the military had a vested interest in preventing Indigenous and other populations with high illiteracy rates from becoming literate. Therefore, the military decided to put an end to Sister Ortiz's work by disappearing her and other educators and students. Such measures are part of a racist colonial project that began more than five hundred years ago and continues into the present and is rooted in ideas about the innate racial inferiority of Indigenous people.[17]

Sister Ortiz occupied another precarious position as a female religious worker who spent much of her time in the company of other women. While the Guatemalan government felt compelled to respond publicly to her disappearance because she was a foreign nun, it simultaneously dismissed her accusations as an attempt to cover up a lesbian relationship. This logic suggests that those who represent a challenge to heteropatriarchy—in this case, a nun, who was assumed to be a lesbian, living among other nuns—are automatically suspect and untrustworthy. The Guatemalan government's attempt to associate women's religious devotion with nonnormative sexuality is nothing new. As Catrióna Rueda Esquibel writes, "Discussions of women's religious communities have [historically] been tied to warnings against carnal emotions and relationships between women."[18] Following this rationale, Guatemalan and US officials hoped to control Sister Ortiz's willingness to talk about her disappearance and torture by accusing her of queer sexual practices—a greater offense, it seems, than torture. As the threats of Alejandro (the American who removed Sister Ortiz from captivity) suggest, both governments expected that speculation about her sexuality would discredit her testimony in the eyes of those disposed to question her in the first place. The construction of Sister Ortiz as a sexual deviant underscores the heteronormative and patriarchal underpinnings of torture and impunity, ranging from the types of torture inflicted on differently gendered and racialized bodies to the court procedures, or lack thereof, to which survivors are subjected. This is important because if disappeared or tortured people can be constructed as deviant and pathological—or, in other words, as a potential threat to the national body—then violations against those persons gain acceptance in the name of protecting the majority of the population.[19]

As a testament to the impunity with which torture occurs, aside from branding her a sexual deviant, the Guatemalan and US governments denied involvement in the crimes committed against Sister Ortiz. Both governments accused her of being a guerrilla operative, being uncooperative in their investigations into her disappearance, and telling inconsistent versions about what happened during the time she was disappeared. The case she pursued in Guatemala was not given importance by Guatemalan officials, and it came to a standstill after her case file was lost by the prosecutor's office. Despite later declassified US government documents and testimony from survivors and witnesses to the contrary, US government officials denied their involvement in torture activities or knowledge of clandestine torture centers.[20] Sister Ortiz initially pushed her case through the Guatemalan court system, the Inter-American Court of Human Rights, the US federal civil court system, and US congressional hearings while continuing to speak to the media. Eventually, she dropped the case due to widespread negligence, accusations against her, and threats carried out by prosecutors, judges, investigators, and law enforcement officials. She came to this decision after the Inter-American Court granted her a hearing and the Guatemalan government responded by accusing her of interfering with their investigation on multiple occasions. Instead of continuing her fight through judicial systems, Sister Ortiz decided to prioritize her own healing process while also redirecting her energy toward anti-torture activism, thereby engaging in more localized and regenerative work. Sister Ortiz's experience as a survivor of disappearance, torture, and rape mirrors the treatment many survivors receive when they appeal to official state systems for redress, leading many to avoid seeking remedy through the state, as Sister Ortiz also decided to do.

Since her reappearance, Sister Ortiz has sought justice and healing for herself and others in ways that do not always appeal to the state for action. Her journey to becoming an anti-torture activist was a difficult one, including learning to cope with the aftermath of her own torture and disappearance. She found strength in the certainty that she survived in order to engage in activist work that calls for the abolition of torture and seeks to provide support services for torture survivors. In *The Blindfold's Eyes*, Sister Ortiz recalls, "The anger was leading me to look beyond my case and beyond Guatemala and to call for more than I would normally dare," leading her to assert that "we must demand an accounting of U.S. actions in *all* of Latin America" to an audience when she gave a keynote at Amnesty International's annual meeting.[21] As an activist, author, and public speaker,

Sister Ortiz has fought for accountability through public presentations and through her work with the Torture Abolition and Survivors Support Coalition International (TASSC) in Washington, DC.

Her case underscores that impunity for those guilty of transgressing national and international laws and conventions that ban torture under all circumstances—such as the UN Declaration of Human Rights (1948), the Geneva Conventions (1949), the UN Convention on Torture (1984), the Inter-American Convention to Prevent and Punish Torture (1985), the Fifth, Eighth and Fourteenth Amendments of the US Constitution, and the American Convention on Human Rights (1969)—makes the United States complicit in those abuses and, by extension, also a perpetrator of violence.[22] In Guatemala, the United States has directly and indirectly participated in brutal torture practices in order to proliferate and protect capitalist and neoliberal interests. Guatemala's post–World War II political instability is often traced to a coup orchestrated by the Central Intelligence Agency (CIA) against President Jacobo Arbenz, who was spearheading land-redistribution efforts that negatively impacted the United Fruit Company and other US interests.[23] After Arbenz's ouster in 1954, Guatemala endured a thirty-six-year civil war that officially lasted from 1960 until 1996, at which time peace accords calling for constitutional reform, demilitarization, and recognition of Indigenous rights were signed between the Guatemalan government and the Guatemalan National Revolutionary Unity (URNG).[24] During the war, more than two hundred thousand people were killed and forty-five thousand were disappeared under the direction of military leaders who were trained at the School of the Americas.[25] Since at least 1946, the United States has been involved in providing military training to more than sixty thousand soldiers at its School of the Americas, known as the Western Hemisphere Institute of Security Cooperation since 2001, including training in interrogation techniques that involve torture. These trainees waged war on civilian populations in Guatemala and other Central American countries during the post–World War II era with US military aid that came in the form of money, training, and equipment.[26] While the United States participated in and supported the violence, the Guatemalan government actively carried out genocide against the Indigenous people of Guatemala.[27] Further, the 1996 peace accords did not bring an end to all war-related violence. Impunity for those who committed war crimes, continued disappearances, and feminicide serve as reminders that achieving peace in a postwar society is a complicated and often illusive process.[28] This is part of the historical context that must be accounted for in order to more deeply understand the motivations behind Sister Ortiz's disappearance, and to critically analyze Castillo's representation of the events surrounding Sister Ortiz's torture, disappearance, and reappearance.

VOICE, RECOGNITION, AND JUSTICE

My reading of each of Castillo's texts focuses on a scene in which Sister Dianna—the character in Castillo's creative writing—is thrown into a mass
grave and a soldier puts a machete in her hand and physically forces her to
kill another woman who is referred to as The Friend.[29] I am particularly
interested in tracing the changing feminist theory of justice for the disappeared that Castillo proposes in her fictional works about Sister Ortiz's life
experiences. By moving among texts and taking up the historical context
that Castillo both wrote within and responded to, I track the ways in which
she eventually arrives at a theory of justice that resists seeking protection,
retribution, reparation, or reconciliation from the very state formations that
either perpetrate or sanction human rights violations. I argue that Castillo
ultimately offers a conceptualization of justice in which the disappeared
and their allies are central to processes of justice-making, allowing for a
more localized and holistic idea about what justice-making processes might
look like, and how to go about claiming justice in the context of torture
and disappearance. Initially, Castillo's imaginary of how justice might be
achieved in Sister Ortiz's case focused on her appeals to the US government.
This was followed by a realization that justice via state-centered models
might not be accessible for Sister Ortiz, even as she continued to struggle
to hold the Guatemalan and US governments accountable. Finally, Castillo
imagines the possibility of justice outside the state apparatus that perpetrated violence against Sister Ortiz by focusing on the role the disappeared
and their allies can play in justice-making. Castillo's intertextual narrative
approach creates the possibility for a feminist conceptualization of justice
that seeks to eliminate all forms of violence, including enacting violence for
the purposes of responding to past injuries. Instead, the feminist theory of
justice that Castillo proposes in her creative writing is rooted in a multiplicity of ideas, commitments, and ways of understanding the world. Castillo's
work underscores that when defined locally, a singular definition of justice
appears to be impossible because, if the goal of seeking justice is healing,
restoration, and regeneration, these things are arrived at differently depending on the needs of people and collectivities on the ground.

Castillo's first publication about Sister Ortiz's disappearance was the
poem "Like the people of Guatemala, I want to be free of these memories"
from the collection *I Ask the Impossible*.[30] She wrote the poem in 1996 after
learning about a six-week candlelight vigil outside the White House that
Sister Ortiz held in order to demand accountability and transparency in
her case and regarding US military intervention in Guatemala. As Sister
Ortiz wrote in a letter to President Bill Clinton, she sought the "declas-
sification of US documents pertaining to my case and all human rights

violations in Guatemala" in order to provide a sense of healing for survivors and for those whose loved ones did not survive.[31] However, as Sister Ortiz learned through government responses to her demands for accountability, the poem begins and ends by representing the impossibility of justice for the disappeared through appeals to the state. Yet, the poem simultaneously suggests that both the speaker and Sister Ortiz embrace the possibility that, through protests, vigils, petitions, and efforts to raise awareness among the US public, the US government would support torture survivors and their allies in their struggle to end torture and in support of healing for survivors of past violations.

In "Like the people of Guatemala, I want to be free of these memories," the murder scene is represented twice, and it repeatedly defies a clear accounting of what transpired in the mass grave, thus raising questions about the importance of voice in Sister Ortiz's search for justice. After Sister Dianna—the poem's subject—and the woman are thrown into the mass grave, a soldier jumps in after them and puts a machete into Sister Dianna's hands. Sister Dianna thinks to herself, "Yes, it is time / to die . . . let me die."[32] At this moment, Sister Dianna imagines death as the only thing that will bring her peace after the violence she has experienced, and while death would foreclose the possibility of healing, it would also bring an end to the physical suffering she endured during and after her disappearance. However, her prayer for death is not answered, as the speaker describes:

> The soldier's hands around hers
> that held the small machete that
> was not used on her own body,
> swung it forward instead and she slashed
> another woman, also in the pit[33]

Together, Sister Dianna and the woman begin to scream, and a question echoed in Castillo's writings about Sister Ortiz's disappearance is posed:

> Who was shouting loudest?
> Sister Dianna Ortíz did
> not know.
> She did not know.[34]

What is it that Sister Dianna and the speaker do not know? Who was shouting loudest? That she would be forced to kill? Who she had killed? Is the speaker performing Sister Ortiz's remorseful conscience because she did not know that the blade would be used against another person instead of against herself? This moment of incomprehensibility underscores the rupture created by the experience of torture in which, Macarena Gómez-Barris argues, "the incommunicability of the experience of torture is not from the inability to narrate experience . . . but the inability to represent the complexity of fullness of that which escapes narrative description."[35] Castillo captures the failure of language and narration by refusing to provide a clear accounting, thereby displacing the privileged US reader whom the speaker assumes in the opening lines of the poem. After all, Sister Ortiz does not have answers to many of her questions, and it is likely she never will. The ruptures and disorientation that torture produces reveal the impossibility of a clear retelling, as the psyche attempts to grapple with the wounds and injuries created by violence. However, this impossibility also becomes part of the logic for denying Sister Ortiz justice through state mechanisms and, symbolically, rejecting claims made by other tortured and disappeared people. The denial of justice for Sister Ortiz—the historical subject—led her to realize that instead of being a benevolent protector, the US government was the arbiter of violence and impunity. In turn, this created an opening for Sister Ortiz and Castillo to begin imagining justice beyond the state, an imaginary of feminist justice that is further explored in Castillo's collection of plays.

In the one-act version of *Psst . . . I Have Something to Tell You, Mi Amor*, Sister Ortiz's character is first introduced twelve years after her torture and is described as being in "the nether space of the perpetual torture chamber of her mind" as she talks to a reporter about the government's response to her disappearance.[36] The trauma of telling and retelling the details of The Friend's death and her own torture takes Sister Dianna back to the temporal space of her abduction. As Sister Dianna recalls her experiences, the woman she was forced to kill is introduced as The Other / The Friend. To symbolize the interconnectedness between Sister Dianna's and The Friend's experiences as characters who have been tortured, Castillo develops a dialogue in which each woman finishes the other's thoughts. In rapid sequence Sister Dianna is put in a cell with The Friend, they comfort each other, they pray, and then they are thrown into a mass grave as their torturers film them. When Sister Dianna first sees The Friend she experiences a moment of profound consciousness and recognition that will guide her after she escapes. In the play, she recalls: "When I came to, the blindfold was off. I realized there was another woman in the room who had also been interrogated. The other woman in the room was weeping, weeping, such inconsolable weeping! I was not crying. I could not cry. I went and put my arms around her."[37] This is a moment of recognition where Sister Dianna's blindfold is both literally and figuratively off, allowing her to see that what is happening to her has happened to many others, including the other woman in the room. Castillo suggests that Sister Dianna's capacity to see allows her to acknowledge that she is not the only person to endure torture in Guatemala, and that if she survives, she must tell what she knows and keep the memory of The Friend, and tens of thousands of others like her, alive. However, while Sister Dianna recognizes the interconnectedness between herself and other disappeared people, the reality of having been tortured and the impossibility of language fully narrating the complexity of that experience is underscored by Sister Dianna's inability to speak and by her being caught in "the perpetual torture chamber of her mind."[38] Thus this moment does not necessarily represent clarity or truth; it does, however, provide increased consciousness about the mass violence perpetrated against people in Central America, and the ways in which such violence simultaneously opened and curtailed multiple possibilities for communication.

The Friend also contributes to the audiences' understanding of the limits of narrating the experience of torture when she states, they "took us outside, naked, burned, violated, from body to soul. All shame, all dignity, all desire to live wrung from us. At least I speak for myself."[39] In these lines, it is important to note the contradiction between The Friend initially speaking in plural for both herself and Sister Dianna, and her subsequent qualification that she is speaking only for herself. The Friend vacillates between understanding what she endured as a shared or collective experience, and understanding her torture as a deeply personal and unique event. Indeed, it is both, and this scene marks the difficulties of recognition and finding voice for survivors and victims of violence. The struggle to find voice indicates the flaws in models of justice that rely upon witnesses and survivors to recount an event precisely because, in the context of horrific violence, there are often obstacles to speaking and remembering. Therefore, collective ways of giving witness to events of violence, that Castillo begins to gesture toward in the one-act play, can be useful when torture has disrupted the circuits of communication. After the first machete slash, The Friend says, "Stop! I wanted to say! . . . You are hurting me! But she couldn't hear or maybe I wasn't speaking anymore."[40] This moment of wounding represents both inevitable death and the silencing of the disappeared, foreclosing the possibility that they can protest on their own behalf and hence necessitating collective witnessing.

However, the impossibility of unambiguously narrating the experience of torture, even through collective witnessing, remains central in Castillo's work, as The Friend's lacerations and lack of voice raise the unanswerable question once again: "Who was shouting loudest?" Was it Sister Dianna or The Friend? As The Friend tried to speak, Sister Dianna was also screaming: "I screamed and screamed until no sound was coming out of my mouth and the laughter above and the woman's bloodied, mutilated body long gone limp on the other bodies!"[41] Neither Sister Dianna nor The Friend knows who was screaming loudest or who protested loudest, as they both lose the ability to scream in the midst of the trauma that torture produces.

Here, voice is recognized as central to demanding and imagining justice. However, the play illustrates the difficulty of claiming voice in the context of mass violence and government-imposed censorship. At the end of the one-act play, the audience is reminded of such censorship as well as the complicity of the United States when a disembodied US ambassador's voice is heard offstage threatening the reporter who interviewed Sister Dianna: "If you insist on writing a story that says what happened, you will be in very hot water, Miss. There's not one shred of evidence."[42] While The Friend's and Sister Dianna's inability to speak emphasizes the importance of having access to information in processes of justice-making, the problem of voicelessness is not necessarily resolved in the one-act version of the play; instead, it is in the two-act version that Castillo imagines the disappeared claiming space to speak in order to create alternative possibilities for justice-making processes.

The two-act version of *Psst . . . I Have Something to Tell You, Mi Amor* takes the audience to a medical facility for torture survivors in the United States. In the opening scene, Sister Dianna is curled up on the floor of her hospital room while her family, several nuns, and a therapist stand around a bed discussing her condition. After the visitors exit the room, the physical manifestations of her torture are described: cigarette burns on her back, bite marks on her breasts, and unevenly cut hair. However, it is the psychological marks of her torture that are most evident in this scene, as Sister Dianna nervously chews on a cross that hangs around her neck and strategically avoids any human touch, moving around the room while pressed against the wall. By paying close attention to both the physical and psychological manifestations of Sister Dianna's torture, Castillo underscores that torture is experienced as a permanent wound that impacts survivors both corporeally and mentally long after the violence has ended; therefore, when thinking about justice for the disappeared, both forms of injury must be addressed.[43]

Act 1, scene 2 introduces the audience to The Friend, a woman who wears a huipil (a traditional embroidered Maya blouse) and is described as Indigenous or ladina in the stage directions. Later, it is revealed that The Friend is the woman who Sister Dianna was forced to kill in the mass grave and the relationship between the two women is more deeply developed. The Friend accompanies Sister Dianna, she talks to her throughout the night, rocks her to sleep when she is afraid, supports her when she must confront José—a janitor at the center for torture survivors who is later revealed to be one of Sister Dianna's and The Friend's torturers—and is a constant part of Sister Dianna's consciousness. However, as Castillo's stage directions indicate, there is a question about The Friend's role in the play: "Is her 'presence' to protect the nun or is it because she has unfinished business with the former soldier?"⁴⁴ Based on the scenes that follow, it seems that The Friend both protects Sister Dianna and wants to hold José accountable for his crimes. She expresses a desire for physical revenge, threatening to torture him as he has tortured so many others. Even while The Friend represents a guardian angel in the two-act play, she also comes to embody the afterlife of torture for Sister Dianna. The Friend serves as a constant reminder of what happened during the twenty-four hours of Sister Ortiz's—the historical subject's—disappearance and of tens of thousands of others who were disappeared and never reappeared. In the play, she reminds Sister Dianna that neither Catholic faith nor US exceptionalist claims can erase the torture she experiences in the present. The Friend is central to creating the conditions of possibility for justice, which is understood as a process of healing wherein the tortured can confront their torturers and hold them accountable for the physical and psychological injuries they perpetrated.

Castillo envisions that Sister Dianna and The Friend can potentially be at the center of ensuring justice for the disappeared by staging a mock trial in act 2, scene 2 of the play. It is here that Castillo's feminist theory of justice for the disappeared begins to more fully emerge. During the mock trial, Sister Dianna and The Friend narrate their experiences and enact solidarity with each other as they confront one of their torturers. The disappeared and torture survivors are thus symbolically placed at the center of justice-making processes that seek accountability and healing for those who have been injured. In the court scene, The Friend fills the role that the state refused to occupy in Sister Ortiz's historical case and acts as judge in the trial for her own assassination, Sister Dianna acts as the defendant, Helen—a therapist at the torture survivors medical center—fills the role of the jury, and José plays the part of the witness. While it is Sister Dianna who is on trial for murdering The Friend, much of the trial focuses on the atrocities committed against Sister Dianna. Castillo's representation of the events turns the tables and it is José, the witness, who is put on trial by the jury and the judge, echoing the contradictions in how government officials treated Sister Ortiz—the historical subject—during the investigation into her torture and disappearance. Despite her self-doubt and with the support of both The Friend and Helen, Sister Dianna confronts José during the mock trial. In solidarity, the two women—one Chicana and one Guatemalteca—confront one of their torturers and speak out against the Guatemalan military's systematic use of torture to combat revolutionary demands for social reform during the country's civil war.

At the trial, The Friend (playing the judge) and Helen (playing the jury) set the stage for Sister Dianna (playing the defendant) to confront José (playing the witness) as she struggles through her trauma. First, Sister Dianna reminds José of his participation in her torture: "All the things you and your men did to me? The burns. My nipples nearly bitten off. I stunk of you for so long. I reeked of your semen, your sweat, your shit-fetid ass-holes, your pubic hair, like nettles digging against my skin. And I could not bear it."[45] When José denies his guilt, The Friend feels compelled to break with her role as judge and becomes a witness, marking the redefini-tion of justice-making processes—in contrast to state-centered models that assume objectivity and impartiality that often prove to be unobtainable within judicial proceedings. In a cathartic scene, Sister Dianna and The Friend begin testifying together, simultaneously praying and recalling what happened in the mass grave. As they describe the bodies—some alive, some dead—in the mass grave, Sister Dianna and The Friend pray a Hail Mary, and the former attempts to comfort the latter by urging "Don't be afraid."[46] In this retelling, when José jumps into the grave, Sister Dianna gratefully thinks: "He wants me to die. . . . Finally, he is helping me to die"; however, "instead of drawing the blade toward my own body, it went forward . . . !"[47] As in the poem and the one-act version of the play, Sister Dianna cannot reconcile having been forced to kill another woman. However, she is able to confront the person who forced her to kill The Friend, and she has a network of support as The Friend and Helen remind Sister Dianna that she is not guilty of any of the offenses that she feels remorse about, thus em-phasizing the importance of voice and solidarity in challenging normative conceptualizations of guilt and witnessing by encouraging her to reach a new understanding of what transpired.

Forcing Sister Ortiz—the historical subject—to kill another person was, in fact, part of her torture, and the remorse and guilt she feels long after that event represent the ways in which torture continues to live on into the present. The repetitive representation of the murder scene captures the afterlife of political violence not only in a fictional sense, but also for Sister Ortiz, who experiences the moment of rupture that torture represents as something that continues to be played out in the present. As Sister Ortiz writes in the preface to *Psst . . . I Have Something to Tell You, Mi Amor*: "Once tortured, that act—those acts—become part of your being, your essence. From that moment on, you always speak as one who was/is tor-tured."[48] Sister Ortiz's assertion that having been tortured lives on in her present and future echoes Elaine Scarry's description of the body's memory of pain: "What is remembered in the body is well remembered; the bodies of massive numbers of [war] participants [people that might also be called survivors or victims] are deeply altered; those new alterations are carried forward into peace."[49] This suggests that experiences of violence simultane-ously alter a person's physical body and their subjectivity and psyche.

At the trial, José's character comes to represent the Guatemalan military when he launches into his own defense by making the familiar Cold War argument that any atrocities he committed were in the name of securing democracy and freedom for Guatemala because he had to work to protect his country from subversive and communist influences: "We processed hundreds, maybe thousands like you. We burned down villages of subversives. Church people? Ha! Nothing but Communists, all of them. They wanted to take our country and turn it upside down, into a dictatorship, another Cuba. Take away democracy and freedom."[50] José articulates the demonization of both Catholic aid workers and the Cuban revolution that created an opening for the United States to increase its intervention in Guatemala during the Cold War and led to the US-supported coup against Arbenz. It is precisely the social conditions that Arbenz was interested in remedying that most disgust José when he characterizes Guatemala as a "hellhole" with a hungry and illiterate population.[51] By giving José's character voice, Castillo underscores the social conditions under which people are recruited into military service and suggests that torture will not be abolished through the punishment of individual perpetrators, since it is governments that create the conditions of possibility for this type of violence. Castillo suggests that in order for justice to be achieved, poverty, illiteracy, and landlessness, as well as military training and funding, must be ended both nationally and internationally. This vision of justice-making proposes that seeking justice cannot be understood through the individualized processes that state models rely upon. Rather, the structural relations that create the conditions of possibility for violence, including torture and disappearance, must be accounted for in demands for remedies to injury. This helps to humanize the perpetrators of violence, and also helps to foster circumstances within which justice-making processes do not enact further violence.

Reemphasizing that justice for the disappeared is illusive, the trial ends when Helen (re)assumes her position as counselor at the torture survivors center and reminds José that he has work to do in the cafeteria. After the trial, Sister Dianna is left "bewildered, devastated" as she returns to bed.[52] Her condition and José's return to work are reminders that accountability and healing are not easily gained in cases of disappearance and torture, in part because even when evidence and testimony are available, perpetrators are allowed to continue living their everyday lives. By ending the trial without granting Sister Dianna and The Friend finality or resolution, Castillo suggests that the wounds and traumas that remain in the aftermath of torture will not be healed or addressed through court trials or punitive measures. As in the one-act version, the play ends with the words: "I have something to tell you, mi amor."[53] This time, the audience knows who the speaker of those words is as José steps out of the bushes before Sister Dianna's disappearance and torture is replayed again. With this ending, Castillo reminds readers, as she does in the poem, that to various degrees, we are

all complicit in the lack of justice for the disappeared through our ignorance, complacency, neglect, the act of witnessing and turning the other
way, and by both willingly and unwillingly providing funding and training
to countries and officials who use torture as a tool of social control, war,
and genocide. More importantly, she suggests that as long as impunity is
pervasive, what happened to Sister Ortiz will continue to play out not only
in a symbolic sense, but also in the social world in which we live.

FICTIONS OF SOLIDARITY?

Although I have argued that The Friend and Sister Dianna stand in solidarity with each other, it is also important to acknowledge that Castillo
addresses the obstacles of working in solidarity by representing the unequal
positionalities that Chicanas and Centroamericanas inhabit. Two of the
ways this imbalance becomes visible are the fact that Sister Ortiz survived
and approximately forty-five thousand disappeared Guatemalans and two
hundred thousand who were killed during the civil war did not, and that
while a multiplicity of voices are represented in Castillo's plays, Sister Ortiz
is still the main subject of Castillo's creative writing on this topic. Thus,
while it is evident that Castillo's poem and plays reflect her support and
collaboration with Sister Ortiz, the ethics of representing torture and disappearance in Guatemala while centering a Chicana subject are not as clear.
As I suggest above, a feminist theory of justice often relies on people who
inhabit different positionalities being willing to work together. Certainly,
as Ariana E. Vigil argues, Castillo's polyvocal approach to developing her
plays creates some space for Guatemalan characters to speak. However, I
want to acknowledge some of the problems with thinking about justice for
the disappeared from a US-centric feminist perspective. It is important to
note that both Castillo and Sister Ortiz are US-based Chicanas who engage
questions of torture and disappearance in Guatemala within the context
of a civil war that was supported by the US government. This creates the
risk of co-opting and marginalizing the struggles and voices of Guatemalans and Guatemalan Americans who also have intimate knowledge about
torture and disappearance, and have represented the violence of the war
through various genres and formats.

In "The Fiction of Solidarity," Ana Patricia Rodríguez argues that anti-imperialist Chicana narratives about the Central American civil wars of
the 1970s and '80s create "a 'fiction of solidarity' predicated on Chicana/
Mexicana subjectivities."[54] Rodríguez asks readers to consider the contradictions of Chicana writers representing the meaning of violence, colonialism, and feminism in the context of, and in relationship to, Central
American struggles for liberation during the post–World War II era. She
cautions, "Solidarity is not transparent or innocent, but rather critically

shaped by borders, power and unequal hierarchical relationships, even within Latina/o feminist communities."[55] Rodríguez contends that Central American–centered Chicana fiction attempts to produce solidarity by representing Chicanas as protagonists in ways that appropriate the pain of Central Americans and elide the specificity of Central American histories and identities, and certainly, though I have not explored it here, Castillo's plays may fall into these pitfalls. Rodríguez suggests that this problem can be remedied by centering narratives that are written by Central Americans and convey Central American subjectivities.

In order to align myself with Rodríguez's argument I will end by mentioning some Guatemalan American writers who represent the violence of the Guatemalan civil war. Novelist and journalist Héctor Tobar is author of *The Tattooed Soldier*, which is often positioned as one of the first novels published in the United States by a US Central American writer.[56] Poet Maya Chinchilla is widely credited for developing the term Central American American to refer to US Central Americans, and many of the poems included in her collection *The Cha Cha Files: A Chapina Poetica* are laced with references to growing up in a home with activist parents that often hosted Central American refugees and meetings about the armed struggle in Guatemala.[57] Another Guatemalan American poet who grapples with how the violence of the Central American civil wars impacted her family through the disappearance of her uncle during the war is Gabriela Ramirez-Chavez. Her poetry can be found in the *Acentos Review* and in the groundbreaking anthology *The Wandering Song: Central American Writing in the United States*. While these works are not at the center of my analysis in this essay, I believe it is essential to mark their significance within these conversations as they insist on recognizing the ways that the past continues to live in the present and how violence and trauma travel across borders and subjectivities through a US Guatemalan perspective. Perhaps such connections can help forge critical collectivities that work toward dismantling the violence Castillo, Tobar, Chinchilla, and Ramirez-Chavez all represent.

CHAPTER 15

CHICANA FEMINIST LITERARY SUBJECTIVITY IN A TRANSNATIONAL FRAME

ELLIE D. HERNÁNDEZ

Ana Castillo has been traversing the transnational terrain throughout her life as a Chicana feminist writer. One of the most prolific writers of our time, Castillo represents the transnational Mexicana/Chicana experience as one shaped by the contours of Mexican culture, geography, and class-revolutionary consciousness. Castillo's style, narrative form, and presentation as a writer draw heavily from her family's ties to Mexico, and her stories offer an array of perspectives about Chicana transnational literary subjectivity. Ana Castillo's story is a familiar one, too, because it represents the well-traveled corridor from Mexico to the US-Mexico *frontera* and ultimately finding a sense of home in Chicago, Illinois. Of course, the general perception of transnational Mexicana/os in the Midwest, especially Chicago, is that they tend to be "mas Mexicano que los Mexicanos." The cultural memory of Mexicanos who settled in the Midwest portions of the United States truly has shaped the transnational literary imaginary among Chicana writers.

Like her literary *comadres*, Norma Alarcón and Sandra Cisneros, whose families also followed the path from Mexico to Chicago, Castillo represents the Chicana literary renaissance of the 1980s, which established a formidable Chicana feminist cultural social movement. Castillo also embodies the Chicana transnational literary experience in such a way as to proffer her own book and recognition as a writer—there is always a concern for Mexico and Latin America throughout Ana Castillo's work. The essayists for this segment on the transnational feminist literary subject, Araceli Esparza, Laura Elena Belmonte, and Rebecca Kennedy de Lorenzini, each offers their own rendition about "the transnational" in Ana Castillo's literary compendium of writings. All engage Ana Castillo as a vital Chicana feminist transnational writer, and each offers a literary critique that is distinctive for its focus on social justice, feminist spiritualities, and ancestral memory.

Those of us who traveled the literary circles in the 1980s and 1990s did not exactly use the term *transnational*. We engaged in *lo Mexicana/o* directly because our ability to travel from the United States to Mexico and back again to the United States was easier—at best, we used the term binational—to convey our comings and goings across the two nations. The transnational merits attention now because it is a term that conveys a critical exegesis or explanation of the grand migration of people across the globe under a pernicious advanced capitalist form that has disrupted so many lives. The term *transnationalism* also signals the emergence of global capital, which we could also say is responsible for the drastic economic restructuring of the past twenty years or so. When we look at transnationalism from a literary perspective, however, the transnational is about entering and exiting semiotic systems with rules, codes, areas of recognition, and grammars that form its basis of communication and power relations—it is its own communicative system.

About the same time that a transnational perspective began to take shape, we also witnessed the borderlands emerge as a vanguard for the transnational that we think of today, a system with its own distinctive language and style within a Chicana literary moment in the 1980s. Ana Castillo recognized the connection to *lo Mexicano* early in her published work. *The Mixquiahuala Letters* details the ostensible friendship bond that seductively and guardedly shows us how women speak to each other using the old-fashioned technology of handwritten letters. Drawing from Julio Cortazar's literary style in *Hopscotch* (1966), Castillo used this self-styled choreographed narrative as a way to decenter the masculine nationalist-revolutionary text, opting for a reader-based approach like the one radicalized by Cortazar's narrative technique. The aim of Cortazar's influence was to decenter a centralized way of telling a story. In the United States, we are accustomed to narratives that unravel sequentially, and we associate this unveiling of information as truth bound texts—even in socialist revolutionary Chicano writings. Instead, *The Mixquiahuala Letters* exists in a state of possibility and uncertainty, with optional approaches to reading the letters. Here the relationship of two women, two nations, and many letters convey all sorts of possibilities for love and friendship. Castillo was able to provide a means to a difficult quandary in Chicana literary subjectivity—what *truth* are Chicanas and Latinas following? Is it the racial colonial narrative? Or gendered feminist texts? Or even the Marxist/socialist story of uprising and reclaiming the language and the land?

Proximity also determines much of what constitutes Chicana feminist transnational subjectivity, as a movement and a reorientation to the new world; proximity to Mexico, Central America, and Latin America all would inform Castillo's connection to women across the Americas. This connection to the Americas typifies the new reality or experience, through characters, settings, and issues that are relevant to Chicanas and Latinas today. This idea of the transnational is about moving from a national perspective into a transnational view of the world. What concerns the Chicana critic in this ever-consuming dialogue is telling: What matters most to Chicanas and Latinas across the Americas? How do women construct a livelihood? How do these women construct a sense of justice, motherhood, love, politics, and cultural identity? Most importantly, how do these women create a sense of self? The literary critics in this section grapple with some of these questions and issues Ana Castillo brings forth incisively and clearly about the Chicana and Mexicana and Latina experience.

TRUTH IN THE MIDST OF CRISIS

For Araceli Esparza, the subject of social justice is critical to her understanding of Ana Castillo in "Feminist Imaginaries of Justice: Ana Castillo, Sister Dianna Ortiz, and Political Violence in Guatemala." Ana Castillo clearly follows a feminist transnational perspective that links the Latina feminist politics of the 1980s to the US interventions in Central America. Esparza associates the plight of Central American women with the Chicana perspective on social justice, and it is fitting to see this time frame mark a shift away from *movimiento*-style politics toward a transnational feminist trajectory. Esparza traces Castillo's notion of "justice" or human rights with particular focus on Sister Dianna Ortiz's disappearance, torture, and reappearance. The main element in this essay is the *notion of truth* in the midst of crisis and social chaos. The *testimonio* tradition underwent a resurgence in Latin American women's writings because of the problematic abuses of authoritarian regimes and covert operations in Latin America (Chile, Argentina, Peru) and Central America (Guatemala, El Salvador, Nicaragua) from the 1970s to the 1990s. The testimonio tradition also forms a unique communicative system of solidarity by situating the voice of women in the midst of political violence that draws largely from female/feminist tropes to uphold their legitimacy as mothers, nuns, spiritual leaders, and educators, all righteous roles for Latina women.

The 1980s under the Reagan administration brought anti-communist interventions in Central America. Among those were military operations in Guatemala and the training of Guatemalan forces by US military intelligence. Esparza examines the disappearance of Sister Dianna Ortiz, who on November 2, 1989, was abducted by Guatemalan security forces from the Posada de Belen convent in Antigua, Guatemala. Tracing the story of Sister Dianna Ortiz, who survived her disappearance, Esparza is also detailing the story of the forty-five thousand other disappeared. Drawing from Ortiz's own testimony in *The Blindfold's Eyes: My Journey from Torture to Truth* and Ana Castillo's poetry and play on the subject of disappearance, Esparza centers on Ana Castillo's poem "Like the people of Guatemala, I want to be free of these memories" from the collection *I Ask the Impossible* (2000) and *Psst . . . I Have Something to Tell You, Mi Amor* (2005). Both renditions of Sister Dianna Ortiz's ordeal are featured in Ana Castillo's perspective as an interlocutor of the truth, a key element in the transnational Latina testimonial tradition. Without revealing all the details, for Esparza's interpretation truly takes to task some of the issues and problems with documenting a lived experience, the telling of the story is what is at the heart of this conundrum of reality.

Esparza's reading is splendid for honing in on the question of "truth" as she lays out some of the complications of the story surrounding Sister Ortiz's disappearance, in particular details of her ordeal and her release from captivity by US-trained Guatemalan military forces. The role of US governmental agencies in matters of torture serves as the critical problem. Esparza notes that governmental accountability may be problematic as she looks closely at Ana Castillo's poem and later her play on the same subject. Herein is the critical question that takes shape as Sister Ortiz reveals she was forced to hold a machete that killed another woman in a pit of murdered and dying captives. The telling of this portion of the story is not quite clear because of the way Sister Dianna Ortiz reveals this part of her experience and the way mind and memory respond to such horrific trauma.

Sister Ortiz, who writes the preface to *Psst . . . I Have Something to Tell You, Mi Amor*, recounts facets of the ordeal, especially the experience of brutality and the object of torture and its effect on the mind and body. The disassembled and overdetermined state of torture and experience of "disappearance" may not be so clear cut since the retelling of the account is shaped and formed by perspectives in accountability in the public's perspective. In a direct approach, Esparza also renders problematic the feminist perspective on solidarity to which a transnational feminist perspective may rely on for its own recognition and sympathetic interpellation.

Esparza notes:

> I want to acknowledge some of the problems with thinking about justice for the disappeared from a US-centric feminist perspective. It is important to note that both Castillo and Sister Ortiz are US-based Chicanas who engage questions of torture and disappearance in Guatemala within the context of a civil war that was supported by the US government. This creates the risk of co-opting and marginalizing the struggles and voices of Guatemalans and Guatemalan Americans who also have intimate knowledge about torture and

disappearance, and have represented the violence of the war through various genres and formats.

In "The Fiction of Solidarity," Ana Patricia Rodríguez argues that anti-imperialist Chicana narratives about the Central American civil wars of the 1970s and '80s create "a 'fiction of solidarity' predicated on Chicana/Mexicana subjectivities." . . . Rodríguez asks readers to consider the contradictions of Chicana writers representing the meaning of violence, colonialism, and feminism in the context of, and in relationship to, Central American struggles for liberation during the post–World War II era."[1]

This is an especially astute assessment of Castillo's and Ortiz's versions of the story of torture and disappearance. Is Esparza questioning a particular kind of feminist ideological tendency espoused and practiced within the United States? Or is there any way in which collectivity and recognition of Chicanas and Latinas exist and can be made manifest outside of the ideological state apparatus's notions of US justice? Even when the intentions are good, the power relations inherent in the horrors of war and retelling of the story therein could not begin to characterize the effect of torture and disappearance on a people. While the aim in all of this is to find a semblance of truth, politics, and solidarity, the matter of telling a story from the collective perspective inevitably shapes a solidarity of sympathy; it is a style of articulation designed to bear a group witnessing as she shares the collective telling of the traumas of war.

Esparza expertly draws out Castillo's social political trajectory to be formed and shaped by her sympathetic alliance with Sister Dianna Ortiz's experience. This approach, Esparza recounts, shapes Castillo's political perspective on the idea of Latina woman agency. This is especially true since the uses of torture post-9/11 have been called into question. At the completion of the essay, Esparza discusses how solidarity and justice across geopolitical borders are not without contradictions, as they have the potential to marginalize and appropriate the pain of Guatemalans and other Central Americans who predominantly experienced the histories of violence Castillo represents. Nevertheless, Castillo and Ortiz are part of legacy of Chicana feminist authors who use their writing as a form of political activism and social theory to mitigate powerlessness.

For Esparza, the issues she lays out in matters of justice touch upon the politics of telling a story; building on the work of Barbara Christian and Sonia Saldívar-Hull,[2] she writes, "Feminists of color have long asserted that creative writing is a site for theorizing and disrupting power relations, particularly for communities that have been historically marginalized. . . . In this context, literature becomes central to both theorizing and fighting for justice by providing frameworks for understanding the way that things are and for imagining the way the world can be otherwise."[3] In this astute examination of Castillo's social justice interventions follows the feminist transnational perspective that links the politics of the 1980s to a very important story of Latina women and war. Esparza is willing to step outside of the ethos of a feminist perspective about the inherent bond of women, even those in the midst of struggle and war. Esparza leaves us with so much to consider in our readings of Chicana and Latina women. But in this we can consider the position of Chicana and Latina women in the United States, where the virtue of citizenship offers no guarantee of social power or legitimacy with the state or military.

SPIRITUAL AUTHORITY *Y LA MADRE*

In "Priestess *y Pastora*: Chicana Feminist Representations of Transnational Female Spiritual Leadership in Ana Castillo's *So Far from God* and María Amparo Escandon's *Esperanza's Box of Saints*," Belmonte follows these novels in an effort to look at the role of women and especially in the "Christian faith through a patriarchal institution."[4] She traces the lead female characters in both novels and locates a morality problem with the church practice, which in turn leads the characters to break away from conventional devotion to the church and find their own spiritual authority. Belmonte looks at the way the characters actively utilize their "motherhood" to transgress their roles and define spaces deemed only for men, both religiously and culturally.

In her analysis of these novels, Belmonte shows how these women are the true spiritual leaders of their communities. As expected, Castillo's own views of the church demonstrate how women in their ordinary lives subvert the dominant and patriarchal structures and challenge "the heteronormative nuclear family by claiming the roles of priestess and *pastora*."[5] Belmonte shows how a Chicana feminist praxis is active and relevant to women who have no claim or formal role in the church. Instead, the incongruences of male-dominated church practices show spiritual authority resides within those who choose a "decolonial love."[6] Both Ana Castillo and María Amparo Escandón focus on the mother as site of defiant roles. Castillo's Sofia of *So Far from God* and Escandon's Esperanza in *Esperanza's Box of Saints* look at spiritual authority within their respective contexts. The role of motherhood in a vast number of writings by Chicana and Mexicana writers uses the trope of the mother to circumvent most patriarchal elements, whether the church or state, the family or the educational system. Mothers occupy a different status within Latina culture where mothers have elevated roles because of their influence in the family and religious communities. Chicana and Mexicana women are also bound by the devotion to Mother Mary and La Virgen de Guadalupe, which redesigns the patriarchal order in the

New World. Sofia and Esperanza own their spiritual authority through their roles as mothers and as women of color who are ever cognizant of the pitfalls and dangers in the global world.

Belmonte looks at Castillo's influence in yet another way; a central aspect of her presentation of the mother as transnational subject is the way these *madres* use their spiritual authority to challenge and transform male religious authority. What is meant by male religious authority is the paternalistic that is guiding and protective. Belmonte is using Castillo's perspective on the male authority within the church and to foreground the failures of the men within the church to offer true moral authority. Belmonte's reading of *So Far from God* recounts how Sofia's youngest daughter dies and comes to life again at her own funeral. Father Jerome, unable to figure out the resurrection of Sofia's daughter as a miracle, questions the child and asks if this is indeed act of God or of the devil. As a grieving mother, Sofia confronts Father Jerome's suggestion that this miraculous event would be an act of the devil. Belmonte is correct to focus on the power of a grieving mother in an effort to mitigate the assertion by Father Jerome. "'Don't you dare!' she screamed at Father Jerome, charging at him and beating him with her fists. 'Don't you dare start this about *my* baby! If our Lord in His heaven has sent my child back to me, don't you start this backward thinking against her; the devil does not produce miracles! And *this* is a miracle, an answer to the prayers of a brokenhearted mother, ¡hombre necio, pendejo . . . !'"[7] Her telling device in this segment is the part where she uses the line ¡hombre necio, pendejo . . . !," which is a clever device drawn from Castillo's not so subtle reference to Sor Juana Inés de la Cruz's famous poem "¡Hombres necios que Acusáis!," which signals one of Sor Juana Inés's most defiant articulations against the Catholic church. For Sofia, this confrontation with Father Jerome signals a defiance of belief and theology, which Belmonte sharply articulates as a mother's faith that has brought back her daughter from the dead. The power of a mother's love shakes Sofia's beliefs so strongly that she is able to confront the priest's misaligned reading of the moment of resurrection. Rather Sofia refutes the possibility of a nefarious devil-like interference and regards the priest's assertion as "backward thinking."

In another reading, Belmonte also looks at Esperanza, a mother, who after an encounter with a saint believes her daughter may still be alive. After an apparition on her dirty stove shows San Judás Tadeo, as he is known in Mexico, the saint tells Esperanza her daughter, Blanca, is not dead. Esperanza (or Hope) confronts Father Salvador's imposing views as she searches for her missing daughter Blanca. Esperanza goes on to exhume Blanca's coffin to find that it is indeed empty, commencing a search of brothels from Tlacotalpán, her hometown in Veracruz, to the US-Mexico border town of Tijuana, and on across the border illegally to Los Angeles. Esperanza's transnational search to the United States borderlands leads her back home to Tlacotalpán. While taking a bath, she hears Blanca's voice and sees her in a rusty stain: "In that stain, I saw Blanca's face. She was wearing a beautiful Jarocha costume. She said, 'Mommy, you and me, we'll always be together'"[8] Anticipating Father Salvador's disbelief, Esperanza goes on to theologize the nature of this miraculous apparition and subverts Father Salvador's misguided view.

What are the implications of having spiritual authority? Belmonte associates spiritual authority with agency and self-empowerment. The power to discern foolish or "backward thinking," and having the common sense to find the answers to those pressing problems mothers encounter on a daily basis are other features. Sometimes, spiritual authority means you have to be simply aware of others or you have to listen and not necessarily act impetuously. In reading Belmonte, I could see a frustration with the way Chicana and Mexicana women have relied too much on male spiritual authority. Ana Castillo and María Amparo Escandón provide the characters necessary to launch a strong critique of the issues that many have faced with the role of the church.

XICANISMA AND ANCESTRAL MEMORY

Rebecca Kennedy de Lorenzini uses the legacy of the Chicano movement to discuss the role of ancestral memory in *The Massacre of the Dreamers: Essays on Xicanisma* (1994). Focusing Castillo's essays on the cultural experience of *Xicana* consciousness in *Massacre of the Dreamers*, Kennedy de Lorenzini utilizes Castillo's *Xicanisma* to explain the power of ancestral memory and to foreground spirituality as "the key to her strength and endurance as a female throughout all the ages."[9] *Xicanisma* becomes a site of empowerment that repudiates widely held beliefs in Western culture that disempower women, such as dualistic or binary thinking that structures the world according to masculine/feminine and active/passive roles for the genders. Pivoting off another notable feminist writer Gloria Anzaldúa in *Borderlands / La Frontera: The New Mestiza* (1987), Castillo's notion of *Xicanisma* bears some resemblance to Anzaldúa's concept of the "new mestiza," which also refuses a binary cultural system and opens the perspective to a connection to the ancestral spaces. Castillo, however, holds on to a much broader perspective of Latin America and the spatial politics of other movements such as the discussions of Central America in the Belmonte segment.

Kennedy de Lorenzini's adept inclusion of other writers such as Anzaldúa and the poetry of Edelma Zapata Pérez frame a prescient discussion of the power of ancestral memory in the writings of women of color. The ancestral memory Kennedy de Lorenzini refers to is a spiritual space, an intellectual sanctuary, and a landscape of the remembrance that refutes the limitations of earth-bound thinking. Ana Castillo, as a writer, has a deep spiritual connection to the ancestral that is tied to the social and political circumstances of the transnational Latina. Looking to Mexico as a return to her own recovery of her identity and sense of being, I could not help but think her frame of reference was a lamentation for the Mexico she never had.

For Kennedy de Lorenzini, the Xicanista consciously, and intentionally, claims the land and the ancestral relationships in an effort to create wholeness and healing from the traumas of colonialism. By seeking to break down binary thinking, *Xicanisma* similarly uses female archetypes and appeals to a sacred feminine aspect as a wellspring of recovery that would lead to a broader awakening into a new consciousness. This new consciousness has been spoken of since the conquest of the Americas and refers to the moment in time when mestizos and indigenas return to their figurative homeland. From this *conscientización*, there is a desire for revolutionary transformation or improved social relations that goes "far beyond class and ethnic divides to address the full being of any individual."[10] Conscientización is a way of viewing the world outside the monikers of identity and divisive, separatist worldviews. The transnationalism of this perspective is evident in the way Kennedy de Lorenzini has flushed out all the critical elements of the ancestral in other women of color poetry. For example, Kennedy de Lorenzini engages Gloria Anzaldúa's borderlands imaginary as a crossing over to the other side. Engaging Anzaldúa's historical/mythological rendition of Aztlán as means to return to the scene of disruption, Kennedy de Lorenzini works with Anzaldúa to acknowledge the deep drive that the ancestral memory calls upon a people's yearning to find their inner truth outside of Western, European constructions. In this reading of Anzaldúa's poem Kennedy de Lorenzini finds one of the most salient and critical aspects of ancestral memory:

[Anzaldúa]

> This is my home
> this edge of
> barbwire.
>
> But the skin of the earth is seamless.
> The sea cannot be fenced,
>   *el mar* does not stop at borders.
>   To show the white man what she thought of his arrogance,
> *Yemayá* blew that wire fence down.

> This land was Mexican once,
>
> Was Indian always
>
>> and is.
>
> And will be again.[11]

Kennedy de Lorenzini masterfully draws upon the transnational ambitions of the new mestiza and of Xicanisma to show how impactful calling upon the ancestral in poetry can be for the reader. The space of ancestral overrides the limits of nations and of boundaries and ties the Southwest to the Indigenous population that inhabited it before Europeans arrived to colonize the regions. Calling forth the African diasporic maternal goddess (*orisha*) of the sea, Yemayá, we can see how Anzaldúa transcends the ethnic geographies, and Kennedy de Lorenzini is correct to link Anzaldúa's poetry to the struggles of the Chicana with the African diasporic struggles, which helps form an alliance and position from which to critique European colonization. Like *Xicanisma*, the deep connection to land and the ancestors is about returning and reclaiming something that has been lost. Like the reference to the West African *cosmovision*, the connection between land, memory, and consciousness are one. In closing, I want to capture an area that Kennedy de Lorenzini writes that resonates strongly with me, and may even apply to all the essays in this section, and that is the ancestral must be "reclaimed." It is an "active process" where Castillo discusses her search for the homeland, Kennedy de Lorenzini writes:

> Castillo explains the inner calling to that ancestral-geographical-spiritual place early in her *Xicanisma* text, "if in search of refuge from the United States I took up residence on another continent, the core of my being would long for a return to the lands of my ancestors. My ethereal spirit and my collective memory with other indigenas and mestizo/as yearn to *claim* these territories as homeland."[12]
>
> Moving one stop beyond simply existing in an ancestral place or homeland, Castillo emphasizes that the homeland must be actively claimed. The Chicana feminist consciously, and intentionally claims the land and the ancestral relationships. Castillo recalled her active seeking of these relationships.[13]

The transnational frame of analysis extends to the realms beyond the time/space realities of the nation/state, so this is clearly a space where the governing rules of state have no determination. Ana Castillo, like Gloria Anzaldúa and Edelma Zapata Pérez, draws heavily from the "social symbolic" in order to form a unifying semiotic system, a cultural space that had been forgotten and now reclaimed. Kennedy de Lorenzini reminds us it is not enough to focus on close readings of literature or texts, for example, when their social context is missing. The social context is a decolonial one, based on principles designed to house a new reality and to offer solace to the weary transnational who has climbed the mountain and crossed the river in an effort to find a sense of home.

TWENTY-FIRST-CENTURY CHICANA TRANSNATIONALISM

For Chicana feminist transnational interventions, this time is unique for its contradictions and upending realities—there's a mix of good times and very bad times. At no other time has there been such a continued surge of impactful writings by Chicanas and Latinas, a long held intellectual renaissance that began in the 1980s and that continues today. There is so much uncertainty about the future, and at the same time, much hope and optimism as we witness a strong flow of Chicanas and Latinas into higher education. Moving beyond the cultural nationalist period has not been easy for a major writer like Ana Castillo; despite the many glories of the civil rights and feminist movements, we find ourselves in precarious times. Throughout all of this, we see the borderlands, a Xicanisma, and a global Latina transnational feminism express its many facets. Ana Castillo's critique of Chicana/o cultural nationalism has since grown to a broad-based feminist literary collection that began in the 1970s and has since evolved into a major literary form that is taught across the United States and beyond. Ana Castillo traversed these decades with the command and grace of a prolific writer who has seen it all. From the matter of social justice and "truth" to the role of women reclaiming their spiritual authority to the power of ancestral memory—the essayists for this segment have profoundly advanced a greater understanding of Ana Castillo's work, especially the ways she invokes the idea of the transnational literary subject, as well as her influence as a writer.

PART V

TEACHING AND PEDAGOGY

CHAPTER 16

REPLANTING YOU AS *WINYAN, UARHITI, KWE*

Transnational Indigena Mothering from Michoacán to Mni Sota Makoce

GABRIELA SPEARS-RICO

Inspired by my experience as a Pirinda[1] and P'urhepecha[2] transnational mother who grew up and was educated in the United States, this essay weaves theory and *testimonio* to propose that Xicanisma, as theorized by Ana Castillo in *Massacre of the Dreamers*, continues to be relevant and important as a political identity and as a mothering and pedagogical practice. In *Massacre of the Dreamers*, Castillo defines Xicanisma as follows: "On a pragmatic level, the basic premise of xicanisma is to reconsider behavior long seen as inherent in the Mexic Amerindian woman's character, such as, patience, perseverance, industriousness, loyalty to one's clan and commitment to our children. Contrary to those who don't understand feminism, we do not reject these virtues. These traits often seen as negative and oppressive to women may be considered strengths."[3] Castillo sees Xicanisma as a reclaiming not only of the caregiver and matriarch roles for Chicanas but also of Chicanas' pride in a rich heritage, which can provide sustainment for surviving a world intent on silencing and erasing them. If we connect her initial theorizing on Xicanisma to her most recent commentary on motherwork, we can see that for Castillo, Xicanisma is closely related to mothering (broadly defined) as a means of changing the world.

In her foreword to *The Chicana Motherwork Anthology*, Castillo acknowledges that there are many ways to mother, and in a sense, the act of caregiving whether for small children or for the environment or the earth is all motherwork. Furthermore, she theorizes motherwork from an acute Xicanista lens: "The blood on these lands—South, North and Central America and the attendant islands near and around—the sweat and tears of original peoples; the buried placentas and ombligos of newborns; the wails of madres sufridas and the war cries of guerrilleras; the prayers of sacerdotas, brujas' incantations, remedios de curanderas y en hecho y en resumen las madre-diosas—whether their words were written or rumoured, echoed or muffled, all have served as the foundation."[4] For Castillo, Xicana motherwork cannot be detached from the legacy of colonial violence and from the legacy of the ancestral. Xicana motherwork (and by extension, pedagogy or other ways we mother) must be informed by the intergenerational knowledge that our foremothers left us both through the survival of violence and the traditions they employed to heal. As a Xicanista savage feminist fiercely positioned in Indigenous epistemologies and educated by Chicana feminists, I insist that Xicanisma braids motherwork, theory, and pedagogy into a radical feminist praxis that is more necessary than ever before. I share how Xicanisma as philosophical practice has been influential in parenting an Indigenous daughter, and on my political activism, teaching, and scholarship since the 2016 presidential election. I draw from Castillo's work in *Massacre of the Dreamers*, *Black Dove*, and *The Chicana Motherwork Anthology*, alongside my own testimonio and theorizing of an Indigenous feminist mothering and teaching praxis, to make my argument.

THE FEAR OF BIRTHING AN INDIGENOUS DAUGHTER

A question to mothers raising daughters: Do you remember the day you were most terrified to be raising a daughter? I sometimes think I carry the fear in me genetically, like my DNA. It is as if the violence against my Pirinda and P'urhepecha *abuelas* were equally woven into my embodied memory as the flesh that makes up my belly, the follicles that birth my hair, and the genes that pour out of my saliva onto my daughter's cheek when I wipe away dust from her face. Because there are moments, yes, moments of terror that I have lived in the six years and three months that I have been carrying and raising Reina. But much of my fear is also a result of the historical violence that is performative and generative, that is not static in its assaults against my memory and psyche, a violence that happened to many of my great-aunties and grandmothers, a violence that never went away.

My understanding of how violence informs the Indigenous experience is rooted in performance theory, postcolonial psychoanalysis, and Indigenous frameworks of historical trauma. French philosopher Michel Foucault, whose theories on punishment as performative are celebrated contributions to performance studies, argues that power is always inter-relational, continuous, and productive, especially when exercised directly on the body. Thus, the performance of power through violence inflicted on the body is not static or contained to the historical moment when the violence occurred but continues being inflicted intergenerationally, especially on racialized, gendered, and sexualized bodies.[5] In *Black Skin, White Masks*, Black Martiniquais psychiatrist Frantz Fanon theorized how trauma informs the postcolonial experiences of colonized subjects. For Fanon, colonial violence informs the psyche of the colonized as one that must internalize inferiority; decolonization happens when the person who has been otherwise thingified gazes back at the violence. However, according to Fanon, this is a slow and difficult process because it involves a racialized individual reclaiming her humanity.[6]

American Indian scholars like Maria Yellow Horse Brave Heart have elaborated on current understandings of intergenerational trauma attached to colonialism by developing a framework of historical trauma for the Indigenous experience. According to Yellow Horse Brave Heart, Indigenous people do not shed the trauma caused by the genocide, forced removal, and institutionalized assimilation such as boarding schools. Instead, she insists, various generations within a family or within a specific tribal context connect remembrances of colonization, dispossession, and internalized racism to suicidal thoughts, internalized inferiority, and depression.[7] A 2014 study by the American Pediatric Association revealed that people's genes can actually carry memories of trauma that occurred to their ancestors and also influence how they react to trauma and stress.[8] I would elaborate on these frameworks that connect violence to trauma by insisting that experiencing intergenerational gender-based terror, such as sexual violence, multiplies how Indigenous women experience and process trauma.

These frameworks of violence explain why I specifically feared having a daughter. A survivor of sexual violence with audible memories of my mother being assaulted and with knowledge of sexual violence being committed against generations of women in both my own and my partner's family, I experienced post-traumatic stress triggered by the knowledge that I would be raising an Indigenous girl. In "The Mother Bond Principle," Castillo acknowledges that both colonial violence and sexual violence inform the Xicana mothering experience and that these violences are intergenerational and continual: "To explore the web of our mother-daughter relationships under ongoing colonization would be a worthwhile and essential study for our self-comprehension as Xicanistas. By observing the repressive conditions under which many of our mothers became mothers, I mean to emphasize that as we become mothers, biologically or otherwise, because of our new Xicanista consciousness, the definition of Mother is altered from the one we experienced as daughters."[9] For me, being my mother's daughter and my grandmothers' granddaughter meant surviving generations of domestic and sexual violence. My experience of becoming a mother from conception to birth was then tainted by the PTSD I was experiencing with the knowledge of another daughter's arrival. In my heart of hearts and in my mind's eye, I knew and analyzed that a daughter of mine would not only face the attempted obliteration of P'urhepecha and Pirinda people, the internalized anti-Indigenous racism in her Mexican family and the deeply embedded patriarchy that comes with growing up Mexicana; a daughter of mine and my partner's would also grow up Dakota and Ojibwe *on land still impacted by settler colonialism* and she would thus face all the dehumanizing stereotypes, attempted genocide, and historical atrocities committed against Native people as well as the disposability historically attributed to Native women's bodies. How would I, an Indigenous woman who had been assaulted by several men both as a child and in adult relationships, be able to teach my daughter survival?

RAPE AS A LEGACY OF BEING *WINYAN, UHARITI, IKWE, MUJER*

I teach Indigenous feminisms and have read much of our herstory and lectured on our ancestral and contemporary feminist theories. Rape for us is a consequence of the postapocalypse of colonialism; rape for us is living in an unnatural state. It is a fact that Indigenous people in the Americas severely punished rape and considered sexual assault an abomination.[10] The targeted violence against Indigenous women, once diplomats, matriarchs, and governesses, intended to trump our power, "correct" our boldness, control our sexualities, and teach Indigenous men how to do the same.[11] According to both legal scholar Sarah Deer and historian Andrés Reséndez, the rape and trafficking of Indigenous women and girls was rampant at the beginning of colonization. In *The Beginning and End of Rape*, Deer presents archival data of both British and Spanish colonizers recounting how they raped Indigenous women.[12] Reséndez presents archival evidence to demonstrate that slavers preferred to export Indigenous women and children to Europe partly because Indigenous slaves were procured for domestic labor in Spain and Italy, but also because "women were less threatening than men and could easily be sexually exploited."[13] Additionally, he claims that "traffickers went to great lengths to procure 'willing' Indians, particularly children, who were more easily tricked and manipulated than adults."[14] The profits from "the other slavery," as Reséndez terms it, were ranked according to gender and age. Reséndez's numerical analysis of the prices paid for Indigenous slaves throughout Latin America revealed a higher cost for women, followed by girls, boys, and then men.[15]

In her foreword to *The Chicana Motherwork Anthology*, Ana Castillo retells the story of the appearance of Itzpapalotl to Mexica emperor Moctezuma, who read it as an omen of a mother-goddess mourning the impending genocide of her Mexica children: "The conquest took place more than five centuries ago. Itzpapalotl wailed one night, 'My children! What will become of my children?' It was a recorded omen of which the Emperor Moctezuma took note and rightly so. He heard a mother's cry and identified it with being representative of his empire."[16] This well-known legend in Mexican storytelling traditions is used to explain Mexican trauma; our mother-goddess's inability to protect us led to our fall or the conquest was so horrific that even our mothers, the most revered figures in our culture, couldn't protect us from death. Yet, Castillo connects the story of this omen to what became historical fact: colonial violence indeed had more devastating consequences on Indigenous women and children. "But on a pragmatic level," she continues, "it was in fact women and their children who would be first most harshly oppressed as a result of the European invasion."[17]

The racist toxic masculinist violence of colonialism has led us to believe that patriarchy is a natural state, but this is hardly the case. Indigenous women in the northern prairies and in the plains were considered strong enough to handle the strenuous physical labor that transitioned their families from one camp to another between seasons.[18] Women's sexuality in Indigenous America was so powerful that it often sealed diplomatic agreements between tribes and nations.[19] Some P'urhepecha women practiced polygamy as they kept the home-fire for the men, who were primarily transient warriors and hunters.[20] Patriarchy, domestication, and capitalism were foreign concepts to most tribes and had to be taught through systematic indoctrination.[21] Hundreds of years of attempts to cement colonialism and teach Indigenous men how to participate in dominating women haven't erased this knowledge, yet violence and femicide that specifically targets Indigenous women remains rampant in Canada, the United States, Mexico, and Central America.[22] It was both living up to the legacy of our foremothers, whose power is as ever present as the violence we have encountered, and having the weapons to protect a new generation of daughters, that scared me when I birthed Reina.

I had no idea that birthing this precious red feminine being would actually inform all aspects of my being from my scholarship to my praxis as a human being to my teaching philosophy and the pedagogy I would rely on to send more empowered, decolonial humans into the world. *The world post-Reina had to be less oppressive and more liberating because it would be a world she would inhabit.* Reina-Xareni. *Reina como la Virgen de Guadalupe. Y Xareni—comienzo de la mañana.* A twilight being connected to my umbilical cord since atoms first formed. *Miskinabiiwinkwe.* A woman drawn by red lightning. But first, for several years, my little girl.

MOTHERING AGAINST 526 YEARS OF ANTI-INDIAN RACISM

Although as an Indigenous migrant, I am constantly longing for P'urhepecherio,[23] my partner and I made a willful decision to raise Reina in Mni Sota Makoce,[24] her Dakota ancestors' traditional homelands and the state that is now home to the Red Lake Nation, where my partner is enrolled. Generations ago, Reina's Santee ancestors were forcibly expelled from Mni Sota and taken to the Crow Creek Reservation. Her father's family archive, documented by Reina's great-great-great-grandfather John Barry, has taught us that her four times great-grandmother, Many Tracks, was taken to Fort Sully in South Dakota in 1863 for "safety."[25] She was only ten years old. I think of Many Tracks as I traverse these Dakota lands with Reina—her expulsion from her homeland at such a young age and her tender marriage to a white officer, which finally allowed her to leave the fort. This is the Mni Sota that we are trying to decolonize by ensuring that Reina's childhood happens here where Many Tracks was born and where the genocide, dispossession, and removal of Reina's Dakota ancestors took place.

After Reina's birth, I began to question whether I knew how to be a Pirinda/P'urhepecha mother while being so far from my homeland. The question lurked all around me as soon as Reina first nursed from my breast: Do I know how to be a Pirinda/P'urhepecha mother without a Pirinda/P'urhepecha community around me? Fiercely informed by my family's experiences of Indigenous displacements and migrations and my coming into political consciousness through Chicana feminism, I realized that Xicanisma had taught me that the answer to these questions was yes. Maybe I won't be the Indigenous mother who immerses her child entirely in a P'urhepecha or Pirinda-speaking environment, but I also have the experience of growing up Chicana/Latina in the United States, and it has been Chicana feminism that has taught me how to survive as a migrant in these lands. An Indigenous migrant contending with her place in the Latinx diaspora, I embraced Xicanisma and became active in Chicanx activism as an adolescent. The guiding philosophy that has informed many of my actions since I came to consciousness through MEChA in high school had been Xicanisma and reading *The Massacre of the Dreamers* specifically. Xicanisma gave me a voice when I felt muted as the undocumented daughter of a single *campesina*,[26] as a survivor of child sexual abuse, and as a first-generation college student. Xicanisma continues to inform my motivations and decisions as a scholar navigating the trials of being overworked as a Woman of Color academic on the tenure track. Xicanisma also offers insights on how to be an Indigenous mother trying to save her daughter from anti-Indigenous racism and toxic masculinity. In her seminal book, *Massacre of the Dreamers*, Ana Castillo insists that Chicanas and Latinas (Mexic Amerindian women) can turn to both their ancestral knowledge and their embodied mestizaje for healing and empowerment:

> Therefore, as Xicanistas (no longer just *obreras culturares pero guerrilleras culturales*) we must simultaneously be archeologists and visionaries of our culture. We may contribute a collective vision toward the development of an alternative social system. Our Mesoamerican indigenous ancestors developed advanced

societies that rivaled that of the Greeks. Our legacy has mostly been vanquished and is widely kept out of the educational curriculum but we can seek it out. From our indigenous background, we can draw examples to understand the endless possibilities and the connections of all things in the realm we perceive as the universe. Our Spanish heritage and its ongoing dynamic in our lives not only connects us with the Eurocentric ideology of dominant society in all of the Americas, but as mestizas it serves to grant a sophisticated and complex perception of dominant society.[27]

Castillo articulates Xicanisma as an integrated philosophy of Paolo Freire's practice of *conscientización*,[28] which she takes to mean a "synthesis of belief systems," for Mexic Amerindian women to live more liberatory lives.[29] With Xicanisma, Castillo actually verbalizes what I read as a Chicana Indígena feminist futurity, a reversive directive to our Indigenous knowledge systems and our legacy of surviving oppression as mestizas to access the resilience that is already in our memory and in our bodies in order to form more liberatory futures for ourselves, our communities, and our families. To achieve conscientización or the Chicana Indígena feminist futurity, Castillo offers what I refer to as "Xicanista savage feminist magic," which includes curanderismo, reclaiming the erotic (reclaiming our bodies as a conscious act against the legacy of rape), the concept of re-matriarchalizing mexicanidad, embracing woman as both sacred and powerful, poetry as an *acto* against linguistic trauma, and most personally significant, reclaiming the ancestral. As Castillo states, "By recalling our blood-tie memories to the Americas and relying on the guidance of our dreams and intuitions, we gradually awaken our female indigenous energies."[30] In Castillo's view, Xicanista feminist magic is present in our embodied memory and can be called upon for healing and empowerment. Xicanista feminist magic is what we find when we follow the Xicanista directive to look for strength in our ancestries and in our familial legacies of resisting oppression. In *The Chicana Motherwork Anthology*, I enumerate several of the places that Xicanista feminist magic has appeared in my own lineage and life.[31] These include coming to embrace the fact that I am the granddaughter of traditional P'urhepecha farmers (milpa growers and *pulqueros*) who traced their existence to Mesoamerican ontologies like the cornstalk and the maguey plant despite the anti-Indigenous racism that I experienced in the United States at the hands of both white Americans and Mexicanos. It means coming to terms with my Pirinda grandfather's insistence not to forget about Charo, our village in Michoacán, and embracing how he mobilized his indigeneity to resist oppression. It also means reclaiming and retelling the stories of fiercely strong P'urhepecha and Pirinda women: documented accounts of leadership and warriorship historically undertaken by P'urhepecha women and contemporary examples of women in my family who practiced traditional spirituality and stood up to racism and sexism.

Despite the question over whether Xicanisma has anything of value to offer Indigenous women by both Latina/o and non-Latina/o literary critics,[32] connecting Xicanisma to my Pirinda/P'urhepecha mothering and pedagogical practices has been useful to me. My intent is not to conflate Xicanisma or other branches of Chicana feminism with traditions of Indigenous feminism, which has been fiercely tied to land and to material investments in decolonization,[33] but rather to place both models in conversation with each other. I argue that both traditions may have useful and valuable tools for Latin American Indigenous women migrants facing not only violence from patriarchal oppression but also systemic racism and everyday white discrimination in the United States. It is also important to distinguish between Chicana and Mexicana feminism. Like Chicana feminism, Mexicana feminism has also defaulted into representing a monogamous mestiza experience rather than prioritizing the voices of Indigenous women.[34] Instead of embracing autonomy, Mexicana feminism has problematically contributed to offering paternalistic indigenista models of development to Mexican Indigenous women.[35] Unlike Mexicana feminism, however, Chicana feminism has had to define itself against a hegemonic nation-state (the United States); in line with Women of Color feminist traditions, Chicana feminists theorize how racialization and intersectionality inform their experience as third-world women in the United States. I believe that despite its reliance on Aztec-centric narratives of indigeneity, Chicana feminism offers valuable insights for Latin American Indigenous female migrants similarly experiencing anti-Mexican violence in the United States. As I raise Reina as Dakota and Ojibwe on her occupied homeland while being racialized as *indigena* and Mexicana, I am instilling both Chicana and Indigenous traditions of feminist resistance into my daughter's upbringing in the Midwest.

HISTORICAL TRAUMA, SETTLER COLONIALISMS, AND TRANSNATIONAL INDIGENEITY IN MNI SOTA MAKOCE

Except when interrupted by American Indian protests, such as those staged by the American Indian Movement and First Nations United (an organization started by my husband and his brothers), and the interventions of Dakota and Ojibwe artists and scholars, settler narratives willfully hide the history of Native removal in Mni Sota Makoce. One of the most trying moments we've had to face as parents happened during Reina's first year of life. In May of 2017, a sculpture by artist Sam Durant titled *Scaffold* was put on display at the Walker Art Center in Minneapolis. The piece broadly addressed the history of capital punishment in the United States but also specifically referenced the 1862 hanging of thirty-eight Dakota men in

Mankato at the conclusion of the Dakota War. President Abraham Lincoln signed off on these lynchings following several Dakota attacks on settler encampments motivated by treaty violations and continuous encroachments on Dakota land. Besides striking me as tone-deaf, the *Scaffold* exhibition also hit a painful chord because it was advertised as a structure that children could climb on, like a playground.[36] It was meant to attract children and toddlers like our daughter. Hardly strangers to activism, my partner and I took Reina to one of the Dakota-led protests demanding its removal. American Indian activists reminded Durant and the Walker that this was not their story to tell. *Scaffold*, as a structure and narrative, had opened an old wound that has not healed in Minnesota. Sam Durant eventually agreed to let Dakota elders burn his sculpture in ceremony. But, for us, the incident was a painful reminder that parenting an American Indian child, a Dakota and Ojibwe child, on her land means continuing to deal with the reality of ongoing settler violence.

The irony is that Minnesota is widely known for its "Minnesota nice" culture. As a dark-skinned Indigenous Mexican woman, I have hardly experienced "Minnesota nice" but instead have become familiar with Minnesota racism. I have experienced both microaggressions in professional spaces as well as white Minnesotan outright aggression. When she is with me, my daughter is read as Mexican and we are both seen as foreigners who, with our bodies and our brownness, invoke the US/Mexico border wall debate when we bump into people at Minnesota establishments. This happened at a Savers thrift store in Burnsville when an elderly white woman berated me for being unable to keep my toddler from crying in the store. She wagged her finger at me, saying, "I don't know where you come from but that is not how we act in stores here!"

The reality of how anti-Indigenous racism feeds anti-Mexican racism concretizes when it affects my daughter in front of me and I choose to practice civility and offer cuddles as answers to her puzzled looks rather than participate in debates. When Reina is older, I will explain that anti-Mexican racism is deeply connected to anti-Indigenous racism and that she will experience both xenophobia and anti-Indigenous sentiment as the daughter of a transnational Indigenous migrant and an Ojibwe/Dakota person. Although my students can intellectually grasp this connection through my lectures, my daughter is still too young to understand why she is a target of hostility if this is indeed her ancestors' land, a truth we have continuously reinforced. This is where Xicanista praxis comes to my aid as a mother. By building her sense of self with the Xicanista feminist magic in her own ancestral and family histories, I am nurturing Reina's whole being so that more isn't stripped from her and she can enjoy a more decolonized future. In Minnesota, Reina enjoys strong ties to Ojibwe and Dakota ontologies and epistemologies through her father's family. She was fortunate to receive her Ojibwe names on the Red Lake Reservation from her great-uncle and hereditary chief, Greeting Spears. She has also participated in Midewin ceremonies,[37] where she is surrounded by Ojibwemowin[38] and her great aunties, aunts, uncles, and cousins. Ojibwes inherit their clan from their fathers and so Reina is solidly tied to Red Lake's crane clan through both ceremonial praxis and intergenerational legacy.

Despite the palpable settler violence in Minnesota, we also live zestful moments of decoloniality, which reinforce our deliberate decision to raise our daughter here. It has been the Minnesota landscape, the earth and the soil, which has revealed truths about Reina's Dakota and Ojibwe ancestors. Her family's Dakota lineage has been traced exclusively matrilineally, which grants power and agency to Many Tracks and to her great-grandmother Pansy, a boarding school survivor. When she was named by her great-uncle Chief Greeting, my daughter was given two names (a unique honoring in and of itself) belonging to her Ojibwe great-grandmothers who lived as monolingual Ojibwemowin speakers at Red Lake. Red Lake prides itself in being sovereign and views itself as separate and independent from the United States. Thus, my daughter traversing these lands as Ikwemakoons (Lady Bear) and as Miskinaabiwinkwe (Red Lightning Woman) somehow quells my fears and gives me hope that if trauma is woven into our DNA as Indigenous people and if gendered fears of sexual assault once informed my fears of raising an Indigenous daughter, resilience is equally woven into who she is.

In *Black Dove*, Castillo acknowledges inherited resilience as she discusses going through Elisabeth Kübler-Ross's five stages of grief after losing her son during his period of incarceration. To acknowledge her suffering, Castillo engages in cutting her hair, a mourning ceremony undertaken by Indigenous people throughout the Americas to release the grief and pain. "When a Mexican indigenous mother loses her son, she mourns the loss of a potential warrior by shearing her hair," she states. "My hair was cut to the scalp. This is not to say that I accepted defeat, only that I acknowledged having lost an important battle. I did not lose hope. It was not in my nature."[39] By acknowledging that losing hope "was not in [her] nature," Castillo, I believe, is motioning toward the resilience that is also embedded in our embodied experiences as racialized Xicanx-Indigenous people. When Castillo's son was imprisoned, she read it as a moment of losing a child to the racist system that more harshly targets and punishes Latino boys and men just for being male and Brown.[40] And, although experiencing this violence sent her through a spiral of isolation and pain, she engaged in ceremony to release her grief while affirming that our ancestral experiences and traditions also imbued us with hope.

As a mother from a matriarchal culture, it is very important to me that my daughter also grows up identifying with her P'urhepecha and Pirinda people. I am physically further from Michoacán than I have ever been, and this is sometimes heartbreaking. However, I continue to maintain strong ties to Michoacán through my creative work, anthropological fieldwork, scholarship, and through familial and community networks and obligations. Reina has accompanied me on fieldwork trips to Michoacán. Her first sweat lodge ceremony was conducted entirely in P'urhepecha; her first visit to a sacred site in Mexico was to the yacatas in Ihuatzio.[41] During her first trip home, I witnessed how my P'urhepecha and Pirinda relatives chart her in our kinship web. She is read as Ojibwe, *norteña*, American but is also claimed as "one of us." In our transnational experience as Pirindas/P'urhepechas, I am ensuring that Reina knows how to identify the symbols and sounds that make us who we are, reminding her that we don't have to be in Michoácan for her to be engaged in these practices. And, braiding Xicanisma with the Zapatista philosophy that we should start the decolonial process of working toward autonomy where we are, we are raising Reina with the decolonial indigenist politics that have been so central to defining contemporary P'urhepechecidad. P'urhepecha politics have been decolonial since the 1970s when the resurgence of P'urhepecha identity became politically tied to the protection of territory. Today P'urhepechas continue to engage in decolonial work through an active armed resistance for political autonomy in face-offs against the Mexican government and Mexican drug cartels in places like Cherán, Arantepacua, and Nahuatzen.[42] It is important that Reina understands the span of anti-Indigenous violence as her people are punished just for being who they are in Michoacán but also in celebrating the resistance integral to who we have always been.

Heeding the call for material decolonization that Indigenous feminists and their allies have insisted upon, we are teaching Reina that decolonization is more than ideological; it is daily practice in the spaces we inhabit. In "Decolonization Is Not a Metaphor," K. Wayne Yang and Aleut scholar Eve Tuck insist that the decolonial project must materialize into commitments to return land and resources to Indigenous people and/or must lead us to consider how we all contribute to forwarding settler colonial logics and settler violence on Indigenous lands.[43] In the Latinx context, I believe that this involves recognizing that all non-Native people in the United States are settlers or arrivants, that there can be settlers of color, immigrant settlers, and Indigenous migrant arrivants, and that we maintain a responsibility to local Indigenous communities and to Latin American Indigenous communities before we further the priorities of the settler governments, which have depended on Indigenous erasure, Indigenous death, and Indigenous resource extraction.[44] Concretizing decolonization, then, also becomes integral to the project I undertake in the classroom and on my campus with Xicanista-informed pedagogy.

XICANISMA AS RADICAL MOTHERING AND PEDAGOGICAL PRAXIS IN THE POST-TRUMP CLASSROOM

In other work, I have insisted that the present moment calls for the saturation of Xicanista savage feminism into our mothering and teaching praxis.[45] During the Trump administration, we witnessed numerous violences that attempted to erase the humanity of targeted communities including immigrants, Latinxs, queer people, and Black people. Last summer, with Reina by our side, we attended local protests at St. Paul City Hall against the practice of child separation along the US/Mexico border that has traumatized a new generation of Central Americans. It was important for me to bring Reina to the protest because the battle I was waging was not only to protect the Central American refugee students I mentor and teach, but it also was a battle for my principles as a Xicanista mother. My husband Chester, Reina, and I were photographed with a delegation of Indigenous people at this protest in St. Paul on June 20, 2018. The photo appeared in the *St. Paul Pioneer Press*, and Chester was also quoted in a *Lillie Suburban Newspaper* article about the event.[46] I knew my colleagues and students would see the press coverage and I questioned what they would think of my actions, but I was so triggered by my own trauma from the deportation of family members during my upbringing in labor camps and so devastated by what was happening to this new generation of Latina/o children that I did not care about being seen engaging in dissent.

If I am going to base my teaching philosophy on the contentions of Cindy Cruz, Manuel Espinosa, Kris Gutierrez, and Carlos Tejeda, who purport that liberatory pedagogy for Indigenous and marginalized students should ensure the integrity of Brown bodies in the college classroom while being intentionally anti-oppressive, then it is important for my students to witness me living Xicanista values.[47] I do not believe that moments of political repression against the most vulnerable should be ignored in the ethnic studies classroom; indeed, this is a teaching passed down to us by Paulo Freire.[48] On the contrary, the present moment calls for radical mothering and for radical teaching. It calls for re-humanizing Latinidad and indigeneity and for valuing LGBT and Latina and Native women's lives. The connection between the current exodus from Central American countries in the Northern Triangle and violence against women and children fueled by the proliferation of gangs in the area, which resulted from the targeted deportation of gang members from the United States, is becoming increasingly apparent even to the mainstream. Indeed, many of the women in the recent caravans from Honduras and El Salvador name fear of femicide and/or the recruitment or murder of their children as their motivation for migrating.[49] This is a time when feminist dissent, when Xicanista dissent, is more necessary than ever before.

During my past two years of teaching, I have noticed more students of color and queer students who are triggered and afraid of experiencing racist, homophobic, and misogynist violence. Teaching at a predominantly white institution, I have also noticed more white students who are excited about ethnic studies and are open to discussing and addressing racism. Although many of the policies of the Trump administration sent clear messages that what he meant by "Making America Great Again" was increased xenophobia and intolerance, the moment is also ripe for utilizing Xicanista pedagogy to engage both marginalized students and white students in critical discussions on how they will intervene to make our society more inclusive, just, and equal. As I mentioned earlier in this essay, working toward a just society became more urgent to me after birthing my daughter. My teaching labor is intertwined with my motherwork.

Besides calling upon my students to learn Minnesota's Dakota history, I also employ pedagogy I learned as a student of Gloria Anzaldúa and Cherríe Moraga. I am developing and workshopping Xicanista curriculum and exercises and revamping syllabi to speak to the diversity of Latinx student experiences today. One way I empower students to tell their stories is by following the advice that Castillo gives us in *Massacre of the Dreamers*, where she names poetry and creative writing as viable outlets for conscientización.[50] I utilize prompts inspired by Xicanisma to encourage my students to express themselves outside of the confines of academic writing. These include prompts like "this stain won't come out," and "these are all things I was supposed to forget." I precede these prompts with engagements with Chicana/Latina art, which may include Frida Kahlo's self-portraits and spoken word or dance performance pieces informed by Chicana feminist ontologies. I also utilize mirrors during writing exercises to promote students' engagement with the concepts of self and identity and regeneration. I spend the semester ensuring that students know how to name the oppressions that impact various marginalized identities as well as the weapons, such as intersectionality, these bodies can use to fight back. Students are armed with and tested on both structural theory and Chicana and Indigenous feminist theory. My experience is that Xicanisma in these times is not only necessary but also effective in teaching students how to survive and thrive beyond oppression.

Intellectual molding and mentoring labor is part of my mothering praxis. If my marginalized students are feeling more empowered and assured of their humanity, I have effectively intervened in the current moment of anti-Indigenous and sexist violence. My goal as a mother is to help my daughter reclaim everything that is sacred about her identity and her body; this is what I mean by "replanting." To firmly replant her as winyan, uhariti, kwe is to ensure that she can experience deep, fulfilling happiness in her Brown Indigenous female existence (or a gender nonconforming existence should she/they desire) without shame, fear of sexual assault, or experiences of racism. Replanting converses with the Chicana Indigena futurity that Castillo articulated when she stated, "Our goal is to achieve joy. We move from victim to survivor, and I advocate, to becoming a warrior to one's cause. That cause may be to achieve personal peace of mind or the cause may spur one to become an activist—*una guerrillera* who has taken her personal tragedy to empower herself and help her environment."[51] This is a Xicanista futurity of empowerment and regeneration that, for Castillo, involves developing "our own alchemy of cures," using our imagination and intuition and reclaiming our bodies.[52] She essentially views this recipe as a means for Xicana-Indigenas to rehumanize. "We will determine for ourselves what makes us feel whole, what brings us tranquility, strength, nerve to face the countless—not for one moment imagined—obstacles in the path of our journey toward being fulfilled human beings."[53] We have not arrived at this rehumanized futurity for Chicanas and Indigenas, but if I can put my own efforts toward shaping more compassionate and educated human beings, I can contribute to the hemispheric movement of regaining our humanity as Women of Color, as queer *familia*, and as Indigenous people.

I would like to end by acknowledging that motherwork and, by extension pedagogy, through Xicanisma is a journey of difficult imperfect work. This is what surviving violence and healing look like. In *Black Dove*, Castillo reflects on how as a Xicanista mother, she ended up raising a son who still looked toward patriarchal models of masculinity to learn how to be a Latino man. Anxious and depressed about not meeting the demands of providing for a family according to capitalist standards, her son turned to robbery, upsetting everything Castillo had taught him about knowing right from wrong and being an honorable man. "As a mother, as a single woman, as a proud self-proclaimed Chicana," she writes, "I had spent over a quarter of a century lighting luminarias just ahead of my boy to lead the way. I strung lights of opportunities to ease the way for this Brown person growing up in a postcolonial society. When he was sixteen, he went to see the last of the matriarchal cultures of the Isthmus of Tehuantepec with me."[54] Despite these lurking questions and her immersion in the five stages of grief, Castillo came to the stage of acceptance and received her son with open arms, assuring him that his life awaited him, post-incarceration. Here, Castillo offers another lesson in hope and resilience for Xicanista mothers and Xicanista feminists. While we can imbue the young people we raise and teach with Xicanista feminist magic such as unconditional love and a trip to the Isthmus of Tehuantepec, we have no control over how the world will hurt them or touch them. It is how we arm them along the way and how we receive them on the other end of healing that makes the love come alive and the journey meaningful. The journey toward the Chicana feminist futurity that Castillo voices with Xicanisma is difficult and messy but worthy of our investment if we are at all committed to our own survival and to that of our next seven generations.

TEACHING ANA CASTILLO

Transnational Feminist Theory, Transvisionaria Poetix, and Practical Tips for the Classroom

LEIGH JOHNSON

Ana Castillo is one of the most well-known and widely published of the Chicana writers, yet the semester I taught *Give It to Me* (2014) at my small, Catholic university, I was pretty sure I'd garner enough student complaints to be reprimanded; after all, the novel is about a polyamorous divorcee who appears to be sexually obsessed with her cousin who has just been released from jail. Instead of focusing on the raunchiness of the text, students found fascinating ways to engage with it as a critique on the American dream. Because Castillo's work is plentiful and versatile (I've taught some element of her work every semester, from plays, poetry, essays, memoir, and novels to short stories), it isn't necessary to convince readers the value of teaching her work. Rather, in this essay, I hope to offer ways to concretely conceptualize the theoretical modes, discussion prompts and class activities, and assignments that will create classroom space revealing how Castillo's work connects cultural, political, and transnational concerns to each other. This essay will focus on how to build a strong unit on Castillo into gender studies courses, upper-level author seminars, Chicana or Latinx literature courses, American literature surveys, or genres and creative writing courses. The first section focuses on a full course devoted to teaching Castillo's Chicana feminist theory and praxis as a foundation to understanding her other creative work. I then turn to a discussion of teaching Castillo's memoir from a transnational social justice framework as a smaller unit in a class on Chicana writers.

As a literature professor, my goal is for students to recognize in literature a transnational, hemispheric feminist movement and the possibilities for agency through literary works. I use writing and literary theory as tools for their approach to literature, which I will explain in discussion of application to various texts, including *So Far from God* (1993), *Give It to Me*, *Black Dove* (2016), *Loverboys* (2008), and *Psst . . . I Have Something to Tell You, Mi Amor* (2005). For instance, in upper-level classes, students need grounding in foundations of Chicana and other feminist theory to understand the transformative power of these texts. Using chapters from Gloria Anzaldúa's *Borderlands / La Frontera* (1987), Norma Alarcón's "Chicana Feminism: In the Tracks of 'the' Native Woman" (1990), Cherríe Moraga's "A Long Line of Vendidas" (1985), and María Herrera-Sobek's "The Politics of Rape: Sexual Transgressions in Chicana Fiction" (1996) among others, grounds the fiction in theory that is accessible to students. More recently, Sylvanna Falcón's work on transnational feminist research is powerful (2016): "By adopting a research approach that acknowledges power dynamics, the importance of political solidarity, and the problematic secular-spiritual divide, then research practices do not empower privatized knowledge over collective knowledge or institutions over communities."[1] Moving to praxis requires what I call *transvisionaria poetix* that imagine and propose ways of being that are not dependent on white- and Western-dominated feminisms. The *trans* is to imply movement and call up transnational theory, while *visionaria* draws on a vision for inclusive, non-monolingual futures, and *poetix* uses the *x* both to challenge the eye and to gesture toward the ways using Latinx has challenged definitions of gender and feminism. Drawing on the theorists above, and showing how their work has been essential to understanding transnational feminist research practices, grounds Castillo's work in a new light—transvisionaria poetix, those that are rooted in a resistant and contestable past, are knowledgeable and hungry in the present, and are focused on a powerful hopeful future for transformative social justice in marginalized and oppressed communities.

With some guidance from their instructor, students should experience reading and deciphering challenging theory and secondary sources firsthand (see appendix 1), but it is equally important for instructors to draw connections to transnational, border, and gender theory that students may not have read. For instance, a discussion of Ana Castillo's *The Guardians* (2008), in which Regina, caring for her undocumented nephew on the US border, has to use her resourcefulness to combat multiple tragedies, can lead to and benefit from Amy Kaminsky's discussion of Indigenous feminisms: "With exposure to different forms of feminism, indigenous feminism recognizes itself as such and develops itself from within, borrowing from whatever is useful in foreign feminism."[2] This example is one of many I could give to show how Castillo's work easily can lead to rich discussions and opportunities to introduce theory that the class may not have read, but can understand via fiction. In the following sections, I will bring in more examples of theory that, if the instructor has familiarity with the approach, can deepen understanding of the text. I regularly draw on hemispheric, border, and gender theories when teaching general education / liberal arts core classes to nonmajors with successful discussion results. Marymount University consistently ranks among the most diverse universities in the South, and Latinx students make up 18 to 22 percent of the student body. Beyond the numbers, students find that by talking with each other in class, they put their family's cultural traditions in context and conversation with their peers' experiences. Since students do not feel like "token" members of an ethnic group, they are more likely to share personal stories that relate to the texts. Clearly, my university is diverse in terms of race, ethnic background, level of preparation, religion, and socioeconomic status, and within those differences, students find questions, and some answers, in these theoretical approaches. In this sense, students interrogate the ways in which any of the characters act with agency despite the odds against them in a country in which they wield little political and economic power.

TEACHING CASTILLO AS A CHICANA FEMINIST THEORIST AND ACTIVIST

Castillo grew up in poverty in Chicago, the youngest daughter of Mexican immigrants. Her memoir, *Black Dove*, details some of the challenges she faced, from police harassment to young motherhood.[3] As she moved to California, furthered her education, divorced, and began raising her son independently, she became more involved in the Chicana feminist movement and activism. Above all, she roots her work in a powerful feminist concept she developed: Xicanisma, "to reconsider behavior long seen as inherent in the Mexic Amerindian woman's character, such as patience, perseverance, industriousness, loyalty to one's clan, and commitment to our children" so that Chicanas can "be self-confident and assertive regarding the pursuing of our needs and desires."[4] As a tenant of this movement's power, she also asserts a kind of feminist collaboration in which women nurture *each other* instead of focusing their attentions where capitalist, patriarchal systems dictate: "A comadre can massage your feet, wash your hair; she can read out loud to you from a novel or poetry . . . we can learn to be each other's mothers, even for one day of the month."[5] This kind of relationship, mutually nurturing and fulfilling, is both self and community care; it is even more powerfully so in that it links women to each other in a way that is woman identified and reciprocal—two theoretical ideas with origins in womanist and Indigenous feminism. However, as discussion of her memoir and novels show, Castillo realizes that theorizing this support and putting it into action can be challenging because of systemic injustices that affect women of color.

I've taught Castillo's work in a variety of contexts from gender studies to American literature. In a summer Major Authors course, she was the major author. That course offered the opportunity to fully explore her work in the context of contemporary Chicana feminist thought. Readings included

Castillo's poetry, novels, essays, plays, and short stories. Students conducted a journal analysis, executed a poetry explication, wrote a researched essay, and presented a creative project using the material from the course. This was an ideal way to teach Castillo, but of course, it's not always feasible to dedicate an entire course to one author. However, teaching her work this way allowed me an opportunity to try multiple pedagogical approaches, from performance pedagogy, to creative presentations, to pairing graduate and undergraduates for writing mentorship, to cognitive mapping. What emerged was Castillo as a theorist, certainly, but also a powerful activist through her literary work; in other words, she engages a transvisionaria poetix. Her fiction and poetry call on the reader to take on a transnational consciousness, in which what happens in another part of the world has an undeniable impact on the communities her characters inhabit. As they come to realize the connectedness, the characters find ways to be activists, empowering themselves within their communities.

When planning a course, I always start backwards, asking myself, what do I want my students to know and be able to do at the end of this course? In this case, I wanted the undergraduates to have the opportunity to use their skills from our literary theories class to read a story through a Marxist, psychoanalytic, or queer theoretical lens, to be able to enter a scholarly conversation about a single novel via a researched paper, and to creatively represent the way that Chicana feminist theory approaches social justice. For the graduate students (many of whom will become teachers), I wanted them to have the opportunity to lecture on one of Castillo's novels for the class and to write a paper for an academic audience that brought something new to Castillo scholarship. To that end, I developed multilayered assignments (see appendices 2–4) for each group of students, even though we met at the same time, in the same place. Two of the graduate students submitted and presented their work at conferences, whereas one of the undergraduates submitted his creative project (poem) to the university's literary magazine, where it was published and won an audience favorite award. Also compelling was the response from the non-English major in the class, a nursing student, who wrote me later that summer to say she was in Guatemala working on LGBT issues, something that she would not have cared about before taking the class. Each student personalized their research to find a way to engage with transvisionaria poetix.

When I taught Castillo as the major author, *Black Dove* had not yet been published, so I started, probably unconventionally, with *Psst . . . I Have Something to Tell You, Mi Amor*. This play dramatizes the 1989 imprisonment and torture of Sister Dianna Ortiz in Guatemala. Because summer classes meet for three hours, three times a week, reading the play aloud permitted us to avoid wasting precious class time in the first meeting. Beginning with it positioned Castillo as a transnational activist and showed my students that I would expect them to physically and creatively engage with the literature. When considering if political activism is possible through literature, the play *Psst . . . I Have Something to Tell You, Mi Amor* tells the harrowing story of the torture and rape of Sister Dianna. There are two versions of the play included in the Wings Press edition, and there are significant differences between them. The first version is thirteen pages with a largely interior monologue of Sister Dianna telling her story to various sympathetic "other" characters, occasionally her mother, friend, and a North American reporter. The second play tells the same story, but incorporates more characters and develops an external narrative. In some ways, this story is almost too traumatic to act out in class, as is often the preferred method of performance pedagogy. However, it's important to read parts of the play out loud so that students can examine the power of *testimonio*.[6] What does it mean to give voice to a traumatic event and tell it to someone versus telling it through action and plot? This play can allow for a good discussion of what kinds of stories women are allowed to tell and who they can tell them to. For instance, it connects well to the spectacle of women testifying in front of committees in the US House and Senate. The focus on personal comportment in order to be believed or seen as credible is something to consider in performance of pieces of these plays. In discussing the effects that "modernization" has had on Latin American peoples and economies, Rosaura Sánchez and Beatrice Pita remark, "The testimonial can in fact serve as a useful way for considering different spheres encompassed by 'postmodernism,' and of examining its position within literary spaces, while at the same time noting its relation to the market and links to various social movements."[7] Understanding the play from this perspective guides students to draw questions such as, what are the stakes of Sister Dianna's story?

Long a part of composition pedagogy to help student writers become more aware of their abilities, applying creative, flexible approaches to texts when reading is a valuable tool in literature pedagogy as well. Performance is both an object of study and a method of study. As Timothy Raphael explains, "Connecting these two processes is a vision of performance as a reciprocal, interactive, and embodied way of knowing that supplements and often challenges text-based epistemologies."[8] Even students who may not be particularly good at acting, being in front of the class, or performing still gain benefits from an approach that allows them to see the effects of the texts as other students close read aloud. This approach balances cognitive goals with pedagogical goals. For instance, using performances of scenes means employing several pedagogical strategies—active learning, group work, kinesthetic learning, performance, close reading, problem solving, and decision-making. The history of performance pedagogy, as summarized by Kay Ellen Capo, is one in which "though practitioners have explored how performance of literature affects social consciousness, theorists have tended to see interpretation in formal or subject-centered (phenomenological) rather than sociopolitical terms."[9] In other words, the action of doing performance can create a social awareness in students that has not been extensively realized by the theories of performance.

Is it too heavy-handed to read this kind of politicized literature in today's classrooms? The play(s) are overtly political, but if one goal of reading them is to assess their style and structure of dramatic devices, then the political aspect is a bonus to help students understand how art can comment on political matters, even years after the fact. In this case, students can even determine for themselves whether an internal or external dialogue and action make for a more powerful literary response in light of the need for social and historical context for persuasion. As Robert Mossman persuasively notes about Demetria Martínez's *Mother Tongue* (which is similar in subject matter to *Psst . . .*), "While [students] agreed it was too sophisticated and too rich to be propaganda, they still objected to being 'manipulated' by the writer, by having their emotions pulled in different directions because the protagonist was so sympathetic."[10] In this case, the text is transparent in its desire to focus attention on a particular political stance, but performance pedagogy opens up so much more space than simply a political reading of the text would do. The revelation constitutes an opportunity for discussing transvisionaria poetix and the ways that movement, change, and action are possible; telling a story changes the way the audience thinks about transnational identity and justice.

The play set the tone for the course, in which we would not only situate Castillo's writing as part of a Chicana feminist tradition, by reading articles by Raúl Coronado, Yvonne Yarbro-Bejarano, Elizabeth Coonrod Martínez, Aída Hurtado, and Sonia Saldívar-Hull, in addition to the previously mentioned Anzaldúa, Moraga, and Alarcón, but also we would use our understanding of the way Castillo yokes Chicana feminist concerns of women living in the United States to women in Mexico and Central America. In addition to the above Chicana feminist theorists, we read Castillo's *Massacre of the Dreamers* together, looking for connections to the other writers, as well as those that Castillo seemed to embody more uniquely, like *comadreo* and motherwork. Graduate students now picked a novel (choosing among *The Guardians, Give It to Me, Peel My Love like an Onion,* and *Sapogonia*) to read that they would teach to the class. More familiar now with Castillo's themes, undergraduates completed a poetry explication, using one of the poems from *My Father Was a Toltec* (1995). Short papers to practice documentation, close reading, and critical analysis, the explications gave students a chance to share their expertise on a poem with peers, causing some to gasp "I didn't think of that at all!" upon a clever analysis of the form of the poem "Napa, California" looking like a heavy grape vine. This assignment gave undergraduates confidence in their voices before moving on to longer works of fiction when the graduate students would weigh in with their extended analysis.

All students then read *So Far from God* (1993), in which four New Mexican daughters die on their quests for the American dream, leaving their mother Sofi to form a support group for mothers who have lost children. I choose this text for all the reasons Danizete Martínez describes in "Teaching Chicana/o Literature in Community College with Ana Castillo's *So Far from God*": it shines "as a Chicana/feminist text that demonstrates the beauty of New Mexico, the traditions of the people, and the value of regional writing, while also challenging the notion of a static cultural identity."[11] However, I would add to this that Castillo, by writing in this regional, folkloric way, highlights the inability of the text to stay within the boundaries of the place; Sofi's daughters challenge region and nation with their seemingly tangential involvement with the Persian Gulf War, but the way imperialism works in the text is via tragic transnational impacts on communities far from the imagined loci. In this way, Castillo provides students and teachers with a way to read the text as critical of geopolitical environmental racism, as Laura Halperin does to strong effect.[12] Theresa Delgadillo's analysis of hybrid spirituality in the novel opens up productive avenues for understanding systemic gender violence.[13] Drawing on theories of space, time, and place, instructors familiar with Mary Pat Brady's foundational *Extinct Lands, Temporal Geographies* (2002) and Chandra Talpade Mohanty's volume on third world women and feminism (1991) can use their knowledge to lead students through the intersections of the critiques Castillo makes on second wave feminist thought and US neoliberal imperialism.

So Far from God is somewhat difficult to read, but when students approach it thinking about questions of social justice and feminist action, it becomes clearer and more manageable (see appendix 5). Each of the five main characters—Sofi and her four daughters, Esperanza, Fe, Caridad, and La Loca—has a specific approach to feminist agency. Through each of the women's confrontation with the violent patriarchal globalized network of oppression, a possibility for action is explored and, subsequently, rejected or affirmed. For instance, Esperanza studies Chicano politics at the University of New Mexico, becomes enamored with American Indian religious traditions, and chooses a career in journalism as a way of engaging feminist action. However, when her boyfriend Ruben leaves her for a white woman, after promising her that as Chicanos they will rise together, she wakes up to the sexism in the Chicano movement. Unfortunately, her journalism career, which was supposed to amplify her voice, ends tragically when she goes to Saudi Arabia as an embedded reporter and is killed by a bomb. Her efforts to be an effective activist are cut short by the news media's complicity in a capitalistic, transnational project of oil exploitation in a country with gender discrimination and violence. According to the novel, by choosing to participate in the war as an embedded journalist, Esperanza has failed to act on the agency she might have had as an educated Chicana.

Using a mapping device, or some other visual organizer (appendix 3), helps students identify what kind of violence each woman has suffered, and what kind of activist approach she takes to resist violence. I ground this activity in Fredric Jameson's (1991) call for cognitive mapping in which the subject enters the Lacanian *imaginary* to see how material conditions of life affect her in the *real*, or in other words, "this is exactly what the cognitive map is called upon to do in the narrower framework of daily life in the physical city: to enable a situational representation on the part of the individual subject to that vaster and properly unrepresentable totality which is the ensemble of society's structures as a whole."[14] In the case of the novel, each daughter's imaginary is connected with the impossibilities of representing her in the nation. What larger networks of oppression exist to stymie her efforts? (For almost all the characters, except Sofi, success is fleeting.) The answer seems to be engagement and dialogue with a community. As students volunteer ideas for the chart, they begin to see what kinds of activism are effective in the community. Most crucially, they can perceive what does not work; white liberal activist approaches that do not take into account the social, cultural, environmental, spiritual, and economic mores of a community are less likely to be effective than those that organically sprout from the community's needs.

So Far from God opens up feminist transnational spaces by rejecting imperialist approaches to globalization. Instructor knowledge of Patricia Hill Collins's "Shifting the Center: Race, Class, and Feminist Theorizing about Motherhood" (1994) is helpful to explaining the ways the novel uses motherhood as social justice. For instance, with regard to motherhood and feminist activism, women whose communities expect them to educate, care for, nurture, and discipline in the face of colonial oppression and racism perform radical motherwork that, as Collins argues, "challenges social constructions of work and family as separate spheres, of male and female gender roles as similarly dichotomized, and of the search for autonomy as the guiding human quest."[15] Rather than glorifying the antagonistic angle of war in the Middle East for career advancement for Esperanza, the novel focuses on the cooperative nature of Sofi's group, M.O.M.A.S. (Mothers of Martyrs and Saints), as an empowering option for women worldwide to think about fighting against the forces of violent globalization that have harmed their children. As the full class discusses these issues and fills in the chart, in a larger class, a group of four students could discuss an assigned character (expanding out with Esmerelda, Doña Felicia, or others).

To heighten connections between theory and text, undergraduates read one scholarly essay about the novel and presented the information to the class. The specifics of the assignment are detailed in the appendix, but their work on this led to three important outcomes: each student had met with me to discuss the rhetorical work the scholar had done, thereby building up my individual mentoring with the students; they practiced concise and clear presentation skills without having the anxiety of having to defend their own analysis of the text; and the annotated bibliography I compiled from their individual entries and distributed to the class was a valuable resource for students working on final papers. Graduate students, meanwhile, presented individually on the novel they had chosen and its secondary body of work, and developed proposals for their conference-style papers. Undergraduates and the other graduate students benefited from these presentations as they became more familiar with the sheer variety and volume of work Castillo has produced; none of the novels is like another.

We indulged a variety of readings of *The Mixquiahuala Letters* (1986), about two women's relationship as they age. Famously, this epistolary novel offers the reader a variety of approaches to read the text—none of which are straight through in the order it appears. In this regard, the text is already queering and crossing the borders of fiction. I will confess that I have sticky notes in the front of my copy with brief comments on what happens in each chapter for the ease of arranging and rearranging. When I taught the book in Major Authors, I had eight students. I had two read as "The Conformist," two as "The Cynic," two as "The Quixotic," and two straight through. As we reconvened in class, I had each pair meet briefly to discuss their understanding of what happened in the novel, and to try to figure out why they had the title they'd been given. Then we scrambled to form two groups of four to share the differences in the story—"Wait, who's Vitorio? Teresa has a son?!"—and to try to figure out if what is left out or included in the different tellings significantly impacts the way we might interpret the story. This exploration brings us to question: Why do we feel a need for understanding the *real* story? Castillo is a genius of narrative play, and for students to experience firsthand the possibilities of jouissance is a powerful opiate for their professor. Reading the novel this way would work especially well in a larger class, too, such as an American literature survey or a creative writing class.

Final essays were strong theoretically and richly engaged with the text. We used a variety of strategies in the revision stages, including a whole class workshop of three pages of graduate student work (pages were selected by the student, based on where she wanted feedback), paired writing mentors with undergraduates benefitting from graduate student colleagues, and individual conferences with me. Graduate students used the University of Pennsylvania English Call for Papers site to find conferences where they might be able to present their work. They posted these conferences to our class Canvas site and explained how their paper would fit the theme of the conference. One student out of the four in class did take her paper to a graduate student conference at a nearby university. This activity exemplified that graduate student writing need not (and should not) occur in a bubble without regard for audience. Taking their interpretations of Castillo's work to a larger stage encouraged graduate students to find their own way through transvisionaria poetix and to share their discoveries with the field. Finally, our class capstones were creative projects, in which students chose elements from their own creative skill sets to engage with elements from Castillo's work. In this class, we had a dance party, a spoken word performance, a student accompanying her original song on the piano, and homemade biscochitos! Students in awe of Castillo's creativity find that they too can create something beautiful and thought-provoking for their classmates.

ADAPTING TO A SMALLER UNIT

Realizing that opportunities to devote an entire course to Ana Castillo do not come around often, I sought a way to engage students in the themes of her work more frequently. Finding a solution to this need resulted in designing my current favorite course, Ethnic Literary Traditions (titled such that colleagues can teach it from other perspectives, and students can repeat with different topics, but my course is on contemporary Chicana memoir and genres), which brings a rich theoretical layer to the works and authors studied, turning students into budding experts grounded in transnational feminist analysis. The class starts by reading some of the foundational texts in Chicana feminist theory, including the entirety of *Borderlands / La Frontera*, the first edition of *Loving in the War Years*, and Norma Alarcón's "Chicana Feminism: In the Tracks of 'the' Native Woman." Depending on the focus of the course, I choose a few other readings to ground us in theory and provide background on the state of the field, for instance, Yvonne Yarbro-Bejarano's "Sexuality and Chicana/o Studies" (2006) and Aída Hurtado's "The Politics of Sexuality in the Gender Subordination of Chicanas" (1998). Our final introductory material includes poetry selections from all the authors we will read over the semester, and students do their first writing project as an explication of a poem supplemented with the theoretical concepts we have introduced—third space, code-switching, *vendida*, Chicana, home, macho, and so forth. One of the benefits of using Hurtado's essay is that she performs an excellent explication of Sandra Cisneros's "Loose Woman" that students can turn to as an example of the sharp thinking expected from them.[16] Each of these theorists lays a foundation for the class to consider how positing transvisionaria poetix might affect our reading of the texts to come.

The course then turns to memoirs (somewhat loosely defined) by Demetria Martínez, Lucha Corpi, Ana Castillo, and Sandra Cisneros (and in a Latina memoir iteration of the course, I swapped Corpi and Martínez for Daisy Hernandez's *A Cup of Water under My Bed* [2015] and Julia Alvarez's *Something to Declare* [1998]). Around midterm and after a complicated selection process of me "pitching" books and assigning difficulty values to each book individually, students find themselves reading a novel or play by one of these writers, meeting with me to discuss their understanding, and presenting on it to the class. Some of these projects are excellent, and some are not, but the value and skill with which many students rise to the occasion is worth the class time. I allow each student twenty minutes to present, and I assign students presenting on books by the same author to go on the same day, so as a group, we get a sense of the author's style and themes. This presentation establishes the primary source material for their final paper, in which they turn their attention to studies of the individual author's work (see appendix 5).

It seems complicated that students work on two multistep projects throughout the semester, but in reality, this gradual approach allows them to keep building on their previous work and renders revision an easy choice. The second major project is an issue analysis essay to compare how these writers deal with one specific theme such as education, the writing process, language, family responsibilities, or sexual orientation (see appendix 4). Students begin this project almost subconsciously by asking questions and thinking about their personal experiences and reactions to the text. As homework, I ask them to bring in an article about Latinx issues in the news. Students share what the article is about and where they found it. This gives us a good opportunity to work on source analysis along with thinking about how current events connect with the concerns of the writers. We also cluster the themes in the articles into the categories above. Students then select two or three themes they are interested in exploring and make a chart filling in how four of the writers take a position or have experience with the theme. Final papers are nuanced as students draw thoughtful comparisons between writers and unexpected contrasts in material or theoretical conditions. It is a highly scaffolded approach meant to turn students into experts in a short time. Furthermore, it sparks a strong vivification of the reality that Chicana feminist theory is not a monolith, and writers can respect each other while they disagree with each other.

In her memoir, Castillo recounts survival of several sexual assaults, none of which she reported to police because the perpetrator of one such assault was a female police officer, searching Castillo for the voyeuristic benefit of the male officers.[17] Among others, she defended herself against a relative left in charge of her, against a "gangbanger" named Shadow, and against the leader of a student organization at her community college. When she comments that she did not trust any of the above, and takes her ability to fight them off matter-of-factly, Castillo describes an egregious violation that seems common as a hallmark of academia's #MeToo reckoning: "I was out with friends and a professor celebrating my twenty-first birthday . . . the professor offered me a ride home. Instead, he took me to his apartment. . . . When trust is ripped away something else comes in its place, ugly and usually permanent."[18] She doesn't say, but the professor was probably white, and the potential damage to her education and career was significant. In the era of #MeToo, the ways that Castillo engages gender and sexual violence is particularly appropriate to incorporate into the classroom. Memoir is useful for these discussions, as the importance of testimony and believing the victim is one of the cornerstones for allies responding to those who report sexual assault. In order to have a productive discussion, it is important to ensure students a safe place for a discussion of the ways in which systemic, institutional sexual violence has shaped Chicanx lives. While this discussion can and should be open-ended, with the professor learning from students and connecting to whatever most recent event nationally or internationally has occurred, some best practices need to be followed. At a minimum, it's important to preface the discussion with an acknowledgment of the nature of the material, to let students know it's okay if they need to take a break from the conversation, and to have prepared yourself with knowledge of on and off campus resources that you can share with students.

Tulsa Studies in Women's Literature editor Jennifer Airey describes the power of speaking about experiences, "The greatest success of the #MeToo movement has been, in my opinion, the defamiliarization of such stories, the act of forcing us to confront and name as Not Okay experiences that we previously shrugged off as an inevitable part of being a woman."[19] Discussing how Castillo's experiences reflect the ways that sexual violence has affected Chicana women's lives reveals how transvisionaria poetix can be a powerful way to reclaim women's voices and power. These discussions in the classroom are important, but also fraught with potential to trigger student responses. For Castillo, despite the constant threat from men and her developing feminist awareness, she finds that women also can betray trust, too, and that the best way to do her work—writing and raising her son—is to realize the following: "While I have had romantic liaisons with women and, later, men, for most of my life I've remained on my own."[20]

These moments in the text can be powerful teaching tools and ways of launching discussion.

Black Dove poses an essential question of writers who care about social justice: Does the art they create have any meaning when the realities of daily and persistent racial, gender, and class violence continue to act on their communities? Reconciling the difficulty of producing art while her son was young, Castillo faces the existential crisis of what was all the sacrifice for if her child is to fall victim to the racist system of American justice and mass incarceration? When her son is a teenager, she remarks, "Reluctantly and painfully, I came to accept that Mi'jo lived in a parallel universe from the one we shared within the walls of the condo and from the activities and travels I offered. From the moment he walked out the door, until his return, he was a brown male on the streets of Chicago."[21] Can she save a community through art if she cannot save the person who matters most? She concludes that the only way she might get him back from the brink is through words and language: "I sent books—many—including my own titles and soon he began to read (again). Over time, he was reading, writing, retaining information—connecting."[22] The process of connection through writing, at a personal and political level, continues the artist's struggle for her son and herself. Students find much to connect with here, as well, and papers that link the concerns in Castillo's memoir to an anti-stereotyping poem such as "We Would Like You to Know" get to the heart of social justice through literature.

I use varied pedagogical strategies to approach any of the texts and authors I teach, but Ana Castillo's work is particularly interesting to apply a variety of strategies to. Ultimately, whether our goals are to help students appreciate the appeal of language as meaningful and beautiful or to have students make connections between transnational capital, trauma, and cultural upheaval and the literature they read, Castillo's work can meet those goals and more. I've offered some points of departure for discussion of the above work, and given context in which I'd use the works, but the bigger message is that you can't go wrong including her work on a syllabus. There are so many layers and pieces of meaning that she manages to bring real delight in language play to the serious ways in which we can look at symbol and meaning in any of her work. I've included assignments mentioned above, as well as some sample quizzes (see appendix 6) for *Black Dove, Give It to Me,* and *So Far from God.* Overall, her work allows teachers and students to engage with her in transvisionaria poetix, an exploration of how social justice and literary activism can profoundly help us complicate the answer she gives to the question at the end of *Black Dove*: "What connects us—not just as citizens from so many walks of life, but to our past and future? Our stories."[23]

APPENDIX 1

Secondary Source Assignment

For your secondary source assignment, you will select (with my approval) one of the secondary sources I've listed on the syllabus. [In this case, the secondary sources are about *So Far from God*, but this assignment could work with any of the texts. —LJ] You'll download the essay from the library databases, and you'll present the essay to your peers during class.

Reading the essay carefully is critical! If you don't understand something, look it up, and then ask me for assistance.

In seven minutes, I'll expect you to:

- Present the thesis of the article, very clearly.
- Give a summary of the author's main points.
- Point to places where the author does a close reading of the text, showing how the evidence supports the argument.
- Highlight some of the most interesting, unusual, and provocative points.
- Address the theoretical perspective the author relies upon.
- You'll need to work from notes, and you may choose to supply a handout to the audience.
- Answer questions from peers and faculty.

I will collect:

- An annotated bibliography of your source, which contains a one-paragraph summary of the author's argument.

Grading Rubric

	Excellent	Good	Average	Needs Improvement	Not Acceptable
Best articulation of the thesis is clearly identified					
Annotated bibliography: MLA format					
Annotated bibliography: Accurate summary					
Presentation clearly identifies author, title, general subject, and basic argument					
Effectively shows theoretical frame example					
Effectively shows close reading / analysis example					
Answers class and faculty questions					

APPENDIX 2

Presentation of Novel Assignment

You'll have thirty minutes to engage the class with the additional novel you read. I'd like you to make sure some basics are covered, but please feel free to be creative and original in your ideas.

Basics:
- Plot
- Setting (a map might be helpful)
- Characters (a character map or list with relationships might be helpful)
- Tone and style of novel
- Themes

Other items that you'll certainly need to cover:
- How does the text relate to other works that we've read by Castillo? Thematically? Stylistically?
- What are the important parts of the text for analysis and interpretation?
- How does the book reflect ideas about Chicana feminist theory?

If applicable . . .
- What have the critics said about this text? Popular or scholarly?
- What are some places (excerpts) that you'd like to look closely at with the class?

Otherwise, it's up to you to make it clear and engaging. Remember the rest of the class has not read these books; I have. You're not presenting to me, but to your peers. They will be hopelessly confused if you're not clear and sure of what happened yourself.

You'll be graded on:
- Basic coverage of information: Is it present and clearly presented?
- Clarity: How well does the class grasp what the novel is about?
- Enthusiasm: How well do you convey interest and excitement about the novel?
- Further development: How well do you open up new ideas for thinking about Castillo's work?
- Extra: What makes your presentation special?

Here is what I add for the class with undergraduates presenting—

Grading for the books will be based on a scale like gymnastics scoring. Each book will have a difficulty level, and your presentation will be worth 100 points for execution. The assignment is worth 150 points. Turn in your notes for the assignment.

Castillo:
  So Far from God (65)
  The Mixquiahuala Letters (55)
  Peel My Love like an Onion (60)
  Give It to Me (60)
  Loverboys (65)
Moraga:
  Heroes and Saints (55)
  Watsonville (55)
  The Hungry Women (55)
  Waiting in the Wings (50)
  A Xicana Codex of Changing Consciousness (60)
Martínez:
  Mother Tongue (50)
  The Block Captain's Daughter (50)
Cisneros:
  The House on Mango Street (50)
  Woman Hollering Creek (55)
  Caramelo (70)
  Have You Seen Marie? (50)
Corpi:
  Eulogy for a Brown Angel (55)
  Crimson Moon (55)
  Cactus Blood (55)
  Death at Solstice (55)
  Black Widow's Wardrobe (55)

APPENDIX 3

	Esperanza	Fe	Caridad	La Loca	Sofi
Type of Violence	War (in service of oil production)	Environmental	Sexual	Absorbs violence her sisters face	Economic
Activism	Reports on the war	Works harder to get ahead	Becomes a healer, hermit	Heals her sisters, speaks to animals	Starts a town co-op and M.O.M.A.S.
Larger network of oppression	Chicano movement	War, reproductive justice	Intimate violence, stalking, sexuality, rape		
Outcome	Death, ghost (the haunting of a lack of recognition of intersectionality)	Cancer from radioactive waste	Jumps from cliff at Acoma (heals through spirit)	AIDS? The lack of touch of community, family only	Works to create new communities and rejects oppression and male privilege

APPENDIX 4

Issue Analysis Paper Assignment

In this essay, you will select an issue of importance to Chicana/Latina writers. As you read, you'll collect information about how each writer portrays her take on the issue you've selected. Generic issues such as "identity" are not what this essay is about. You want something more substantial. A thesis statement should look something like this: While Latina writers agree education is necessary to successful rejection of gender roles, it is clear that differences in socioeconomic status affect how much education can change the material conditions of life.

First—issue exploration. Find an article about Latina issues in the news, and bring to class for discussion.

Second—narrowing and exploring. Complete an issue summary chart with a minimum of four writers and evidence from their texts.

Third—draft. Minimum five pages, four writers put in conversation. You should not merely summarize what the writer says about the issue, but probe for ways in which they are speaking to each other and to society about these issues. HARD DEADLINE: 11/3 IN CLASS. I will still comment on your drafts after this time (and you will not be allowed to submit a final copy without a draft), but you will not receive credit for the draft.

Final papers—submit all prior materials. If Hernandez and Cisneros have something to say about your issue, you should include them in the conversation. Revision is essential to your grade. Essays that have not been revised cannot score higher than a B-.

The essay should make a strong argument, using textual evidence to support the argument throughout. Careful attention to the material and a strong thesis are essential, but you should also plan to attend to writing conventions that assist your argument, such as topic sentences, transitions, and mechanics of presentation. You must have a bibliography page with all sources consulted accounted for, including your peers. If you have visited the CTL for help with the essay (and I encourage you to make an appointment on Starfish to do so), make a note of that on your bibliography page. If you have had ANY outside help, it must be documented; failure to do so will jeopardize your grade.

APPENDIX 5

Author Study Paper Assignment

In this essay, you will develop an argument about your writer's work—specifically as it relates to the memoir we read by her and the additional reading you presented to the class. You're not aiming for a biography of the writer or a plot summary of the additional work you encountered. Rather, you want to say something important about how the writer uses a particular theme, idea, or event. You want something substantial. A thesis statement should look something like this: In the collection of short stories *Woman Hollering Creek*, Sandra Cisneros develops what is a central theme in her work—liberated women working to liberate others, to varying degrees of success.

Proposal Due

This should include a tentative thesis, an introduction, a brief outline, and at least two outside sources you're considering using (2–3 pages, due 11/21). You will receive credit for submitting the proposal, but there will a deduction of 10 percent in your final paper grade if you do not submit a proposal on time.

Draft Due

The draft should be well-developed with your thesis clearly articulated and your main points clearly written out. You should have a draft, for rigorous in-class work (5 pages, due 12/5). By 12/8, you should also have located the four sources you will use for your essay and have incorporated them into the essay (7-page draft, due 12/8).

Final Draft with Presentations

The culminating project for the course is the presentation of your comparison essay. You will have 5–7 minutes in class to creatively and interestingly share your research with the class. What, after all this time, still excites you about your project? You should aim to get classmates to respond to your ideas (8-page final, with presentation on 12/12, 3:00–5:30 p.m.). Submit all prior materials. Revision is essential to your grade. Essays that have not been revised cannot score higher than a B-.

The essay should make a strong argument, using textual evidence to support the argument throughout. Careful attention to the material and a strong thesis are essential, but you should also plan to attend to writing conventions that assist your argument, such as topic sentences, transitions, and mechanics of presentation. You must have a bibliography page with all sources consulted accounted for, including your peers. If you have visited the CTL for help with the essay (and I encourage you to make an appointment on Starfish to do so), make a note of that on your bibliography page. If you have had ANY outside help, it must be documented; failure to do so will jeopardize your grade.

APPENDIX 6

Black Dove Quiz, pages 1–142

1. Why do Castillo's grandparents have to go back to Mexico? Where had they lived before?
2. Describe the difference(s) between Tia Flora and Castillo's mother, Raquel.
3. What are the pitfalls in Castillo's feminist domestic relationship with her lover? (Did you figure out who this was?)
4. What is so funny (surreal, not ha-ha, really) about Castillo having died in Oaxaca?
5. Describe Castillo's efforts to educate her son.

Black Dove Quiz, Part Two

1. What does Castillo track down from the neighborhood boys for her son? How does she get it back?
2. Describe the conversation between Castillo and her granddaughter.
3. What are some of the books her son reads in prison?
4. What does Castillo mean by survival?

So Far from God Quiz

1. Where does Esperanza (oldest daughter) go when given the opportunity of a lifetime?
2. What attacks Caridad (prettiest daughter)?
3. Who does La Loca visit at the creek?
4. Tell me some things about Sofi and Domingo's relationship.
5. What is different about Fe's death?

Give It to Me Quiz

1. Why is Palma so angry with her *abuela*?
2. How does Palma get even with Chana the chef?
3. Which member of her family actually welcomes Palma?
4. Where does Randall's sister Claire live?
5. There are a lot of graphic descriptions in the novel. What is the point of Palma's sexual exploits in the scope of the theme of the novel?

CHAPTER 18

"NEVER *STAY* SILENT"

A Pedagogical Approach to Teaching *The Guardians*

SANDRA RUIZ

The first time I heard Ana Castillo speak was at the 2009 Los Angeles Times Festival of Books. Usually held in the month of April, at the time it was hosted on the University of California, Los Angeles (UCLA) campus. She was at the festival promoting her latest novel, *The Guardians* (2007), set in a fictitious border city of New Mexico and centered on a Mexican American woman, Regina, who is searching for her undocumented brother who did not return home after crossing the Mexico-US border. Castillo and her fellow panelists of writers had filled up one of the largest university lecture halls,[1] one that holds nearly 450 people. During the question-and-answer portion of the panel, I recall a tall white male dressed in military fatigues approach the podium and ask a question about "anchor babies,"[2] and what the group of Chicanx/Latinx authors thought could be done about *them*. The question from our recollection was: "I am a veteran and fought for the citizens of this country; what can you do about illegals and their anchor babies?"[3] One of the panelists immediately responded by stating that his cousins are "anchor babies" who have also served this country, but I cannot recall verbatim what Castillo's response was to this person, mostly because I, at that moment of *his* question and definition, would be an anchor baby. What I do remember is my body's temperature rising and my cheeks turning flushed. Castillo's response calmed my spirit. With a controlled "do-not-start-with-me" tone of voice that did not feed into his trap, she did not engage him. The audience watched him do an about-face and he left the crowded lecture hall. Castillo, instead, decided to address the attendees and asked us to consider how the undocumented immigrant as a whole is exploited economically and then used as a political scapegoat and pawn.

As a young graduate student at the time, I felt an immense sense of relief and admiration for the author, whose work I had begun to read as an undergraduate and whose narratives and poetry I had connected with as a first-generation, underrepresented, and working-class Chicana-Latina. As I approached Castillo during her book signing, I thanked her for her response during the Q-and-A. She then turned up to look at me and I clearly remember her saying, "Never *stay* silent."[4] I evoke the memory of an event that occurred more than ten years ago because now as a professor and educator in higher education, I ask: How do we teach our current generation of college students about one of the most radical Chicana writers of the twenty-first century? When teaching literary texts whose characters and settings are fictional, but whose narratives reverberate real life experiences, what is our responsibility as educators? How do we create interventions and interruptions where our students can participate actively in challenging local, state, and national policies that are detrimental to targeted communities such as immigrants, women, and people of color? How do we empower our students, especially if they are a part of the communities we are studying and reading about? The novel lends itself to having in-depth conversations about mixed-status families, transborder politics, faith, and intergenerational trauma. Once this framework has been established, my students and I work together to create possible interventions, such as using social media to create digital interruptions, to bring awareness, and, I hope, to push forward for changes at local, state, and national levels.

For this essay, I will discuss a series of pedagogical activities I use in my classroom when teaching *The Guardians* to college/university students in Southern California. It is important to note that the state of California forms part of what Héctor Calderón defines as Greater Mexico, implying "that there is more than one Mexico beyond the Mexican Republic."[5] With this state forming part of the borderlands, students from or residing in Southern California come into significant contact with Mexican and Mexican American culture. For example, the Tijuana–San Diego border is one of the busiest, if not *the* busiest, entry into Mexico and the United States. In 2018, the US Department of Transportation reported that the agency had processed a total of 34.6 million individual border crossers and more than 14.5 million individual vehicles.[6] Taking into consideration my student population, my methodology serves to challenge and teach students into becoming community activists against inhumane practices. By bringing in "the personal is political"[7] along with other elements of plausibility found in the novel, we can further understand the battles marginalized and transnational communities confront in the United States and abroad.

With *The Guardians*, I start with the novel's dedication: "*To all working for a world without borders and to all who dare to cross them*,"[8] opening a conversation with my students about why Castillo would dedicate her novel to these two seemingly distinct groups. Asking: "Which group are you a part of? Or, can you become a part of one of these two groups, is this at all possible?" The conversation helps establish an understanding in our classroom that we as readers will refuse to be idle and/or complicit; together as a collective we will work through some of the themes we uncover in the novel such as border politics, immigration reform, and family separation, and in turn we will work on developing actions centered on bringing attention to these issues and/or to actively fight against them.

As a professor, I have taught at three levels of California's public institutions of higher education: the University of California, California State University, and California Community/City College. My current institution is a Hispanic Serving Institution (HSI) with nearly 45 percent of our student population self-identifying as Chicanx and/or Latinx.[9] While *The Guardians* has been heart-wrenching to teach in my academic career, it has been made especially difficult during this current decade of the 2010s, with the long-term detention of unaccompanied minors,[10] active travel bans against the Muslim community, and the 2019 zero-tolerance border policy that has separated families, specifically immigrant parents, the majority from Central America, from their children as young as eight months old,[11] without any solid reunification plan in the near future.

Establishing a curriculum where a portion of the methodology serves to challenge and potentially teach students how to become active accomplices against inhumane practices locally and abroad becomes not only a necessary tool but one that assists in the creation of other forms of belonging, one that does not require an authority or governmental documents to acknowledge and value your worth and position. In my classroom, I encourage students to share personal experiences by bringing forth my own and intertwining them with the source material. This practice allows me to set a more palpable tone for my students, opening the door for them to feel free to do the same when reading the novel, with the understanding that while we are collectively reading a fictional novel, its events, experiences, histories, and outcomes might not be fictional to all. Taking cues from the 1960s and 1970s feminist movement, the use of the "personal is political" provides an alternative methodology to studying a fictional narrative. I guide my students with the formative 1969 essay by Carol Hanisch "The Personal Is Political," along with Audre Lorde's essay "The Transformation of Silence into Language and Action,"[12] Gloria E. Anzaldúa's "Speaking in Tongues: A Letter to Third World Women Writers,"[13] and Kimberlé Crenshaw's work on intersectionality, "Mapping the Margins: Intersectionality, Identity Politics, and Violence against Women of Color."[14] When what you are reading on the page is far from the objective, detached reader experience because this could be *you, your* family, and these experiences speak to your own, then national discourses and political decisions are personal, as they directly influence and impact your and your family's everyday lives. I introduce students to primary sources, government documents such as *Mendez v. Westminster* (1947), a federal court case in Southern California that challenged public school segregation and was the predecessor to *Brown v. Board of Education* (1954), or California Proposition 187 (1994), which attempted to deny public services to undocumented residents, such as public education and nonemergency medical care. This pedagogical method assists in creating a more in-depth understanding of decision-making practices taking place at the state and national level.

Framing Ana Castillo's novel within its historical time period provides insight into the history of US national and political discourses that have taken place (or not) regarding the immigrant community residing in the United States. From 2005 to 2007, a series of immigration reform bills were introduced in the US Congress, each one failing. In the classroom, we do a close reading of one specific Senate bill, the last one of the 2005–2007 series, introduced in May 2007 by former senator Harry Reid. Known as the "Comprehensive Immigration Reform Act of 2007,"[15] it promised a pathway to citizenship for undocumented residents, while also providing funding for the US-Mexico border and its related agencies. It lasted under discussion for only four weeks before it was effectively dismissed by the Senate majority.

With the publication of the novel within this specific time period, Castillo inserts an alternative narrative to the debate, one that is not taking place within the realm of mainstream national politics, but rather within the communities that are directly affected by the lack of immigration reform and the inhumane policies in place. Her novel also contributes to a historical conversation on how US immigration policies of the past and present affect Mexicans and Mexican Americans as well as Central American migrants. The inclusion of secondary reading material, such as Castillo's introductory essay from her memoir *Black Dove: Mamá, Mi'jo, and Me* (2016), where she interlaces her family history with Mexican and US history, demonstrates the impact these policies have had in displacing people on both sides of the border and beyond.

Castillo's essay focuses on the racist policy of the early twentieth century, Operation Wetback, which forced deportation of documented and undocumented Mexican and Mexican American residents. Her essay provides startling statistics: "Sixty percent of those deported were American citizens. . . . It has been estimated by historians and acknowledged by US Citizenship and Immigration Services that in the two years after the crash, at least two hundred thousand Mexicans left the United States. Over the next ten years, altogether an estimated four hundred thousand to one million Mexicans and Mexican Americans were deported to México."[16] While Castillo's essay provides statistical data on how many Mexicans and Mexican Americans were deported during Operation Wetback, *The Guardians* gives a brief history lesson on how US anti-immigrant practices have been a part of systemic forms of oppression via governmental agencies. One of the novel's characters, Abuelito Milton, recalls the origins of the Border Patrol and the complexities behind being a Chicano soldier and living in the borderlands: "The Border Patrol got started up in 1924, the year I was born. That's when Mexicans got to be fugitives on our own land. Whether you lived on this side or that side, all Mexicans got harassed. Sometimes the police would come knocking on your door and pull you out. It didn't matter if you were born over here or not. When I went to fight in Germany I'd tell people, Here los Anglos are fighting the Nazis. Over there, where I live, they treat us Mexicans as if they were the Nazis."[17] In the twenty-first century, the Border Patrol continues to play a prominent part in anti-immigrant policies and the novel itself serves as a precursor to understanding the battles marginalized and transnational communities would continue to confront over ten years after *The Guardians*'s publication and nearly one hundred years after Abuelito Milton's experience as a Mexican American soldier in New Mexico.

One of the most justified critiques I have heard surrounding a discipline like Chicana/o studies centers on the exclusion of Central American experiences. Castillo's text works to create a context for higher learning by including a Chicana feminist principle of the critical examinations of commonalities between transnational migrants in the Americas. Two central ideas bridging diverse communities unfold: first, how the Central American community is deeply embedded within the Mexican and Mexican American experience in the United States, and second, the saliency of parallel experiences across the southern border in Mexico among immigrants of the Americas. If we can consider the US Southwest, specifically California as part of "Greater Mexico," then there also exists the possibility of a "Greater Latin America" or in the case of California, which houses the largest Central American population in the United States, "Greater Central America." In *The Guardians*, one of the few Chicano male high school teachers, Miguel, expresses his frustration with having to teach history according to the approved curriculum of his school, which does not include ethnic studies or a holistic approach to the hemispheric relationship between the United States and Latin America. Explaining the complicated history between his family and the School of the Americas (his father was an instructor for the school), Miguel uses his own archival research through the Freedom of Information Act and explains how US imperialism has been detrimental to Latin America. He states, "It was a US Army center located at Fort Benning in Columbus, Georgia, that trained more than sixty thousand soldiers and police, mostly from Latin America, in counterinsurgency and combat-related skills since 1946. Its graduates became experts in torture, murder, and political repression."[18] These US intervention tactics have destabilized many Latin American countries, even sparking decades-long civil wars as we have seen in Central America. Castillo's feminist praxis has not shied away from performing intersectional connections between the Chicana/x/o experiences and those of her Central American brethren. Two years prior to the publication of *The Guardians*, Castillo published *Psst . . . I Have Something to Tell You, Mi Amor* (2015), one poem and two plays centered around the Guatemalan civil war. Her poem "Like the people of Guatemala, I want to be free of these memories" discusses the importance of not staying silent in the face of the oppressor: "Let us shout louder than her memory, / louder then [*sic*] the unheard cries / of 200,000 disappeared, / buried alive in pits, / thrown alive from airplanes, / butchered and bayoneted / defenseless and blindfolded / in the name of democracy."[19] By framing *The Guardians* in 2018/2019, we are able to create saliency to the cross-cultural and transnational outside the Mexican and Mexican American experience. One case would be the Central American migration from the summer and fall of 2018.

Before we, as a class, can understand why Central American migration has happened and continues to happen in 2018/2019, it is important to consider the historical context of Central America and its complex and contentious relationship with the United States. In the nineteenth century, like most of Latin America, the region was exploited for its natural resources and land. Alvarado et al. provide one of the most thorough history lessons on Central America in the introduction to their anthology, *U.S. Central Americans: Reconstructing Memories, Struggles, and Communities of Resistance* (2017):

> The (mis)fortunes of the Central American countries have been tied to the creation of the Canal Zone and the development of the banana plantation economy and other export crops, such as coffee. Imperialist adventurers and capitalist magnates had designs on Central American territory since the nineteenth century. They dreamed of a railroad system, built a canal, took over the land, and turned it into a plantation, which produced the twentieth-century golden crop—bananas and, later, coffee plantations. This land takeover would later produce the internal social upheaval of the 1980s, subdued to U.S. international interests in confrontation with the socialist bloc.[20]

Alvarado et al. state that while Central America was never authoritatively colonized by the United States, twentieth-century political, economic, and social interventions along with "the legacies of colonialism that promote patriarchal ideologies of whiteness and male heterosexual superiority"[21] have indisputably tied Central America to the United States. In the past thirty years the region has experienced civil wars, with the majority of the Indigenous population targeted and massacred,[22] and the rise of the *mara salvatrucha*, an urban gang with beginnings in Los Angeles, California, in the 1970s and 1980s, which now has a prominent presence in countries like Honduras and El Salvador. While multiple factors have contributed to the reasons for Central American migration, one issue remains constant: How do families fare with past and present US policies on immigration, refugees, and asylum seekers?

In December of 2018, the Pew Research Center published a report about the steady decline of undocumented Mexican immigrants into the United States, with the apprehension of non-Mexicans climbing in the past five years.[23] During the summer and fall of 2018, it was reported that a group of Central American migrants were forming a caravan, originating in Honduras, with the hopes of reaching the US-Mexico border for the opportunity to apply for asylum. US news media outlets began reporting the migration, highlighting the different gender and age groups who joined the caravan. One of its most striking qualities has been the inclusion of families, with children as young as three months old migrating, and even a child reportedly having been born somewhere in Mexico in the midst of the migration.[24] Family migration is also centered in *The Guardians* as its central character Regina witnesses her own family's experiences as migrating border crossers and the consequences that unfold such as the murder of her sister-in-law and the mystery behind her missing brother. Castillo's ability to humanize the anxiety and trauma families experience resonates and connects with the transnational experiences of Central American families, as well. In her seminal study on Central American migration and transnational families, *Sacrificing Families* (2014), scholar Leisy J. Abrego discusses the consequences for transnational families: "Illegality for undocumented transnational parents, therefore, means that they will have to experience family separations that are prolonged over several years."[25] While Donald Trump and his presidential administration used anti-immigrant rhetoric to publicly admonish the Central American migrants and forcibly separate families, UCLA's recent project "Re-imagining Migration" (reimaginingmigration.org), helmed by scholars and educators of immigration and education, works toward creating a more holistic understanding to migration, seen as a human condition. Their database, "Talking and Teaching about the Fall 2018 Migrant Caravan," provides a wealth of scholarship and mixed media to assist educators and students who want to challenge misconceptions surrounding the immigrant community. The database debunks myths as well as the anti-immigrant discourse that has been nationalized by the US government.

Now supplied with a historical framework, government documentation, and the sharing of personal testimonies and experiences, we as a class collective can work toward creating an intervention. One assignment I propose is the use of social media tools to perform "digital interruptions" (see appendix). Using Jill Lane's article, "Digital Zapatistas" (2003), and her definition surrounding electronic disturbances, I focus on one of the three proposed approaches: "*semantic*, which involves engaging and undermining the discursive norms and realities of the system as a whole. . . . Semantic resistance is an effective—and viable—form of contesting power from the margins."[26] As a class we use one of the most popular smartphone applications, Instagram. Using an app like Instagram, with more than half a billion active accounts used daily, and employing the use of hashtags to create digital and visual interventions surrounding immigration issues in the United States, gives the students the power to curate their own content via video stories, memes, photography, and gifs. When students become their own content creators with the guidance of the literature, scholarship, classroom lectures, and historical documents, they can then be part of what Lane identifies as effective forms that challenge systems of oppression even while possibly being a part of a marginalized community. One example that I have is from a former student who decided to deconstruct the pejorative term "wetback" given to anyone who has crossed the Mexico-US border. Its etymology might reference the river dividing the two nations: Rio Grande on the US side and Rio Bravo in Mexico. While the original class Instagram account is no longer available, I blogged about my student's work on my own website,[27] and it got picked up by one of the largest undocumented immigrant media-activist groups, UndocuMedia.[28]

With their nearly half a million followers on Instagram and nearly three hundred thousand members on their official Facebook page, the organization shared the Instagram post on Facebook; it received nearly one thousand shares and comments.[29] By focusing on the term and breaking it down, I interpret my student's written reflection as her exercising her agency; her post, which appeared on the class-shared Instagram account as well as her personal account, demonstrates that her engagement is not limited to a classroom assignment. Her post's content demands a pause, creating an interruption of mindless scrolling, and instead forcing the viewer to take a moment to analyze the image and read her written reflection, hence using one of the most powerful tools of the twenty-first century, the Internet, as a site for digital interruptions, protest, and, I hope, justice.

In the 2008 edition of *The Guardians* published by Random House, Castillo provides a reader's guide at the end of the novel. There is a short essay explaining the genesis of her novel and how the narrative came to be. She states:

> But it's a challenge to go from an oral tradition to the page, and a challenge to stay true to the hearts of those who are powerless to speak for themselves. It

would be presumptuous, even arrogant, to say that I give voice to the otherwise silenced. What would they say if they thought they'd be heard? And would they really trust anyone with the authority to let them say it? Honestly, I don't know the answers to those questions. I can only hope that I can summon the very real voices of the people I grew up with.[30]

This quote forces me to return to my memory, the words Castillo said to me at the festival of books ten years ago. At the time I knew what she meant, but what I was not aware of was how influential her words would be for my teaching philosophy and classroom pedagogy. With a novel like *The Guardians*, it would be a disservice to my students and scholarship to remain silent, idle, and ignore its call. I would like to think that the novel was written with someone like me in mind, a first-generation, working-class Chicana who has crossed many borders and will continue working toward breaking them down.

APPENDIX

Sample Handout

CCS 111

Dr. Sandra Ruiz

Digital Interventions Instagram Project (20 percent)
Ana Castillo's *The Guardians*

As we read Castillo's novel *The Guardians*, I want you to keep in mind how the book, through its written form, performs literary interruptions on preconceived ideas and prejudicial perceptions about immigrants; Chicanas/os; who is considered a citizen, and who isn't, and why; women; undocumented residents; language; Latin America; education, etc.

For this project, you will create a "critical-visual intervention" using Instagram as your platform. Because we live in an era when technology and social media infiltrate our every day, for this assignment, you will create an image/video of what you critically conclude to visually represent an intervention/interruption to any subject matter or topic from the novel that speaks to you, your histories, and/or experiences.

This project will be your active participation in a *digital interruption and visual archive*, documenting how a work of fiction can stir up dialogue and discussions that could lead to action at the local, state, or national level. You may use whatever is at your disposal to take your photograph or video (e.g., phone, computer, camera, tablets, etc.).

Make sure you have read the excerpt of the article "Digital Zapatistas" (Lane) to help you understand how we can use digital technology to create these intervening digital and visual dialogues. If you need guidance or would like to brainstorm some ideas, feel free to speak with me after class or come by and visit me during office hours.

Note: You will also respond/comment on two other images from our course with your own interpretation/comment/questions to earn FULL credit for this assignment. Each photograph and visual analysis must be uploaded and submitted by Sunday at 11:59 p.m.; comments must be made by Monday at 11:59 p.m.

During lecture, I will select Instagram posts submitted to moderate our class discussion.

What to Do:
1. Open an Instagram account.
2. Follow the account @XicFictionaLives and the account will follow you back.

3. Use the following three hashtags when you post your image to your account: #CCS111; #ChicanaLit; #AnaCastillo

4. Upload your chosen photograph/video to your account; make sure that you
tag @XicFictionaLives

5. If your photograph/video is from a specific location, include an address or
street intersections; sometimes Instagram helps with locations.

6. With your photograph provide a 450–500 word critical-visual analysis, see
guiding questions below.

7. Make sure you sign your photograph with your first and last name.

8. Take a look at the Instagram accounts I mentioned in lecture that are
performing different digital interruptions: @vetaranas_and_rucas; @
latinarebels; @undocumedia

Format

Word Count: at least 450 to 500 words

Please make sure to check your spelling, syntax, and grammar before you submit.

Questions to Consider:

1. What is the significance of your photograph/image/video?

2. How/why does the image connect to Castillo's novel *The Guardians*?

3. Is there a direct quote from the novel that speaks to your image? Is there a
specific scene it is inspired from?

4. How does the image relate to issues of immigration, gender, sexuality, and/
or race?

5. What digital intervention/interruption is your image making?

6. How does the image relate to topics, readings, films and/or discussions
from our class?

7. Does the image challenge any preconceived notions regarding this particular ethnic group; does it express a personal experience; does it contain a
scholarly connection?

CHAPTER 19

TEACHING CHICANA LITERATURE IN COMMUNITY COLLEGE

Social, Ethnic, and Linguistic Hybridity in Ana Castillo's *So Far from God*

DANIZETE MARTÍNEZ

Ana Castillo's 1993 novel, *So Far from God*, covers two decades of the life of a Chicana family originally from Tomé, New Mexico—a land grant community in Valencia County, roughly thirty-five miles south of Albuquerque and within walking distance of the University of New Mexico Valencia campus where I taught for more than nine years. The story is told through a series of historical, ethnic, and gender juxtapositions, or rather, collisions. In a quixotic manner, Castillo depicts the life of Sofia/Sofi and her ill-fated daughters, Fe, Esperanza, Caridad, and La Loca, as they navigate Chicana/o confluences of Indigenous and westernized ways of life, language, social, and spiritual beliefs. Additionally, she emphasizes the uniqueness of place and indigeneity characteristic of culture blending in New Mexico that can be important to readers unfamiliar with this history. For these reasons, *So Far from God* is an exceptional and effectual novel to introduce students to regional writing and how it fits within a larger global conversation about ethnic identity from a Chicana perspective.

I should preface that while my previous institution at was a stone's throw away from the novel's setting, I had to do some convincing to get the green light from the administration to teach a section on Chicana/o literature, primarily because they were worried that local students would not want to take a course titled with what they considered to be a pejorative term. This was in part due to the fact that Valencia County, in general, is very conservative, and most of my colleagues were not familiar with the popularity of Chicano/a literary studies in urban colleges. This is a major distinction between teaching the course at a rural community college versus at a research institution. Knowing that history courses at my campus focused on local customs were often well attended, I pitched my course under a similar umbrella of regionalism in the hopes that our students would sign up for it.

I initially approach teaching the novel from a regionalist perspective by focusing on the speech, expressions, and customs idiosyncratic to the area mainly to draw in my community college students who are inclined to take more interest in a text if they can connect with the characters and sense of place. Eventually, I introduce a transnational component in the classroom, since many issues confronted by the characters in the novel are indeed based on long-standing national and transnational discussions that center race, class, and gender in a global context that expands the discussion of Chicanx identity more broadly. This sequence works quite well since my students can first identify with the characters in the text, and then make more global connections between traditions and customs in their community and those beyond state and national boundaries.

This method is on the increase in the rising field of Chicanx and Latinx critical studies. As Michelle Hall Kells states: "Given the prevailing theories in cultural studies, linguistics, rhetoric and composition, shifting notions of transcultural citizenship and identity among Latino/as provide critical exigencies for reshaping pedagogical practices, educational systems, and public policies in the 21st century. This entry considers the underlying support, both theoretical and empirical, for pedagogies in K–16 education promoting critical literacy, linguistic pluralism, and transcultural rhetorical practices for Latino/a students."[1] Arguably, our goal as educators is to make a point to stress the interconnectivity between our students and the world at large. This connection is a central theme in Castillo's *So Far from God*. At some point Sofi and each of her daughters literally or figuratively cross borders and boundaries because of their vocations, as is the case with Esperanza who was an international journalist, and Fe whose work at Acme International exposes her to toxic chemicals. Because of La Loca and Caridad's heightened sensitivities, La Loca is able to commune with the dead, and Caridad, through a spiritual awakening, is motivated to jump off a mesa with her lover Esmeralda in order to commune with their Native ancestors. And Sofi, through her political convictions at the end of the novel, is able to help organize her community based on national and international models of social and economic change.

To establish context for the novel, I give an overview of Chicana/o writing to help students understand the emergence of Chicana/o literature and *So Far from God's* position in this cultural production. Early forms of Chicana/o literature include autobiographies, memoirs, and testimonials of landowners, as well as *corridos*: popular narrative songs and poetry derived from Mexican ballads. Yet in the heyday of the 1960s civil rights movement, Chicano literature underwent critical changes that included a

flowering of letters, narratives, novels, short stories, and poetry committed to representing the social consciousness of the Chicana/o. The Chicano
movement of the 1960s and 1970s encompassed a broad cross-section of issues—from restoration of land grants, to farmworkers' rights, to enhanced
education, to voting and political rights, as well as emerging awareness of
collective history. Socially, the movement addressed what it perceived to be
negative ethnic stereotypes of Mexicans in mass media and the American
consciousness. A major element of the movement was the burgeoning of
Chicano art fueled by heightened political activism and energized cultural
pride. Chicano visual art, sculpture, music, literature, dance, theater, and
other forms of expression flourished, as well.

The Chicano art movement of the 1960s opened a gate for novels, poetry, short stories, essays, and plays to flow from the pens of contemporary
Chicana/o writers. Chicano, Mexican American, and Hispanic cultural
centers, theaters, film festivals, museums, galleries, and numerous other
arts and cultural organizations have also grown in number and impact
since this time. The movement also provided an opportunity for Chicanas who felt oppressed by Chicanos and masculinist ideologies embedded
within the movement to raise their voices; the 1980s saw a flood of Chicanx
writers including Gloria Anzaldúa, Cherríe Moraga, and Richard Rodriguez producing feminist and queer texts. The popularity and success of this
new pluralistic Chicana writing continued into the 1990s with the work of
authors such as Sandra Cisneros, Denise Chávez, and Ana Castillo.

With this groundwork laid, I teach *So Far from God* as a Chicana/femi-
nist text that demonstrates the beauty of New Mexico, the traditions of the
people, and the value of regional writing, while also challenging the notion
of a static cultural identity. The novel, rich in folklore, also provides a great
opportunity to discuss myth and legend in contemporary Chicana writing.
In Chicana literary production, the presence of Mexican folklore demonstrates a symbolic re-membering, resurrection, and return to what Américo
Paredes identifies as the "Folk Base of Chicano Literature."[2] This return
signals an ideological rebirth of Chicana/o cultural identity that is neither
androcentric nor nostalgic for "old Mexico"; instead, it marks a resurgence
that foregrounds the potential for cultural empowerment in Chicana discourse.[3] Paredes attributes the molding and inciting of folk traditions in
the United States to colonization, the westward movement, slavery, immigration, regionalism, the rhetoric of democracy, and the influence of the
mass media.[4] When looking specifically at Mexican folklore, we need to
account for the various groups of the Spanish, creole, mestizo, and Indian
viewpoints that were engaged in the process of storytelling and consider
how their experiences of social contact among themselves and to each other
further influenced their narrative cultural production.

Drawing on folkloric elements, Chicana literary cultural production is simultaneously a repository for past and future traditions: it takes elements from the past in the form of myth and legend, and ensures their sustainability by retelling them to a new generation of Chicanas/os. This new audience, as a result of language or geographical boundaries, would not previously have had access to these tales, which became particularly resonant after the Chicano movement when Chicanas/as turned to Aztec and Mayan myths and legends for inspiration. Inspiration for the production of a distinct Chicana/o folklore also came out of the cultural conflicts that took place during the Spanish colonization of Mexico in the late 1500s and early 1600s, out of the cultural conflicts between the United States and Mexico between 1821 and 1848 when Anglos were beginning to settle in Texas, during the Mexican-American War (1846–1848),[5] and when the first postwar generation of Mexicans after the Mexican-American War were becoming US citizens (1848–1910).[6]

This symbolic re-membering emerges as a critical tool for understanding Chicana notions of identity, politics, aesthetics, and the conflicted dynamics of their culture. However, contemporary Chicana writers are not reiterating the damaging mythology that reinforces a fragmented female subjectivity; instead, they are revising Chicana/o mythology to depict female figures as a whole, and thus rewriting the history of Chicana/o culture. Castillo's novel is an enactment of this shift in masculinist ideology. In *The Decolonial Imaginary*, Emma Pérez states: "I am, in a sense, exposing how historians have participated in a politics of historical writing in which erasure—the erasure of race, gender, sexualities, and especially differences—was not intentional, but rather a symptom of the type of narrative emplotment unconsciously chosen by the historians."[7] Pérez asserts lesbians have since created their own historical identity and identity politics through their own writing. This concept is key when I am teaching *So Far from God* in the classroom; Castillo inverts the notion of patriarchy through her projections of strong and vulnerable women willing to blur the boundaries between their traditional upbringing in a provincial community and to propel themselves out into the larger world either physically or psychically. This is the intersection where regionalism and transnationalism merge, and the text resonates with my students as they see themselves in the plights of Castillo's characters, in these women's curiosity about the world, as well as in their adventures. To further students' abilities to connect their experiences to those articulated in *So Far from God*, I assign a "Learning and Community Narrative" assignment (see appendix 1) in which they are asked to draw from one of the characters' formative experiences in the novel to share a meaningful experience in their personal history that relates to learning and/or community. This assignment allows them not only to reflect on their own personal growth, but also to reflect critically on how Castillo employs different narrative strategies, such as the use of myth, to describe the experiences of the characters in the novel as processes of growth and community-centered identity.

Female writers' nontraditional representation of ancient and colonial myth reformulates and ultimately queers existing paradigms at work in both Chicana/o and Anglo cultures. In "From Chingada to Chingona: La Malinche Redefined, Or, A Long Line of Hermanas," Rita Cano Alcalá maintains that the re-evaluation of female mythological figures "constitutes a symbolic reclaiming of a feminine indigenous voice, one that has been silenced and discredited because of its threat to institutionalized patriarchy, beginning with the ideological state apparatus of the family and ending in the pages of its national myths and histories."[8] This same rhetorical impulse is enacted in the rewriting of pre-Columbian and post-conquest myth and legend by contemporary Chicanas. Gloria Anzaldúa argues that myth and fiction create reality, and have historically been used against women to control, regulate, and manipulate them; thus, rewriting mythology is a way of responding to oppressing paradigms and correcting the historical malaise of women perpetuated through a negative mythology.[9] While this rewriting is subversive and disruptive, its inherent power leads to communal healing within both the Chicana community and within the larger Chicana/o body politic. Again, this reinvention is enacted through Sofi and her activism. While these divisions represent a fragmentation and a division in the community, they foreshadow a rupture with male-centered, heteronormative assumptions about Chicana/o identity. Thus, through revisionist myth-making, Chicana writers are picking up the pieces and "re-membering" the Chicana/o body.

In class, I use an "Artifact Reflection" assignment (see appendix 2) in which students are instructed to locate an artifact in *So Far from God*, such as a myth like that of La Malogra or another element of Chicana folklore, and describe how the artifact links a specific character to their community. The assignment allows students to further explore the historical depth of the narrative and to consider how Chicana writers like Castillo use folklore to rewrite the "fate" of their female protagonists. The Spanish colonial period is the most historically significant period in the establishment of Chicana folklore, since it is during this time that the myths and legends of La Malinche (1519), the much maligned interpreter, advisor, lover, and intermediary for Hernán Cortés; the Virgin of Guadalupe (1531), the Mexican iteration of Mother Mary; and La Llorona emerged as models of *meztizaje-ness* born out of the dominant European and Indigenous cultural strands. In *So Far from God*, Castillo narrates how myths from this colonial period, specifically La Llorona and La Malogra, are perpetuated in Hispanic New

Mexican culture. La Llorona, the Wailing or Weeping Woman, is a confluence of European and Indigenous cultural influences. Legend has it that La Llorona was a mestiza woman who was jilted by her Spanish lover, and in an act of revenge, drowned their children. As a result of God's punishment, she forever roams the earth's waterways looking for her children while wailing in the night. A Native American version relates her to the Aztec goddess Cihuacótl who steals babies from their cribs and leaves behind an obsidian knife; another version dates back to preconquest and has her appearing before men, covered with chalk and wailing, while wearing obsidian earplugs. Mexican Americans often use the folk legend to socialize their children: they better not misbehave or La Llorona will get them.

In *So Far from God*, La Llorona and other examples of traditional Mexican American mythology figure prominently in the narrative and are rewritten to challenge narrow androcentric understandings of Chicana/o discourse. Castillo's La Llorona account is rewritten to portray a strong female identity, and critically explores the complexities of class, sexuality, and spiritualism within a hybrid existence. Similar to the original story, Castillo's La Llorona functions as a cautionary tale; yet, La Llorona specifically functions as an agent of change in the lives of Sofi's daughters Fe and La Loca. Castillo employs the myth of La Llorona to not only pay homage to Mexican American culture, but also to addresses modern concerns about environmental racism and other areas of socioeconomic oppression that directly impact the Chicana characters. For example, for Fe, La Llorona's resistance is manifested over environmental concerns, while for La Loca, her resistance materializes in the rejection of a westernized logocentrism (both discussed below). Castillo draws on myth to underscore the psychic and physical consequences that can result from internalizing oppressive dominant ideologies (as is the case with Fe), and from challenging them (as La Loca demonstrates). *So Far from God* nods to a variety of feminisms including the reclamation of the La Llorona figure, through which Castillo challenges the cultural hegemony of an Anglo American dominant culture.

Additionally, Castillo's La Llorona departs from these negative associations and appears as a sympathetic presence, one that is able to relate to the simple ways of Sofi's youngest, beatific, and idiotic daughter, La Loca. La Loca's constant communication with La Llorona enables her to predict other people's deaths. In the chapter partially titled "Wherein Sofia Discovers La Loca's Playmate by the Acequia Has an Uncanny Resemblance to the Legendary Llorona . . . ," La Llorona gives La Loca the news of her oldest sister's death: "Who better but La Llorona could the spirit of Esperanza have found, come to think of it, if not a woman who had been given a bad rap by every generation of her people since the beginning of time and yet, to Esperanza's spirit-mind, La Llorona in the beginning (before men got in the way of it all) may have been nothing short of a loving mother goddess."[10] Referred to by the narrator as "the Chicana international astral-traveler," La Llorona is reinvented and reclaimed as a feminist force. As a phenomenon and a mestiza, La Llorona is represented in the novel as a hybridized figure dealing with four distinct spheres: reality and fantasy, and a European and Indigenous status. She is also a well-known regional figure who, like La Loca, transcends borders physically, culturally, spiritually, and geographically. Seen through the eyes of La Loca who does not privilege reality over phenomena, La Llorona's presence posits one of the many marvelous sequences of events surrounding La Loca's life, which many critics have characterized as a form of magical realism. Unlike the traditional Western version of realism, which is narratively singular, objective, and thus intended to be universally ideological and hegemonic, the eccentricity of magical realism creates space for interactions of diversity. Lois Parkinson Zamora and Wendy B. Faris argue that "in magical realist texts, ontological disruption serves the purpose of political and cultural disruption: magic is often given as a cultural corrective, requiring readers to scrutinize accepted realistic conventions of causality, materiality, motivation."[11]

By having narratives that are drawn from non-Western cultures that value mystery, empathy, and tradition over empiricism, technology, and innovation, magical realist texts call attention to cultural and political contrasts. In this context, magical realism is a mode suited to exploring and transgressing ontological, political, and geographical boundaries by displacing mind/body, spirit/matter, life/death, real/imaginary, self/other, and male/female normative oppositions. This suspension of traditional logic is inherent to the grotesque since it also displaces, confuses, interpenetrates, and distorts the different spheres of the "magic" world with the "real" world through hyperbolic narrative. The subversive power in Castillo's rewrite of La Llorona shifts power from the dominant paradigm to an alternative outlook, thus redefining conceptions of reality from a marginal perspective and legitimizing the Chicana point of view.

Loca's older sister, Fe, similarly has a twofold connection to La Llorona; it lies in the nickname, *la gritona*, given to her by her family after she was deserted by her fiancé and cried "one continuous scream" for weeks, and also in the parallels between her personal life and the traditional legend surrounding La Llorona. In this regard, Castillo is drawing on the version of La Llorona that serves as a cautionary tale against crossing boundaries but rewrites the story so that instead of killing her children, Fe dies childless as a result of being exposed to poisonous chemicals produced by a factory that exploits its poor female laborers. Instead of having Fe bear the responsibility of killing her children and aligning her with a misogynistic interpretation of La Llorona, Castillo shifts the responsibility to the patriarchal institution of the military arms industry that leaves Fe sterile and inverts the tale of La Llorona into a critique of the institutions responsible for the environmental crises affecting countless regions that are populated by poor minorities.

Barbara Cook points out Castillo's criticism of dominant ideology when Fe, dying of cancer, is questioned by the FBI about the plant's illegal use of chemicals rather than her terminal illness that resulted from exposure to the chemicals: "In Castillo's revision of the story of female cultural history, female strength appears and creates other opportunities and possibilities at the same time she is calling attention to environmental issues. The story embodies the weeping so it becomes a voice that calls attention to both loss and the possibilities of resistance."[12] While Fe dies as a consequence of internalizing an oppressive construction of the American dream, at the end she is able to draw the strength to protest the toxic environmental state that is a ramification of the ideology behind that dream. In this sense, Castillo is channeling a nationalistic political subtext for the local Chicana/o community to illustrate a contemporary need to collectively protest violence directed at ethnic laborers, but instead of relying on a masculinist-based ethos of the 1960s and 1970s, she transposes the mythology to be inclusive of the female perspective. Fe's act of resistance parallels Castillo's rhetorical impulse to rewrite, or heal, the ways in which Chicanas/os and other minorities interact with dominant systems of power.

In an interview Castillo states: "I cannot say I am a citizen of the world as Virginia Woolf, speaking as an Anglo woman born to economic means, declared herself; nor can I make the same claim to US citizenship as Adrienne Rich does despite her universal feel for humanity. As a mestiza born to the lower strata, I am treated at best, as a second-class citizen, at worst as a nonentity."[13] We see this treatment, this dismissal, manifested in the attack on Sofia's most beautiful daughter, Caridad. Returning home "as mangled as a stray cat,"[14] Caridad's extensive damages include bite, burn, and stab wounds; yet, despite her massive bleeding and mangled body, the sheriff's department refuses to investigate her case and fails to convict anyone. After being prodded, tubed, and stapled together by the hospital, Caridad is sent home looking like a "nightmare incarnated."[15]

It is only after Caridad is healing and preparing to be a *curandera* (a traditional folk healer) with Doña Felicia that Caridad first speaks of the attack; this leads Doña Felicia to identify the violator as La Malogra. According to New Mexican folklore, the Malora, also pronounced *malogra*, or "the evil one," wanders about during night, namely at crossroads, and terrorizes women who wander alone. The Malogra is said to usually don a large lock of wool or the whole fleece of a sheep and rarely takes on a human form. According to folklorist Aurelio M. Espinosa, "It is generally believed that a person who sees *la malora*, like one who sees a ghost (*un difunto*), forever remains senseless. When asked for detailed information about this myth, the New Mexicans give the general reply, '*es cosa mala*' it is an evil thing."[16] In *So Far from God*, Caridad's Malogra is described as: "[Something] made of sharp metal and splintered wood. Of limestone, gold, and brittle parchment. It held the weight of a continent and was indelible as ink, centuries old and yet as strong as a young wolf. It had no shape and was darker than the night, and mostly, as Caridad, would never, ever forget, it was pure force."[17] With its amorphous shape, its tools and mined minerals, and its brittle parchment of old maps, La Malogra embodies colonial impact, imperialistic violence, and the effects of war resulting in redistribution of property that speaks to Tomé's history as a land grant. At the same time, the Malogra proves to be a pivotal force that razes boundaries and necessitates change. Caridad's encounter with La Malogra does affect change: she stops drinking and engaging in pernicious relationships and becomes interested in *curanderismo*—a form of folk healing that includes various techniques such as prayer, herbal medicine, healing rituals, spiritualism, massage, and psychic healing—certainly a "senseless" practice in the eyes of traditional Western biomedicine, but the only effective treatment for Caridad's broken body and broken heart. Her so-called senselessness is what leads to her physical and spiritual healing. Instead of simply re-telling this tale, Castillo inverts La Malogra's original interpretation as an oppressive force against women into a way of re-evaluating problematic constructs that still need to be addressed in Chicana/o communities.

For Caridad, and like all of her sisters, her life is cut short in an unusual way; she plunges off a cliff with her unrequited love, Esmeralda, but their remains are never found: "There were no morbid remains of splintered bodies tossed to the ground, down, down, like bad pottery or glass or old bread. There weren't even whole bodies lying peaceful. There was nothing."[18] Instead of suicide, Caridad's death is a mythical re-enactment and return home to her Indigenous roots. Ralph E. Rodriguez calls it a tender connection to the earth and a form of rebirth through which "they have returned to what the Acoma myth of creation refers to as the earth's womb."[19] In the Acoma origin myth, the spirit Tsichtinako instructs the two sisters Nautsiti and Iatiku to give life to the earth. Yet, before they are able to proceed, they need to grow underground. Caridad and Esmeralda respond to Tsichtinako's call and fall back into the earth in a symbolic return home: "*Tsichtinako was calling!* . . . The Acoma people heard it and knew it was the voice of the Invisible One who had nourished the first two humans, who were also both female, although no one had heard it in a long time and some had never heard it before. But all still knew who It was."[20] Just as the myth of Montezuma suggests, the Acoma creation story has its origins beneath the earth and in the grotesque. Caridad's death becomes an expression of what

Rodriguez calls "a deep feeling of spirituality" that she has been seeking since her encounter with La Malogra.[21] While Castillo relies on traditional folklore to narrate Caridad's attack and suicide, her feminist rewriting of these events sublimates a feminine and nonlinear worldview to invoke a holistic interpretation of Chicana/o mythology.

Castillo's treatment of Caridad, as well as Moraga's, Anzaldúa's, and Cisneros's revisionist mythmaking, show how Chicanas can counter issues of poverty, environmental racism, and gendered violence being perpetuated by oppressive dominant cultures and institutions. By rewriting Chicana/o mythology from a feminist perspective, Chicana writers demonstrate how the grotesque is a disruptive, subversive, and powerful agent for transformation and collective healing. Most importantly, their contributions to Chicana/o cultural production demonstrate the interdependency between self-writing and self-formation. In this symbolic act of giving birth to one's self all over again, these writers "re-member" the dismembered history of Chicana identities.

Pedagogically, Castillo's *So Far from God* is not only useful in introducing students to regional writing; it also helps us teach the importance of myth in cultural identity and the value of healthy opposition inherent in larger transnational Chicanx discussions. While conventional writing is dominated by values that are patriarchal, rationalistic, logocentric, and linear, *So Far from God*, especially through folkloric representations, breaks out of these conceptual molds and provides creative alternatives for thinking about cultural identity. By re-membering mythology and legend into contemporary literature, Castillo explores and transgresses ontological, political, and gendered boundaries by displacing life/death, self/other, and male/female normative oppositions. Her novel demonstrates that old myths, stories, and legends are indeed culturally active forces in our present lives, and ultimately reminds us of the power of mystery intrinsic in the Southwest, while at the same time demonstrating how a regional text has the theoretical capacity to connect to larger cultural, political, and transnational concerns.

APPENDIX 1

So Far from God Assignment 1: Artifact Reflection

Purpose

Students will identify an artifact in *So Far from God* that is central to one of the character's identity by exploring how the object connects the character to their values and to their community, and then reflect on their own meaningful object and how it connects them to their own culture and community.

Overview of Your Task

Anchoring Question: "How does our relationship to objects express our cultural experiences?"

"Artifact Resource Page." Campus at Plymouth State University, 2020. https://campus.plymouth.edu/nwpnh/resources-for-fellows/artifact-resource-page/.

1. Describe the artifact (an item of your choice) objectively so that someone who could not see it would get a good visual picture of it. Your aim is to be very objective and precise in your description.
2. Tell a story about the artifact by reflecting on these critical stances. These questions can lead to thinking about artifacts in terms of their place in the global economy. They can help students to consider artifacts critically.
   a. Value—reconsidering types of value—what is the value of this object? What kinds of value could we look at?
   b. Timescale—historical and personal—where does this object fit into the character's cultural history?
   c. Space—what spaces has it occupied? Where has it traveled?
   d. Production—who made it or found it and under what conditions?
   e. Relations to institutions of power—how does this object relate to global or local institutions of power? Who controls the artifact and its attendant communities?
3. Answer questions 1 and 2 about one of your own meaningful artifacts.

APPENDIX 2

So Far from God Assignment 2: Learning and Community Narrative

Purpose

Drawing from one of the character's formative experiences in the novel, share with your readers a meaningful experience in your personal history that relates to learning and/or community.

Overview of Your Task

Anchoring Question: "How have my lived experiences shaped who I am today?"

1. This assignment asks you reflect on an episode in Castillo's novel that depicts one of the character's personal growth or connection to their community in one or two paragraphs, describing how the example impacted their worldview.

2. Then, continue to write a narrative (i.e., tell a story) that captures a meaningful experience about a learning process, experience, or involvement within a community that has influenced who you are today.

Your essay should incorporate both *narrative strategies* (sequencing, vivid description, dialogue, etc.) and *analysis* (in other words, you should closely "read" and critically reflect on the experience to help your readers understand the narrative's significance). To make your essay manageable, you should focus on one key "event" or experience rather than trying to share your life story—the narrower your topic, the more likely you are to be successful. Once you choose an experience to describe, unpack it, dig deeper, think about it critically—tell your readers how *you* interpret its broader significance.

CHAPTER 20

POR TODOS LADOS

Reading and Teaching as Feminist Xicanisma Practice

NORMA E. CANTÚ

Ana Castillo, poet, playwright, memoirist, and fiction writer, offers teachers an array of topics and themes that serve as a springboard for multiple lessons. In any number of disciplines—literature, of course, sociology, ethnic studies, migration studies—we find work unpacking the complex theories of identity and of literatures. We can trace her influence over a number of disciplines and across these often artificial boundaries. In her oeuvre, including her play *Psst . . . I Have Something to Tell You, Mi Amor* and her fiction—*The Mixquiahuala Letters, Sapogonia, So Far from God, The Guardians, Give It to Me, Loverboys,* and *Peel My Love like an Onion*—and her poetry collections *Women Are Not Roses* and *My Father Was a Toltec,* as well as her nonfiction, *Massacre of the Dreamers* and the foreword to the anthology *Chicana Motherwork,* we find the essence of twentieth- and twenty-first-century life for a Brown woman living in the United States. One could say that Castillo provides a panoramic view of a world where Chicana womanhood is shaped by the social realities of life in the United States in the late twentieth and early twenty-first centuries. Revealing that what we pursue in our feminist work is at once affirming on an individual and collective level as well as an indictment of what this world means for Brown women and often for women in general, Castillo takes the pulse of our discomfort, and of our rage—a rage that is a reaction to the attacks that come *por todos lados,* from all sides. Her work, though, is a way to deflect these attacks.

As a teacher of literature, I have taught Castillo's texts over the years and have found them to be rich and fertile ground for discussions about ideas, politics, religion, sexuality, and the material condition of the Chicanx population in particular. Moreover, I have found her work to be all that good literature should be, stimulating and informative as well as entertaining. As do the authors of several of the essays I am responding to, I usually begin lessons on Chicana feminism with Gloria Anzaldúa and then proceed to Castillo's *Massacre of the Dreamers* and to the literary analysis of the texts. My pedagogical inclinations lead me to incorporate the notion of

Xicanisma, and I guide my students' lived experiences as they dismantle the racist structures that they live in and which have formed their educational experiences. Through entering *The Guardians*'s protagonist Regina's world, we understand the educational frames that we have been through as she and Miguel, a history teacher, discuss their position within the educational system. In *So Far from God*, and through Sofia's New Mexican landscape, we see the consequences of life in a capitalist racist society, of the neoliberal assault on our traditional cultures. I want my students to understand the complexities of life on the borderlands, of life in the United States, for Brown women. Similarly, reading *Massacre of the Dreamers* proves useful as we prepare to enter the fictional worlds Castillo constructs; we accept the tools that Xicana feminist thought gives us to push the boundaries of our complacency. My aim is to equip students with the tools necessary to critically engage with the world and to do as Anzaldua urged, "work that matters," because as she wrote, "vale la pena, it is worth the pain."[1] Similarly, our seemingly innocuous forays into Castillo's poetry and plays are deeply political and spiritual as we approach these texts with those tools.

I began this essay in the midst of one of the strongest attacks against immigrants; due to the current political climate even more insidious violations of human rights persist in our country. It was with all this in mind that I agreed to respond to four of the essays in this much anticipated anthology on Castillo's work. Because of my interest in and familiarity with Castillo's work, I was eager to read and engage the work of these four scholars. I was not disappointed. Indeed, these teachers are preparing critical readers who will engage with the issues Castillo presents, that we are all confronted with in today's world. As a folklorist, I applaud Castillo's use of traditional culture and her revision of cultural practices. They may be the mainstay of our identity, that which remains to ground us during the onslaught against our very existence. Through teaching Castillo, then, we can achieve permanence; we will survive, endure.

The authors of the four essays I am responding to here take vastly different approaches to Ana Castillo's work; yet all similarly weave their first-person narratives—sometimes almost stream of consciousness—with their teaching strategies. Approaching Castillo's texts—either a single one or a number of them—through a lens that illuminates its potential for teaching a myriad of topics, the authors share their goals and aspirations for their students, or in Gabriela Spears-Rico's case, for her daughter, Reina. In this braided essay, I reflect on the individual essays and render a response that is at once seeking to elucidate some of the issues these essays raise and also point to further exploration or discussion of the works. In my usual style of using *testimonio*, perhaps poetry, and critical analysis, I respond in writing to these four essays.

Spears-Rico's exploration of the way Indigenous women mother, informed by Castillo's own narratives of mothering, overlays a patina of normalcy, and yet it is a radical resistance she promotes and the most salient message is that parenting under certain circumstances becomes layered and complicated. The author alludes to very real threats and macroaggressions. She asks: How do you explain racism to children? How do I prepare my child for "life among the whites," as Jennine Capó Crucet might put it? Moreover Spears-Rico's first-person narrative draws from personal encounters in Minnesota with that white midwestern world I know so well from living in Nebraska and Missouri: the part of the country where Brown people—Indigenous and mestizo—are constantly erased and subsumed at best and killed at worst.

In Laredo, Texas, my hometown, I recently saw a billboard for bus service to Kansas City, not an unusual advertisement. But, it was in Spanish and it was not for Greyhound but for one of the alternative bus lines (Tornado, El Conjeo, etc.) that have sprung up in the past twenty years and that cater almost exclusively to a segment of a traveling public that is neglected or ignored by the mainstream Greyhound bus lines, if not overtly, then covertly with all-English signage and such. What does this have to do with the essay? Well, for one, it signals the shifting demographics, a population that is increasingly Brown, increasingly working poor, and whom we must account for. They will be our students in a few years, if they are not already sitting in our classrooms ready to learn and acquire tools to dismantle the master's house.[2] Similarly, while discussing public transportation in Laredo, I recently found out that the line with the most riders is the one that goes to the north, specifically that one that serves the more affluent areas of town; the bus system provides public transportation for the Indigenous and mestiza women domestic workers who go to work in the richest subdivisions of our communities whether in Laredo or San Antonio. Gabriela Spears-Rico's chapter "Replanting You as *Winyan, Uarhiti, Kwe*: Transnational Indigena Mothering from Michoacán to Mini Sota Makoce" came to mind as I went on and imagined the Mexicana and Indigenous people who would be boarding that bus headed to Kansas City, heading into a world that would not welcome them, or boarding the city bus to go work in the affluent family home in an equally inhospitable world.

Spears-Rico's chapter is a personal and testimonio-based paper that weaves Spears-Rico's own story "as a Pirinda and P'urhepecha transnational mother" in Minnesota and the ferreting out of lessons or guidance from Castillo's writings, specifically from the nonfiction work: the foreword to *The Chicana Motherwork Anthology*, *Black Dove*, and *Massacre of the Dreamers*. While the purpose of this chapter is not to provide a teaching methodology or approaches to teaching Castillo, I find that it does inform the application of the ideas posited by Castillo in her work to the ways women of color exist and survive in academia and in the greater social reality of the United States, especially in the Midwest. Drawing from the writings of American Indian scholars and from performance theory, Spears-Rico arrives at a discussion of both mothering and of violence and aggression, themes that she also tackles in her teaching of Indigenous feminisms. I enjoyed the way that Spears-Rico discusses these topics within the framework of Castillo's texts, particularly *Massacre of the Dreamers*. Moreover, as a backdrop to all her discussions her daughter Reina appears with all the potential and concern her presence elucidates.

I was moved by her testimonio and the fact that she came to consciousness through MEChA in high school. Finding solace in Castillo's words even then, she learns lessons that she still holds onto as she is now the mother of an Indigenous child, and no longer in the familiar space of Michoacán but in Minnesota. She clarifies that "Despite the question over whether Xicanisma has anything of value to offer Indigenous women by both Latina/o and non-Latina/o literary critics, connecting Xicanisma to my Pirinda/P'urepecha mothering and pedagogical practices has been useful to me."[3] She elaborates and clarifies that her:

> Intent is not to conflate Xicanisma or other branches of Chicana feminism with traditions of Indigenous feminism . . . but rather to place both models in conversation with each other and to argue that both traditions may have useful and valuable tools for Latin American Indigenous women migrants facing not only violence from patriarchal oppression but also systemic racism and everyday white discrimination in the United States.[4]

These are powerful goals, and I must say that I am heartened by her articulation of ways that such tools can be useful. Her heartwarming narrative illustrates how her daughter, Reina, is included in both the Ojibwe and Pirinda/P'urepecha groups through ritual and practice; therefore, Spears-Rico, in my view, answers her own questions about how to mother, how to realize and integrate an Indigenous feminist practice: through bold action. She says: "We are teaching Reina that decolonization is more than ideological; it is daily practice in the spaces we inhabit." This notion of working "where we are" is rooted in "the decolonial indigenist politics that have been central to defining contemporary P'urepechecidad." She then proceeds to explain how she practices a liberatory pedagogy. She recounts her participation in a June 20, 2018, protest against the practice of child separation along the border where she and her family were photographed with a delegation of Indigenous people. I finished reading the chapter with a renewed sense of hope. While Spears-Rico is in a classroom in Minnesota teaching through her own actions, and as she teaches her daughter the Indigenous ways of all her people, there is hope. She is continuing to do what so many Chicanas like Ana Castillo and Inés Hernández Avila have done. With a liberatory pedagogy and with Castillo's writings, she is realizing our dream for our university spaces to be sites of *conocimiento*.

My reaction to Leigh Johnson's essay is also one of hope, for the chapter details the teaching of a course on a single author—in this case Castillo—using a transnational feminist theory. She too begins class with readings from Chicana feminist thought including Anzaldúa, Alarcón, and others before delving into Castillo's varied texts. Johnson's most profound contribution through this chapter is the specifics of how she introduces students to the theoretical texts and then proceeds to offer a teaching schedule that contains detailed explanations of her presentation of the material to her students. Johnson writes that the chapter will: "Offer ways to concretely conceptualize the theoretical modes, discussion prompts and class activities, and assignments that will create a classroom space revealing how Castillo's work connects cultural, political and transnational concerns to each other."[5]

The chapter presents two main sections—the first develops a course for a single-author semester-long class focusing on "teaching Castillo's Chicana feminist theory and praxis,"[6] and the second a smaller unit plan for teaching "Castillo's memoir from a transnational social justice framework"[7] designed as a stand-alone unit within the overall syllabus of a class on Chicana writers. Overall, Johnson achieves the goal and lays out how these two class plans come about and includes specific assignments in the appendix. It is apparent that the courses work and Johnson presents evidence by noting that students develop multilayered assignments that yield conference presentations for graduate students and a publication for one of the undergraduate students. Students taking the course include non-English majors who then become familiar with Castillo and perform close readings of the texts and create their own work grounded on Castillo's theories of Xicanisma.

In my view, the approaches Johnson describes fit the texts beautifully as Castillo's novels, poetry, plays, and essays form the corpus of a serious engagement with Chicana literature as a transfronteriza literary practice. Like Sandra Ruiz, whose chapter also focuses on the international perspective, Johnson inserts the transnational nature of the plots and underscores the ways Castillo sets narratives that exist on borders but that transcend borders.

Because the classes are intense and delve deeply into a number of texts, Johnson is able to present the pedagogical framing and the various approaches to the different genres to students. Moreover, the analysis also becomes unique. For example, the way the class reads *The Mixquiahuala Letters* illustrates the engagement at the level of narratology and how Castillo's narrative play is integral to the plot and the development of character. I found the pairing of graduate and undergraduate students particularly significant as the intergenerational "audience" is more real; further, the writing mentorship appears to function on various levels. The graduate students do not write in a vacuum; they have a real audience in the workshop part of the class. Also impressive was the multilayered feedback or layered revision process as students had ample time to revise and refine their writing and thinking. Similarly, in the second section I found the discussion rich and firmly grounded in similar pedagogical issues. Overall, this chapter explores the teaching of Castillo's oeuvre and because it is based on the author's own teaching strategies, a wonderful tool for teachers who may not have taught Castillo or who may want to hone their assignments and teaching strategies.

Sandra Ruiz's "Never *Stay* Silent: A Pedagogical Approach to Teaching *The Guardians*" surprised me with its matter-of-fact style, and Ruiz's focus on only one of Castillo's texts, *The Guardians*. While presenting an approach to teaching this novel, Ruiz is also engaged in a discussion of the relevance of such a text to current realities. As already mentioned, Ruiz highlights the way the novel is a transfronteriza narrative. Ruiz deftly includes a section on how Castillo weaves in the transnational nature of Chicanx realities through a discussion of Miguel's father and his involvement with the School of the Americas where Central American soldiers are trained. She further notes how Castillo includes a discussion on the origins of the Border Patrol, as told through Miguel's grandfather, Abuelito Milton. In her class, Ruiz includes historical information on Central America and prepares students for an "intervention" that follows the preparation. She discusses one successful strategy, the use of digital interruptions through the use of social media tools. She presents one example of such an activity to demonstrate the success of this strategy. It was so successful that Undocu-Media picked it up from her blog about the student's work. The student "decided to deconstruct the pejorative term 'wetback' given to anyone who has crossed the Mexico-US border."[8] Using a class site on Instagram, students shared their posts. The students then, "part of what Lane identifies as effective forms that challenge systems of oppression even while possibly being a part of a marginalized community,"[9] impact and engage in social media activism. Solidly framed using a culturally relevant pedagogy, the students in Ruiz's class, through their discussion of *The Guardians*, gain an understanding of the historical backdrop and the social justice issues that surface in the apparently simple plot that nevertheless gathers multiple historical events that have impacted the Chicano community such as origins of the Border Patrol in 1924. Also the chapter discusses how Ruiz contextualizes the current influx of Central American migrants. A discussion of why they have been dispossessed and deterritorialized to such a degree that they seek to escape to the north, to the United States, leads to a discussion of how the novel weaves together the various factors of a weakened social fabric due to the United States's interventions in Central America and its twentieth-century neoliberal policies.

I found Danizete Martínez's "Teaching Chicana Literature in Community College: Social, Ethnic, and Linguistic Hybridity in Ana Castillo's *So Far from God*" to be revealing of how transformative the novel can be for students. As do the other authors, Martínez speaks from a first-person perspective of how she approaches Castillo's work, specifically *So Far from God*, and tells how at one time she taught at an institution that "was a stone's throw away from the novel's setting,"[10] but she encountered resistance from the administration "worried that local students from the community would not want to take a course titled with what they considered to be a pejorative term."[11] She doesn't say what the term is, but we can glean that the word is "Chicano." Her solution was to pitch the course as "regional" and then initially to teach "the novel from a regionalist perspective by focusing on the speech, expressions, and customs idiosyncratic to the area."[12] The strategy of beginning with a regional focus and then guiding the discussion and analysis to a national and transnational purview worked well with her students. *So Far from God* lends itself beautifully for such an approach. Perhaps it is because of the reluctant administration, and certainly to contextualize the plot, she includes a discussion of Chicano literature in general and the historical basis for the existence of the political Chicano movement of the 1960s and 1970s.

As a folklorist and as someone who often reads Castillo through a folklorist's lens, I was very pleased to see that Martínez uses the same. She expertly draws from various scholars like Rita Cano Alcalá and Gloria Anzaldúa for her analysis. Centering the use of folklore and of revisioning of myth, she writes, "In *So Far from God*, La Llorona and other examples of traditional Mexican American mythology figure prominently in the narrative and are rewritten to challenge narrow androcentric understandings of Chicana/o discourse."[13] One of Mexican folklore's most famous figures, La Llorona, then functions as a pivotal figure whereby Castillo hangs a tale of "environmental racism and other areas of socioeconomic oppression."[14] The lengthy discussion of this key figure and of Castillo's character of the same name allows Martínez to conclude that "the subversive power in Castillo's rewrite of La Llorona shifts power from the dominant paradigm to an alternative outlook, thus redefining conceptions of reality from a marginal perspective and legitimizing the Chicana point of view."[15]

Martínez also brings into conversation social justice issues alongside the unpacking of the figure of La Llorona who is the victim of environmental crises that ultimately kill her. Rightly so, Martínez points out that Castillo is channeling a nationalistic political subtext for the local Chicana/o community to illustrate a contemporary need to collectively protest violence directed at ethnic laborers, but instead of relying on a masculinist-based ethos of the 1960s and 1970s, she transposes the mythology to be inclusive of the female perspective. Also, strongly tying the novel to Indigenous cosmology, Martínez ends the chapter with an insight that "Chicana writers demonstrate how the grotesque is a disruptive, subversive, and powerful agent for transformation and collective healing."[16] Finally, she concludes that "the novel demonstrates that old myths, stories, and legends are indeed culturally active forces in our present lives, and ultimately reminds us of the power of mystery intrinsic in the Southwest, while at the same time demonstrating how a regional text has the theoretical capacity to connect to larger cultural, political, and transnational concerns."[17] Although it is a straightforward approach, Martínez's pedagogical choices are rooted in serious resistance tenets that she and her students pursue while reading and discussing Castillo's work. Martínez claims that the novel is "a form of magical realism" and adds, "unlike the traditional Western version of realism, which is narratively singular, objective, and thus intended to be universally ideological and hegemonic, the eccentricity of magical realism creates space for interactions of diversity."[18] She explains that Castillo uses a form of magical realism because it "is a mode suited to exploring and transgressing ontological, political, and geographical boundaries by displacing mind/body, spirit/matter, life/death, real/imaginary, self/other, and male/female normative oppositions."[19] I want to argue with her that indeed Castillo has denied that it is magical realism but that it is "our" realism. But, because Castillo told me this in a conversation shortly after the novel was published and I cannot find it in any publication, I must defer. After all, there are a number of articles, master's theses, and dissertations where the claim is used to analyze *So Far from God*. So, given her argument, I agree with her concluding that "the subversive power in Castillo's rewrite of La Llorona shifts power from the dominant paradigm to an alternative outlook, thus redefining conceptions of reality from a marginal perspective and legitimizing the Chicana point of view."[20] My response to Martínez's chapter focuses on her literary analysis and on how *So Far from God* works for her classes as she instills a sense of regionalism and demythifies myth by revealing how Castillo (and Anzaldúa and Moraga) revise or rewrite the old myths for their purposes.

For Martínez, *So Far from God* allows for an approach to teaching about identity that is firmly grounded in first, regional literary studies, and secondly, folklore or cultural studies. In her view, "Castillo explores and transgresses ontological, political, and gendered boundaries by displacing life/

death, self/other, and male/female normative oppositions."[21] For Martínez, there is an "intrinsic" mystery in the Southwest. While I may agree with such a general statement, I would say that there is a mystery in all places, especially if coupled with the myths, stories, and legends that inherently grow attached to a particular place. What I do agree wholeheartedly with is that "a regional text has the theoretical capacity to connect to larger cultural, political, and transnational concerns"[22] and that Castillo achieves such in *So Far from God*—indeed, she does so in many of her works. That is, she transcends the world of the novel and moves beyond the genre borders or expectations to create memorable characters and plots that weave a fabric made of various threads that include folklore as well as history and contemporary social justice issues.

As I conclude my reactions or reflection upon reading these four chapters, I arrive at a crossroads. On one side is the pedagogical side of the essays, as they intend to offer guidance for teachers, and on the other, the critical literary analysis. Martínez's chapter has more of the latter while Johnson's more of the former. I also conclude that much work remains to be done along both of these paths. This book's chapters are achieving a rare thing as the authors come to Castillo's texts with keen insights and well-argued critical positions for teaching and for reading her work. No doubt there will be more articles written on Castillo's work for years to come, but these contribute to an ongoing critical discussion on the pedagogical approaches to teaching her work. These authors are but teasing out some salient points, offering clear and coherent teaching approaches, and sharing their own paths with us as they have come to Castillo's work and are sharing it with their students.

PART VI

AN INTERVIEW WITH ANA CASTILLO

CHAPTER 21

AN INTERVIEW WITH ANA CASTILLO

FRANCISCO J. GALARTE

I was asked by the editors of this volume to interview Ana Castillo, whom I first met during her visit to the University of Illinois at Champaign Urbana (UIUC) in March of 2011. At the time of her visit, I was a graduate student and was fortunate to be invited to participate in a writing workshop with her. I had recently begun a new phase of my transition and had started taking testosterone just three months before, so in this workshop, I wrote a personal narrative about the relationship between my childhood and shifting understandings of Chicana and Latina feminism as a transgender Chicano. Castillo's writing workshop was a transformative experience for me and other participants and impacted my understanding of Castillo's own writing process and texts. This experience very much informs the questions I chose to include as part of the interview. The interview was conducted over email in November of 2019. The interview transcript has been minimally edited for clarity.

Francisco J. Galarte: Over the years I have noticed that space (urban, rural, *la frontera*) and place (Chicago, New Mexico) and notions of belonging and isolation figure significantly in your work. Can you talk a bit about the relationship between these concepts in your work?

Ana Castillo: In terms of belonging and isolation (versus need for solitude) as a poet and writer, up until the current era of social media, most people were living relatively private lives. Getting [or] pursuing [a] degree to become a poet or novelist was also rare. Many writers had to have a regular paying job to supplement their writing. (Many still do.) I was born, raised, went to college, and grad school in Chicago and in fact, spent most of my life in that city. As secondary homes, as an adult I've lived for extended periods in New Mexico and California.

Place in relation to culture is fascinating to my writer's sensibilities. It is also of interest as a WOC, who must go out and earn a living, a single mother, caretaker of her own mother, who may use public transportation, who has taught in higher ed. In other words, interacts with her environment on a regular basis.

There are many ways I might address the question of a sense of "isolation." Again, there is the necessity of "solitude," to write. (I also paint and draw and these activities also necessitate extended periods of solitude.) In general, a writer spends a lot of time writing and revising, researching and in reflection.

As a woman whose family members were factory and field workers and who grew up in the city of Chicago, attending public schools during the height of the civil rights movement, I have been aware of the marginalization cast upon the demographics I was born into by class, gender, ethnicity, and color.

Place and isolation also become important from this perspective. Marginalization hasn't been limited to living in Chicago or even the United States, but as many are becoming aware today, [it is] the ongoing consequences of centuries of colonialism. In 2019, with the anti-immigrant sentiment throughout varying countries against POC, I think marginalization is as profound as ever. When you are conscious of these stratifications, it does give way to a certain ongoing sense of "isolation." For me, being bisexual in a patriarchal, misogynist world added another dimension to the sense of disenfranchisement (on the one hand, and from my own traditional communities, rejection, being outcast, seen as "insurgent," or a troublemaker, etc.). I've addressed these realities in most of my writing for decades.

FG: We're living in a moment of what most would call unprecedented visibility for trans folks. Were trans identities and politics a part of how you understood Chicana/o and Latina/o politics and culture? What are your thoughts about the "transgender turn"? I know you have included trans characters in your work before—what motivated you to include these kinds of subject positions in your work? (I'm thinking of the transgender woman in *Give It to Me*. I also remember a trans character in *Loverboys*.)

AC: As a Chicana feminist who began to formulate ideas in the mid-seventies, female sexuality was key to my thinking of oppression and exploitation of the "woman figure," specifically what we think of as "feminine."[1]

In my view as a self-termed "Xicanista" (a term I came up with to describe the Chicana feminist[2]), I believed that whether an individual was born biologically female, chose to cross-dress (male to female), or identified as a transgendered person or trans woman or woman (male to female) in a patriarchal world, the consequences would be similar. A feminine figure (considered [an] object of beauty) is considered a commodity. Commodities are exploited on the market. Demonstrating this point, Carmen, the protagonist of *Peel My Love*, goes through a lot. In the novel both of the *feminine* [characters] who are biologically male characters are killed. (One is gay and the other trans.) The idea around homophobia is that "woman" is considered inferior to men and, again, a commodity. She is considered inferior biologically, and her worth (despite changes made by feminist activism) is usually appraised by the objectification of her body. Following this line of patriarchal capitalist thinking, a transgendered individual and a gay man are not just relegated to the same level of "inferiority," or secondary status in society as "woman," but held in contempt for rejecting male privilege.

The novel is loosely based on the classic novella *Carmen*. In the original narrative, Carmen is a Gypsy woman (i.e., considered dark, exotic, poor, without social status, from a "minority" group. Despite this, Carmen insists she owns her body and sexual desire. This is perceived as a threat to capitalist patriarchy. Because of her defiance to patriarchal authority, the traditional story line must be that she must be annihilated. (In *Carmen*, she [is] killed.) In my novel I didn't want the Carmen character to end this way. However, demonstrating the point [of] how a feminine figure attempt[s] to subvert male authority and superiority gets castigated, two minor characters are destroyed.

In everyday life, anywhere in the world, I think, femicide—the concept of being killed for the sole reason of being female—is real.

In my most recent novel, *Give It to Me*, the main character (of Mexican descent born and raised in Chicago) is not a feminist or politically aware. In today's parlance, she is not exactly "woke." But she's not unaware of her desires. Perhaps because it is the only aspect of her existence that she knows she owns and therefore may be able to negotiate with for other things she wants (love and attention, yes, and also material things). Palma, the protagonist, has taken ownership of her body. She doesn't outright commodify her body, as let's say, an "exotic dancer," "Instagram model," or "sugar baby" might today. Instead, it seems she may use her body in relationships because it is a way to connect. Meanwhile, time and again, [in addition to] her lack of power in society, lack of support and true allies (again, your first question regarding "isolation," comes to mind), patriarchy subjects her to further marginalization, even humiliation. In one scene, Palma is attracted to a transgendered character in a bar but is pulled away by a male bisexual companion who uses her masculinity to dominate his partners. In another scene, Palma is raped by a woman who has used her privilege to control. For a time, she negotiates her body with this woman in exchange for goods and a sense of control in the relationship. For the "feminine figure," this negotiation is basically a survival tactic.

As mentioned, early on as a writer and feminist I understood sexuality to be key to how women (and all things feminine) were controlled. Woman as the feminine is controlled in every way in society, government, media, and religion. Regardless of the half trillion-dollar beauty industry [that] promotes itself today to woman as *adding* to their power (viewed as inner and outer beauty), I'd argue that racism and misogyny remain present.

Characters in my prose and poetry, which include transgender, have frequently attempted to demonstrate subversion to that control. In my view, rarely is such a character or individual in life fully successful. By successful I mean to be "at peace." Even in the example of full political consciousness and, let's say, economically self-sufficient individuals who do everything in their power to subvert society's control over their lives, the struggle to feel [at] peace and safe is constant. Capitalist patriarchy is violent.

FG: On a related note, alongside the surge of transgender politics within the public sphere, the marker of the "x," as in "Latinx" and "Chicanx," has provoked a bit of a linguistic and gender debate within Chicana/o/x and Latina/o/x communities. What are your thoughts on the turn to the "x"?

AC: The debate appears to be mostly academic. I appreciate the discussion because it is looking for inclusion with not only women (or the feminine) but LGBTQ. By the way, as Latinx is getting some wind in its sails, linguistic anthropology is offering an alternative to the alternative a/o: Latinu (the universal "u" is gender neutral, while respecting Spanish phonology).

As I wrote in the first edition of *Massacre of the Dreamers: Essays on Xicanisma* (1994) and reiterated in the twentieth anniversary edition, each generation has a right to identify as it seems appropriate for its time. We tend to think of generations as homogenous, but I think it's important to say in no generation has everyone been in agreement [with] one political or social identification.

Sometimes a term gets out there and is misinterpreted or turned on its head, and ironically, the contradictory definition gets accepted. Moreover, let's never underestimate the power and influence capitalist white supremacist patriarchy has to subvert any sign of insurgency. I'll use "Hispanic" vs "Latino/a" as an example. In the 1970s activists used Latino/a to include all who were from "Latin American and the Caribbean," and [their] descendants. In the 1980s, fearing the growing numbers of people who were identifying as of "Latino/a" origin (US born, migrants and immigrants), the Reagan administration moved to whitewash, so to speak, the population. It aimed to neutralize any to White power and chose the term "Hispanic" in the census. By the nineties, the term Hispanic was successfully used in government and institutions and a new generation grew up identifying themselves with it.

There are groups at all margins of this thinking and certainly today there are those who object to Latino/a and Hispanic. They may feel both terms negate African and Indigenous heritage and accept colonization. The binary use of feminine and masculine in Spanish (and language of Latin origin) has been questioned by feminists for a long time. (In the 1980s, as the Spanish translator of *This Bridge Called My Back*, I chose to make *puente* feminine.) Today, as we work toward understanding nonbinary gender identification and a transgendered population, scholars and public thinkers are looking for terms that may be applicable and inclusive.

Finally, I reiterate: it is my personal opinion not to tell others whether or how to label themselves. My first novel, *The Mixquiahuala Letters* (1986), which takes place in the 1970s, grapples with the questions that were being asked by feminists at that time within a traditional "Latino/Mexican Catholic" context. In that novel, too, there is a chapter dedicated to men who chose the feminine in a macho society. As I recall the chapter ends in near chaos with local police showing up. The grappling of female sexuality is always present in all my books, nonfiction, fiction, and poetry. It is central in my one published play, which is based on the true-life story of a contemporary nun.

FG: Following up on the previous questions, I wonder if you could elaborate a bit more on what you do with genre in your work. For example, *The Mixquiahuala Letters* might be described by some as multi-genre and *So Far from God* is genre-bending, by which I mean you bend the genre of magical realism. What do you think leads you to engage in this kind of practice of form in your work?

AC: The short answer here is that I am a self-taught poet and writer. I was never in a program that led my thinking. In college, I first majored to teach art in high school and then moved on to the social sciences. I have been a voracious reader and learned about writing through writers I discovered and admired. Add to that two other factors. I was dedicated to being a writer and poet, and it appears I was born an artist. I can't remember a time in my existence that I wasn't reading, valuing all forms of art, drawing, and writing with the constant urge to participate in the arts.

FG: Finally, can you share your thoughts about the current state of Chicana/x and Latina/x feminism? As someone whose work (*Massacre of the Dreamers*) is foundational to Chicana feminism, what gaps and silences within Chicana/x and Latina/x feminism continue to persist? What advice do you have for writers, artists, [and] activists today?

AC: We who identify as feminists and Latina/o/x or u, Chicana/x, or Xicanx, in my opinion, are a modest demographic, mostly (but not necessarily) restricted to academic discourse. It stands in contradiction at times to the aspirations of ideas that challenge the world we live in—fraught with all the isms that today are as unjust to large populations as ever. It calls to mind a poem of mine that appeared in my book *I Ask the Impossible*. Its title, "Women Don't Riot." A real argument may be made that it's an inaccurate statement to say women haven't rebelled against their circumstances. There have been courageous people who stood up against injustice throughout the world. My point in the poem and now, trying to address your questions, is that while there are those who find inequality of any kind worth opposing, so many more do not. Fortunately, those who do oppose fight hard with heart and soul; they fight with body and mind. Sometimes change is made and that change benefits everyone. So, women following my own generation are the beneficiaries of such activism. Each subsequent generation is welcome to pick up the banner or carry on the torch, so to speak. Each generation faces new challenges.

Technology has in many ways made the world smaller because we are more accessible to each other. Ideas may be transmitted instantly via the Internet.

Regarding the silences, in general I would say the challenge is not so much the silences but how much apathy and indifference continues to exist among these overlapping demographics. Personal gain often takes precedence for individuals. Further disturbing today are those who side with the kind of divisive conservative politics dominating government, even as they'd argue that they take apart mainstream politics, too. Unsettling and in my view, an unproductive tack, is to invest your time attacking people who, for all intents and purposes, could be your allies. Ironically, Paulo Freire's *Pedagogy of the Oppressed* (a book I used in the 1970s as an assigned text in the classroom) is being touted to serve this end.

At this writing, regarding the direction "creatives" may go, I'll offer some recommendations and practices that I follow to stay centered from day to day. It's critical to stay focused on the priorities of your current life. We may feel conflicted with personal and professional goals or personal and economic needs. But if you think about it, your life may not be cubbyholed. All the pieces comprise your current life. All those pieces are consequences of origins, yes, but also decisions, goals, and actions.

I'm not sure there are "silences" to be addressed as much as the divisions and very heated opinions today, even at extremes within similar communities—blood-related families, religious, academic discourse, economic, etc.— that keep groups of people from being united on the basis of long-term common goals. These heated political divisions are even breaking up personal social units such as same-sex marriages and immigrant families. It's also disturbing to see younger generations invest their time attacking their elders—whether at home or on the Internet. That kind of passionate energy could go toward actually doing something. Divide and conquer is an effective strategy on the very part of the powers-that-be, always has been.

As a final note, as I discussed in *Massacre of the Dreamers: Essays on Xicanisma* ([1994] 2014), I believe labels are important in as much you have chosen how you want to be called (Latinx, Xicanx, Chicana feminist, etc.). It's a point of reference and an indication of where your thinking has arrived. It may also be a point of departure. Societal changes move slowly, but they do move. As human beings, we change from decade to decade. How you feel about yourself today may not be how you feel a decade from now or what your expectations were a decade before. On the other hand, most people, from what I've observed, don't tend to change all that much after their twenties. My advice in general? As a grownup, if things aren't working for you in life, look honestly within. If the world is the problem, besides badmouthing, what will you *do* about it?

LATINX/CHICANX FEMINIST FUTURES

KAREN R. ROYBAL AND BERNADINE M. HERNÁNDEZ

Our impetus in organizing this collection was to draw attention to the expansive oeuvre of Ana Castillo's literary, theoretical, and feminist work that has impacted multiple generations over time. As we conclude this collection that traces the ways Castillo has contributed to these areas and helped reconfigure them, we want to emphasize that the essays making up this volume offer new ways of thinking about transnational feminisms, Chicana/o/x and Latina/o/x studies, gender and sexuality studies, and literature that encourage us to read Castillo's work as significant beyond confining it to being solely read as Chicana literature. While we set out to pose new questions and critiques on Castillo and her huge body of work, we also set out to open the conversation for more questions. What is the future of Chicana feminism? How can we historicize the critical importance of Chicana feminism within and outside of the movement, while simultaneously considering how it can contribute to conversations within transnational feminism? Our contributors have identified and posited how her poetry, novel, critical essays, and memoir render the "always becoming" Chicanx subject visible in societies that often designate them invisible. It is within the "X" that we find something that we haven't quite reached yet. It is within the "X" where possibility flourishes.

WHAT IS THE FUTURE OF THE X?

Over time, the "X" has become a signifier of political and historical meaning. Jennie Luna and Gabriel Estrada trace the genealogy of the "X" saying, "The X arguably stem[med] from the X in Mexico that was fought for as a national reminder of Nahuatl roots."[1] This signifier is steeped in debate about how it neutralizes the Spanish language but its adoption needs to be situated within a critical assessment of its value for acknowledging "discrepant gender politics."[2] Luna and Estrada further remind us that the "X" "stems from the resurgence of 'Indigenismo/Indigeneity/Indianismo'" that symbolizes the "recognition of a more profound political and spiritual grounding."[3] Castillo contributed to the significance of the "X" in her work when she coined the term *Xicanisma* in *Massacre of the Dreamers* (1994), which she used to invoke a political and active feminism that reclaims Chicanx subjectivity, honors Indigenous ideology and Xicanas' Indigenous identities, *and* centers female power. Through these actions, Castillo made and continues to make room for the Latinx body in her work and in broader discussions of race, class, gender, and sexuality in literature, Chicana and transnational feminist theory, and Chicanx/Latinx studies. Similar to the ways in which nonbinary, trans* and gender nonconforming folx have adopted the "X" as a decolonial move against heteropatriarchal and normative structures (broadly speaking), since the 1990s, Castillo's use of the "X" has allowed her to deconstruct colonial and white supremacist confines around gender, sexuality, race, and ethnicity. We read Castillo's X as dynamic—she also bends genre, form, and aesthetics; she interrogates subjectivities that cannot be contained; and she makes room for indeterminacy embodied by Chicanx subjects.

This indeterminacy results in what Alan Pelaez Lopez proposes when he suggests "that we think of the 'X' as a scar that exposes four wounds" signified by each corner of the "X": the wound of settlement; the wound of anti-blackness; the wound of femicides; and the wound of inarticulation.[4] López's assertions, considered alongside Castillo's body of fiction and nonfiction work, remind us that Latinx *and* Chicanx identities are firmly rooted in the history of settler colonialism and using the "X" encourages debate about where the "borders of Latin America start and end."[5] Further, we must acknowledge that "Latinidad" not only includes settler colonial and genocidal practices against our Indigenous brothers and sisters, but also enslavement of our Afro-Latinx brothers and sisters who were enslaved throughout Latin America and the Caribbean;[6] our histories are rooted in both narratives. This colonial violence also resulted in the wound created by femicides enacted by European colonizers against Indigenous women, whom they often raped, and Black female slaves who were raped by plantation owners. This continued colonial violence against "those who are identified as women by Western society (not just self-identified women), which includes cisgender women, trans women, trans men experiencing intentional targeted violence from transphobic cultures, gender nonconforming people who have their nonconformity questioned and erased and identify as 'women,' butch women . . . and third, fourth and fifth gendered NDNs who the state will not recognize[,]"[7] must also be acknowledged in order to address the final wound identified by Lopez—inarticulation, which signifies "the inability to articulate violence and denounce it."[8] As we consider the ways in which the "X" is *becoming*, we must also recognize its symbolic and material importance in our Chicanx past. In this volume, we have considered how Castillo's oeuvre has contributed to acknowledging this complex history and its (dis)articulations of Chicanx identity.

However, there are also critiques of the X with which peers of Castillo might agree. In an opinion piece that came out in *Yes!* magazine in 2019, Kurly Tlapoyawa states, "While it may be in vogue to adopt trendy terms like 'Latinx' in an attempt to be more inclusive, [the X] erases a part of history that many consider very important. . . . The participants in the Chicano Moratorium most certainly did not identify as 'Latinx' or 'Chicanx,' and no amount of historical revisionism is going to change that."[9] Castillo's writings put us right in the middle of the debates on gender neutrality and historical geopolitical space. The Feminist Press, which published *Give It to Me* in 2014, promoted the novel on their website as the "Chicana Sex in the City," a type of sexual liberation narrative that showed the agency of the Chicana protagonist, Palma Piedras. However, Palma's sexual escapades mark her position as a racialized Chicana, while simultaneously putting forth the language for Palma to choose gender nonconforming partners throughout the entire novel.

In the context of Chicana feminism and Chicana literature, Palma differs historically from other sexually excessive Chicana protagonists because she refuses to negotiate or question the dialectic of power and abjection in terms of gender and race. The foundational work of Chicana feminists Cherríe Moraga and Emma Peréz centers Chicana sexuality in the context of larger issues of Chicano nationalism, patriarchy, and state-sanctioned violence and offers alternative political imaginaries with which their protagonists eventually come to terms. Palma remains disengaged from desire, political consciousness, and community throughout the entire novel. We contend that Castillo engages in such a hyperbolic representation of excessive sex as a metaphor for the unproductive nature of the Chicana racialized body in the social imaginary. This in turn requires us as readers to not only come to terms with Palma's historical position as a Chicana but also how she is moving in and out of gender nonconforming spaces. The X gives us room to read *Give It to Me* through Chicana feminism but also up against Chicanx literature.

INDIGENEITY, RACIALIZATION, AND COLONIALISM

Castillo utilizes the X to understand herself in relation to the world that is yielding and based on integration, not dualism. Her early work, as noted in this collection, takes the X from the Mexica tribe, the descendants of the Aztecs. In this move to trace Chicana lineage to a precolonial subjectivity, Chicana feminists like Anzaldúa, Moraga, and Castillo rewrite the problems of difference through Indigenous networks throughout the Americas, which is a transnational move. However, the debate within Chicana/o/x and Latina/o/x studies reveals the persistent transborder erasure, generalization, and co-opting of specific Indigenous people. What did it mean during the Chicano/a movement to trace Chicana roots back to Indigeneity when there were many dispossessed tribes in the Americas attempting to exist? How can Chicana/o/x and Latina/o/x studies engage in a productive dialogue with Indigenous feminist studies, and what does liberation look like in relation to a hemispheric movement? For as Jodi Byrd has eloquently put forth, "Indianness" created conditions of possibility for US imperialism to manifest its intent and allows "Indianness" to move not through absence but through reiteration.[10] Chicana/o/x and Latina/o/x studies must contend with its genealogy of Indigenous utility not only in the movement, but also after. It is our hope this collection will put these large debates in the field into conversation. The importance of a transnational perspective in this collection is important for evident and not so evident reasons. Castillo's consciousness about the history of subjugation and maltreatment of ethnic others extends geographical lines. In *Massacre of the Dreamers* she connects the histories of colonization, genocide, and marginality of peoples of color across the globe when she says:

> We are not the only people wronged by racism and conquest, whose records have been destroyed, who themselves, in fact, were nearly all annihilated. The black diaspora is a long, mournful wail reminding us of the inhumane history of greed. In México, too, there had been slavery and a slaughtering of millions of indigenous peoples. Latinos and Hispanos from the United States, originally from the Southwest, share this legacy with the African Americans. Off the mainland United States, the Aleuts and Inuits north of us and the Polynesian ancestors of the native Hawaiians have also been stripped of their ways and Christianized.[11]

Acknowledging the global reaches of imperialist projects as she does above, Castillo's critical work makes clear that she is influenced, too, by international issues that form her sociopolitical perspective. In part, this reading of Castillo's work echoes Olga Herrera's claim that she challenges Latinidad as static,[12] and Marissa K. López's assertion that in her novels, "a core concern . . . is what happens to the nation when bodies move."[13]

Castillo's literary work cognizes the relationship between mestiza/o identity, the geographical body, *and* the physical body—one that not only calls attention to the importance of spaces like Chicago as sites of hemispheric and colonial history, but that also help us conceive of biological race and geographic space in a more fluid way. Through this critical mestizaje framework, Castillo uses spaces such as Chicago to decolonize the assumed connection between racialization and colonization, a methodology called for by Byrd. This collection recognizes the difference between racialization and colonization and attempts to contend with those contours in Chicana/o/x studies. Thus, Castillo herself and her writing embody and represent a hemispheric consciousness rooted in Indigenous identity.

Sapogonia (1990) is a prime example of the way Castillo decenters what in interviews she has labeled as a "white-dominated city" as part of a dominant "U.S. culture" by de-racializing Chicago in such a way that she ensures that "different racial and ethnic groups not only live with each other and interact closely, but mix."[14] At first glance, *Sapogonia* appears to be a narrative that centers solely on the relationship between the two protagonists, Máximo Madrigal and Pastora Velásquez Aké. Máximo is the quintessential antihero—a character readers love to hate because his machismo leads him to treat people exploitatively. As an expatriate of Sapogonia, Máximo traverses Europe and North America, from New York to Chicago to California, and back to Chicago, in search of an identity to which he can lay full claim, one that separates him from his mestizo past. Pastora, on the other hand, embodies strength and a strong sense of Indigenous and spiritual identity, making her the ideal and often out-of-reach counterpoint to Máximo's arrogant persona. Though he is a Sapogón, throughout most of the narrative Máximo's narcissism blinds him to the fact that "the Sapogón is besieged by a history of slavery, genocide, immigration, and civil uprisings, all of which have left their marks on the genetic make-up of the generation following such periods as well as the border outline of its territory."[15] This description counters the way Máximo presents himself and emphasizes that the Sapogón, the mestiza/o body, is "marked" by the region's colonial history.

Through her discussion of the fissures that mark the Sapogón's physical, psychological, and geographical body, Castillo emphasizes the mestiza/o hemispheric history of colonization, civil wars, and resistance. She also invites her reader to consider the ways the geographical body, much like the physical body, is constructed on "some realm of 'the real,'"[16] an idea based on the assumption that the mestiza/o has a place to which she/he can return. Castillo challenges this idea through her description of Sapogonia as a place located "somewhere in the Americas," and by setting the majority of the novel in Chicago, a city that represents hybridity in cultures, race, and history. Herrera echoes this reading of *Sapogonia* and suggests that the novel is "transnational in its reach."[17] When asked to describe *Sapogonia*, Castillo says in part, "it is to get an understanding of who we are as Latinos throughout the Americas and particularly with our relationship to the U.S."[18] Through this novel, she makes clear the entanglements between the United States and the broader Americas, but acknowledges that understanding that relationship and mestiza/o identity will never be absolute: "The question of identity . . . the search for identity is always there."[19]

For more than forty years, Castillo's body of work has pressed her readers to confront and to think deeply about the ways her Chicanx characters and she herself, have defied social and cultural norms; addressed the ways misogyny and white supremacist structures of power impact Brown bodies and geographical spaces; and rejected the limitations of a heteropatriarchal society that has historically attempted to reinforce fixed places for women, people of color, and queers—in other words, her work over time situates what Frederick L. Aldama and Arturo J. Aldama (2020) call "the decolonial turn of using X."[20] It is worth reiterating in this conclusion Castillo's own contention that "the very act of self-definition is a rejection of colonization." In other words, the X allows for that self-definition and rejection to occur simultaneously. We read Castillo's work as an intervention in Western conceptions of Chicanx identity and ask how might we build on the scholarship included in this volume to further consider Castillo's work. We are invested in how Chicanx studies is in conversation with Indigenous studies, as well as trans and disability studies and how each critically engages with the X.

TRANS* AND DISABILITY STUDIES IN CHICANA FEMINISM

Although they are growing fields, trans and disability studies are two areas that remain minimized in the literature, especially in their intersections with the Chicanx body. The late 1990s were not necessarily ripe with literary texts addressing these areas. However, in 1999, Castillo gave us her novel *Peel My Love like an Onion*, in which she addresses disability and transgender identity when she places at center stage Carmen "La Coja" ("the cripple") Santos as her protagonist. Santos is a flamenco dancer whose childhood affliction of polio left her with a crippled leg. A story one-part telenovela-esque narrative, one-part tragic comedy, *Peel My Love like an Onion* epitomizes the intersectionality of Castillo's work. Centering a disabled Chicana as the protagonist in her novel, Castillo was already pushing the boundaries of American *and* Chicana/o/x literature at the end of the twentieth century.[21] To further the ways she addressed subjects most mainstream writers may have avoided, she also included a direct confrontation with sexuality and gender identity when she becomes one of the first Chicana authors to include a transgender character in her literary work. True to Castillo's integrity as a writer who knows no bounds, this move reveals how she confronted gender politics in fiction writing in a significant way. In *Peel My Love like an Onion*, she introduces her audience to Chichi, a transgender woman. There has not been critical work on the characterization of Chichi and it is a definite gap in the criticism in relation to the Latinx body.

The relationship between Chichi and "La Coja" is noteworthy because it further reveals the entanglement between embodiment and identity. Although Chichi appears only minimally in the novel, she serves as Carmen's teacher about sexual identity, love, and sense of self. Carmen says, "I learned a lot about being a woman from Chichi, who was a lot of woman for being a man."[22] Matthew Teorey notes, Carmen's relationship with Chichi is not underpinned by Carmen's transphobia; rather he says their exchanges reveal "more about her [Carmen's] own gender unhappiness and sexual insecurities."[23] When Chichi asks Carmen if she's gay after she relays a story to Chichi about her threesome with a brother and sister who both "come out" as gay after having slept with her, Carmen doesn't know how to react and, in fact, gets a bit defensive when she retorts, "No, are *you?*" (italics original).[24] Suzanne Bost reminds us that Carmen's identity is unpredictable, which challenges how we read this character and perhaps becomes the reason why "critics invested in Chicana/o studies and disability studies have not, or at least not yet, celebrated this novel."[25] On the one hand, Castillo uses Carmen to push the boundaries of corporeality and disability, as she critiques how Brown bodies are already always rendered immobile, but she also forces the reader to rethink the politics of embodiment and identity.[26]

Another way Castillo does this in *Peel My Love like an Onion* is in how she addresses the elision of transgender representation, as she makes evident the complexity of sex, sexuality, and identity and the vexed relationships between her characters of color. Francisco J. Galarte asserts, "'Trans-' has the potential to provoke the kind of paradigmatic shift necessary to critically engage gender and sexuality in such a way that disrupts the heteronormative patriarchal authority and conformity with which Chicana/o Studies is currently entangled."[27] Castillo reveals these entanglements within *Peel My Love like an Onion* by addressing, for example, the significance of various kinds of embodiments, that include trans and disabled bodies. Castillo successfully accomplishes this through a Chicana feminist lens that "further complicate[s] and destabilize[s] approaches to theorizing gender and sexuality in the current Chicana/o context."[28] Although Chichi is a secondary character to the main character, Carmen, Castillo's decision to include a transgender character was a significant move because it reveals that the author was attempting to begin a dialogue about trans Latinidad in 1999. This move resonates with contemporary calls for such conversations in trans* and jotería studies. Although there are limitations in the work within *Peel My Love like an Onion*, Castillo emphasizes notions of gender identity, queerness, and trans-ness that are emblematic of what Susana Peña calls the "borderlands between transgender and gay," or between "gender and sexual non-conformity."[29] The border Castillo leaves unsettled, however, is that she does not develop Chichi's character further than existing narratives about transgender people[30]—Chichi is brutally murdered and her body is found in a hallway "broken forever" because she is killed "just before [she] was able to have the operation that would have made her a total woman."[31] In fact, as the narrative progresses, we come to learn that Carmen, not Chichi, remains fragmented, much like the "porcelain figures," "plates and china [sic] cups, [and] Danish crystal candy dishes"[32] she collected and displayed in her rundown home.

The gender and sexual politics with which Chichi is faced, when considered alongside Carmen's disabled body in *Peel My Love like an Onion*, provides furtive ground for examining the ways in which "trans* Chican@ bodies, politics and communities" should be read as "integral sites of inquiry, but not as objects of study,"[33] as Galarte so keenly notes in his examination of jotería studies. After *Peel My Love like an Onion*, in the early 2000s other Chicana/o/x authors followed suit and pushed the boundaries of gender identity even further, as noted by T. Jackie Cuevas[34] when she states that Felicia Luna Lemus's novel *Like Son* (2007) "features a transgender protagonist and may be the first Chicanx novel to do so."[35] Almost twenty years before Lemus, Castillo brings to the forefront of mainstream literature a direct confrontation with sexual identity. Although we certainly cannot expect Castillo's work in the 1990s to include the language and ideas posited by contemporary queer, trans*, and disability studies, in *Peel My Love like an Onion* and in much of her work, Castillo demonstrates the lived reality of border crossers and many queer people of color. As Maria Esther Quintana Millamoto notes, "Castillo shows how difficult it is for non-normative bodies to find social support within society's institutions."[36] Her stories don't conclude with easy resolutions—instead, Castillo reveals what it means to live on the edge, and through the plots of her narratives, she demonstrates the complexities of being a racialized, sexualized, disabled, and classed subject.

Despite some of the shortcomings within Chicano/a studies to contend with indigeneity, blackness, disability, or gender-neutrality within the X, this collection attempts to bridge these very conversations together in relation to Chicana feminism. We thought it was crucial to revisit the foundational Chicana feminist, Ana Castillo, in a way that critically looks at how her work has connected to the social, historical, and political struggles beyond the US nation-state and beyond the confines of Chicana/o literature. What can Chicana feminism offer us in this contemporary moment? While a US president (Trump) is referring to Central American migrants as "really bad people" and "animals," how can we form discussions and connections of solidarity through a political discourse, such as Chicana feminism?[37] More importantly, where does Chicana feminism lead us when we think about its beginnings, which are firmly rooted in anti-racist and critical class-consciousness work? As history proved during westward expansion and over again thereafter, President Trump is not the first person to label Latinx people as uncivil and likened to animals. In fact, the language of colonialism from centuries before cemented a language of primitiveness to dark Spanish-speaking peoples and Indigenous populations. However, what this edited collection has examined are the difficult cross-cultural connections and deep fissures of feminist politics that mostly disengage with a Chicana feminist politics. We are attempting to make those connections visible.

Castillo's work lends theoretical, pedagogical, and cultural practices to Chicanx feminist and trans-border politics. It is our hope that this volume helps shape our understandings of Chicanx identities from a more transnational perspective that acknowledges global impacts of capitalist structures, legacies of colonization, and reductionist heteropatriarchal narratives that construct Chicanx identities in ways that minimize their heterogeneity. In tracing the ways Castillo's poems, novels, memoir, and critical essays transcend borders of literature and theory, this volume pays tribute to Castillo's contributions to the growing body of more current Chicanx feminist politics and scholarship.

NOTES

INTRODUCTION

1. Guidotti-Hernández, "Affective Communities and Millennial Desires," 143.

2. Castillo, *So Far from God* (Plume, 1994), 22.

3. Castillo, *So Far from God*, 22.

4. Faris, "Scheherazade's Children," 167.

5. Carpentier, "On the Marvelous Real in America," 86.

6. Caminero-Santangelo, "Pleas of the Desperate," 83.

7. The German art critic Franz Roh first used the term "Magischer Realismus" ("magical realism") to describe a new tendency in art. When Roh's 1925 book, *Nach Expressionisms: Magischer Realismus* (*After Expressionism: Magical Realism*), was translated into Spanish, it became a literary phenomenon in Latin America. For *lo real maravilloso* or magical realism in Latin American literature, see *The House of the Spirits* by Isabel Allende, *One Hundred Years of Solitude* by Gabriel García Márquez, *Like Water for Chocolate* by Laura Esquivel, *Ficciones* by Jorge Luis Borges, and *The Kingdom of This World* by Alejo Carpentier. For more reading on Ana Castillo and magical realism, see "'The Pleas of the Desperate': Collective Agency versus Magical Realism in Ana Castillo's *So Far from God*" by Marta Caminero-Santangelo, *Postethnic Narrative Criticism: Magicorealism in Oscar "Zeta" Acosta, Ana Castillo, Julie Dash, Hanif Kureishi, and Salman Rushdie* by Frederick Luis Aldama, "Ecocritical Chicana Literature: Ana Castillo's "Virtual Realism" by Kamala Platt, and "Ana Castillo's *So Far from God*: Intimations of the Absurd" by B. J. Manríquez.

8. In "Forms of Chicana Feminist Resistance," Theresa Delgadillo similarly contends, "It is not unusual for the literature of this heterogenous [Chicana/o] community to grapple with conflicting claims and demands, for its characters engage a discourse of identity in which issues of power and opposition to the dominant society are central" (893).

9. Castillo, *So Far from God*, 23.

10. Delgadillo, "Forms of Chicana Feminist Resistance," 891.

11. Manríquez, "Ana Castillo's *So Far from God*," 38.

12. Castillo, *Massacre of the Dreamers* (University of New Mexico Press, 2014), 9–10.

13. Hong, *Death Beyond Disavowal*, 47.

14. In *Chica Lit: Popular Latina Fiction and Americanization in the Twenty-First Century*, Tace Hedrick argues that "chica lit" is popular fiction written by Latinas that is aimed at twenty- to thirty-something upwardly mobile Latina readers. Castillo takes this neoliberal narrative of "success" and uses it to illuminate the position of Chicanas who deal directly with the intersection of gender violence, racism, and classism. She does this while appealing to mass readers by adding "magical" elements of Latino people to the narrative in ways that undercut the entire genre.

15. Cooper Alarcón, "Literary Syncretism," 145.

16. Castillo, *So Far from God*, 160.

17. Castillo, *So Far from God*, 161.

18. Castillo, *So Far from God*, 161.

19. Jameson, in *Postmodernism, Or, The Cultural Logic of Late Capitalism*, states that postmodernism is an attempt to think about the present historically in an age that has forgotten how to think historically in the first place. In that case, postmodernism either "expresses" some deeper irrepressible historical impulse (in however distorted a fashion) or effectively "represses" and diverts it, depending on the side of the ambiguity you happen to favor. Postmodernism, and postmodern consciousness, may then amount to not much more than theorizing the condition of possibility (ix).

20. Szeghi, "Literary Didacticism," 405–6.

21. Larkin, "Reading as Responsible Dialogue," 141.

22. Soto, "Queering the Conquest," 63.

23. Espinoza, Cotera, and Blackwell, *Chicana Movidas*, 1–2.

24. Saldívar-Hull, *Feminism on the Border*, 30.

25. Hong, *Death Beyond Disavowal*, 47.

26. "Combahee River Collective," *Bridge Called My Back*, 210–18.

27. "About," Third Woman Press website, accessed November 5, 2019, http://www.thirdwomanpress.com/about/.

28. Ramírez, "Alternative Cartographies," n.p.

29. The performance of gender and sexuality within the feminist movement is thoroughly explained in "Decolonizing Gender Performativity: A Thesis for Emancipation in Early Chicana Feminist Thought (1969–1979)" by Daphne V. Taylor-García. Early Chicana feminists were already thinking about breaking through the gender binary in the 1960s and 1970s. Anna Nieto Gómez (Anna NietoGomez) was one of the main voices during this time period that spoke to these silences. In "La Chicana: Legacy of Suffering and Self-Denial" in *Chicana Feminist Thought: The Basic Historical Writings*, she begins by addressing the "roots of the psyche of la Chicana [that] lies deep within the colonial period in Mexico" (48). Like deco-

lonial feminists, Chicana feminists were calling for the recognition of how legacies of colonial violence perpetuate and shift throughout history and modern times. María Lugones in "Heterosexualism and the Colonial/Modern Gender System" states, "Colonialism imposed a new gender system that created very different arrangements for colonized males and females than it did for white bourgeois colonizers" (186). The normative constructions of feminine and masculine that are tied to constructions of "female" and male" are in need of a poststructuralist reading of racialized gender and sexuality, which interrogate the meaning, historical positionality, and performativity embedded within these notions of differentiation. Chicana feminists were calling for a decolonization of gender and sexual performativity and took seriously not only how economic systems in place shaped gender and sexuality, but also how "the conquest, the encomienda system and the colonial Catholic Church were to a play a major role in formatting the sexual-social roles of the Mexican women" (48). The multiple tools of colonization like rape, marriage, the church, and the peon relationship to the *patrón* all aided in creating structures of violent oppression through the biopolitical and necropolitical. Mirtha Vidal in "New Voice of La Raza: Chicanas Speak Out" states, "The inferior role of women in society does not date back to the beginning of time. In fact, before the European came to this part of the world women enjoyed a high position of quality with men. The submission of women, along with institutions such as the church and the patriarchy, was imported by European colonizers" (21–23).

30. Castillo, *Mixquiahuala Letters* (New York: Anchor Books, 1992), n.p.

31. Jameson, *Postmodernism* (New York: Verso, 1991), 17.

32. Bost, "Movement: Ana Castillo's Shape Shifting Identities," in *Encarnación*, 152.

33. Guidotti-Hernández, "Affective Communities," 143.

34. Castillo, *So Far from God*, 77.

35. Guidotti-Hernández, "Affective Communities," 142.

36. Rodriguez, *Latinx Literature Unbound*.

37. Milian, *Latining America*.

38. Milian, "Extremely Latin, XOXO," 25.

39. Aldama, *Brown on Brown*, chapter 4.

40. Hong, *Death Beyond Disavowal*, 11.

41. Mitchell, "Transnational Discourse," 104.

42. Libman, "Ana Castillo Takes the Fifth," n.p.

43. In 1848, Mexico and the United States signed the Treaty of Guadalupe Hidalgo as a way to end the Mexican-American War (1846–1848). This legal document not only drew new geographical lines that clearly demarcated the border between the two countries, but it also ruptured people's identities, cultures, and their relationships with the land. Mexicans were forced to choose whether they wanted to remove themselves from the United States, to become permanent resident aliens, or to become US citizens one year after the signing of the treaty. Each

of the offered choices came with consequences. Even those who chose to return to Mexico would later flee north during and after the Mexican Revolution and had to become US citizens along with their fellow former Mexican peers who had already been through that process post-1848. Although the move north and subsequent citizenship appeared to promise a new and better life, in the United States Mexicans were treated as second-class citizens as the newly developing capitalistic nation became even more racialized and class-based.

44. Castillo, *Black Dove*, 55.

45. Alarcón, Kaplan, and Moallem, "Introduction," *Between Woman and Nation*, 15.

46. Alarcón, Kaplan, and Moallem, "Introduction," *Between Woman and Nation*, 15.

47. Castillo, *Black Dove*, 16.

48. Arredondo et al., *Chicana Feminisms*, 4.

49. Moraga and Anzaldúa, *Bridge Called My Back* [1981] (1983), 23.

50. Orchard and Padilla, *Bridges, Borders, and Breaks*, 12.

51. Orchard and Padilla, *Bridges, Borders, and Breaks*, 12.

52. López, *Chicano Nations*, 6.

53. López, *Chicano Nations*, 7.

54. Herrera, "Finding Mexican Chicago," *Bridges, Borders, and Breaks*, 104.

55. Saldívar, "Chicano Narrative Now," *Bridges, Borders, and Breaks*, 175.

56. López, *Chicano Nations*, 10.

57. González, "Transnational Field Imaginaries," 602.

58. Gallegos, "Building Transnational Feminist Solidarity Networks," *Decolonizing Feminism*, 231–56.

59. Crenshaw, "Demarginalizing the Intersection of Race and Sex," 139–67.

CHAPTER 1. LETTERED ENCOUNTERS

1. In fact, *The Mixquiahuala Letters* opens with a dedication to the Argentine author and his acclaimed postmodern text. It says: "In memory of the master of the game, Julio Cortázar."

2. Larkin, "Reading as Responsible Dialogue," 142.

3. Castillo, *Mixquiahuala Letters* (Anchor Books, 1992), 23.

4. Benjamin, *Illuminations*, 257.

5. Benjamin, *Illuminations*, 255.

6. Eakin, *Fictions in Autobiography*, 63.

7. Bower, *Epistolary Responses*; Kauffman, *Discourses of Desire*.

8. Bower, *Epistolary Responses*, 15.

9. Earle, *Epistolary Selves*, 2.

10. Bower, *Epistolary Responses*, 14 (italic type in original).

11. Moraga and Anzaldúa, *This Bridge Called My Back* (Persephone Press, 1981), 23.

12. Among the critiques that point to the unusual epistolary language and framing of Teresa's letters is Anne Bower's critique of a review that took issue with the "lack of analysis" of past events on Teresa's part, as in most occasions, her letters simply narrate their stories of travel. Bower, *Epistolary Responses*, 135.

13. In her presentation of potential reading paths, Ana Castillo closes her own "letter to the reader" by stating: "For the reader committed to nothing but short fiction, all the letters read as separate entities. Good luck whichever journey you choose! A.C."

14. Castillo, *Mixquiahuala Letters*, 32.

15. Castillo, *Mixquiahuala Letters*, 34.

16. Castillo, *Mixquiahuala Letters*, 49.

17. Castillo, *Mixquiahuala Letters*, 51.

18. Castillo, *Mixquiahuala Letters*, 52

19. Castillo, *Mixquiahuala Letters*, 62.

20. Castillo, *Mixquiahuala Letters*, 65.

21. Castillo, *Mixquiahuala Letters*, 126.

22. *Desvío* stands for a "detour" or "diversion" in Spanish. It points to acts of "going off the course," as it points to the act of "losing the path."

23. Castillo, *Mixquiahuala Letters*, 45.

24. Castillo, *Mixquiahuala Letters*, 46.

25. Castillo, *Mixquiahuala Letters*, 45.

26. Castillo, *Mixquiahuala Letters*, 46.

27. Castillo, *Mixquiahuala Letters*, 50.

28. Castillo, *Mixquiahuala Letters*, 119.

29. Castillo, *Mixquiahuala Letters*, 38.

30. Castillo, *Mixquiahuala Letters*, 27–28.

31. Castillo, *Mixquiahuala Letters*, 65.

32. Although we do not have record of the possible dates of reference in *The Mixquiahuala Letters*, its incorporation of historical markers like the Chicano movement locate the time of travel for these two women as around the 1970s and early 1980s.

33. Castillo, *Mixquiahuala Letters*, 100.

34. Castillo, *Mixquiahuala Letters*, 91.

35. Alarcón, "The Sardonic Powers of the Erotic," 103.

36. Soto, *Reading Chican@*, 70–71.

37. Bower, *Epistolary Responses*, 132.

38. Linda Margarita Greenberg writes on the matter: "[Teresa and Alicia's] erotic friendship and national ties are performative endeavors, continually and strategically reimagined. The lack of a fixed authentic homeland pains the characters, who can neither lay easy claim to the United States nor nostalgically yearn for Mexico." Greenberg, "Epistolary Women," 288.

39. Taylor, *Archive and the Repertoire*, 94 (italic type in original).

40. Castillo, *Mixquiahuala Letters*, 27.

41. The letters without any signature include letters 3, 14, 15, 19, 21, 23, 26, 28, 29, 30, 36, and 38.

42. Castillo, *Mixquiahuala Letters*, 24.

43. Khanna, *Dark Continents*, 30.

44. Castillo, *Mixquiahuala Letters*, 31.

45. Castillo, *Mixquiahuala Letters*, 31.

46. Castillo, *Mixquiahuala Letters*, 31.

47. Khanna, *Dark Continents*, 230.

48. Khanna, *Dark Continents*, 230.

49. Castillo, *Mixquiahuala Letters*, 126.

50. Sweeney, "Race and Reproductive Rights," 85.

51. Krase, "History of Forced Sterilization."

52. Krase, "History of Forced Sterilization."

53. Castillo, *Mixquiahuala Letters*, 126.

54. Castillo, *Mixquiahuala Letters*, 127.

55. Castillo, *Mixquiahuala Letters*, 127.

56. Castillo, *Mixquiahuala Letters*, 133.

57. Castillo, *Mixquiahuala Letters*, 133–34.

58. Pérez, *Decolonial Imaginary*.

59. Pérez, *Decolonial Imaginary*, xiv.

60. Alarcón, "Sardonic Powers of the Erotic," 9.

61. Castillo, *Mixquiahuala Letters*, 25.

62. Larkin, "Reading as Responsible Dialogue," 153.

63. Castillo, *Mixquiahuala Letters*, 117.

64. Barad, "Troubling Time/s and Ecologies," 83.

65. Ahmed, *Cultural Politics of Emotion*, 5.

66. Larkin, "Reading as Responsible Dialogue," 143.

67. Lugones, "Purity, Impurity, and Separation," 458.

68. Cvetkovich, *Archive of Feelings*.

69. *An Archive of Feelings* gathers personal stories, letters, memories, documentary films, and music of LGBTQ communities that have been continually been subject to "institutional neglect." The book aims to capture and make public the often "ephemeral and unusual traces" gay and lesbian cultures have left behind. Cvetkovich, *Archive of Feelings*, 8.

CHAPTER 2. FOR THE PLEASURE OF THE CHICANX POET

1. Castillo, *My Father Was a Toltec* (Anchor Books, 2004), 1–8.

2. Castillo, "A Christmas Gift," *My Father Was a Toltec*, 17; 18–19.

3. Castillo, "A Christmas Gift," *My Father Was a Toltec*, 41; 31–32; 46–49.

4. Castillo, "A Christmas Gift," *My Father Was a Toltec*, 55–56.

5. I use Latina/o/x when discussing Latinidad more broadly, and Chicana/o/x

to discuss the distinct Chicanx poetics demonstrated in Castillo's work, to honor her identity as a Chicanx writer, and to describe the Mexican American literary experience and the Chicana/o movement.

6. Castillo, *My Father Was a Toltec*, xxvi.

7. Brady, *Extinct Lands*.

8. Brady, *Extinct Lands*, 7.

9. Wilder, *Ebony and Ivy*.

10. Newfield, *Unmaking the Public University*.

11. McLaren, *Life in Schools*.

12. Gutiérrez y Muhs et al., *Presumed Incompetent*.

13. Brady, *Extinct Lands*, 8.

14. Castillo, *Black Dove*, 264–65.

15. Cisneros, *House of My Own*, 134.

16. Castillo, *Black Dove*, 265.

17. Cisneros, *House of My Own*, 136.

18. Cisneros, *House of My Own*, 136.

19. Castillo, *Black Dove*, 265.

20. Castillo, *My Father Was a Toltec*, xxiii–xxiv.

21. Castillo, *My Father Was a Toltec*, xxiv.

22. Cisneros, *House of My Own*, 99.

23. Cisneros, *House of My Own*, 127–28.

24. Cisneros, *House of My Own*, 128.

25. Cisneros, *House of My Own*, 130.

26. Castillo, *My Father Was a Toltec*, xxv–xxvi.

27. Limón, *Mexican Ballads*, 4.

28. Limón, *Mexican Ballads*, 4.

29. Arteaga, *Chicano Poetics*, 10.

30. Arteaga, *Chicano Poetics*, 25.

31. Ordóñez, "Sexual Politics," 68.

32. Ordóñez, "Sexual Politics," 60.

33. Alarcón, "Sardonic Powers of the Erotic," *Breaking Boundaries*, 96.

34. Alarcón, "Sardonic Powers," *Breaking Boundaries*, 96–97.

35. Gaspar de Alba, *[Un]framing the Bad Woman*, 116.

36. Rodríguez, *Queer Latinidad*, 5.

37. Brady, *Extinct Lands*, 6.

38. Castillo, *My Father Was a Toltec*, 69–71.

39. Pérez-Torres, *Mestizaje*, 90.

40. Pérez-Torres, *Mestizaje*, 90.

41. Pérez-Torres, *Mestizaje*, 90.

42. Castillo, "In My Country," *My Father Was a Toltec*, 1–3.

43. Castillo, "In My Country," *My Father Was a Toltec*, 8–10.

44. Castillo, "In My Country," *My Father Was a Toltec*, 40.

45. Castillo, "In My Country," *My Father Was a Toltec*, 55–57.

46. Castillo, "In My Country," *My Father Was a Toltec*, 85–90.

47. Castillo, *Massacre of the Dreamers* (Plume, 1994), 171.

48. Castillo, *My Father Was a Toltec*, xxvi.

49. Castillo, *My Father Was a Toltec*, xxvi.

50. Castillo, *Massacre of the Dreamers*, 171.

51. Castillo, *My Father Was a Toltec*, xxiv.

52. Castillo, "A Christmas Gift," *My Father Was a Toltec*, 20.

53. Castillo, "A Christmas Gift," *My Father Was a Toltec*, 21–22.

54. Castillo, "A Christmas Gift," *My Father Was a Toltec*, 25–28.

55. Castillo, "The Toltec," *My Father Was a Toltec*, 8; 9.

56. Castillo, "The Toltec," *My Father Was a Toltec*, 10–11.

57. Castillo, "The Toltec," *My Father Was a Toltec*, 2.

58. Castillo, *My Father Was a Toltec*, 1–7.

59. Castillo, "Saturdays," *My Father Was a Toltec*, 8–9.

60. Castillo, "Saturdays," *My Father Was a Toltec*, 14–16.

61. Castillo, *My Father Was a Toltec*, 71–81.

62. Castillo, "Daddy with Chesterfields in a Rolled Up Sleeve," *My Father Was a Toltec*, 136–46.

63. Soto, *Reading Chican@*, 5.

64. Soto, *Reading Chican@*, 1 (emphasis mine).

65. Soto, *Reading Chican@*, 6.

66. Castillo, *My Father Was a Toltec*, 1–19.

67. Castillo, "Alternatives," *My Father Was a Toltec*, 30–31.

68. Castillo, *My Father Was a Toltec*, 8–11.

69. Pérez, *Decolonial Imaginary*, 101.

70. Castillo, *My Father Was a Toltec*, 1–4.

71. Castillo, "Wyoming Crossing Thoughts," *My Father Was a Toltec*, 25–41.

72. Castillo, "An Idyll," *My Father Was a Toltec*, 1–9.

73. Castillo, "An Idyll," *My Father Was a Toltec*, 54–55.

74. Gutiérrez-Jones, *Rethinking the Borderlands*, 111.

75. Castillo, "An Idyll," *My Father Was a Toltec*, 15–17.

76. Castillo, "An Idyll," *My Father Was a Toltec*, 75–78.

77. Castillo, "An Idyll," *My Father Was a Toltec*, 79–82.

78. Castillo, "The Invitation," *My Father Was a Toltec*, 1–2.

79. I have chosen not to ascribe line numbers to this poem. To do so would mean foreclosing the poem's possibilities as afforded by its architecture. By electing not to assign a particular sequence to the stanzas, I have allowed the qualities integral to this poem to remain.

CHAPTER 3. UNBOUNDED AND LIMITLESS

1. Castillo, *Peel My Love like an Onion* (Anchor Books, 2000), 16.

2. Borislavov, "Poetics."

3. Noel, "Bodies that Antimatter," 856.

4. Noel, "Poetry," 291.

5. Salinas, ch. 2 (this volume), "For the Pleasure of the Chicanx Poet," 49.

6. Salinas, ch. 2 (this volume), "For the Pleasure of the Chicanx Poet," 49.

7. Salinas, ch. 2 (this volume), "For the Pleasure of the Chicanx Poet," 49.

8. Castillo, *I Ask the Impossible*, xvi.

9. Keogh Serrano, ch. 1 (this volume), "Lettered Encounters," 33.

10. Salinas, ch. 2 (this volume), "For the Pleasure of the Chicanx Poet," 49.

11. Keogh Serrano, ch. 1 (this volume), "Lettered Encounters," 33.

12. Keogh Serrano, ch. 1 (this volume), "Lettered Encounters," 33.

13. Keogh Serrano, ch. 1 (this volume), "Lettered Encounters," 33.

14. Keogh Serrano quoting Bower, *Epistolary Responses*, 132.

15. Keogh Serrano, ch. 1 (this volume), "Lettered Encounters," 33.

16. Keogh Serrano, ch. 1 (this volume), "Lettered Encounters," 33.

17. Keogh Serrano quoting Greenberg, "Epistolary Women," 288.

18. Castillo, *Massacre of the Dreamers*, 21.

19. Castillo, *Massacre of the Dreamers*, 41.

20. I emphasize my use of the terms "affinities," "affiliations," and "kinships" for Castillo's engagement with experiences of other women of color, over arguing for a collective identity in these examples. I argue for a Latinidad that strategically emphasizes a collective identity for political and social purposes, but that recognizes specific national and cultural identities. I suggest that we see this distinction in Castillo's work, especially in *Sapogonia*. See Arlene Dávila and Suzanne Oboler for their discussions of Latinidad.

21. Castillo, *Massacre of the Dreamers*, 226.

22. Castillo, *Peel My Love Like an Onion*, 124.

23. Castillo, *Peel My Love Like an Onion*, 124.

24. Castillo, "Like the People of Guatemala," *I Ask the Impossible*, 46.

25. Castillo, *Massacre of the Dreamers*, 226.

26. Castillo, *Sapogonia* (Anchor Books, 1994), 1.

27. Castillo, *Sapogonia*, 2.

28. Salinas, ch. 2 (this volume), "For the Pleasure of the Chicanx Poet," 000.

29. Pérez-Torres, *Movements in Chicano Poetry*, 90.

30. Pérez-Torres, *Movements in Chicano Poetry*, 91.

CHAPTER 4. "¿A'CA'O QUÉ, COMADRE?"

1. Alfred Arteaga, *An Other Tongue*, 1.

2. I use the term "fragmented English" instead of the commonly used "broken English" because the latter often reinforces xenophobic and ableist rhetorics of belonging and inclusion.

3. It is important to acknowledge that Spanglish and fragmented English are only a couple out of many border languages that enact decolonial thinking. For instance, Indigenous and some Black communities who live on or near the border

use neither Spanglish nor fragmented English yet still enact decolonial thinking to resist white heteropatriarchal society.

4. Mignolo, "Geopolitics of Sensing and Knowing," 137.

5. Mignolo, *Local Histories / Global Designs*, 256.

6. Castillo, *So Far from God* (Norton, 1993), 177.

7. Castillo, *So Far from God*, 23.

8. Castillo, *So Far from God*, 33.

9. Castillo, *So Far from God*, 165.

10. Castillo, *So Far from God*, 247.

11. hooks, *Yearning: Race, Gender, and Cultural Politics*, 44.

12. Paredes, *Folklore and Culture on The Texas-Mexican Border*, xv.

13. Castillo, *So Far from God*, 251.

14. Castillo, *So Far from God*, 7.

15. Morales, *Living in Spanglish*, 31.

16. Castillo, *So Far from God*, 52.

17. Castillo, *Massacre of the Dreamers* (University of New Mexico Press, 2014), 37.

18. Castillo, *Massacre of the Dreamers*, 21.

19. Hurtado, *Voicing Chicana Feminisms*, 217.

20. Hurtado, *Voicing Chicana Feminisms*, 205.

21. Freire, *Pedagogy of the Oppressed*, 35.

22. Castillo, *So Far from God*, 138.

23. Castillo, *So Far from God*, 137.

24. Castillo, *So Far from God*, 137.

25. Castillo, *So Far from God*, 137.

26. Castillo, *So Far from God*, 137.

27. Castillo, *So Far from God*, 137–38.

28. Castillo, *So Far from God*, 138.

29. Castillo, *So Far from God*, 137.

30. Castillo, *So Far from God*, 138.

31. Castillo, *So Far from God*, 138.

32. Castillo, *So Far from God*, 138.

33. Castillo, *So Far from God*, 138.

34. Castillo, *So Far from God*, 138–39.

35. Castillo, *So Far from God*, 139.

36. Castillo, *So Far from God*, 138.

37. Manríquez, "Ana Castillo's 'So Far from God,'" 39.

38. Castillo, *So Far from God*, 138.

39. Castillo, *So Far from God*, 139.

40. Castillo, *So Far from God*, 140.

41. Castillo, *So Far from God*, 139.

42. Castillo, *So Far from God*, 148.

43. Castillo, *So Far from God*, 138.

44. Ángeles et al., "Entrevista con Ana Castillo," 24. "I have thought about this for ten years, how as Chicanas, as Mexicans, and as Latinas in the United States we have inherited from our grandmothers espiritualidad. And it is the same with politics, because anyway most Chicanas and Latinas who work in the United States with political awareness are healers in their own way, because there is a lot of work to be done in our communities. . . . We are not necessarily doing witchcraft, or anything like that, but we have a lot in common, we are doctors, medics, social workers, and all that is healing; we are looking for ways to blend our Latina Chicana feminist spirituality." This is my translation.

45. Castillo, *So Far from God*, 29.

46. Castillo, *Massacre of the Dreamers*, 21.

47. Castillo, *Massacre of the Dreamers*, 21.

48. Castillo, *So Far from God*, 9.

49. Castillo, *So Far from God*, 177.

50. Castillo, *So Far from God*, 177.

51. Castillo, *So Far from God*, 177.

52. Castillo, *Massacre of the Dreamers*, 38.

53. Castillo, *So Far from God*, 181.

54. Castillo, *So Far from God*, 181.

55. Castillo, *So Far from God*, 182.

56. Castillo, *Massacre of the Dreamers*, 34.

57. Mignolo, *Local Histories / Global Designs*, 256.

CHAPTER 5. IDENTITY FORMATION AND DISLOCATION

1. In my article entitled "Literary Didacticism and Collective Human Rights in US Borderlands: Ana Castillo's *The Guardians* and Louise Erdrich's *The Round House*," I argue that both authors "reject conventional approaches to the role of literature in effectively promoting human rights—which tend to emphasize literature's capacity to spur empathy—by blurring the line between literary, legal, and political realms. Castillo and Erdrich weave into their narratives overt statements about the laws, policies, and colonially rooted biases that contribute to human rights violations in the United States today. They do not just appeal to readers' emotions but also offer readers and would-be activists guidance about what can be done to effect change (e.g., citing specific policies that need to be overhauled) in order to increase the odds that their novels will prompt readers to take action." Szeghi, "Literary Didacticism," 404.

2. See Kandiyoti, "Multiplicity and Its Discontents," and Torres-Saillant, "Nothing to Celebrate."

3. Castillo, *Mixquiahuala Letters* (Bilingual Review Press, 1992), 7.

4. See Kaup, *Rewriting North American Borders*, 82 and 201.

5. Castillo, *Mixquiahuala Letters*, 83.

6. Castillo, *Mixquiahuala Letters*, 130.

7. Castillo, *Mixquiahuala Letters*, 129.

8. Castillo, *Mixquiahuala Letters*, 98.

9. Castillo, *Mixquiahuala Letters*, 100.

10. Castillo, *Mixquiahuala Letters*, 100.

11. As Greenberg observes, "While Mexico proves a vexed homeland, neither does the United States offer Teresa safe haven. The central core of letters suggests that to the extent that Chicana agency and interethnic coalition occur in the United States, their potential is undercut through the exclusion of Mexican bodies. While letter 10 describes San Francisco as a site of burgeoning Chicana feminism and interethnic bonds (42–43), the policing of national others undermines this solidarity. Letter 10 also depicts the deportation of 'long, lost kin / husbands lost to immigration officials taken on a bus / and never heard from again' (43)." See Greenberg, "Epistolary Women," 292.

12. For instance, in one letter Teresa characterizes the women's "shared consciousness" as being as inseparable as "two huge slabs of stone placed adjacent with inexplicable precision by the Incas." Castillo, *Mixquiahuala Letters*, 24. Notably, here there is some slippage between Teresa's attachment to Mexican Indigeneity specifically and Latin American Indigeneity more broadly.

13. Larkin, "Reading as Responsible Dialogue," 150.

14. Castillo, *Mixquiahuala Letters*, 35.

15. Castillo, *Mixquiahuala Letters*, 28–29.

16. Greenberg takes a different view of the role of traveling through Mexico in the formation of Teresa and Alicia's relationship. She argues that "the ancient Mexican homeland for which Teresa longs is not so much a female refuge as a site of male control. To the extent that Mexico is an 'embracing bosom,' it is also a 'homeland/of spiritual devastation' (61)—a space rife with men's betrayal of women. To the extent that female friendship remains viable in the quixotic's narrative, it is despite nations rather than through them." Greenberg, "Epistolary Women," 297. What Greenberg points to here is that whichever narrative path readers choose for reading the letters (Castillo specifies different reading routes for the quixotic, conformist, or cynic) can lead to a different take on any one of the novel's themes, with greater emphasis on one element or another. Nonetheless, I regard it as a misreading not to see Mexico, for all the perils the women face there and even periods of estrangement, as a distinct space in which the women find themselves able to cultivate their friendship in a way they seemingly cannot in the United States.

17. See Szeghi, "Indigeneity and Mestizaje."

18. Indigenismo, in this sense, is a nostalgic idealization of selective aspects of Indigenous cultures that fails to address the experiences and needs of living Indigenous peoples themselves.

19. Alberto, "Topographies of Indigenism," 41.

20. Larkin, "Reading as Responsible Dialogue," 150.

21. Castillo, *Mixquiahuala Letters*, 25.

22. See Szeghi, "Indigeneity and Mestizaje."

23. Castillo, *Guardians*, 4 and 50.

24. Castillo, *Guardians*, 51.

25. Castillo, *Guardians*, 52.

26. Castillo, *Guardians*, 187.

27. Castillo, *Guardians*, e.g., 29.

28. Castillo, *Guardians*, 117.

29. Castillo, *Guardians*, 118.

30. See also Regina's wish that the United States would just acknowledge its need for labor from the South and open the border. Castillo, *Guardians*, 29.

31. Castillo, *Guardians*, 116.

32. Castillo, *Guardians*, 116.

33. Castillo, *Guardians*, 7.

34. Castillo, *Guardians*, 3.

35. Castillo, *Guardians*, 39.

36. Castillo, *Guardians*, 85.

37. Castillo, *Guardians*, 85.

38. Castillo, *Guardians*, 5.

39. Gonzales, "Joaquín," 16.

40. Regarding the Trump administration's limitations on asylum seekers, see Lind, "US has made migrants," and Hesson, "In legal setback."

41. See "Migrant caravan: Trump defends tear gas."

42. According to Sieff, "In some cases, passport applicants with official US birth certificates are being jailed in immigration detention centers and entered into deportation proceedings. In others, they are stuck in Mexico, their passports suddenly revoked when they tried to reenter the United States. As the Trump administration attempts to reduce both legal and illegal immigration, the government's treatment of passport applicants in South Texas shows how US citizens are increasingly being swept up by immigration enforcement agencies." Sieff, "U.S. is denying passports."

43. The Trump administration announced within its first year, on September 5, 2017, that it was ending the Deferred Action on Childhood Arrivals program ("Trump Ends DACA"). Since that time, multiple federal judges and the Supreme Court have blocked the administration from terminating the program (Redden, "Third Judge Blocks"; Dickerson and Shear, "Judge Orders Government").

44. See Shear, Goodnough, and Haberman, "Trump Retreats on Separating Families."

45. See Alvarez, "Parents of 628 migrant children."

46. Lopéz, *Chicano Nations*, 12.

CHAPTER 6. SELLING THE "AUTHENTIC"

1. Giddens, "Consequences of Modernity," 181.

2. Cheng, *Inauthentic*, 5.

3. Cheng, *Inauthentic*, 5.

4. Malefyt, "Gender Constructions," 65.

5. Baltanás, "Fatigue of the Nation," 151.

6. Bhabha, *Location*, 201.

7. Federico García Lorca dedicates many of his poems in his book *Romancero Gitano: Poema del Cante Jondo* to denounce the persecution of the Gypsy. In "Romance de la Guardia Civil Española," for example, the poet creates a *Guernica*-like atmosphere in order to condemn the marginalization of the Gypsy. Enrique Baltanás rightly argues that for García Lorca "the gypsy was the embodiment of protest, the impossibility of the assimilation of the individual by the system, the negation of the status quo." Baltanás, "Fatigue of the Nation," 152.

8. Bhabha, *Location*, 203.

9. Bhabha, *Location*, 106.

10. Baltanás, "Fatigue of the Nation," 153.

11. Simonari, "Bringing," 193.

12. Simonari, "Bringing," 193.

13. Bhabha, *Location*, 107.

14. Paco de Lucía, a participant in Saura's *Carmen*, was one of the many musicians involved in the creation of a hybridized form of flamenco, or "flamenco fusion." Steingress explains that after the constraints flamenco suffered during the years of the Franco dictatorship (only the "authentic" was to be performed), in the years of "La Movida" flamenco was reevaluated as it merged with other music styles. Steingress, "Flamenco Fusion," 192. Steingress makes clear, however, that Paco de Lucía and the others who were the precursors of flamenco fusion "never abandoned their basic musical orientation although they stimulated the creative work of a whole generation of young international flamenco guitarists." Steingress, "Flamenco Fusion," 196.

15. Steingress, "Flamenco Fusion," 198.

16. Mujčinović, *Postmodern*, 5.

17. Castillo, *Peel My Love* (Anchor Books, 1999), 98.

18. Castillo, *Peel My Love*, 84.

19. Castillo, *Peel My Love*, 35.

20. Simonari, "Bringing," 194.

21. Simonari, "Bringing," 195.

22. Castillo, *Peel My Love*, 39.

23. While this chapter focuses on the artistic implications of the transition from dictatorship to democracy, it is important to note different views on the transition as a national narrative. Critics such as Gregorio Morán and Txetxu Aguado

demystify the concept of "transición" in their work. Rather than seeing it as a complete cut with the Francoist dictatorship, they question the official narrative surrounding the transition. As Morán explains: "Lo cierto es que el franquismo no se desmoronó, ni fue derribado, y que los planteamientos políticos del conjunto de las fuerzas democráticas hubieron de ser rápidamente adaptados para afrontar el año 1977 y las primeras elecciones" (The truth is that the Franco regime didn't fall and wasn't overthrown, and that the political proposals made by the group of democratic forces had to be quickly adapted to face the year 1977 and the first elections). Morán, *Precio*, 25. Aguado approaches the transition from the framework of postmodernism, maintaining that "el avance democrático durante la transición nunca ha de significar olvido" (the democratic progress during the transition should never mean forgetting). Aguado, *La tarea*, 167. Both Morán and Aguado see the transition as a fluid concept rather than an abrupt cut from the old regime that culminates in a new democracy and society.

24. Heng, "Nationalism," 31.

25. Heng, "Nationalism," 31.

26. Bhabha, *Location*, 94.

27. Steingress, "Flamenco Fusion," 183.

28. Steingress, "Flamenco Fusion," 184.

29. Castillo, *Peel My Love*, 42.

30. Bhabha, *Location*, 96.

31. Castillo, *Peel My Love*, 33.

32. As Erich Hatala Matthes remarks: "There is general agreement that if cultural appropriation is morally objectionable, it is only objectionable when a member of a dominant cultural group appropriates from a member of a marginalized group." Matthes, "Cultural Appropriation," 347. While Carmen's appropriation of Gypsy culture can be construed as problematic, Carmen's marginal background as described in the novel is socially comparable to that of the Gypsy within Spanish society, rendering it difficult to observe a dominant/marginal dynamic. Carmen's nemesis, La Courtney, would be a more fitting example of a "morally objectionable" appropriator of culture.

33. Corbalán, "Otredad," 74.

34. Anzaldúa, "Homeland," 25.

35. Castillo, *Peel My Love*, 160.

36. Castillo, *Peel My Love*, 3.

37. Bhabha, *Location*, 200.

38. Shohat and Stam, *Unthinking*, 193.

39. Castillo, *Peel My Love*, 30.

40. Castillo, *Peel My Love*, 30.

41. Castillo, *Peel My Love*, 30–31.

42. Castillo, *Peel My Love*, 74.

43. Castillo, *Peel My Love*, 84.

44. Mujčinović, *Postmodern*, 58.

45. Mujčinović, *Postmodern*, 3.

46. Castillo, *Peel My Love*, 187–88.

47. Castillo, *Peel My Love*, 213.

48. Lorente-Murphy, "El baile y canto," 129.

49. Malefyt, "Gender Constructions," 63.

50. Castillo, *Peel My Love*, 80.

51. Huggan, *Post-Colonial*, 157.

52. Cheng, *Inauthentic*, 36.

53. According to Antonio Gades there are two sides to flamenco: "el 'duende' y la perseverancia" ("soul" and persistence). Lorente-Murphy, "El baile y canto," 129.

54. Castillo, *Peel My Love*, 49.

55. Castillo, *Peel My Love*, 50.

56. Castillo, *Peel My Love*, 50.

CHAPTER 7. SO FAR FROM NATION

1. Anzaldúa, *Borderlands* (Aunt Lute Books, 2012), 81.

2. Rasquache derives from the Nahuatl language and is translated in Spanish as "rascuache" (with a "c"). It was a derogatory term meaning "of the lower classes" or that which is "crude or base." And it is exactly because of this meaning that Chicanx artists and writers applied the term to their work mixing high and low art, elevating "street art" to an aesthetic that then defies what is meant by a "pure language" or "art."

3. Anzaldúa, *Borderlands*, 80.

4. Bonifacio, ch. 4 (this volume), "'¿A'ca'o qué, comadre?'," 75.

5. Bonifacio, ch. 4 (this volume), "'¿A'ca'o qué, comadre?'," 75.

6. Bonifacio, ch. 4 (this volume), "'¿A'ca'o qué, comadre?'," 75.

7. Bonifacio, ch. 4 (this volume), "'¿A'ca'o qué, comadre?'," 75.

8. Anzaldúa, *Borderlands*, 38.

9. Anzaldúa, *Borderlands*, 77.

10. Szeghi, ch. 5 (this volume), "Identity Formation and Dislocation," 86.

11. Szeghi, ch. 5 (this volume), "Identity Formation and Dislocation," 86.

12. Rutherford, "The Third Space," 211.

13. Szeghi, ch. 5 (this volume), "Identity Formation and Dislocation," 86.

14. Fielding, ch. 6 (this volume), "Selling the 'Authentic'," 100.

15. Fielding, ch. 6 (this volume), "Selling the 'Authentic'," 100.

16. See Benavides, "Flamenco Fusion."

17. See Peinete Revuelta, "About the Huge Racism."

18. Valentish, "Commodification of Frida Kahlo."

CHAPTER 8. QUEERING SPACE IN ANA CASTILLO'S *GIVE IT TO ME*

1. On the educational aspects of pornography, see, for instance, Rodríguez, *Sexual Futures*, 146–47, and Hartley, "Porn." For readers unfamiliar with queer theory, Nikki Sullivan's *A Critical Introduction to Queer Theory* remains a helpful overview of important ideas in the field. For an introduction to queer theory from a Latinx perspective, see Hames-García, "Queer Theory Revisited."

2. Morales, *Latinx*, 56, 87.

3. Ahmed, *Living a Feminist Life*, 255.

4. Ahmed, *Living a Feminist Life*, 230.

5. Castillo, *Black Dove*, 1.

6. Further examples include Jack Halberstam's *In a Queer Time and Place*; Kate Eichhorn's *The Archival Turn in Feminism*; Juana María Rodríguez's *Sexual Futures, Queer Gestures, and Other Latina Longings*; and Tim Dean, Steven Ruszczycky, and David Squires's *Porn Archives*. Lawrence La Fountain-Stokes's *Queer Ricans* is one of my favorite Latinx examples.

7. Reed, "Whiter the Bread," 61 (emphasis in original).

8. Rodríguez, *Queer Latinidad*, 31–32.

9. Mills, "Creating a Resistant Chicana Aesthetic," 317.

10. Castillo, *Give It to Me*, 3. Further references to this novel are given in parentheses in the text.

11. Castillo describes her own work as a translator in *Black Dove*; see p. 103.

12. On incest as a queer subject, see Cvetkovich, *Archive of Feelings*, 83–117 (chapter 3).

13. On the various facets of biphobia, see Eisner, *Bi*, 59–93 (chapter 2).

14. Eisner, *Bi*, 35.

15. Gómez-Vega, "Homoerotic Tease," 80.

16. Berlant and Warner, "Sex in Public," 171.

17. Castillo, *Massacre*, 72–73.

18. Perkins, *Secret Record*, 129. Eric Schaefer discusses the development of this structure throughout "Gauging a Revolution."

19. Castillo, *Massacre*, 145.

20. Rodríguez, *Sexual Futures*, 2. Ariane Cruz concurs that color is a form of queerness; Cruz, *Color of Kink*, 3.

21. Rodríguez, *Queer Latinidad*, 135–38; Rodríguez, *Sexual Futures*, 55–60, 120.

22. Castillo, "Evolution," 50.

23. Castillo, "La Macha," 25. Chapter 6 of Castillo's *Massacre of the Dreamers* is a revision of this essay, but I cite the older version to show how little attitudes have changed since then.

24. I am unaware of any accounts of this story in print, but I know it because Castillo and I were colleagues when she was the Writer in Residence during the fall 2012 semester at Westminster College in Salt Lake City, Utah. She was revising *Give It to Me* at this time and discussed the novel's publication difficulties in several of our conversations. Castillo has written some about the genesis of the novel, noting that it was "inspir[ed]" by her reading of Charles Bukowski's fiction and that when she was having difficulty completing what would become *Black Dove*, which was already under contract with the Feminist Press, they happily took *Give It to Me* first (*Black Dove*, 203n1, 281–82).

25. Castillo, "La Macha," 24.

26. Cuevas, *Post-Borderlandia*, 10. Catrióna Rueda Esquibel and Alicia Gaspar de Alba each examine the lineage of queer Chicana literature, though they both erase Castillo's bisexuality by considering her as a "lesbian" writer.

27. Note that Palma would have barely been born when *Numbers* was published because she is forty-two when *Give It to Me* takes place, and it takes place during the Great Recession, which began in 2008, so 1966 is the earliest she could have been born; Castillo, *Give It to Me*, 7. Her highlighting of Rechy's good looks at the time might thus be considered anachronistic, a memory of Castillo's rather than Palma's. Nevertheless, its inclusion remains the important thing because of how it gestures toward the Latinx queer tradition.

28. Cuevas, *Post-Borderlandia*, 60.

29. Rechy, *Sexual Outlaw*, 28, 206.

30. Rechy, *Sexual Outlaw*, 16; e.g., 23.

31. Rechy, *Sexual Outlaw*, 48.

32. Castillo, "Interview," 61.

33. I use this gendered term (Chicano) here because it was the term used by the movement itself at the time.

34. Castiglia and Reed, *If Memory Serves*, 170–71, 172. I first learned of *The Sexual Outlaw* from *If Memory Serves*, thus my writing about Rechy here is an example of the queer academic lineage building they call for throughout their book. I must acknowledge, however, that more recently a statement Reed posted on his professional website (since removed) has been named as transphobic by Grace Lavery and others. Although I have been unable to read the statement, it is the oppressed who get to define what actions are oppressive rather than their oppressors, so I accept Lavery's claims. In this instance, Reed and Castiglia (who joined Reed in his response to Lavery) fail to live up to their ideals of queer community building from *If Memory Serves*. However, I do not feel that this failure invalidates the ideals themselves. For more on the controversy, see Lavery, "Grad School"; Castiglia and Reed, "Conversion Therapy"; and Adair et al., "Open Letter."

35. Cheng, *Radical Love*, 60; Pellegrini, "Queer Structures," 240–41. I discuss this issue further in *Queering Mennonite Literature*; see pp. 6, 129.

36. Mills, "Creating a Resistant Chicana Aesthetic," 329; Wallace, *Of Women Borne*, 125–67.

37. Castillo, *Massacre*, 229.

38. Lopez, "Introduction," xi–xii.

39. Castillo, *Black Dove*, 68.

40. Cuevas, *Post-Borderlandia*, 55.

CHAPTER 9. QUEER(ING) MOTHERHOOD IN ANA CASTILLO'S *BLACK DOVE: MAMÁ, MI'JO, AND ME*

1. Pérez, *Decolonial Imaginary*, 116, 123.

2. Pérez, *Decolonial Imaginary*, 122.

3. Pérez, *Decolonial Imaginary*, 120.

4. Pérez, *Decolonial Imaginary*, 122.

5. Park, *Mothering Queerly, Queering Motherhood*, 17.

6. Rodríguez, *Sexual Futures*, 20.

7. Sánchez, *Essays on la mujer*; Norma Alarcón, "Traddutora, Traditora; Del Castillo, *Between Borders*; Moraga, *Last Generation*; Trujillo, *Chicana Lesbians*.

8. In the sequel to *Chicana* (1979), *A Crushing Love: Chicanas, Motherhood and Activism* (2009) offers Morales the opportunity to continue amplifying the subjective meaning-making process of mothers, mothering, and motherhood. I reference this documentary because it records the struggle of women in their roles as mothers and cements what I find to be the most important contribution of Castillo's positionality in *Black Dove*: the account of a single mother.

9. Castillo, *Black Dove*, 159.

10. Castillo, *Black Dove*, 159.

11. Castillo, *Black Dove*, 1.

12. Bermudez, Stinson, Zak-Hunter, and Abrams, "Mejor Sola Que Mal Acompañada," 622–41.

13. Bermudez, Stinson, Zak-Hunter, and Abrams, "Mejor Sola Que Mal Acompañada," 635.

14. Castillo, *Black Dove*, 251.

15. Castillo, *Black Dove*, 267.

16. To understand the manner in which Castillo's queer motherhood lens relates to the Virgin of Guadalupe, see *Goddess of the Americas: Writings on the Virgin of Guadalupe* (1997).

17. "Día de la Madre," np. English translation: "At the beginning of the 20th century, a feminist movement emerged, encouraged by the Mexican Revolution, which discussed maternity, contraceptive methods, and defended the emancipation and rights of women. As a response to this movement, according to the book 'El ten de mayo' by Marta Acevedo, in 1922, the newspaper 'Excélsior,' the Archdiocese, the then Secretary of Public Education and other entities began to celebrate Mother's Day on May 10. The newspaper requested the participation of readers to propose a holiday for the mothers and, in this way, it was established on May 10.

The media reported that it did so to 'pay homage of affection and respect to the mother.'"

18. Chicana m(other)work is a concept and project informed by our specific gendered, classed, and racialized experiences. Chicana m(other)work offers a new interpretation of motherwork that looks at the layers of care work we do in our communities through activism, self-care, teaching, and mothering (https://www .chicanamotherwork.com).

19. "Given it to the globe" makes an intertextual reference to Castillo's novel *Give It to Me* (2014), precisely because of the bisexual politics that center the narrative.

20. Pérez, *Decolonial Imaginary*, 22.

21. Cohen, "Punks, Bulldaggers, and Welfare Queens," 437–65.

22. On page 11 in the *Decolonial Imaginary*, Pérez reminds us that:

> the writings of Chicano history have focused on social change, but the discourse has been shaped so that gender/sex does not have to be part of the paradigm. In this way, I believe that postmodern questions provide a fresh look at Chicana/o history and the manner in which gender and sex is contemplated and negated. Paradigms that take into account only the cultural condition of the worker have been useful, but constricting. While I would not abandon historical materialism, I would build upon a model with Sandoval's differential consciousness, with the interstitial space where Bhabha locates culture, and with Foucault's dream of "a history that would be both an act of long, uninterrupted patience and the vivacity of a movement, which, in the end, breaks all bounds"—in essence, an archaeology in which movement does not rely on a teleological history.

23. Soto, *Reading Chican@*, 9.

24. Furthermore, José David Saldívar's argument that "decolonial expressions restructure minoritized identities by reframing their position as stakeholders in hemispheric and spherical understanding of the world as a system" in *Trans-Americanity* (2012), in tandem with Sandra Soto's theorizations about radicalized sexuality and the ways "a range of Chican@ thinkers have been invested in asking complex questions about the relationship between collective circumstances and individual desires, between material realities and interiority, and particularly about why we love the way we do," in *Reading Chican@ like a Queer* (2011), extend Pérez's significance of the importance for Chicanas to amass a *"sitio y lengua"*; this is outlined in Pérez's "Sexuality and Discourse: Notes from a Chicana Survivor," which appears in Carla Trujillo's *Chicana Lesbians: The Girls Our Mothers Warned Us About* (1991).

25. Castillo, *Black Dove*, 132.

26. Castillo, *Black Dove*, 138.

27. Castillo, *Black Dove*, 140.

28. Castillo, *Black Dove*, 147.

29. The work of Juana María Rodríguez permits a further understanding of "failed." *Sexual Futures, Queer Gestures, and Other Latina Longings* (2014) empha-

sizes the importance of queer theory in understanding queer social bonds and why sex matters for new definitions of other sexual futures. Drawing from José Esteban Muñoz's concept of "futurity" and "horizon," Rodríguez discusses theories on gesture to argue that a "Latina longing" exists for understanding queer sexual futures outside deficit models, hence notions of failure. Similarly, in the article "Queer Politics, Bisexual Erasure: Sexuality at the Nexus of Race, Gender and Statistics" (2016), Rodríguez debunks the idea of bisexuality as a failure and critiques such opinions as a colonial symptom of both heterosexual and homosexual thought that is bound to normative frameworks.

30. Castillo, *Black Dove*, 141.

31. Sandoval, *Methodology of the Oppressed*.

32. Caballero and Castillo, "Chicana Motherwork Anthology: Porque sin madres no hay revolución," xiii.

33. Caballero, Martínez-Vu, Pérez-Torres, Téllez, and Vega, *Chicana Motherwork Anthology*.

34. Caballero and Castillo, "Chicana Motherwork Anthology," ix.

35. Castillo, *Black Dove*, xii.

36. Castillo, *Black Dove*, 47.

37. Mesa-Bains, "Domesticana"; McMahon, *Domestic Negotiations*.

38. Castillo, *Black Dove*, 49.

39. Castillo, *Black Dove*, 49.

40. Castillo, *Black Dove*, 47.

41. Pertusa and Torres, *Tortilleras*.

42. Moraga, *Giving Up the Ghost*, 35.

43. Moraga, *Waiting in the Wings*, 15–22.

44. Castillo, *Black Dove*, 101.

CHAPTER 10. NOSTALGIA FOR A FUTURE

1. Soto, "Queerness," 76.

2. Anzaldúa, *Borderlands* (Aunt Lute Books, 2007), 41.

3. Moraga, "Queer Aztlán," 147.

4. Moraga, "Queer Aztlán," 150.

5. Keeling, *Black Futures*, 35.

6. Keeling, *Black Futures*, 35.

7. Castillo, *Mixquiahuala Letters* (Anchor Books, 1992), 36–37.

8. Williams, *Marxism*, 129.

9. Rodríguez, *Sexual Futures*, 11.

10. Rodríguez, *Sexual Futures*, 11.

11. Rodríguez, *Sexual Futures*, 11.

12. Quiroga, *Tropics of Desire*, 72.

13. Quiroga, *Tropics of Desire*, 75.

14. Quiroga, *Tropics of Desire*, 19.

15. Castillo, *Mixquiahuala Letters*, 25.

16. Castillo, *Mixquiahuala Letters*, 65.

17. Castillo, *Mixquiahuala Letters*, 29.

18. Castillo, *Mixquiahuala Letters*, 52.

19. Nieto-Gómez, "La Chicana," 48.

20. Castillo, *Mixquiahuala Letters*, 27.

21. Cisneros, "Guadalupe the Sex Goddess," 44.

22. Castillo, *Mixquiahuala Letters*, 65.

23. Castillo, *Mixquiahuala Letters*, 35.

24. Castillo, *Mixquiahuala Letters*, 35.

25. Esquibel, "Memories of Girlhood," 645.

26. Esquibel, "Memories of Girlhood," 649.

27. Weissberger, "Queer Don Quijote," 12.

28. Weissberger, "Queer Don Quijote," 12.

29. Castillo, *Mixquiahuala Letters*, 63.

30. Castillo, *Mixquiahuala Letters*, 106.

31. Castillo, *Mixquiahuala Letters*, 110.

32. Castillo, *Mixquiahuala Letters*, 110.

33. Castillo, *Mixquiahuala Letters*, 7.

34. Castillo, *Mixquiahuala Letters*, 57.

35. Castillo, *Mixquiahuala Letters*, 57.

36. Castillo, *Mixquiahuala Letters*, 51.

37. Castillo, *Mixquiahuala Letters*, 51.

38. Castillo, *Mixquiahuala Letters*, 52.

CHAPTER 11. GIVING IT TO THE GLOBE

1. Avilés, ch. 9 (this volume), "Queer(ing) Motherhood," 000.

2. Soto, *Reading Chican@ like a Queer*, 1.

3. Pérez, *Decolonial Imaginary*, 1.

4. Muñoz, *Cruising Utopia*, 1.

5. Muñoz, *Disidentifications*, 1.

6. Rodríguez, *Sexual Futures*, 1, 89.

7. Muñoz, *Sense of Brown*, 1.

8. Avilés, ch. 9 (this volume), "Queer(ing) Motherhood," 134.

9. Avilés, ch. 9 (this volume), "Queer(ing) Motherhood," 134.

10. Avilés, ch. 9 (this volume), "Queer(ing) Motherhood," 134.

11. Cruz, ch. 8 (this volume), "Queering Space," 123.

12. Cruz, ch. 8 (this volume), "Queering Space," 123.

13. Cruz, ch. 8 (this volume), "Queering Space," 123.

14. Cruz, ch. 8 (this volume), "Queering Space," 123.

15. Cruz, ch. 8 (this volume), "Queering Space," 123.

16. González, ch. 10 (this volume), "Nostalgia for a Future," 148.

17. González, ch. 10 (this volume), "Nostalgia for a Future," 148.

18. González, ch. 10 (this volume), "Nostalgia for a Future," 148.

19. González, ch. 10 (this volume), "Nostalgia for a Future," 148.

20. González, ch. 10 (this volume), "Nostalgia for a Future," 148.

21. González, ch. 10 (this volume), "Nostalgia for a Future," 148.

CHAPTER 12. PRIESTESS *Y PASTORA*

1. The use of the verb "theologize" is purposeful as the word is defined as to "engage in theological reasoning or speculation" in the *Oxford English Dictionary*. This act of engaging is transgressive for a woman particularly with a Catholic priest, as the gendered hierarchies are delineated to prescribe male authority over all theological questions. Raab, *When Women Become Priests*, 39.

2. Castillo, *So Far from God* (Norton, 1993), 23.

3. Castillo, *So Far from God*, 23.

4. Escandón, *Esperanza's Box of Saints*, 244.

5. Escandón, *Esperanza's Box of Saints*, 244–45.

6. Alarcón, Kaplan, and Moallem, *Between Woman and Nation*, 1.

7. Alarcón, Kaplan, and Moallem, *Between Woman and Nation*, 2.

8. Mohanty, *Feminism without Borders*, 1–2.

9. Pérez, *Chicana Art*, 19.

10. Johnson, "Covert Wars in the Bedroom and Nation," 159.

11. Johnson, "Covert Wars in the Bedroom and Nation," 157.

12. Sandoval, *Methodology of the Oppressed*, 58.

13. Sandoval, *Methodology of the Oppressed*, 61.

14. *Penitentes* are a "lay Catholic penitential brotherhood of New Mexican flagellants, who long have called themselves Los Hermanos de Nuestro Padre Jesus Nazareno," and have existed since the eighteenth century. Espinosa explains that their most important purpose is "to commemorate the Passion and Death of Christ during the Lenten season and especially during Holy Week" by flagellating themselves, carrying a large wooden cross, and even wrapping cacti around their bodies to perform the "disciplinas" of their rituals. Espinosa, "The Origin of the Penitentes of New Mexico," 1–2.

15. Alarcón, "Native Woman," 68.

16. Alarcón, "Native Woman," 68.

17. Definition of trafficking: "The recruitment, transportation, transfer, harbouring or receipt of persons, by means of the threat or use of force or other forms of coercion, of abduction, of fraud, of deception, of the abuse of power or of a position of vulnerability or of the giving or receiving of payments or benefits to achieve the consent of a person having control over another person, for the purpose of exploitation. Exploitation shall include, at a minimum, the exploitation of

the prostitution of others or other forms of sexual exploitation, forced labour or services, slavery or practices similar to slavery, servitude or the removal of organs." UNDOC, "Protocol to Prevent, Suppress and Punish," n.p.

18. Escandón, *Esperanza's Box of Saints*, 49.

19. Some Protestant denominations also prescribe roles and expectations regarding gender but with different theological bases than Catholicism.

20. Although the Roman Catholic church is categorized under the inclusive term "Christianity," Catholicism must not be confused with Protestant Christian denominations, many of which do allow women to take on leadership roles. According to the Pew Research Center, the Protestant denominations that do *not* allow female leadership at an executive level (pastoral, deaconry) are The Church of Jesus Christ of Latter-day Saints (Mormons), the Missouri Synod Lutheran Church, and the Southern Baptist Convention. In addition, even though it is not Protestant or Catholic, the Orthodox Church of America falls under the category of "Christianity" but also does not allow female leadership. Maschi, "The Divide over Ordaining Women," n.p.

21. Raab, *When Women Become Priests*, 39.

22. These documents are "Declaration *Inter Insigniores* on the Question of Admission of Women to the Ministerial Priesthood" (1976), which contains "four drafts of a pastoral letter on women" and an apostolic letter written by Pope John Paul II in 1994 titled "Ordinatio Sacerdotalis."

23. Raab, *When Women Become Priests*, 36.

24. According to the *Encyclopedia of Religion*, Thomas Aquinas (1225–1274) was an Italian Dominican theologist whose teachings were, and continue to be, influential in Catholic doctrine. He wrote *Summa Theologica*, which contains all of the teachings of Christianity and five famous arguments supporting the existence of God. Aquinas was canonized July 18, 1323, by Pope John XXII.

25. Aquinas, *Summa Theologica*, part 3, supplement, question 39, article 1.

26. Segura and Pesquera, "Beyond Indifference and Antipathy," 72.

27. Segura and Pesquera, "Beyond Indifference and Antipathy," 73.

28. Anzaldúa, *Borderlands*, 58.

29. Many Chicana feminists have theorized and posited that Malinche, being a slave to the Mayas and subsequently to Hernán Cortés, used her ability of speech to survive her oppressive situation. Chicana literature thus paints Malinche as a visionary, who saw beyond her circumstances. La Llorona is also a figure that has been reappropriated by Chicana feminists. While she is not a historical figure like Malinche, La Llorona has been represented as a murderous mother seeking revenge, who then feels remorse for eternity seeking her dead children; she is a well-known folkloric cautionary tale. Chicana feminists have taken the vituperative representation of La Llorona to theorize how a woman in dire circumstances will look for her lost children as long as it takes. She will be transgressive and commit the taboo acts in order to find her children. Anzaldúa, *Borderlands*, 52, 55.

30. Schoeffel, *Maternal Conditions* , 46.

31. Castillo, *So Far from God*, 28.

32. A. Espinosa wrote about *la Malogra* in Nuevomexicano folklore:

> The myth about the evil one, *la malora* (*mala hora*), also pronounced *malogra* (literally, "the evil hour"), is indeed interesting, both from the purely folk-lore side as well as from the philological side. How mala hora, the evil hour, ill fate, bad luck, came to be thought of as a definite concrete idea of an individual wicked spirit, is interesting from more than one point of view. This myth is a well-known one. *La malora* is an evil spirit which wanders about in the darkness of the night at the cross-roads and other places. It terrorizes the unfortunate ones who wander alone at night, and has usually the form of a large lock of wool or the whole fleece of wool of a sheep (*un vellón de lana*). Sometimes it takes a human form, but this is rare; and the New Mexicans say that when it has been seen in human form, it presages ill fate, death, or the like. When it appears on dark nights in the shape of a fleece of wool, it diminishes and increases in size in the very presence of the unfortunate one who sees it. It is also generally believed that a person who sees la malora, like one who sees a ghost (*un difunto*), forever remains senseless. When asked for detailed information about this myth, the New Mexicans give the general reply, "It is an evil thing" (*es cosa mala*). (Espinosa, "New Mexican Folk-Lore," 400)

33. Castillo, *So Far from God*, 39.

34. Castillo, *So Far from God*, 39.

35. Castillo, *So Far from God*, 32.

36. La Llorona "is a figure of mourning that weeps for the losses Chicanas and Chicanos have sustained in contemporary mainstream American culture, especially women, who suffer gender as well as ethnic oppression. *She is, at the same time, a figure of revolt against those same losses.*" Perez, *There Was a Woman*, 35.

37. hooks, *Yearning*, 41.

38. Maringer, "Priests and Priestesses in Prehistoric Europe," 101.

39. Sandoval, *Methodology of the Oppressed*, 139.

40. Rabuzzi, *Sacred and the Feminine*, 42.

41. Etymological history of "home"; "Despite the fact that home is a concept deeply embedded in our thinking, no distinct word exists for it in classical Greek or ancient Hebrew. . . . Despite the absence of a separate word to distinguish it from the closely related house, the underlying idea is implicit at times in classical Greek. For instance, it sometimes attaches to the word 'family' (oikia, oikikos), as occurs in the Septuagint, the Greek translation of the Old Testament." Rabuzzi, *Sacred and the Feminine*, 44.

42. Rabuzzi, *Sacred and the Feminine*, 55–56.

43. Castillo, *So Far from God*, 55.

44. Castillo, *So Far from God*, 138.

45. Escandón, *Esperanza's Box of Saints*, 76.

46. Sandoval, *Methodology of the Oppressed*, 142.

47. John 10:11, New International Version.

48. A *limpia* is "a ritual sweeping designed to protect a person from harm, to remove bad influences, and to provide spiritual strength." Trotter and Chavira, *Curanderismo: Mexican American Folk Healing*, 181.

49. Pérez, *Chicana Art*, 20.

50. In August of 2016, Pope Francis announced that he would establish a commission for the study of deaconship for women, comprised of six men and six women. The announcement indicates that the commission's purpose is to consider the calling of deaconship for women "especially with regard to the first ages of the Church." "Pope Institutes Commission," Vatican Radio, 2016.

CHAPTER 13. THE UNBREAKABLE LINK

Epigraph. Giddings, "Some Themes in the Poetry of Margaret Walker," 20.

1. Loubet, "Ana Castillo Reveals Her Own Life."

2. Cole, "Interview with Ana Castillo," 61.

3. *Xicanista* is a term that I use to describe someone who supports the ideas of Xicanisma. Castillo uses the term in the twentieth anniversary edition of *Massacre of the Dreamers* (2014); see pp. 2, 223, 227.

4. Quoted in Ricardo F. Vivancos Pérez, *Radical Chicana Poetics*, 14.

5. Filipino labor organizer Larry Itliong also played a crucial role in the founding and expansion of the United Farm Workers of America and was one of the organization's early leaders.

6. These movements include the US civil rights movement, Chicano movement, and the *movimiento negro* of Colombia; they all took place in the twentieth century.

7. African American poets Margaret Walker (1915–1998) and Maya Angelou (1928–2014) are two examples of active female authors of the US Black freedom movement.

8. Castillo and Cantú, "Conversation with Ana Castillo," 61.

9. Castillo, *Massacre of the Dreamers* (Plume, 1994), 95.

10. Castillo, *Massacre of the Dreamers*, 116.

11. There are direct links between the writings of Gloria Anzaldúa and Ana Castillo that move beyond the theoretical and thematic. In her notes to *Massacre of the Dreamers*, Castillo directs the reader to *This Bridge Called My Back: Writings by Radical Women of Color* (1981), edited by Cherríe Moraga and Gloria Anzaldúa. Castillo translated the book into Spanish.

12. Anzaldúa, *Borderlands* (Aunt Lute Books, 2007), 100.

13. Anzaldúa, *Borderlands*, 100–101.

14. Castillo, *Massacre of the Dreamers*, 226.

15. Castillo, *Massacre of the Dreamers*, 6.

16. "Diaspora," traditionally used to describe the movement of Jewish peoples throughout the world, was first applied to people of African descent beginning in the 1960s when anti-colonial freedom movements in Africa and the civil rights

struggle in the United States brought attention to racist systems and an international Black world and cultures that encompass what came to be known as the African Diaspora. Butler, "Defining Diaspora," 195.

17. Anzaldúa, *Borderlands*, 33.

18. Anzaldúa, *Borderlands*, 25.

19. Anzaldúa, *Borderlands*, 102.

20. Afolabi A. Epega and Philip John Neimark explain that in the West African Yoruba tradition, "We are literally part of a *body* that includes every life form and energy in our universe. While we are overwhelmingly human, within each of us reside small, fractionated particles of energy that represent the rest of our *body*. Poets and philosophers have often written that within all of us is the sea, the sky, the trees, the lion, and so on. In the Yoruba tradition, that is literally true." See Epega and Neimark, *Sacred Ifa Oracle* (1995), viii.

21. Castillo, *Massacre of the Dreamers*, 21.

22. Castillo, *Massacre of the Dreamers*, 17.

23. See Anzaldúa, *Borderlands*, 48. While this conceptualization of ancestral knowledge was a shift from culturally dominant forms of understanding power, it should be noted that it does not reflect universal understandings of the ancestors for the Chicano or Indigenous communities. Some Chicana feminists have critically called attention to the tendency in "New Tribalism" to essentialize native-ness and assume an Aztec or Mexic Amerindian perspective when the authors themselves may have been quite distant temporally and culturally from those societies. This critique, relevant to current debates within Indigenous studies, sheds light on the multiple uses of ancestral memory by the poets. This essay focuses more closely on the ways in which the language of ancestral memory was used in a particular historical moment of the late twentieth century that ran parallel to African Diasporic poetic discussions of the same themes. For more on this body of literature, see Pérez, "New Tribalism."

24. Castillo, *Massacre of the Dreamers*, 166.

25. Zapata Peréz, "Esbozo autobiográfico," 210. I translate the Spanish to English as follows: "the compass that has known me, since my earliest age, to access the path of ethnic and cultural reaffirmation, and the understanding of the world."

26. Castillo, *Massacre of the Dreamers*, 164.

27. Castillo, *Massacre of the Dreamers*, 164.

28. Castillo, *Massacre of the Dreamers*, 171.

29. When using the term *conscientización*, Castillo draws from the work of Paulo Freire, the author of *Pedagogy of the Oppressed* (1968).

30. Castillo, *Massacre of the Dreamers*, 13.

31. Castillo, *Massacre of the Dreamers*, 170.

32. Zapata Pérez, "Esbozo autobiográfico," 203. I translate the Spanish into English as follows: "goddess of death and life, enchained to me in time" and "Creation of profound spiritual resistance that ignited the suffering."

33. Zapata Pérez, "Consciousness-Raising," 367.

34. Zapata Pérez, "Consciousness-Raising," 367.

35. To my knowledge, Zapata Pérez did not use the term Afro-Latinx. I use it here as a capacious and inclusive term that applies to people of African descent with origins in Latin America, including Haiti.

36. After completing a pilgrimage to Harlem to meet Langston Hughes in the 1940s, he spent the rest of the twentieth century fighting for the civil and cultural rights of Afro-Colombians. His work, and that of other activists, led to the ratification Law 70, Article 55, of the Colombian Constitution in 1993. This radical legislation recognized the need to protect Indigenous and Afro-Colombian rights and territories that had long been exploited as a result of Spanish colonialism in the country.

37. As explained in Cuesta Escobar and Ocampo Zamorano, *Antología de mujeres*, 240.

38. Zapata Pérez, "Consciousness-Raising," 359.

39. Zapata Pérez, "Consciousness-Raising," 366.

40. Zapata Pérez, "América," 163. I translate the Spanish to English as follows: "America / My loins / speak ancient memories / Magical moments / populate my veins. / Through me, history bleeds. / The link / unbreakable bond / that unites me to the ancestors. / Whispers: / black, Indian, white. / Voices palpitate! / voices call me! / Mestiza! / Shaman! / Christian! / I am / Alienated dance in / the night of drums / Sadness of an Indian flute / Conqueror of breastplate and arquebus. / Voices palpitate, Voices call me. / They flow together: / the waters, the bloods, the rivers. / America!"

41. Zapata Pérez states in her brief autobiography that "la saga del mestizaje" is "de la africanización." I translate the Spanish to English as "the saga of mestizaje" is "from the Africanization." See "Esbozo autobiográfico," 203.

42. While the Americas have a significant and influential population of Asian descent, this ethnic and cultural group is not included in the tri-ethnicity that Zapata Pérez discusses. This might be due to the fact that fewer Asian people and their descendants settled in Colombia than in countries such as Cuba, Mexico, Panama, and the United States.

43. Cuesta Escobar and Ocampo Zamorano, *Antología de mujeres*, 245. I translate the Spanish to English as follows: "Today I will give you my song and joy / we will not speak of your night nor mine. / We will embroider a dress in honor of Coatlicue: / you will put nails from your moon heart / I will pour to the wind a Rain of feathers. / We will watch her skirt fly in the gardens."

44. Castillo, *Massacre of the Dreamers*, 166.

45. Castillo, *Massacre of the Dreamers*, 17.

46. Castillo, *Massacre of the Dreamers*, 146.

47. Castillo, *Massacre of the Dreamers*, 17.

48. Moreno Vega, "Ancestral Sacred Creative Impulse," 46.

49. Moreno Vega, "Ancestral Sacred Creative Impulse," 47.

50. Zapata Pérez, "Esbozo autobiográfico," 213. I translate the Spanish to English as follows: "Let's leave the pious acts for the pious and free ourselves from their chains the intuitive being, the creator of verses, the fire and the silence, the goddesses of love. Let's give back life to the dark night that the dawn frees."

CHAPTER 14. FEMINIST IMAGINARIES OF JUSTICE

1. Ana Castillo Papers, "Margo del Salvador," CEMA 2, University of California, Santa Barbara; Castillo, *Sapogonia*; Castillo, *Watercolor Women, Opaque Men*; Castillo, "Like the people of Guatemala, I want to be free of these memories"; Castillo, *Psst . . . I Have Something to Tell You, Mi Amor.*

2. Ortiz, *Blindfold's Eyes.*

3. The Latin American Federation of Associations of Relatives of Detainees-Disappeared (FEDEFFAM) defines *disappearance* as "any act or omission intended to hide the fate of an opponent or political dissident whose whereabouts are unknown to his/her family, friends or associates, undertaken with the intent to repress, ban or obstruct opposition or dissidence, by persons exercising governmental functions or public agents of any kind or by organized groups of private citizens acting with the support or tolerance from the above mentioned persons" (qtd. in Brody and González, "Nunca Más," 370). See Esparza, "Toward a Feminist Theory of Justice for the Disappeared," for an extended discussion of feminist conceptualizations of justice.

4. See, for example: Anzaldúa, *Borderlands*; Anzaldúa and Keating, *This Bridge We Call Home*; Moraga, *Loving in the War Years* and "Art in América Con Acento"; Moraga and Anzaldúa, *This Bridge Called My Back*; Viramontes "The Writes Ofrenda"; Kevane and Heredia, "Praying for Knowledge: An Interview with Helena María Viramontes."

5. See, for example: Christian, "Race for Theory," and Saldívar-Hull, *Feminism on the Border.*

6. See, for example: Beverly, *Subalternity and Representation*; Beverly and Zimmerman, *Literature and Politics in the Central American Revolutions*; de la Campa, *Latin Americanism*; Gugelberger, *Real Thing*; Saldaña-Portillo, *Revolutionary Imagination in the Americas.*

7. Cantú, "Conversation with Ana Castillo," 61.

8. Castillo, *Ana Castillo Blog*, accessed April 9, 2010, http://anacastillo.com/ac/blog/archives/2007_11_01_index.shtml (site discontinued).

9. Castillo, *Ana Castillo Blog.*

10. Huerta, *Chicano Theatre*, 9.

11. Huerta, *Chicano Theatre*, 103.

12. Yarbro-Bejarano, "Female Subject in Chicano Theatre"; Broyles-González, "Living Legacy of Chicana Performers" and *El Teatro Campesino*; Ramírez, *Chicanas/Latinas in American Theatre*; Huerta, *Chicano Drama.*

13. Yarbro-Bejarano, "Teatropoesía by Chicanas in the Bay Area" and "Female Subject in Chicano Theatre."

14. Yarbro-Bejarano, "Teatropoesía by Chicanas in the Bay Area" and "Female Subject in Chicano Theatre."

15. Martínez, "Still Treading Water."

16. Archbishop of Guatemala, *Guatemala: Never Again!*

17. See Mignolo, *Darker Side of the Renaissance*, for an extended discussion about the coloniality of power.

18. Esquibel, *With Her Machete in Her Hand*, 69. The case of Sor Juana Inés de La Cruz, a sister at the convent of Saint Jerónimo in colonial Mexico City—an order dedicated to penance, contemplation, and study—is instructive because she was persecuted for her intellectual activities and defense of women's educational rights. However, this alone did not ignite the wrath of the church hierarchy. Sor Juana's sexuality has been the subject of much speculation precisely because she was a nun who had many close female friends and wrote poems dedicated to some of them (Rebolledo, *Chronicles of Panchita Villa and Other Guerrilleras*, 56, 210).

19. Inda's "The Value of Immigrant Life" is particularly insightful on such matters.

20. National Security Archive, "Relevant Declassified U.S. Documents from the National Security Archive's Guatemala Collection."

21. Ortiz, *Blindfold's Eyes*, 427.

22. Burgers and Danelius, *United Nations Convention against Torture.*

23. McPherson, *Intimate Ties, Bitter Struggles*, 36–39.

24. United States Institute of Peace, "Peace Agreements."

25. Gill, *School of the Americas*; Sanford, *Buried Secrets*, 6.

26. LaFeber, *Inevitable Revolutions.*

27. La Comisión para el Esclarecimiento Histórico (CEH), *Guatemala.*

28. Sanford, *Buried Secrets.*

29. Moving forward I will distinguish between Castillo's character—Sister Dianna—and Sister Ortiz the historical subject who inspired Castillo's creative writing by using "Sister Dianna" to refer to the subject of Castillo's writing and "Sister Ortiz" to refer to the historical person, Sister Dianna Ortiz.

30. Castillo, *I Ask the Impossible.*

31. Ortiz, *Blindfold's Eyes*, 337.

32. Castillo, *Psst . . . I Have Something to Tell You, Mi Amor*, xi.

33. Castillo, *Psst . . . I Have Something to Tell You, Mi Amor*, xi.

34. Castillo, *Psst . . . I Have Something to Tell You, Mi Amor*, xi–xiii.

35. Gómez-Barris, *Where Memory Dwells*, 99.

36. Castillo, *Psst . . . I Have Something to Tell You, Mi Amor*, 3.

37. Castillo, *Psst . . . I Have Something to Tell You, Mi Amor*, 12–13.

38. Castillo, *Psst . . . I Have Something to Tell You, Mi Amor*, 3.

39. Castillo, *Psst . . . I Have Something to Tell You, Mi Amor*, 13.

40. Castillo, *Psst . . . I Have Something to Tell You, Mi Amor*, 14.

41. Castillo, *Psst . . . I Have Something to Tell You, Mi Amor*, 15.

42. Castillo, *Psst . . . I Have Something to Tell You, Mi Amor*, 16.

43. See Scarry, *Body in Pain*, for a discussion of torture as a permanent physical and psychological wound.

44. Castillo, *Psst . . . I Have Something to Tell You, Mi Amor*, 40.

45. Castillo, *Psst . . . I Have Something to Tell You, Mi Amor*, 56.

46. Castillo, *Psst . . . I Have Something to Tell You, Mi Amor*, 58.

47. Castillo, *Psst . . . I Have Something to Tell You, Mi Amor*, 59.

48. Castillo, *Psst . . . I Have Something to Tell You, Mi Amor*, xv.

49. Scarry, *Body in Pain*, 113.

50. Castillo, *Psst . . . I Have Something to Tell You, Mi Amor*, 45.

51. Castillo, *Psst . . . I Have Something to Tell You, Mi Amor*, 42.

52. Castillo, *Psst . . . I Have Something to Tell You, Mi Amor*, 67.

53. Castillo, *Psst . . . I Have Something to Tell You, Mi Amor*, 67.

54. Rodríguez, "Fiction of Solidarity," 200.

55. Rodríguez, "Fiction of Solidarity," 221.

56. Tobar, *Tattooed Soldier*.

57. Chinchilla, *Cha Cha Files*.

CHAPTER 15. CHICANA FEMINIST LITERARY SUBJECTIVITY IN A TRANSNATIONAL FRAME

1. Esparza, ch. 14 (this volume), "Feminist Imaginaries of Justice," 000.

2. Christian, "The Race for Theory"; Saldívar-Hull, *Feminism on the Border*.

3. Esparza, paraphrasing Christian, "Race for Theory," and Saldívar-Hull, *Feminism on the Border*, in ch. 14 (this volume), "Feminist Imaginaries of Justice," 000.

4. Belmonte, ch. 12 (this volume), "Priestess *y Pastora*," 169.

5. Belmonte, ch. 12 (this volume), "Priestess *y Pastora*," 169.

6. Belmonte, ch. 12 (this volume), "Priestess *y Pastora*," 169.

7. Castillo, *So Far from God* (Norton, 1993), 23.

8. Escandón, *Esperanza's Box of Saints*, 244.

9. Castillo, *Massacre of the Dreamers* (Plume, 1994), 95.

10. Kennedy de Lorenzini, ch. 13 (this volume), "Unbreakable Link," 188.

11. Anzaldúa, *Borderlands*, 25.

12. Castillo, *Massacre of the Dreamers*, 21.

13. Kennedy de Lorenzini, ch. 13 (this volume), "Unbreakable Link," 188.

CHAPTER 16. REPLANTING YOU AS *WINYAN, UARHITI, KWE*

All of these words translate into "woman" in Lakota, P'urhepecha, and Dakota respectively.

1. The Pirinda people are a small Indigenous ethnic group in Mexico. My father and grandfather belong to the Yepez and Chora families from the Pirinda town Charo, Michoacán. In historical and anthropological records, Pirindas are more

commonly known by our Nahuatl name, "Matlatzincas," "the expert net makers." According to my grandfather and community members in Charo, Pirinda is what we call ourselves. Throughout this essay, I use Pirinda.

2. P'urhepechas are the largest Indigenous ethnic group in Michoacán, with approximately 124,000 speakers. I identify as Pirinda because my paternal family still lives Charo, but P'urhepecha culture is matrilineal, and because my mother's family are ejidatarios who migrated from the region of Uruetaro, land originally ceded to Inahuatzi (Tangaxuan II's sister), P'urhepechas claim me, and I embrace the identity out of reverence and respect in acknowledgment of my P'urhepecha grandmother, Emma Tapia.

3. Castillo, *Massacre of the Dreamers* (University of New Mexico Press, 2014), 37.

4. Castillo, foreword to *Chicana Motherwork Anthology*, x.

5. Foucault, "Body of the Condemned," in *Discipline and Punish*, 23.

6. Fanon, *Black Skins, White Masks*, xiv–xv.

7. Brave Heart, "Historical Trauma," 284–85.

8. Pember, "Trauma May Be Woven into DNA of Native Americans," n.p.

9. Castillo, *Massacre of the Dreamers*, 201.

10. Deer, *Beginning and End of Rape*, 21–22.

11. Deer, *Beginning and End of Rape*, 18–20.

12. Deer, *Beginning and End of Rape*, 33.

13. Reséndez, *Other Slavery*, 50.

14. Reséndez, *Other Slavery*, 51.

15. Reséndez, *Other Slavery*, 50.

16. Castillo, "Foreword," x.

17. Castillo, "Foreword," x.

18. Jager, *Malinche, Pocahontas and Sacagewea*, 40.

19. Jager, *Malinche, Pocahontas and Sacagewea*, 48.

20. Cruz, "Interview with Pedro Victoriano Cruz," n.p.

21. Glenn, "Settler Colonialism as Structure," 56–57.

22. Hundreds of cases of femicide that specifically targeted Indigenous women have been occurring in Canada, Mexico, and Guatemala since the mid-1990s. More than 1,500 women have been murdered in Guatemala since 2001 (Chazaro and Casey, "Getting Away with Murder," 141). More than 1,000 cases of missing and murdered Indigenous women in Canada remain unresolved (McDiarmid, "How Many Indigenous Women and Girls," n.p.). In Mexico, more than 2,200 women have been victims of femicide in Ciudad Juarez, Chihuahua, while a new wave of femicide is impacting women in Estado de Mexico (Suarez, "Los Feminicidios No Cesan," n.p.; Fernandez, "EdoMex Primer Lugar," n.p.). In the United States, 506 cases of missing and murdered Indigenous women and girls were identified in 71 US cities in 2017 (Echo-Hawk, "Missing and Murdered," n.p.). According to the National Congress of American Indians, 56.1 percent of American Indian and

Alaska Native women experience sexual assault in their lifetimes, the highest rate of any ethnic group in the United States (National Congress of American Indians, "Research Policy Update," n.p.).

23. P'urhepecherio is "the land of the P'urhepechas," how some P'urhepechas refer to Michoacán.

24. "Land where the waters reflect the clouds," Dakota name for Minnesota.

25. Barry, "Big Bend," n.p.

26. Female farm worker.

27. Castillo, *Massacre of the Dreamers*, 227.

28. Freire, *Pedagogy of the Oppressed*.

29. Castillo, *Massacre of the Dreamers*, 158.

30. Castillo, *Massacre of the Dreamers*, 158–59.

31. Spears-Rico, "Decolonial P'urhepecha," 254–56.

32. See Chacón, "Metamestizaje," 182–200, and Torres-Saillant, "The Indian in the Latino," 587–607.

33. Native feminism critically engages with the imposition of patriarchy and the gender binary on Native societies. It critiques the exclusion of Native women from feminism as well as mainstream feminism's appropriation of Indigenous feminism. Native feminist theories insist that the issues facing Native people are inseparable from the issues facing Native women and therefore can only be resolved through decolonization and sovereignty. For further reading, see Tuck et al., "Decolonizing Feminism," 8–34.

34. See Hernandez-Castillo, *Multiple InJustices*, 136; and Altamirano-Jimenez, "Zapatista Movement," 164.

35. Mexican intellectuals Manuel Gamio and José Vasconcelos theorized the ideology of indigenismo, which institutionally translated into a set of policies meant to obliterate any trace of Indigenous culture among Indigenous peoples while assimilating them into Mexican national identity and bringing them into "modernity."

36. Regan, "After Protests," n.p.

37. Midewin: The Grand Medicine Society, a religion that is exclusively open to Anishinaabe/Ojibwe people.

38. The Ojibwe language.

39. Castillo, *Black Dove*, 169.

40. Castillo, *Black Dove*, 172.

41. Yacatas are pyramid structures built by P'urhepechas in precolonial times.

42. Spears-Rico, "In Times of War and Hashtags," 189.

43. Tuck and Yang, "Decolonization Is Not a Metaphor," 7.

44. Byrd, *Transit of Empire*, 39.

45. Spears-Rico, "Decolonial P'urhepecha," 256–57.

46. Melo, "St. Paul City Council," n.p.; Otto, "Marchers Go from Eastside," n.p.

47. Espinoza et al., "Towards a Decolonizing Pedagogy," 7; Cruz, "Toward an Epistemology," 658.

48. Freire, "Pedagogy of Freedom" 93.

49. Kinzer, "How Femicide Drove the Caravan," n.p.

50. Castillo, *Massacre of the Dreamers*, 182.

51. Castillo, *Massacre of the Dreamers*, 158.

52. Castillo, *Massacre of the Dreamers*, 159.

53. Castillo, *Massacre of the Dreamers*, 160.

54. Castillo, *Massacre of the Dreamers*, 174.

CHAPTER 17. TEACHING ANA CASTILLO

1. Falcón, "Transnational Feminism," 188.

2. Kaminsky, *Reading the Body Politic*, 22.

3. Castillo, *Black Dove*.

4. Castillo, *Massacre of the Dreamers* (Plume, 1994), 40.

5. Castillo, *Massacre of the Dreamers*, 192.

6. See the foundational work by Sonia Saldívar-Hull, *Feminism on the Border: Chicana Gender Politics and Literature*, for a discussion of how testimonio becomes feminist transnational practice, both in personal reflection and feminist literary analysis.

7. Sánchez and Pita, "Mapping Cultural/Political Debates," 495.

8. Raphael, "Teaching, Performance, and the Shifting Stage," 14.

9. Capo, "Performance of Literature as Social Dialectic," 31.

10. Mossman, "Teaching Demetria Martínez' *Mother Tongue*," 39.

11. Martínez, "Teaching Chicana/o Literature in Community College," 217.

12. Halperin, *Intersections of Harm*, 92.

13. Delgadillo, "Forms of Chicana Feminist Resistance," 894.

14. Jameson, *Postmodernism* (Duke University Press, 1991), 51.

15. Collins, "Shifting the Center," 47.

16. Hurtado, "Politics of Sexuality," 389–93.

17. Castillo, *Black Dove*, 80.

18. Castillo, *Black Dove*, 72–73.

19. Airey, "Preface," 7.

20. Castillo, *Black Dove*, 107.

21. Castillo, *Black Dove*, 146.

22. Castillo, *Black Dove*, 188.

23. Castillo, *Black Dove*, 278.

CHAPTER 18. "NEVER *STAY* SILENT"

1. The panel was held on Sunday, April 26, 2009.

2. See Lugo-Lugo and Bloodsworth-Lugo, "'Anchor/Terror Babies,'" 1–21.

3. This quote has been paraphrased with the help and recollection of my friends and colleagues who were also present at the panel.

4. Emphasis is mine.

5. Calderón, *Narratives of Greater Mexico*, 22.

6. US Department of Transportation, "Bureau of Transportation Statistics."

7. Hanisch, "The Personal Is Political."

8. Emphasis is mine.

9. West Los Angeles College, "Fall 2016 Student Profile."

10. See Luiselli, *Tell Me How It Ends*, based on her time as an interviewer of unaccompanied minors detained in the New York state area.

11. Baldas, "Torn from Immigrant Parents."

12. Lorde, *Sister Outsider*, 40–44.

13. Moraga and Anzaldúa, *This Bridge Called My Back* (Third Woman Press, 2002), 183–93.

14. Crenshaw, "Mapping the Margins," 1241–99.

15. United States Congressional Senate, "Comprehensive Immigration Reform Act of 2007."

16. Castillo, *Black Dove*, 7.

17. Castillo, *Guardians*, 72.

18. Castillo, *Guardians*, 32.

19. Castillo, *Psst . . . I Have Something*, xiii.

20. Alvarado et al., *U.S. Central Americans*, 5.

21. Alvarado et al., *U.S. Central Americans*, 20.

22. For example, Alvardo et al., in *U.S. Central Americans*, provide the following data regarding how the Central American civil wars included genocide: using data from the United Nations Truth Commission and Commission for Historical Clarification, they report "of the approximately 200,000 killed and forcefully disappeared, 83 percent were Maya" (p. 10); this was known as the "Silent Holocaust."

23. Gonzalez-Barrera and Krogstad, "What We Know."

24. Moraleda and Luna, "Guadalupe, la primera niña."

25. Abrego, *Sacrificing Families*, 71.

26. Lane, "Digital Zapatistas," 136.

27. Ruiz, "Opticourses VI: Subverting Semiotics."

28. In late 2018, the nonprofit organization had to reckon with accusations of sexual harassment and conflicts; the group appears to no longer be active on their social media accounts. See Latino Rebels, "Current UndocuMedia Mess."

29. UndocuMedia Facebook.

30. Castillo, *Guardians*, 219.

CHAPTER 19. TEACHING CHICANA LITERATURE IN COMMUNITY COLLEGE

1. Hall Kells, "Latino/as in the United States," n.p.

2. Paredes, *Folktales of Mexico*, xii.

3. Paredes, *Folktales of Mexico*, xii.

4. Paredes, *Folktales of Mexico*, xii.

5. Herrera-Sobek, *Chicano Folklore: A Handbook*, 8–11.

6. Herrera-Sobek, *Chicano Folklore: A Handbook*, 11–17.

7. Pérez, *Decolonial Imaginary*, 27.

8. Alcala, "From Chingada to Chingona," 52.

9. Anzaldúa, *Interviews/Entrevistas*, 219.

10. Castillo, *So Far from God*, 163.

11. Faris and Parkinson Zamora, *Magic Realism*, 3.

12. Cook, "La Llorona and a Call for Environmental Justice in the Borderlands," 130.

13. Madsen, *Understanding Contemporary Chicana Literature*, 80.

14. Castillo, *So Far from God*, 32.

15. Castillo, *So Far from God*, 33.

16. Espinosa, "New Mexican Folk-Lore," 401.

17. Castillo, *So Far from God*, 77.

18. Castillo, *So Far from God*, 211.

19. Rodriguez, "Chicana/o Fiction from Resistance to Contestation," 77.

20. Castillo, *So Far from* God, 211.

21. Rodriguez "Chicana/o Fiction from Resistance to Contestation," 77.

CHAPTER 20. *POR TODOS LADOS*

1. Anzaldúa, "Let Us Be the Healing of the Wound," 102.

2. I allude here to Audre Lorde's often quoted title of her essay "The Master's Tools Will Never Dismantle the Master's House," 110.

3. Spears-Rico, ch. 16 (this volume), "Replanting You," 231.

4. Spears-Rico, ch. 16 (this volume), "Replanting You," 231.

5. Johnson, ch. 17 (this volume), "Teaching Ana Castillo," 246.

6. Johnson, ch. 17 (this volume), "Teaching Ana Castillo," 246.

7. Johnson, ch. 17 (this volume), "Teaching Ana Castillo," 246.

8. Ruiz, ch. 18 (this volume), "Never *Stay* Silent," 265.

9. Ruiz, ch. 18 (this volume), "Never *Stay* Silent," 265.

10. Martínez, ch. 19 (this volume), "Teaching Chicana Literature," 276.

11. Martínez, ch. 19 (this volume), "Teaching Chicana Literature," 276.

12. Martínez, ch. 19 (this volume), "Teaching Chicana Literature," 276.

13. Martínez, ch. 19 (this volume), "Teaching Chicana Literature," 276.

14. Martínez, ch. 19 (this volume), "Teaching Chicana Literature," 276.

15. Martínez, ch. 19 (this volume), "Teaching Chicana Literature," 276.

16. Martínez, ch. 19 (this volume), "Teaching Chicana Literature," 276.

17. Martínez, ch. 19 (this volume), "Teaching Chicana Literature," 276.

18. Martínez, ch. 19 (this volume), "Teaching Chicana Literature," 276.

19. Martínez, ch. 19 (this volume), "Teaching Chicana Literature," 276.

20. Martínez, ch. 19 (this volume), "Teaching Chicana Literature," 276.

21. Martínez, ch. 19 (this volume), "Teaching Chicana Literature," 276.

22. Martínez, ch. 19 (this volume), "Teaching Chicana Literature," 276.

CHAPTER 21. AN INTERVIEW WITH ANA CASTILLO

1. AC: I will note here a couple of secondary characters in my novel *Peel My Love Like an Onion*, one gay and the other identified as transvestite in the early 1990s, but today would have been considered transgendered. The novel takes place in Chicago, and all the characters are POC, hustling one way or the other. There [are] also references to two spirit characters in my novel in verse, *Watercolor Women, Opaque Men*. My more recent novel, *Give It to Me*, has references to similar characters. My first collection of poems and novel, *The Mixquiahuala Letters*, written in the 1970s, also focus on the power and disempowerment by society of the feminine, especially with regard to expressed sexuality.

2. Castillo, *Massacre of the Dreamers* ([1994], 2014).

CONCLUSION. LATINX/CHICANX FEMINIST FUTURES

1. See Luna and Estrada, "Trans*lating the Genderqueer -*X* ," 256; and Guidotti-Hernández, "Affective Communities and Millennial Desires," 142–47, for a more in-depth discussion of "Historicizing the X."

2. R. T. Rodriguez, "X Marks the Spot," 212.

3. Luna and Estrada, "Trans*lating the Genderqueer -*X* ," 257.

4. Pelaez Lopez, "The X in Latinx Is a Wound, Not a Trend," n.p.

5. Pelaez Lopez, "The X in Latinx Is a Wound, Not a Trend," n.p.

6. Pelaez Lopez, "The X in Latinx Is a Wound, Not a Trend," n.p.

7. Pelaez Lopez, "The X in Latinx Is a Wound, Not a Trend," n.p.

8. Pelaez Lopez, "The X in Latinx Is a Wound, Not a Trend," n.p.

9. Tlapoyawa, "What 'Latinx' Doesn't Include."

10. Byrd, "Introduction," *Transit of Empire*, xvii.

11. Castillo, *Massacre of the Dreamers* [1994] (2014), 5.

12. Herrera, "Geographies of Latinidad," 159–69.

13. López, *Chicano Nations*, 150.

14. Herrera, "Geographies of Latinidad," 159–69.

15. Castillo, *Sapogonia*,1.

16. Pérez-Torres, *Mestizaje*, xv.

17. Herrera, "Geographies of Latinidad," 168.

18. Hector Torres Papers, "Ana Castillo," undated interview.

19. Hector Torres Papers, "Ana Castillo," undated interview.

20. See Aldama and Aldama, "Introduction," *Decolonizing Latinx Masculinities*, 16.

21. Chichi and Carmen exemplify the ways in which trans and disabled identities intersect. See Puar, "Disability," 77–81, on the need for more intersectional approaches between trans- and disability studies.

22. Castillo, *Peel My Love like an Onion*, 45.

23. Teorey, "Empowering Femininity," 52–69.

24. Castillo, *Peel My Love like an Onion* , 47.

25. Bost, *Encarnación*, 153.

26. For a detailed discussion of the ways Castillo addresses embodied disability, mobility, and identity, see Bost, *Encarnación*, chapter 4 ("Movement: Ana Castillo's Shape-Shifting Identities").

27. Galarte, "Transgender Chicana/o Poetics," 120.

28. Galarte, "Transgender Chicana/o Poetics,"121.

29. See Peña, "Gender and Sexuality," 768.

30. See section on "Representation" in Galarte, "Transgender Studies."

31. Castillo, *Peel My Love like an Onion*, 62.

32. Castillo, *Peel My Love like an Onion*, 62.

33. See Galarte, "On Trans* Chicanos," 229.

34. See Cuevas, *Post-Borderlandia*.

35. See Cuevas, *Post-Borderlandia*.

36. Quintana Millamoto, "Redefinition of the Disabled Chicana," 35.

37. White House, "What You Need to Know."

BIBLIOGRAPHY

Abrego, Leisy J. *Sacrificing Families: Navigating Laws, Labor, and Love across Borders.* Stanford: Stanford University Press, 2014.

Adair, Cassius, et al. "An Open Letter from Queer Studies Scholars." Blarb blog, *Los Angeles Review of Books.* December 13, 2018, https://blog.lareviewofbooks .org/essays/open-letter-queer-studies-scholars/.

Adams, Rachel. "Have We Crossed a Border?: The Hemispheric Americas of *Citizen Suarez.*" In *Hemispheric American Studies,* edited by Caroline Field Levander and Robert S. Levine, 313–27. New Brunswick: Rutgers University Press, 2008.

Aguado, Txetxu. *La tarea política: Narrativa y ética en la España posmoderna.* Barcelona: El Viejo Topo, 2004.

Ahmed, Sara. *The Cultural Politics of Emotion.* New York: Routledge, 2004.

Ahmed, Sara. *Living a Feminist Life.* Durham, NC: Duke University Press, 2017.

Airey, Jennifer. "Preface." *Tulsa Studies in Women's Literature* 37, no. 1 (2018): 7–13.

Alarcón, Norma. "Chicana Feminism: In the Tracks of 'the' Native Woman." *Cultural Studies* 4, no. 3 (1990): 248–56.

Alarcón, Norma. "Chicana Feminism: In the Tracks of 'the' Native Woman." In *Between Woman and Nation : Nationalisms, Transnational Feminisms, and the State,* edited by Caren Kaplan, Norma Alarcón, and Minoo Moallem, 63–71. Durham, NC: Duke University Press, 1999.

Alarcón, Norma. "The Sardonic Powers of the Erotic in the Work of Ana Castillo." In *Breaking Boundaries: Latina Writing and Critical Readings,* edited by Asunción Horno-Delgado, Eliana Ortega, Nancy Saporta Sternbach, and Nina M. Scott, 94–107. Amherst: University of Massachusetts Press, 1989.

Alarcón, Norma. "Traddutora, Traditora: A Paradigmatic Figure of Chicana Feminism." In *Dangerous Liaisons: Gender, Nation, and Postcolonial Perspectives,* edited by Anne McIntlock, 278–97. Minneapolis: University of Minnesota Press, 1998.

Alarcón, Norma, Caren Kaplan, and Minoo Moallem. "Introduction: Between Woman and Nation." In *Between Woman and Nation: Nationalisms, Transna-*

tional Feminisms, and the State, edited by Caren Kaplan, Norma Alarcón, and Minoo Moallem, 1–18. Durham, NC: Duke University Press, 1999.

Alberto, Lourdes. "Topographies of Indigenism: Mexico, Decolonial Indigenism, and the Chicana Transnational Subject in Ana Castillo's *Mixquiahuala Letters*." In *Comparative Indigeneities of the Americas: Toward a Hemispheric Approach*, edited by M. Bianet Castellanos, Lourdes Gutiérrez Nájera, and Arturo J. Aldama, 38–52. Tucson: University of Arizona Press, 2012.

Alcalá, Rita Cano. "From Chingada to Chingona: La Malinche Redefined, Or, A Long Line of Hermanas." *Aztlán* 26 (2001): 33–61.

Aldama, Arturo J., and Frederick Luis Aldama. "Decolonizing Latinx Masculinities: An Introduction." In *Decolonizing Latinx Masculinities*, edited by Arturo J. Aldama and Frederick Luis Aldama, 3–20. Tucson: University of Arizona Press, 2020.

Aldama, Frederick Luis. "Ana Castillo's and Sheila Ortiz Taylor's Bent Chicana Textualities." In *Brown on Brown: Chicano/a Representations of Gender, Sexuality, and Ethnicity*. Austin: University of Texas Press, 2005.

Altamirano-Jiménez, Isabel. "The Zapatista Movement: Place-Driven Recognition?" In *Indigenous Encounters with Neoliberalism: Place, Women and the Environment in Canada and Mexico*, 149–75. Vancouver: University of British Columbia Press, 2013.

Altman, Janet Gurkin. *Epistolarity: Approaches to a Form*. Columbus: Ohio State University Press, 1982.

Alvarado, Karina, Alicia Ivonne Estrada, and Ester E. Hernández, eds. *U.S. Central Americans: Reconstructing Memories, Struggles, and Communities of Resistance*. Tucson: University of Arizona Press, 2017.

Ángeles, María Toda Iglesia, Ramón Espejo, Juan-Ignacio Guijarro, Jesús Lerate, and Pilar Marín. *Critical Essays on Chicano Studies*. New York: Peter Lang, 2004.

Anzaldúa, Gloria. *Borderlands / La Frontera: The New Mestiza*. First edition. San Francisco: Aunt Lute Books, 1987.

Anzaldúa, Gloria. *Borderlands / La Frontera: The New Mestiza*. Fourth edition. San Francisco: Aunt Lute Books, 2012.

Anzaldúa, Gloria. *Borderlands / La Frontera: The New Mestiza*. Third edition. San Francisco: Aunt Lute Books, 2007.

Anzaldúa, Gloria. "The Homeland, Aztlán." In *Borderlands / La Frontera: The New Mestiza*, 1–14. First edition. San Francisco: Aunt Lute Books, 1987.

Anzaldúa, Gloria. "Let Us Be the Healing of the Wound: The Coyolxauhqui Imperative—La sombra y el sueño!" In *One Would for Another / Una herida por otra: Testimonios de Latin@s in the U.S. through Cyberspace*, edited by Claire Joysmith and Clara Lomas, 92–103. Cd. de Mexico: Universidad Autónoma de Mexico, 2005.

Anzaldúa, Gloria, and AnaLouise Keating, eds. *This Bridge We Call Home: Radical Visions for Transformation*. New York: Routledge, 2002.

Anzaldúa, Gloria, and Cherríe Moraga. *This Bridge Called My Back: Writings by Radical Women of Color*. New York: Kitchen Table Press, 1983.

Aquinas, Thomas. *Summa Theologica*. www.sacred-texts.com/chr/aquinas/summa/.

Archbishop of Guatemala, Human Rights Office. *Guatemala: Never Again!* Maryknoll, NY: Orbis Books, 1998.

Arredondo, Gabriella, Aída Hurtado, Norma Klahn, Olga Nájera-Rámirez, and Patricia Zavella, eds. *Chicana Feminisms: A Critical Reader*. Durham, NC: Duke University Press, 2003.

Arteaga, Alfred. *Chicano Poetics: Heterotexts and Hybridities*. Cambridge: Cambridge University Press, 1997.

Arteaga, Alfred. *An Other Tongue: Nation and Ethnicity in the Linguistic Borderlands*. Durham, NC: Duke University Press, 1994.

Asunción Horno-Delgado, Eliana Ortega, Nancy Saporta Sternbach, and Nina M. Scott, eds. *Boundaries: Latina Writing and Critical Readings*. Amherst: University of Massachusetts Press, 1989.

Baldas, Tresa. "Torn from Immigrant Parents, 8-Month Old Baby Lands in Michigan." MSN News. Published June 20, 2018. Accessed November 11, 2018. https://www.wusa9.com/article/news/nation-now/torn-from-immigrant-parents-8-month-old-baby-lands-in-michigan/465-1c8813f6-4d09-4df4-a033-48dc33635462.

Baltanás, Enrique. "The Fatigue of the Nation: Flamenco as the Basis of Heretical Identities." In *Songs of the Minotaur: Hybridity and Popular Music in the Era of Globalization*, edited by Gerhard Steingress, 139–86 Münster: Lit Verlag, 2003.

Barad, Karen. "Troubling time/s and ecologies of nothingness: Re-turning, re-membering, and facing the incalculable." *New Formations* 92.92 (2017): 56–86.

Barry, John. "The Big Bend." *Hughes County History*. Pierre: Office of the County Superintendent of Schools, 1937.

Beatley, Meaghan. "Grammy Nominee Rosalía's Flamenco Fame Is Questioned by Spain's Roma Community." PRI GlobalPost. November 11, 2018. https://www.pri.org/stories/2018-11-14/award-winning-rosal-flmnco-fame-questioned-spains-roma-community.

Bejarano, Cynthia L. "Serpent Tongues, Social Hierarchies, and National Citizenship: The Splitting of Border Languages and Cultures between Latina/o Youths." In *Border Culture*, edited by Ilan Stavans, 93–138. Westport, CT: Greenwood Press, 2010.

Benavides, Lucía. "Flamenco Fusion: Rosalía Offers a Modern Take on Spanish Traditions." *All Things Considered*, National Public Radio (NPR). Published November 14, 2018. Accessed August 1, 2019. https://www.npr.org/2018/11/14/667436267/flamenco-fusion-rosal-a-offers-a-modern-take-on-spanish-traditions.

Benjamin, Walter. *Illuminations: Essays and Reflections*. New York: Schocken Books, 1968.

Berlant, Lauren, and Michael Warner. "Sex in Public." In *The Routledge Queer Studies Reader*, edited by Donald E. Hall and Annamarie Jagose, 165–79. New York: Routledge, 2013.

Bermudez J., Maria, M. A. Stinson, L. Zak-Hunter, and B. Abrams. "Mejor sola que mal acompañada: Strengths and challenges of Mexican-origin mothers parenting alone." *Journal of Divorce and Remarriage* 52.8 (2011): 622–41.

Beverley, John. *Subalternity and Representation: Arguments in Cultural Theory.* Durham, NC: Duke University Press, 1999.

Beverley, John, and Marc Zimmerman. *Literature and Politics in the Central American Revolutions.* Austin: University of Texas Press, 1993.

Bhabha, Homi. *The Location of Culture.* New York: Routledge, 1994.

Borislavov, Rad. "Poetics." *The Chicago School of Media Theory.* Accessed Nov. 4, 2019. https://lucian.uchicago.edu/blogs/mediatheory/keywords/poetics/.

Bost, Suzanne. *Encarnación: Illness and Body Politics in Chicana Feminist Literature.* New York: Fordham University Press, 2009.

Bower, Anne. *Epistolary Responses: The Letter in Twentieth-Century American Fiction and Criticism.* Tuscaloosa: University of Alabama Press, 1997.

Brady, Mary Pat. *Extinct Lands, Temporal Geographies: Chicana Literature and the Urgency of Space.* Durham, NC: Duke University Press, 2002.

Brave Heart, Maria Yellow Horse, Josephine Chase, Jennifer Elkins, and Deborah B. Altschul. "Historical Trauma among Indigenous Peoples of the Americas: Concepts, Research, and Clinical Considerations." *Journal of Psychoactive Drugs* 43, no. 4 (2011): 282–90.

Brody, Reed, and Felipe González. "Nunca Más: An Analysis of International Instruments on 'Disappearances.'" *Human Rights Quarterly* 19, no. 2 (1997): 365–405.

Broyles-González, Yolanda. *El Teatro Campesino: Theater in the Chicano Movement.* Austin: University of Texas Press, 1994.

Broyles-González, Yolanda. "The Living Legacy of Chicana Performers: Preserving History through Oral Testimony." *Frontiers: A Journal of Women Studies* 11, no. 1 (1990): 46–52.

Burgers, J. Herman, and Hans Danelius. *The United Nations Convention against Torture: A Handbook on the Convention against Torture and Other Cruel, Inhuman or Degrading Treatment or Punishment.* Dordrecht: Martinus Nijhoff Publishers, 1988.

Butler, Kim. "Defining Diaspora, Refining a Discourse." *Diaspora* 10, no. 2 (2001): 195.

Byrd, Jodi. *Transit of Empire: Indigenous Critiques of Colonialism.* Minneapolis: University of Minnesota Press, 2011.

Caballero, Cecilia, Yvette Martínez-Vu, Judith Pérez-Torres, Michelle Téllez, and Christine Vega, eds. *The Chicana Motherwork Anthology.* Tucson: University of Arizona Press, 2019.

Calderón, Héctor. *Narratives of Greater Mexico: Essays on Chicano Literary History, Genre, and Borders.* Austin: University of Texas Press, 2004.

Cáliz-Montoro, Carmen. *Writing from the Borderlands: A Study of Chicano, Afro-Caribbean and Native Literatures in North America.* Toronto: TSAR, 2000.

Caminero-Santangelo, Marta. "'The Pleas of the Desperate': Collective Agency versus Magical Realism in Ana Castillo's *So Far from God.*" *Tulsa Studies in Women's Literature* 24, no. 1 (Spring 2005): 81–103.

Cantú, Norma E. "A Conversation with Ana Castillo." *World Literature Today* 82, no. 2 (2008): 59–62.

Capo, Kay Ellen, "Performance of Literature as Social Dialectic." *Literature in Performance* 4, no. 1 (1983): 31–36.

Carmen. Dir. Carlos Saura. Perf. Antonio Gades, Laura del Sol, and Paco de Lucía. Suevia Films, 1983.

Carpentier, Alejo. "On the Marvelous Real in America." In *Magical Realism: Theory, History, Community,* edited by Louis Parkinson Zamora and Wendy B. Faris, 75–88. Durham, NC: Duke University Press, 1995.

Castiglia, Christopher, and Christopher Reed. "Conversion Therapy v. Re-education Camp: An Open Letter to Grace Lavery." *Los Angeles Review of Books,* Dec. 11, 2018. https://blog.lareviewofbooks.org/essays/conversion-therapy-v-re-education-camp-open-letter-grace-lavery/.

Castiglia, Christopher, and Christopher Reed. *If Memory Serves: Gay Men, AIDS, and the Promise of the Queer Past.* Minneapolis: University of Minnesota Press, 2012.

Castillo, Ana. *Ana Castillo Blog.* http://anacastillo.com/ac/blog/archives/2007_11_01_index.shtml (site discontinued).

Castillo, Ana. "Ana Castillo Papers." No date. CEMA 2, Department of Special Collections, University Libraries, University of California, Santa Barbara.

Castillo, Ana. *Black Dove: Mamá, Mi'jo, and Me.* New York: The Feminist Press at CUNY, 2016.

Castillo, Ana. "The Evolution of Chicana Erotica." *Heresies* 6, no. 4 (1989): 50–53.

Castillo, Ana. Foreword to *The Chicana Motherwork Anthology,* edited by Cecilia Caballero, Yvette Martínez-Vu, Judith Pérez-Torres, Michelle Téllez, and Christine Vega, ix–xiii. Tucson: University of Arizona Press, 2019.

Castillo, Ana. "Interview with Ana Castillo," by Alicia Cole. *Femspec* 18, no. 1 (2017): 60–64.

Castillo, Ana. *Massacre of the Dreamers: Essays on Xicanisma.* New York: Plume, 1994.

Castillo, Ana. *Massacre of the Dreamers: Essays on Xicanisma.* Twentieth anniversary updated edition. Albuquerque: University of New Mexico Press, 2014.

Castillo, Ana. *Give It to Me.* New York: The Feminist Press at CUNY, 2014.

Castillo, Ana, ed. *Goddess of the Americas: Writings on the Virgin of Guadalupe.* New York: Riverhead Books, 1997.

Castillo, Ana. *The Guardians: A Novel*. New York: Random House, 2007.

Castillo, Ana. *The Guardians*. Paperback reprint, New York: Random House, 2008.

Castillo, Ana. *I Ask the Impossible: Poems*. New York: Anchor Books, 2001.

Castillo, Ana. "La Macha: Toward a Beautiful Whole Self." *Chicana Lesbians: The Girls Our Mothers Warned Us About*, edited by Carla Trujillo, 24–48. Berkeley, CA: Third Woman Press, 1991.

Castillo, Ana. "Like the people of Guatemala, I want to be free of these memories . . ." In *I Ask the Impossible*, 41–46. New York: Anchor Books, 2001.

Castillo, Ana. *Loverboys*. Paperback reprint, New York: Norton, 2008.

Castillo, Ana. *Loverboys: Stories*. New York: Norton, 1996.

Castillo, Ana. *The Mixquiahuala Letters*. New York: Anchor Books, 1992. First published 1986.

Castillo, Ana. *The Mixquiahuala Letters*. Tempe, AZ: Bilingual Review Press, 1992.

Castillo, Ana. *My Father Was a Toltec*. New York: Anchor Books, 1995.

Castillo, Ana. *My Father Was a Toltec and Selected Poems*. New York: W. W. Norton, 1985.

Castillo, Ana. *My Father Was a Toltec and Selected Poems, 1973–1988*. New York: Anchor Books, 2004.

Castillo, Ana. *My Father Was a Toltec: Poems*. Albuquerque, NM: West End Press, 1988.

Castillo, Ana. *Otro Canto*. Chicago: Alternativa Publications, 1977.

Castillo, Ana. *Peel My Love like an Onion*. Paperback reprint, New York: Anchor Books, 2000. First published 1999.

Castillo, Ana. *Psst . . . I have Something to Tell You, Mi Amor*. San Antonio, TX: Wings Press, 2005.

Castillo, Ana. "Righteous White Boyz." In *Watercolor Women, Opaque Men: A Novel in Verse*, 153–58. Willimantic, CT: Curbstone Press, 2005.

Castillo, Ana. *Sapogonia: An Anti-Romance in 3/8 Meter*. Reprint, New York: Anchor Books / Doubleday, 1994.

Castillo, Ana. *So Far from God*. New York: W. W. Norton & Company, 1993.

Castillo, Ana. *So Far from God*. Paperback, New York: Plume, 1994.

Castillo, Ana. *Watercolor Women, Opaque Men*. Willimantic, CT: Curbstone Press, 2005.

Castillo, Ana, and Norma E. Cantú, "A Conversation with Ana Castillo." *World Literature Today* 82, no. 2 (March–April 2008): 59–62.

Cervantes Saavedra, Miguel de. *El Ingenioso Hidalgo Don Quijote de La Mancha*. Newark, DE: Juan de la Cuesta, 2000.

Chacón, Gloria. "Metamestizaje and the narration of political movements from the South." *Latino Studies* 15, no. 2 (2017): 182–200.

Chazaro, Angelica, and Jennifer Casey. "Getting Away with Murder: Guatemala's Failure to Protect Women and Rody Alvarado's Quest for Safety." *Hastings Women's Law Journal* 17, no. 2 (2006): 141–85.

Chinchilla, Maya. *The Cha Cha Files: A Chapina Poética*. San Francisco: Kórima Press, 2014.

Christian, Barbara. "The Race for Theory." *Cultural Critique* 6 (Spring 1987): 51–63.

Cheng, Patrick S. *Radical Love: An Introduction to Queer Theology*. New York: Seabury, 2011.

Cheng, Vincent J. *Inauthentic: The Anxiety over Culture and Identity*. Brunswick, NJ: Rutgers University Press, 2004.

Ciria, Concepción Bados. "Escrito en el tiempo: Ensayo epistolar como práctica autobiográfica femenina." *Estudios Humanísticos. Filología* 19 (1997): 127–32.

Cisneros, Sandra. "Guadalupe the Sex Goddess: Unearthing the Racy Past of Mexico's Most Famous Virgin." *Ms.* July–August1996, 43–46.

Cisneros, Sandra. *A House of My Own: Stories from My Life*. New Work: Vintage, 2015.

Cole, Alicia. "Interview with Ana Castillo." *Femspec* 18, no. 1 (2017): 60–64.

Collins, Patricia Hill. "Shifting the Center: Race, Class, and Feminist Theorizing about Motherhood." In *Mothering: Ideology, Experience, and Agency*, edited by Evelyn Nakano Glenn, Grace Chang, and Linda Rennie Forcey, 45–66. New York: Routledge, 1994.

Combahee River Collective. "A Black Feminist Statement." In *This Bridge Called My Back: Writings by Radical Women of Color*, edited by Cherríe Moraga and Gloria Anzaldúa, 210–18. London: Persephone Press, 1981.

La Comisión para el Esclarecimiento Histórico (CEH). *Guatemala: Memory of Silence, Tz'ninil Na'tab'al*. 12 vols. Guatemala City: United Nations, 1999.

Cook, Barbara J. "La Llorona and a Call for Environmental Justice in the Borderlands: Ana Castillo's *So Far from God*." *Northwest Review* 39 (2001): 124–33.

Cooper Alarcón, Daniel. "Literary Syncretism in Ana Castillo's *So Far from God*." *Studies in Latin American Popular Culture* 23 (2004): 145–52.

Corbalán, Ana. "Otredad e hibridez cultural: *Peel My Love like an Onion*, de Ana Castillo y *Salsa*, de Clara Obligado." *Confluencia* 21.2 (2006): 71–82.

Crenshaw, Kimberlé. "Demarginalizing the Intersection of Race and Sex: A Black Feminist Critique of Antidiscrimination Doctrine, Feminist Theory and Antiracist Politics." *University of Chicago Legal Forum* 1989, iss. 1, article 8: 139–67.

Crenshaw, Kimberlé. "Mapping the Margins: Intersectionality, Identity Politics, and Violence against Women of Color." *Stanford Law Review* 43, no. 6 (July 1991): 1241–99.

Cruz, Ariane. *The Color of Kink: Black Women, BDSM, and Pornography*. New York: New York University Press, 2016.

Cruz, Cindy. "Toward an Epistemology of a Brown Body." *International Journal of Qualitative Studies in Education* 14, no. 5 (2001): 657–69.

Cruz, Daniel Shank. *Queering Mennonite Literature: Archives, Activism, and the Search for Community*. University Park: Pennsylvania State University Press, 2019.

Cruz, Pedro V. Interviewed by Gabriela Spears-Rico at San Lorenzo, Michoacán, Mexico, November 3, 2017.

Cuesta Escobar, Guiomar, and Alfredo Ocampo Zamorano, eds. *Antología de mujeres poetas afrocolombianas*. Bogotá: Ministerio de Cultura, 2010.

Cuevas, T. Jackie. *Post-Borderlandia: Chicana Literature and Gender Variant Critique*. New Brunswick, NJ: Rutgers University Press, 2018.

Cvetkovich, Ann. *An Archive of Feelings: Trauma, Sexuality, and Lesbian Public Cultures*. Durham, NC: Duke University Press, 2003.

Davila, Arlene. *Latinos Inc.: The Marketing and Making of a People*. Berkeley: University of California Press, 2001.

Dean, Tim, Steven Ruszczycky, and David Squires, eds. *Porn Archives*. Durham, NC: Duke University Press, 2014.

DeCosta-Willis, Miriam, ed. *Daughters of the Diaspora: Afra-Hispanic Writers*. Kingston, Jamaica: Ian Randle Publishers, 2003.

Deer, Sarah. *The Beginning and End of Rape: Confronting Sexual Violence in Native America*. Minneapolis: University of Minnesota Press, 2015.

de la Campa, Román. *Latin Americanism*. Minneapolis: University of Minnesota Press, 1999.

Del Castillo, Adelaida R., ed. *Between Borders: Essays on Mexicana/Chicana History*. Encino, CA: Floricanto Press, 1990.

Delgadillo, Theresa. "Forms of Chicana Feminist Resistance: Hybrid Spirituality in Ana Castillo's 'So Far from God.'" *Modern Fiction Studies*, no. 4 (1998): 888–916.

"Día de la Madre: ¿Por qué en México se celebra el 10 de mayo?" *El Periódico*, Oct. 5, 2017. https://www.elperiodico.com/es/extra/20170510/dia-de-la-madre-mexico-6028174.

Díaz del Castillo, Bernal. *Historia verdadera de la Conquista de la Nueva España*. Mexico: Tipografía de Angel Bassols y Hermanos, 1981.

Eakin, Paul J. *Fictions in Autobiography: Studies in the Art of Self-Invention*. Princeton, NJ: University Press, 1985.

Earle, Rebecca. *Epistolary Selves: Letters and Letter-Writers, 1600–1945*. New York: Routledge, 1999.

Echo-Hawk, Abigail. "Missing and Murdered Indigenous Women and Girls: A Snapshot of Data from 71 Urban Cities in the United States." Seattle: Urban Indian Health Institute, 2017.

Eichhorn, Kate. *The Archival Turn in Feminism: Outrage in Order*. Philadelphia: Temple University Press, 2013.

Eisner, Shiri. *Bi: Notes for a Bisexual Revolution*. Berkeley, CA: Seal Press, 2013.

Epega, Afolabi A., and Philip John Neimark. *The Sacred Ifa Oracle*. San Francisco: HarperSanFrancisco, 1995.

Escandón, María Amparo. *Esperanza's Box of Saints*. New York: Scribner Paperback Fiction, 1999.

Esparza, Araceli. "Toward a Feminist Theory of Justice for the Disappeared: Ana Castillo's Creative Writing and the Case of Sister Dianna Ortiz." *Feminist Formations* 25, no. 3 (2013): 1–32.

Espinosa, Aurelio M. "New Mexican Folk-Lore." *Journal of American Folklore* 23, no. 90 (1910): 395–418.

Espinosa, J. Manuel. "The Origin of the Penitentes of New Mexico: Separating Fact from Fiction." *Catholic Historical Review* 79, no. 3 (1993): 454–77.

Espinoza, Dionne, María Eugenia Cotera, and Maylei Blackwell, eds. *Chicana Movidas: New Narratives of Activism and Feminism in the Movement Era.* Austin: University of Texas Press, 2018.

Espinoza, Manuel, Carlos Tejeda, and Kris Gutierrez. "Toward a Decolonizing Pedagogy: Social Justice Reconsidered." In *Pedagogies of Difference: Rethinking Education for Social Justice*, edited by Peter Pericles Trifonas, 10–40. New York: RoutledgeFalmer, 2003.

Esquibel, Catrióna Rueda. "Memories of Girlhood: Chicana Lesbian Fictions." *Signs: Journal of Women in Culture and Society* 23, no. 3 (1998): 645–82.

Esquibel, Catrióna Rueda. *With Her Machete in Her Hand: Reading Chicana Lesbians.* Austin: University of Texas Press, 2006.

Falcón, Sylvanna M. "Transnational Feminism as a Paradigm for Decolonizing the Practice of Research: Identifying Feminist Principles and Methodology Criteria for US-Based Scholars." *Frontiers: A Journal of Women Studies* 37, no. 1 (2016): 174–94.

Fanon, Frantz. *Black Skin, White Masks.* Translated by Richard Filcox. New York: Grove Press, 2008.

Faris, Wendy B. "Scheherazade's Children: Magical Realism and Postmodern Fiction." In *Magical Realism: Theory, History, Community*, edited by Lois Parkinson Zamora and Faris, 163–90. Durham, NC: Duke University Press, 1995.

Fernandez, Emilio. "Edomex, primer luger en número de femicidios." *El Universal*, March 7, 2018. https://www.eluniversal.com.mx/metropoli/edomex/edomex-primer-lugar-en-numero-de-feminicidios.

Fielding, Electra Gamón. "Crossing Borders, Boundaries, and Identities—A Conversation with Ana Castillo." *Weber: The Contemporary West* 32, no. 2 (2016): 103–15.

Freire, Paulo. *Pedagogy of Freedom: Ethics, Democracy, and Civic Courage.* Translated by Patrick Clarke. Lanham, MD: Rowman and Littlefield, 1998.

Freire, Paulo. *Pedagogy of the Oppressed.* Fiftieth anniversary edition. New York: Bloomsbury, 2012.

Foucault, Michel. "The Body of the Condemned." In *Discipline and Punish: The Birth of the Prison.* New York: Vintage Books, 1979.

Foucault, Michel. "The Body of the Condemned." In *Discipline and Punish: The Birth of the Prison*, translated by Alan Sheridan, 3–31. Second edition. New York: Vintage Books, 1995.

Galarte, Francisco J. "On Trans* Chicanos." *Aztlán: A Journal of Chicano Studies* 39, no. 1 (Spring 2014): 229–36.

Galarte, Francisco J. "Transgender Chicana/o Poetics." *Chicana/Latina Studies* 13, no. 2 (Spring 2014): 118–39.

Galarte, Francisco J. "Transgender Studies and Latina/o/x Studies." In *Oxford Encyclopedia of Latina/o Literatures*, edited by Louis Mendoza, Arturo Arias, Raúl Coronado, Yolanda Martinez San Miguel, Ben V. Olguín, and Sandra Soto, n.p. New York: Oxford University Press, 2019. March 31, 2020. Accessed Dec. 22, 2020. https://oxfordre.com/literature/view/10.1093/acrefore/9780190201098.001.0001/acrefore-9780190201098-e-349.

Gallegos, Sergio A. "Building Transnational Feminist Solidarity Networks." In *Decolonizing Feminism*, edited by Margaret McLaren, 231–56. London: Rowman and Littlefield International, 2017.

Gallop, Jane. *Anecdotal Theory*. Durham, NC: Duke University Press, 2002.

García Lorca, Federico. *Romancero Gitano: Poema del Cante Jondo*. México: Espasa-Calpe, 1992.

Gaspar de Alba, Alicia. "Thirty Years of Chicana/Latina Lesbian Literary Production." In *The Routledge Companion to Latino/a Literature*, edited by Suzanne Bost and Frances R. Aparicio, 462–75. New York: Routledge, 2013.

Gaspar de Alba, Alicia. *[Un]framing the Bad Woman: Sor Juana, Malinche, Coyolxauhqui, and Other Rebels with a Cause*. Austin: University of Texas Press, 2014.

Giddens, Anthony. "The Consequences of Modernity." In *Colonial Discourse and Post-Colonial Theory: A Reader*, edited by Patrick Williams and Laura Chrisman, 181–90. New York: Columbia University Press, 1994.

Giddings, Paula. "Some Themes in the Poetry of Margaret Walker." *Black World / Negro Digest*, Dec. 1971, 20–25.

Gill, Lesley. *The School of the Americas: Military Training and Political Violence in the Americas*. Durham, NC: Duke University Press, 2004.

Glenn, Evelyn N. "Settler Colonialism as Structure." *Sociology of Race and Ethnicity* 1, no. 1 (2015): 52–72.

Goldsmith, Elizabeth C., ed. *Writing the Female Voice: Essays on Epistolary Literature*. Boston: Northeastern University Press, 1989.

Gómez-Barris, Macarena. *Where Memory Dwells: Culture and State Violence in Chile*. Berkeley: University of California Press, 2009.

Gómez-Vega, Ibis. "The Homoerotic Tease and Lesbian Identity in Ana Castillo's Work." *Crítica Hispánica* 25, no. 1–2 (2003): 65–84.

Gonzales, Rodolfo "Corky." "I Am Joaquín: An Epic Poem, 1967." *Message to Aztlán: Selected Writings*. Houston: Arte Público Press, 2001.

González, John M. "Transnational Field Imaginaries and the Transformation of Chicano/a Literary Studies." *American Literary History* 26, no. 3 (Fall 2014): 592–602.

Gonzalez-Barrera, Ana, and Jens Manuel Krogstad. "What We Know about Illegal Immigration from Mexico." PEW Research Center. Published December 3, 2018. Accessed April 10, 2019. https://www.pewresearch.org/fact-tank/2018/12/03/what-we-know-about-illegal-immigration-from-mexico/.

Greenberg, Linda Margarita. "Epistolary Women: Navigating Ethnicity and Autonomy in Ana Castillo's *Mixquiahuala Letters* and Hualing Nieh's *Mulberry and Peach*." *Genre* 49, no. 3 (2016): 273–302.

Griswold del Castillo, Richard. *The Treaty of Guadalupe Hidalgo: A Legacy of Conflict.* Norman: University of Oklahoma Press, 1990.

Gugelberger, Georg M., ed. *The Real Thing: Testimonial Discourse and Latin America.* Durham, NC: Duke University Press, 1996.

Guidotti-Hernández, Nicole. "Affective Communities and Millennial Desires: Latinx, or Why My Computer Won't Recognize Latina/o." *Cultural Dynamics* 29, no. 3 (2017): 141–59.

Gutiérrez-Jones, Carl. *Rethinking the Borderlands: Between Chicano Culture and Legal Discourse.* Berkeley: California University Press, 1995.

Gutiérrez y Muhs, Gabriella, et al., eds. *Presumed Incompetent: The Intersections of Race and Class for Women in Academia.* Logan: Utah State University Press, 2012.

Haggerty, George E. *A Companion to Lesbian, Gay, Bisexual, Transgender, and Queer Studies.* Malden, MA: Blackwell, 2007.

Halberstam, J. Jack. *In a Queer Time and Place: Transgender Bodies, Subcultural Lives.* New York: New York University Press, 2005.

Hall Kells, Michelle. "Latino/as in the United States: Transnationalism, Language, and Identity." In *The International Encyclopedia of English Language Teaching,* edited by John Liontas. Wiley, 2018. https://doi.org/10.1002/9781118784235.eelt0308.

Halperin, Laura. *Intersections of Harm: Narratives of Latina Deviance and Defiance.* New Brunswick, NJ: Rutgers University Press, 2015.

Hames-García, Michael. "Queer Theory Revisited." In *Gay Latino Studies: A Critical Reader,* edited by Michael Hames-García and Ernesto Javier Martínez, 19–45. Durham, NC: Duke University Press, 2011.

Hanisch, Carol. "The Personal Is Political" (1969). Accessed June 1, 2014. www.carolhanisch.org.

Hartley, Nina. "Porn: An Effective Vehicle for Sexual Role Modeling and Education." *The Feminist Porn Book: The Politics of Producing Pleasure,* edited by Tristan Taormino, Celine Parreñas Shimizu, Constance Penley, and Mireille Miller-Young, 228–36. New York: The Feminist Press, 2013.

Hector Torres Papers. "Ana Castillo," undated interview. University of New Mexico Center for Southwest Research.

Hellier-Tinoco, Ruth. *Embodying Mexico: Tourism, Nationalism and Performance.* New York: Oxford University Press, 2011.

Heng, Geraldine. "'A Great Way to Fly': Nationalism, the State, and the Varieties of Third-World Feminism." In *Feminist Genealogies, Colonial Legacies, Democratic Futures*, edited by M. Jacqui Alexander and Chandra Talpade Mohanty, 30–45. New York: Routledge, 1997.

Hernandez-Castillo, R. Aida. *Multiple InJustices: Indigenous Women, Law, and Political Struggle in Latin America*. Tucson: University of Arizona Press, 2016.

Hernández-Linares, Leticia, et al., eds. *The Wandering Song: Central American Writing in the United States*. Evanston, IL: Northwestern University Press, 2017.

Herrera, Cristina. *Contemporary Chicana Literature: (Re)writing the Maternal Script*. Amherst, MA: Cambria Press, 2014.

Herrera, Olga H. "Finding Mexican Chicago on Mango Street: A Transnational Production of Space and Place in Sandra Cisneros's *The House on Mango Street* and *Caramelo*." In *Bridges, Borders, and Breaks: History, Narrative, and Nation in Twenty-First-Century Chicana/o Literary Criticism*, edited by William Orchard and Yolanda Padilla, 103–20. Pittsburgh: University of Pittsburgh Press, 2016.

Herrera, Olga H. "Geographies of Latinidad in Ana Castillo's *Sapogonia*." *Confluencia: Revista Hispánica de Cultura y Literatura* 31, no.1 (2015): 159–69.

Herrera-Sobek, María. "The Politics of Rape: Sexual Transgression in Chicana Fiction." In *Chicana Creativity & Criticism: New Frontiers in American Literature*, second edition, edited by María Herrera-Sobek and Helena María Viramontes, 245–56. Albuquerque: University of New Mexico Press, 1996.

Hesson, Ted. "In legal setback, U.S. judge strikes down Trump asylum restriction." Reuters, July 1, 2020. https://www.reuters.com/article/us-usa-immigra tion-courts-asylum/in-legal-setback-u-s-judge-strikes-down-trump-asylum-re strictions-idUSKBN2426EQ.

Hoffman, Joan M. "'Hope Is the Last to Die': The Quixotic Adventure of 'Esperanza's Box of Saints.'" *Bilingual Review* 25, no. 2 (May 2000): 163–71.

Hong, Grace Kyungwon. *Death beyond Disavowal: The Impossible Politics of Difference*. Minneapolis: University of Minnesota Press, 2015.

hooks, bell. *Yearning: Race, Gender, and Cultural Politics*. Boston: South End Press, 1990.

Huerta, Jorge A. *Chicano Drama: Performance, Society and Myth*. Cambridge: Cambridge University Press, 2000.

Huerta, Jorge A. *Chicano Theater: Themes and Forms*. Ypsilanti, MI: Bilingual Press / Editorial Bilingue, 1982.

Huggan, Graham. *The Post-Colonial Exotic: Marketing the Margins*. New York: Routledge, 2001.

Hughes, Langston. In *The Black Poets: A New Anthology*, edited by Dudley Randall, 78–91. New York: Bantam Books, 1985.

Hurtado, Aída. "The Politics of Sexuality in the Gender Subordination of Chicanas." In *Living Chicana Theory*, edited by Carla Trujillo, 383–428. Berkeley, CA: Third Woman Press, 1998.

Hurtado, Aída. *Voicing Chicana Feminisms: Young Women Speak Out on Sexuality and Identity*. New York: New York University Press, 2003.

Inda, Jonathon Xavier. "The Value of Immigrant Life." In *Women and Migration in the U.S.–Mexico Borderlands: A Reader*, edited by Denise A. Segura and Patricia Zavella, 134–57. Durham, NC: Duke University Press, 2007.

Jager, Rebecca K. *Malinche, Pocahontas, and Sacagewea: Indian Women as Cultural Intermediaries and National Symbols*. Norman: University of Oklahoma Press, 2015.

Jameson, Fredric. *Postmodernism, Or, The Cultural Logic of Late Capitalism*. Durham, NC: Duke University Press, 1991.

Jameson, Fredric. *Postmodernism, Or, The Cultural Logic of Late Capitalism*. New York: Verso, 1991.

Johnson, Leigh. "Covert Wars in the Bedroom and Nation: Motherwork, Transnationalism, and Domestic Violence in Black Widow's Wardrobe and Mother Tongue." *Meridians: Feminism, Race, Transnationalism* 11, no. 2 (2013): 149–71.

Kaminsky, Amy K. *Reading the Body Politic: Feminist Criticism and Latin American Women Writers*. Minneapolis: University of Minnesota Press, 1993.

Kandiyoti, Dalia. "Multiplicity and Its Discontents: Feminist Narratives of Transnational Belonging." *Genders* 37, no. 1 (April 2003). https://www.colorado.edu/gendersarchive1998-2013/2003/04/01/multiplicity-and-its-discontents-feminist-narratives-transnational-belonging.

Kaplan, Caren, Norma Alarcón, and Minoo Moallem, eds. *Between Woman and Nation: Nationalism, Transnational Feminisms, and the State*. Durham, NC: Duke University Press, 1999.

Kauffman, Linda S. *Discourses of Desire: Gender, Genre, and Epistolary Fictions*. Ithaca, NY: Cornell University Press, 1986.

Kaup, Monica. *Rewriting North American Borders in Chicano and Chicana Narrative*. New York: Peter Lang, 2001.

Keeling, Kara. *Queer Times, Black Futures*. New York: New York University Press, 2019.

Kevane, Bridget, and Juanita Heredia, eds. "Praying for Knowledge: An Interview with Helena María Viramontes." *Latina Self-Portraits: Interviews with Contemporary Women Writers*. Albuquerque: University of New Mexico Press, 2000.

Khanna, Ranjana. *Dark Continents: Psychoanalysis and Colonialism*. Durham, NC: Duke University Press, 2003.

Kinzer, Stephen. "How Femicide Drove the Caravan." *Boston Globe*, December 5, 2018. https://www3.bostonglobe.com/opinion/2018/12/05/how-femicide-drove-caravan/5lktZE3HNESy7AwLksW5LJ/story.html?arc404=true.

Krase, Kathryn. "The History of Forced Sterilization in the United States." Ourbodiesourselves.org. Oct. 1, 2014. https://www.ourbodiesourselves.org/book-excerpts/health-article/forced-sterilization/.

LaFeber, Walter. *Inevitable Revolutions: The United States in Central America.* 2nd ed. New York: W. W. Norton, 1993.

La Fountain-Stokes, Lawrence. *Queer Ricans: Cultures and Sexualities in the Diaspora.* Minneapolis: University of Minnesota Press, 2009.

Lamke, Sherece, dir. *The Past Is Alive within Us: The U.S. Dakota Conflict.* Documentary. Minneapolis: Twin Cities PBS, 2013.

Lane, Jill. "Digital Zapatistas." *Drama Review* 4, no. 2 (Summer 2003): 129–44.

Lanza, Carmela Delia. "Hearing the Voices: Women and Home and Ana Castillo's *So Far from God.*" *MELUS: Multi-Ethnic Literature of the U.S.* 23, no. 1 (1998): 65–79.

Larkin, Lesley. "Reading as Responsible Dialogue in Ana Castillo's *The Mixquiahuala Letters.*" *MELUS: Multi-Ethnic Literature of the U.S.,* 37, no. 3 (2012): 141–65.

Latino Rebels. "The Current UndocuMedia Mess Just Got Messier." Aug. 15, 2018. https://www.latinorebels.com/2018/08/15/undocumediamess/.

Lavery, Grace. "Grad School as Conversion Therapy." *Los Angeles Review of Books,* October 29, 2018. https://blog.lareviewofbooks.org/essays/grad-school-conversion-therapy/.

Levander, Caroline Field, and Robert S. Levine, eds. *Hemispheric American Studies.* New Brunswick, NJ: Rutgers University Press, 2008.

Libman, Daniel. "Ana Castillo Takes the Fifth." In Taking the Fifth with Daniel Libman. *Fifth Wednesday Journal* 10 (Spring 2012), n.p.

Limón, José Eduardo. *Mexican Ballads, Chicano Poems: History and Influence in Mexican-American Social Poetry.* Berkeley: California University Press, 1992.

Lind, Dara. "The US has made migrants at the border wait months to apply for asylum. Now the dam is breaking." *Vox,* November 28, 2018. https://www.vox.com/2018/11/28/18089048/border-asylum-trump-metering-legally-ports.

Lopez, Donald S., Jr. "Introduction: Digesting the Dharma." In *Buddhist Scriptures,* edited by Donald S. Lopez Jr., xi–xlii. New York: Penguin, 2004.

López, Marissa K. *Chicano Nations: The Hemispheric Origins of Mexican American Literature.* New York: New York University Press, 2011.

Lorde, Audre. *Sister Outsider: Essays and Speeches.* Berkeley, CA: Crossing Press, 1984.

Lorde, Audre. "The Master's Tools Will Never Dismantle the Master's House." In *Sister Outsider: Essays and Speeches,* 110–14. Berkeley, CA: Crossing Press, 1984.

Lorente-Murphy, Silvia. "El baile y canto flamencos como metáfora de la vida en Peel My Love like an Onion de Ana Castillo." Congreso Internacional de Literatura Iberoamericana 34 (2002): 127–32.

Loubet, Susan Thom. "Ana Castillo Reveals Her Own Life." Women's Focus. *KUNM,* July 15, 2016.

Lugo-Lugo, Carmen R., and Bloodsworth-Lugo, Mary K. "'Anchor/Terror Babies' and Latina Bodies: Immigration Rhetoric in the 21st Century and the Feminization of Terrorism." *Journal of Interdisciplinary Feminist Thought* 8, no. 1 (Summer 2014): 1–21.

Lugones, María. "Heterosexualism and the Colonial/Modern Gender System." *Hypatia* 22, no. 1 (Winter 2007): 186–209.

Lugones, Maria. "Purity, Impurity, and Separation." *Signs* 19, no. 2 (1994): 458–79.

Luiselli, Valeria. *Tell Me How It Ends: An Essay in Forty Questions*. Minneapolis: Coffee House Press, 2017.

Luna, Jennie, and Gabriel Estrada. "Trans*lating the Genderqueer -X through Caxcan, Nahua, and Xicanx Indígena Knowledge." In *Decolonizing Latinx Masculinities*, edited by Arturo J. Aldama and Frederick Luis Aldama, 251–74. Tucson, AZ: University of Arizona Press, 2020.

Malefyt, Timothy Dewaal. "'Inside' and 'Outside' Spanish Flamenco: Gender Constructions in Andalusian Concepts of Flamenco Tradition." *Anthropological Quarterly* 71, no. 4 (1998): 63–73.

Manríquez, B. J. "Ana Castillo's *So Far from God*: Intimations of the Absurd." *College Literature* 29, no. 2 (2002): 37–49.

Maringer, Johannes. "Priests and Priestesses in Prehistoric Europe." *History of Religions* 17, no. 2 (1977): 101–20.

Mariscal, Jorge. "Cesar and Martin, March '68." In *The Struggle in Black and Brown: African American and Mexican American Relations during the Civil Rights Era*, edited by Brian Behnken, 148–78. Lincoln: University of Nebraska Press, 2012.

Martínez, Danizete. "Dismemberment in the Chicana/o Body Politic: Fragmenting Nationness and Form in Oscar Zeta Acosta's *The Revolt of the Cockroach People* and Alejandro Morales's *The Rag Doll Plagues*." *Disclosure: A Journal of Social Theory* 21 (2012): 38–53.

Martínez, Danizete. "Teaching Chicana/o Literature in Community College with Ana Castillo's *So Far from God*." *Rocky Mountain Review of Language and Literature* 65, no. 2 (2011): 216–25.

Martínez, Marcos. "Still Treading Water: Recent Currents in Chicano Theater." In *The State of Latino Theatre in the United States*, edited by Luis A. Ramos-García, 15–29. New York: Routledge, 2002.

Maschi, David. "The Divide over Ordaining Women." *Fact Tank: News in the Numbers*. Pew Research Center, September 9, 2014. www.pewresearch.org/fact-tank/2014/09/09/the-divide-over-ordaining-women/.

Matthes, Erich Hatala. "Cultural Appropriation without Cultural Essentialism?" *Social Theory and Practice* 42, no. 2 (2016): 343–66.

McDiarmid, Margo. "Still No Way to Tell How Many Indigenous Women and Girls Go Missing in Canada Each Year." CBC News, December 21, 2017. https://www.cbc.ca/news/politics/indigenous-missing-women-police-data-1.4449073.

McLaren, Peter. *Life in Schools: An Introduction to Critical Pedagogy in the Foundations of Education.* Fifth edition. New York: Pearson, 2006.

McMahon, M. R. *Domestic Negotiations: Gender, Nation, and Self-Fashioning in US Mexicana and Chicana Literature and Art.* New Brunswick, NJ: Rutgers University Press, 2013.

McPherson, Alan. *Intimate Ties, Bitter Struggles: The United States and Latin America since 1945.* Washington, DC: Potomac Books, 2006.

Melo, Frederick. "St. Paul City Council Condemns Trump Administration Border Policies." *St. Paul Pioneer Press,* June 20, 2018. https://www.twincities.com/2018/06/20/st-paul-city-council-condemns-trump-administrations-border-policies/.

Mercedes Jaramillo, María, and Lucía Ortiz, eds. *Hijas del muntu: Biografías críticas de mujeres afrodescendientes de América Latina.* Bogotá: Panamericana Editorial, 2011.

Mesa-Bains, Amalia. "Domesticana: The Sensibility of Chicana Rasquachismo." In *Chicana Feminisms: A Critical Reader,* edited by Gabriela F. Arredondo, 298–315. Durham, NC: Duke University Press Books, 2003.

Mignolo, Walter. *The Darker Side of the Renaissance: Literacy, Territoriality, and Colonization.* Ann Arbor: University of Michigan Press, 2003.

Mignolo, Walter. "Geopolitics of Sensing and Knowing: On (de)coloniality, Border Thinking, and Epistemic Disobedience." *Confero: Essays on Education, Philosophy and Politics* 1, no. 1 (2013): 129–50.

Mignolo, Walter. *Local Histories / Global Designs: Coloniality, Subaltern Knowledges, and Border Thinking.* Princeton, NJ: Princeton University Press, 2012.

"Migrant caravan: Trump defends tear gas on Mexican border." BBC, Nov. 27, 2018. www.bbc.com/news/world-us-canada-46355258.

Miguela, Antonia Domínguez. "Tropicalizing the Other's Culture and Language in Latino/a Literature." *Asociación Española de Estudios Anglo-Norteamericanos,* 1999, 1–7.

Milian, Claudia. "Extremely Latin, XOXO: Notes on LatinX." *Cultural Dynamics* 29, no. 3 (July 2017): 121–40.

Milian, Claudia. *Latining America: Black-Brown Passages and the Coloring of Latino/a Studies.* Athens: University of Georgia Press, 2013.

Mills, Fiona. "Creating a Resistant Chicana Aesthetic: The Queer Performativity of Ana Castillo's *So Far from God.*" *CLA Journal* 46, no. 3 (March 2003): 312–36.

Mitchell, Katharyne. "Transnational Discourse: Bringing Geography Back In." *Antipode* 29, no. 2 (1997): 101–14.

Mohanty, Chandra. *Feminism without Borders : Decolonizing Theory, Practicing Solidarity.* Durham, NC: Duke University Press, 2003.

Mohanty, Chandra Talpade. "Introduction: Cartographies of Struggle: Third World Women and the Politics of Feminism." In *Third World Women and the*

Politics of Feminism, edited by Chandra Talpade Mohanty, Ann Russo, and Lourdes Torres, 1–50. Bloomington: Indiana University Press, 1991.

Moraga, Cherríe. "Art in América Con Acento." *The Last Generation: Prose and Poetry*. Boston, MA: South End Press, 1993.

Moraga, Cherríe. *Giving Up the Ghost*. Albuquerque: West End Press, 1986.

Moraga, Cherríe. *The Last Generation: Prose and Poetry*. Boston: South End Press, 1993.

Moraga, Cherríe. *Loving in the War Years*. Boston: South End Press, 1983.

Moraga, Cherríe. "Queer Aztlán: The Re-formation of Chicano Tribe." *The Last Generation: Prose and Poetry*. Boston, MA: South End Press, 1993.

Moraga, Cherríe. *Waiting in the Wings: Portraits of a Queer Motherhood*. New York: Firebrand Books, 1997.

Moraga, Cherríe, and Gloria Anzaldúa, eds. *This Bridge Called My Back: Writings by Radical Women of Color*. Third edition. Berkeley, CA: Third Woman Press, 2002.

Moraga, Cherríe, and Gloria Anzaldúa, eds. *This Bridge Called My Back: Writings by Radical Women of Color*. Watertown, MA: Persephone Press, 1981.

Moraga, Cherríe, and Ana Castillo, eds. *Esta Puente, mi espalda: Voces de mujeres tercermundistas en los Estados Unidos*. San Francisco: Ism Press, 1988.

Moraleda, Alba, and Olga Luna. "Guadalupe, la primera niña que nace en la caravana migrante que cruza México." *Noticias Telemundo*. Published November 1, 2018. Accessed November 15, 2018. https://www.telemundo.com/noticias/2018/11/01/guadalupe-la-primera-nina-que-nace-en-la-caravana-migrante-que-cruza-mexico.

Morales, Ed. *Latinx: The New Force in American Politics and Culture*. London: Verso, 2018.

Morales, Ed. *Living in Spanglish: The Search for Latino Identity in America*. New York: St. Martin's Press, 2010.

Morales, Sylvia, Dolores Huerta, Elizabeth Sutherland Martínez, Cherríe Moraga, Alicia Escalante, and Martha Cotera, eds. *A Crushing Love: Chicanas, Motherhood and Activism*. New York: Distributed by Women Make Movies, 2009.

Morales, Sylvia, Anna Nieto-Gomez, Carmen Zapata, and Carmen Moreno. *Chicana*. New York: Distributed by Women Make Movies, 1979.

Morán, Gregorio. *El precio de la transición*. Madrid: Ediciones Akal, 2015.

Moreno Vega, Marta. "The Ancestral Sacred Creative Impulse of African and the African Diaspora: Ase, the Nexus of the Black Global Aesthetic." *Lenox Avenue: A Journal of Interarts Inquiry* 5 (1999): 45–57.

Mossman, Robert. "Teaching Demetria Martínez' *Mother Tongue*." *English Journal* 86, no. 8 (1997): 38–41.

Mujčinović, Fatima. *Postmodern Cross-Culturalism and Politicization in U.S. Latina Literature*. New York: Peter Lang Publishing, 2004.

Muñoz, José Esteban. *Cruising Utopia: The Then and There of Queer Futurity*. New York: New York University Press, 2009.

Muñoz, José Esteban. *Disidentifications: Queers of Color and the Performance of Politics*. Minneapolis: University of Minnesota Press, 1999.

Nájera-Ramírez, Olga, Norma Elia Cantú, and Brenda M. Romero, eds. *Dancing across Borders: Danzas y Bailes Mexicanos*. Urbana: University of Illinois Press, 2009.

National Congress of American Indians. *Research Policy Update: Violence against American Indian and Alaska Native Women*. Washington, DC: NCAI Policy Research Center, 2019.

National Security Archive. "Relevant Declassified U.S. Documents from the National Security Archive's Guatemala Collection." George Washington University, Washington, DC, posted May 20, 1999. http://www.gwu.edu/~nsarchiv/NSAEBB/NSAEBB15/index.html.

Newfield, Christopher. *Unmaking the Public University: The Forty-Year Assault on the Middle Class*. Reprint. Cambridge, MA: Harvard University Press, 2011.

NietoGómez, Anna. "La Chicana: Legacy of Suffering and Self-Denial." In *Chicana Feminist Thought: The Basic Historical Writings*, edited by Alma M. García, 48–49. New York: Routledge, 1997.

Noel, Urayoán. "Bodies that Antimatter: Locating U.S Latino/a Poetry, 2000–2009." *Contemporary Literature* 52, no. 4 (2011): 852–82.

Noel, Urayoán. "Poetry." In *The Routledge Companion to Latino/a Literature*, edited by Suzanne Bost and Frances R. Aparicio, 285–98. New York: Routledge, 2012.

Oboler, Suzanne. *Ethnic Labels, Latino Lives: Identity and the Politics of (Re)Presentation in the United States*. Minneapolis: University of Minnesota Press, 1995.

O'Gorman, Edmundo. *The Invention of America: An Inquiry into the Historical Nature of the New World and the Meaning of Its History*. Bloomington: Indiana University Press, 1961.

Orchard, William, and Yolanda Padilla, eds. *Bridges, Borders, and Breaks: History, Narrative, and Nation in Twenty-First-Century Chicana/o Literary Criticism*. Pittsburgh: University of Pittsburgh Press, 2016.

Ordóñez, Elizabeth. "Sexual Politics and the Theme of Sexuality in Chicana Poetry." *Letras Femeninas* 32, no. 1 (Summer 2006): 67–92.

Ortiz, Sister Dianna. *The Blindfold's Eyes: My Journey from Torture to Truth*. Maryknoll, NY: Orbis Books, 2002.

Otto, Marjorie. "Marchers go from Eastside to City Hall Condemning Separation of Children." *Lillie Suburban Newspapers*, June 25, 2018. http://www.lillienews.com/articles/2018/06/25/marchers-go-east-side-city-hall-condemning-separation-children.

Paredes, Américo. *Folklore and Culture on the Texas-Mexican Border*. Austin: University of Texas Press, 1993.

Park, Shelley M. *Mothering Queerly, Queering Motherhood: Resisting Monomaternalism in Adoptive, Lesbian, Blended, and Polygamous Families*. Albany: State University of New York Press, 2013.

Paul VI. 1976. "Declaration Inter Insigniores on the Question of Admission of Women to the Ministerial Priesthood." *Sacred Congregation for the Doctrine of the Faith*. http://www.vatican.va/roman_curia/congregations/cfaith/documents/rc_con_cfaith_doc_19761015_inter-insigniores_en.html.

Paz, Octavio. *Laberinto de la soledad*. Mexico D.F.: Fondo de Cultura Económica, 1959.

Peinete Revuelta. "About the Huge Racism from Singer Rosalía to Roma People." *Peineta Revuelta. Revolución Flamenca*. January 25, 2019. Accessed August 1, 2019. https://peinetarevuelta.wordpress.com/2019/01/25/about-the-huge-racism-from-singer-rosalia-to-roma-people/.

Pelaez Lopez, Alan. "The X in Latinx Is a Wound, Not a Trend." *Efniks*. Published September 13, 2018. Accessed May 29, 2020. https://www.colorbloq.org/the-x-in-latinx-is-a-wound-not-a-trend.

Pellegrini, Ann. "Queer Structures of Religious Feeling: What Time Is Now?" In *Sexual Disorientations: Queer Temporalities, Affects, Theologies*, edited by Kent L. Brintnall, Joseph A. Mitchell, and Stephen D. Moore, 240–57. New York: Fordham University Press, 2018.

Pember, Mary A. "Trauma May Be Woven into DNA of Native Americans." *Indian Country Today*, October 3, 2017. https://newsmaven.io/indiancountrytoday/archive/trauma-may-be-woven-into-dna-of-native-americans-CbiAxpzar0WkMALhjrcGVQ/.

Peña, Susana. "Gender and Sexuality in Latina/o Miami: Documenting Latina Transsexual Activists." *Gender & History* 22, no. 3 (November 2010): 768.

Pérez, Domino Renee. "New Tribalism and Chicana/o Indigeneity in the Work of Gloria Anzaldúa." In *The Oxford Handbook of Indigenous American Literature*, edited by James H. Cox, Daniel Heath Justice, and Domino Renee Perez, 489–502. Oxford: Oxford University Press, 2014.

Perez, Domino Renee. *There Was a Woman: La Llorona from Folklore to Popular Culture*. Austin: University of Texas Press, 2008.

Pérez, Emma. *The Decolonial Imaginary: Writing Chicanas into History*. Bloomington: Indiana University Press, 1999.

Pérez, Emma. "Sexuality and Discourse: Notes from a Chicana Survivor." In *Chicana Lesbians: The Girls Our Mothers Warned Us About*, edited by Carla Trujillo, 159–84. Berkeley, CA: Third Woman Press, 1991.

Pérez, Laura E. *Chicana Art: The Politics of Spiritual and Aesthetic Altarities*. Durham, NC: Duke University Press, 2007.

Pérez, Laura E. "*El desorden*, Nationalism, and Chicana/o Aesthetics." In *Between Woman and Nation: Nationalisms, Transnational Feminisms, and the State*, edited by Caren Kaplan, Norma Alarcón, and Minoo Moallem. Durham, NC: Duke University Press, 1999.

Pérez-Torres, Rafael. *Mestizaje: Critical Uses of Race in Chicano Culture*. Minneapolis: University of Minnesota Press, 2006.

Pérez-Torres, Rafael. *Movements in Chicano Poetry: Against Myths, against Margins*. Cambridge: Cambridge University Press, 1995.

Perkins, Michael. *The Secret Record: Modern Erotic Literature*. New York: William Morrow, 1976.

Perry, Ruth. *Women, Letters, and the Novel*. Vol. 4. New York: AMS Press, 1980.

Pertusa, Inmaculada, and Lourdes Torres. *Tortilleras: Hispanic and U.S. Latina Lesbian Expression*. Philadelphia: Temple University Press, 2003.

"Pope Institutes Commission to Study the Diaconate of Women." Vatican Radio, August 2, 2016. en.radiovaticana.va/news/2016/08/02/pope_institutes _commission_to_study_the_diaconate_of_women/1248731.

Pratt, Mary Louise. "'Yo Soy La Malinche': Chicana Writers and the Poetics of Ethnonationalism." *Callaloo* 16, no. 4 (Autumn1993): 859–73.

Priewe, Marc. "Making a Home away from Home: Traveling Diasporas in María Escandón's *Esperanza's Box of Saints*." *Journal of Transnational American Studies* 4, no. 2 (2012): 581–93.

"Protocol to Prevent, Suppress and Punish Trafficking in Persons Especially Women and Children, Supplementing the United Nations Convention against Transnational Organized Crime." United Nations. Adopted November 15, 2000. https://www.ohchr.org/Documents/ProfessionalInterest/Protocolon Trafficking.pdf.

Puar, Jasbir K. "Disability." *Transgender Studies Quarterly* 1, nos. 1–2 (May 1, 2014): 77–81.

Quintana, Alvina E. "Ana Castillo's *The Mixquiahuala Letters*: The Novelist as Ethnographer." In *Criticism in the Borderlands: Studies in Chicano Literature, Culture, and Ideology*, edited by Héctor Calderón and José David Saldívar, 72–83. Durham: Duke University Press, 1991.

Quintana Millamoto, María Esther. "The Redefinition of the Disabled Chicana in Ana Castillo's *Peel My Love like an Onion*." In *Disability in Spanish-Speaking and U.S. Chicano Contexts: Critical and Artistic Perspectives*, edited by Dawn Slack and Karen L. Rauch, 28–43. Cambridge: Cambridge Scholars Publishing, 2019.

Quiroga, José. "Nostalgia for Sex." In *Tropics of Desire: Interventions from Queer Latino America*. New York: New York University Press, 2000.

Quiroga, José. *Tropics of Desire: Interventions from Queer Latino America*. New York: New York University Press, 2000.

Raab, Kelley A. *When Women become Priests: The Catholic Women's Ordination Debate*. New York: Columbia University Press, 2000.

Rabuzzi, Kathryn Allen. *The Sacred and the Feminine: Toward a Theology of Housework*. New York: Seabury Press, 1982.

Ramírez, Catherine. "Alternative Cartographies: The Impact of Third Woman on Chicana Feminist Literature, 1981–1986." http://www.thirdwomanpress.com/about/history/.

Ramírez, Elizabeth C. *Chicanas/Latinas in American Theatre: A History of Performance*. Bloomington: Indiana University Press, 2000.

Ramirez-Chavez, Gabriela. *The Wandering Song: Central American Writing in the United States*. San Fernando: Tia Chucha Press, 2017.

Raphael, Timothy. "Teaching, Performance, and the Shifting Stage." *Transformations* 20, no. 1 (2009): 14–18.

Rebolledo, Tey Diana. *The Chronicles of Panchita Villa and Other Guerrilleras*. Austin: University of Texas Press, 2005.

Rebolledo, Tey Diana, and Eliana S. Rivero. *Infinite Divisions: An Anthology of Chicana Literature*. Tucson: University of Arizona Press, 1993.

Rechy, John. *The Sexual Outlaw: A Documentary; A Non-Fiction Account, with Commentaries, of Three Days and Nights in the Sexual Underground*. New York: Grove, 1977.

Reed, Alison. "The Whiter the Bread, the Quicker You're Dead: Spectacular Absence and Post-Racialized Blackness in (White) Queer Theory." In *No Tea, No Shade: New Writings in Black Queer Studies*, edited by E. Patrick Johnson, 48–64. Durham, NC: Duke University Press, 2016.

Regan, Sheila. "After Protests from Native American Community, Walker Art Center Will Remove Public Sculpture." *Hyperallergic Media*, May 29, 2017. https://hyperallergic.com/382141/after-protests-from-native-american-community-walker-art-center-will-remove-public-sculpture/.

Resendez, Andres. *The Other Slavery: The Uncovered Story of Indian Enslavement in America*. Boston: Houghton Mifflin Harcourt, 2016.

Rodríguez, Ana Patricia. "The Fiction of Solidarity Transfronterista Feminisms and Anti-Imperialist Struggles in Central American Transnational Narratives." *Feminist Studies* 34, no. 1–2 (2008): 199–226.

Rodriguez, Jeanette. "Mestiza Spirituality: Community, Ritual, and Justice." *Theological Studies* 65, no. 2 (2004): 317–39.

Rodríguez, Juana María. *Queer Latinidad: Identity Practices, Discursive Spaces*. New York: New York University Press, 2003.

Rodríguez, Juana María. "Queer Politics, Bisexual Erasure: Sexuality at the Nexus of Race, Gender, and Statistics." *Lambda Nordica* 1, no. 2 (2016): 169–82.

Rodríguez, Juana María. *Sexual Futures, Queer Gestures, and Other Latina Longings*. New York: New York University Press, 2014.

Rodriguez, Ralph E. "Chicana/o Fiction from Resistance to Contestation: The Role of Creation in Ana Castillo's *So Far from God*. *MELUS* 25, no. 2 (2000): 63–82.

Rodriguez, Ralph E. *Latinx Literature Unbound: Undoing Ethnic Expectation*. New York: Fordham University Press, 2018.

Rodriguez, Richard T. "X Marks the Spot." *Cultural Dynamics* 29, no. 3 (2017): 202–13.

Román-Odio, Clara. "Global-Local Parodies in María Amparo Escandón's 'Esperanza's Box of Saints.'" *Letras Femeninas* 2 (2008): 87.

Ruiz, Sandra. "Opticourses VI: Subverting Semiotics." Published October 3, 2016. Accessed May 28, 2020. https://ruizsandra.com/2016/10/03/opticourses -vi-subverting-semiotics/.

Rutherford, Jonathan. "The Third Space: Interview with Homi Bhabha." *Identity: Community, Culture, Difference.* London: Lawrence Wishart, 1990.

Saeta, Elsa. 1997. "A MELUS Interview: Ana Castillo." *MELUS* 22 (3): 133–49.

Saldaña-Portillo, María Josefina. *The Revolutionary Imagination in the Americas in the Age of Development*. Durham, NC: Duke University Press, 2003.

Saldívar, José David. *Trans-Americanity: Subaltern Modernities, Global Coloniality, and the Cultures of Greater Mexico*. Durham, NC: Duke University Press, 2012.

Saldívar, Ramón. "Chicano Narrative Now: Literary Discourses in an Age of Transnationalism." In *Bridges, Borders, and Breaks: History, Narrative, and Nation in Twenty-First-Century Chicana/o Literary Criticism*, edited by William Orchard and Yolanda Padilla, 171–76. Pittsburgh: University of Pittsburgh Press, 2016.

Saldívar-Hull, Sonia. *Feminism on the Border: Chicana Gender Politics and Literature*. Berkeley: University of California Press, 2000.

Sanchez, Paloma V., Natalie de Marinis, Bertha Patricia Rosette Xotlanihua, and Raul Martinez Navarro. *Violencia Contra las Mujeres en Zonas Indigenas en Mexico*. Mexico: Secretaria de Gobernacion, 2007.

Sánchez, Rosaura. *Essays on la Mujer*. Los Angeles: University of California Press, 1979.

Sánchez, Rosaura. "Reconstructing Chicana Gender Identity." *American Literary History* 9, no. 2 (1997): 350–63.

Sánchez, Rosaura, and Beatrice Pita. "Mapping Cultural/Political Debates in Latin American Studies." In *Chicana/o Cultural Studies Reader*, second ed., edited by Angie Chabram-Dernersesian, 492–516. New York: Routledge, 2006.

Sandín, Lyn Di Iorio. *Killing Spanish: Literary Essays on Ambivalent U.S. Latino/a Identity*. New York: Palgrave Macmillan, 2004.

Sandoval, Chela. *Methodology of the Oppressed*. Minneapolis: University of Minnesota Press, 2000.

Sandoval, Chela. "U.S. Third World Feminism: The Theory and Method of Oppositional Consciousness in the Postmodern World." *Genders* 10 (1999): 1–24.

Sanford, Victoria. *Buried Secrets: Truth and Human Rights in Guatemala*. New York: Palgrave Macmillan, 2003.

Sanford, Victoria. "From Genocide to Feminicide: Impunity and Human Rights in Twenty-First Century Guatemala." *Journal of Human Rights* 7, no. 2 (2008): 104–22.

Sauer, Michelle M. "'Saint-Making' in Ana Castillo's *So Far from God*: Medieval Mysticism as Precedent for an Authoritative Chicana Spirituality. *Mester* 29, no. 1 (2000): 72–91.

Scarry, Elaine. *The Body in Pain*. Oxford: Oxford University Press, 1985.

Schaefer, Eric. "Gauging a Revolution: 16 mm Film and the Rise of the Pornographic Feature." In *Porn Studies*, edited by Linda Williams. Durham, NC: Duke University Press, 2004.

Schoeffel, Melissa A. *Maternal Conditions: Reading Kingsolver, Castillo, Erdrich, and Ozeki*. New York: Peter Lang, 2008.

Segura, Denise A., and Beatriz M. Pesquera. "Beyond Indifference and Antipathy: The Chicana Movement and Chicana Feminist Discourse." *Aztlán: A Journal of Chicano Studies* 19, no. 2 (1988), 69–92.

Shohat, Ella, and Robert Stam. *Unthinking Eurocentrism: Multiculturalism and the Media*. London: Routledge, 1994.

Sieff, Kevin. "U.S. is denying passports to Americans along the border, throwing their citizenship into question." *Washington Post*, Sept. 13, 2018, www.washington post.com/world/the_americas/us-is-denying-passports-to-americans-along -the-border-throwing-their-citizenship-into-question/2018/08/29/1d630e84 -a0da-11e8-a3dd-2a1991f075d5_story.html?utm_term=.2f7b0d48bcc0.

Simonari, Rosella. "Bringing 'Carmen' Back to Spain: Antonio Gades's Flamenco Dance in Carlos Saura's Choreofilm." *Dance Research: The Journal of the Society for Dance Research* 26, no. 2 (2008): 189–203.

Sirias, Silvio, and Richard McGarry. "Rebellion and Tradition in Ana Castillo's *So Far from God* and Sylvia López-Medina's *Cantora*." *MELUS* 25, no. 2 (2000): 83–100.

Smith Silva, Dorsía. *Latina/Chicana Mothering*. Toronto: Demeter Press, 2011.

Soldatenko, Michael. "The Genesis of Academic Chicano Studies, 1967–1970: Utopia and the Emergence of Chicano Studies." *Chicano Studies: The Genesis of a Discipline*. Tucson: University of Arizona Press, 2009.

Soto, Sandra K. "Queerness." In *The Routledge Companion to Latino/a Literature*, edited by Suzanne Bost and Frances R. Aparicio, 91–99. New York: Routledge, 2012.

Soto, Sandra K. *Reading Chican@ like a Queer: The De-Mastery of Desire*. Austin: University of Texas Press, 2010.

Soto, Sandra K. "Queering the Conquest with Ana Castillo." In *Reading Chican@ like a Queer: The De-Mastery of Desire*. Austin: University of Texas Press, 2010.

Spears-Rico, Gabriela. "Decolonial P'urhepecha Maternalista Motherwork and Pedagogy." In *The Chicana Motherwork Anthology*, edited by Cecilia Caballero, Yvette Martínez-Vu, Judith Pérez-Torres, Michelle Téllez, and Christine Vega, 243–62. Tucson: University of Arizona Press, 2019.

Spears-Rico, Gabriela. "In a Time of War and Hashtags: Rehumanizing Indigeneity in the Digital Landscape." In *Indigenous Interfaces: Spaces, Technology, and Social Networks in Mexico and Central America*, edited by Gloria Elizabeth Chacon and Jennifer Menjivar Gomez, 180–200. Tucson: University of Arizona Press, 2019.

Steingress, Gerhard. "Flamenco Fusion and New Flamenco as Postmodern Phenomena: An Essay on Creative Ambiguity in Popular Music." In *Songs of the Minotaur: Hybridity and Popular Music in the Era of Globalization*, edited by Gerhard Steingress, 169–216. Münster: Lit Verlag, 2003.

Suarez, Karina. "Los Femicidios no cesan en Ciudad Juarez." *El Pais*, November 23, 2017. https://elpais.com/internacional/2017/11/22/mexico/1511307168 _804661.html.

Sullivan, Nikki. *A Critical Introduction to Queer Theory*. New York: New York University Press, 2003.

Sweeney, Kelly. "Race and Reproductive Rights: Eugenic Practices throughout 20th Century American History." *Susquehanna University Political Review* 9, no. 1 (2018): 4.

Szeghi, Tereza M. "Indigeneity and Mestizaje in Ana Castillo's *The Mixquiahuala Letters* and Leslie Marmon Silko's *Almanac of the Dead*." *Comparative Literature* 65, no. 4 (2013): 429–49.

Szeghi, Tereza M. "Literary Didacticism and Collective Human Rights in US Borderlands: Ana Castillo's *The Guardians* and Louise Erdrich's *The Round House*." *Western American Literature* 52, no. 4 (Winter 2018): 403–33.

Tamboukou, Maria. "Interfaces in Narrative Research: Letters as Technologies of the Self and as Traces of Social Forces." *Qualitative Research* 11, no. 5 (2011): 625–41.

Taylor, Diana. *The Archive and the Repertoire: Performing Cultural Memory in the Americas*. Durham, NC: Duke University Press, 2003.

Taylor-García, Daphne V. "Decolonizing Gender Performativity: A Thesis for Emancipation in Early Chicana Feminist Thought (1969–1979)." In *Performing the US Latina and Latino Borderlands*, edited by Arturo J. Aldama, Chela Sandoval, and Peter J. García, 107–24. Bloomington: Indiana University Press, 2012.

Tejeda, Carlos, Manuel Espinoza, and Kris Gutierrez. "Toward a Decolonizing Pedagogy: Social Justice Reconsidered." In *Pedagogies of Difference: Rethinking Education for Social Justice*, edited by Peter Pericles Trifonas, 9–38. New York: Routledge, 2003.

Teorey, Matthew. "Empowering Femininity through Trans Discourse." *Community College Humanities Review* 3 (Fall 2017): 52–69.

Third Woman Press. "About." Accessed November 5, 2019. http://www.thirdwom anpress.com/about/.

Tlapoyawa, Kurly. "What 'Latinx' Doesn't Include." *Yes! Magazine.* November 22, 2019. Accessed May 29, 2020. https://www.yesmagazine.org/peace-justice/lat inx-indigenous-history-heritage-20191122?fbclid=IwAR2rHBuzU4eCQgIqJ UAj7SHl4JvBqqphl-IXcxwbGswBP73x92PvP_cgJxQ.

Tobar, Héctor. *The Tattooed Soldier.* New York: Penguin, 1998.

Torres-Saillant, Silvio. "The Indian in the Latino: Genealogies of Ethnicity." *Latino Studies* 10, no. 4 (2012): 587–607.

Torres-Saillant, Silvio. "Nothing to Celebrate." *Culturefront: A Magazine of the Humanities* 8, no. 2 (1999): 41–44.

Trotter, Robert T., and Juan Antonio Chavira. *Curanderismo: Mexican American Folk Healing.* Athens: University of Georgia Press, 1981.

Trujillo, Carla. *Chicana Lesbians: The Girls Our Mothers Warned Us About.* Berkeley, CA: Third Woman Press, 1994.

"Trump Ends DACA, Calls on Congress to Act." *NPR*, Sept. 5, 2017. www.npr.org/2017/09/05/546423550/trump-signals-end-to-daca-calls-on -congress-to-act.

Tuck, Eve, Malie Arvin, and Angie Morrill. "Decolonizing Feminism: Challenging Connections between Settler Colonialism and Heteropatriarchy." *Feminist Formations* 25, no. 1 (2013): 8–34.

Tuck, Eve, and K. Wayne Yang. "Decolonization Is Not a Metaphor." *Decolonization: Indigeneity, Education and Society* 1, no. 1 (2012): 1-40.

UndocuMedia Facebook. August 25, 2016. Accessed April 6, 2019. https://www .facebook.com/undocumedia/posts/true-story-must-read-alondra-correa-bau tista-my-father-works-two-jobs-six-out-of/1237565532943145/.

United States Congressional Senate. Comprehensive Immigration Reform Act of 2007. S. 1348, 110th Cong. (2007). Accessed April 14, 2019. https://www .congress.gov/bill/110th-congress/senate-bill/1348.

United States Institute of Peace. "Peace Agreements: Guatemala." Peace Agreements Digital Collection, posted November 20, 1998. http://www.usip.org/ publications/peace-agreements-guatemala.

UNODC. "Global Report on Trafficking in Persons." United Nations Publications, 2016. https://www.unodc.org/documents/data-and-analysis/glotip/2016 _Global_Report_on_Trafficking_in_Persons.pdf.

UNODC. "Protocol to Prevent, Suppress and Punish Trafficking in Persons." United Nations Publications, 2000. https://www.ohchr.org/en/professionalin terest/pages/protocoltraffickinginpersons.aspx.

US Department of Transportation. "Bureau of Transportation Statistics." Accessed April 3, 2019. https://explore.dot.gov/t/BTS/views/BTSBorderCross ingAnnualData/BorderCrossingTableDashboard?:embed=y&:showShareOp tions=true&:display_count=no&:showVizHome=no.

Valdes, Marcela. "Rosalía's Incredible Journey from Flamenco to Megastardom." *New York Times*, October 8, 2019.

Valentish, Jenny. "The Commodification of Frida Kahlo: Are We Losing the Artist under the Kitsch?" *Guardian*, December 28, 2018. https://www .theguardian.com/artanddesign/2018/dec/29/the-commodification-of-frida -kahlo-are-we-losing-the-artist-under-the-kitsch.

Vidal, Mirtha. "New Voice of La Raza: Chicanas Speak Out." In *Chicana Feminist Thought: The Basic Historical Writings*, edited by Alma M. García, 21–23. New York: Routledge, 1997.

Vigil, Ariana E. *War Echoes: Gender and Militarization in U.S. Latina/o Cultural Production*. New Brunswick, NJ: Rutgers University Press, 2014.

Viramontes, Helena María. "Four Guiding Principles to a Lived Experience." *La Herencia / The Heritage: I Encuentro De Escritoras Chicanas*. México City: Universidad Nacional Autónoma de México, 2003.

Viramontes, Helena María. "The Writes Ofrenda." In *Mascaras*, edited by Lucha Corpí, 125–31. Berkeley, CA: Third Woman Press, 1997.

Vivancos Pérez, Ricardo F. *Radical Chicana Poetics*. New York: Palgrave Macmillan, 2013.

Wallace, Cynthia R. *Of Women Borne: A Literary Ethics of Suffering*. New York: Columbia University Press, 2016.

Walker, Margaret. *Prophets for a New Day*. Detroit, MI: Broadside Press, 1970.

Weissberger, Barbara F. "Ana Castillo's *The Mixquiahuala Letters*: A Queer Don Quijote." *Letras Femeninas* 33, no. 2 (2007): 9–23.

West-Durán, Alan "Introductory Essays." *Latino and Latina Writers*. Vol. 1. New York: Charles Scribner's Sons, 2004.

West Los Angeles College. "Fall 2016 Student Profile." Accessed April 3, 2019. http://www.wlac.edu/WLAC/media/documents/research/planning/Student_ Profile_Fall_2016.pdf.

White House. "What You Need to Know about the Violent Animals of MS-13." Published May 21, 2018. Accessed January 5, 2021. https://www.whitehouse .gov/articles/need-know-violent-animals-ms-13/.

Wilder, Craig Steven. *Ebony and Ivy: Race, Slavery, and the Troubled History of America's Universities*. London: Bloomsbury Press, 2013.

Williams, Raymond. *Marxism and Literature*. Vol. 392. Oxford: Oxford Paperbacks, 1977.

Yarbro-Bejarano, Yvonne. "The Female Subject in Chicano Theatre: Sexuality, 'Race,' and Class." *Theatre Journal* 38, no. 4 (1986): 389–407.

Yarbro-Bejarano, Yvonne. "Sexuality and Chicana/o Studies." In *The Chicana/o Cultural Studies Reader*, edited by Angie Chabram-Dernersesian, 224–32. New York: Routledge, 2006.

Yarbro-Bejarano, Yvonne. "Teatropoesía by Chicanas in the Bay Area: Tongues on Fire." *Revista Chicano-Riqueña* 1, no. 1 (1983): 78–94.

Zamora, Lois Parkinson. *Magic Realism: Theory, History, Community.* Durham, NC: Duke University Press, 1995.

Zapata Pérez, Edelma. "The Consciousness-Raising of an Afro-Indo-Mulatto Woman Writer in Colombia's Multiethnic Society." In *Daughters of the Diaspora: Afra-Hispanic Writers*, edited by Miriam DeCosta-Willis, 357–72. Kingston, Jamaica: Ian Randle Publishers, 2003.

Zapata Pérez, Edelma. "Esbozo autobiográfico." *Afro-Hispanic Review* 28, no. 1 (Spring 2009): 203–13.

Zapata Pérez, Edelma. "América." *Afro-Hispanic Review* 27, no. 2 (Fall 2008): 163.

CONTRIBUTORS

Elena Avilés is an assistant professor of Spanish at West Los Angeles College. She earned her PhD in Hispanic languages and literatures at the University of New Mexico. Her research brings new insights to the study of contemporary US Latina/o and Chicana/o cultural production with more than a decade of experience in higher education focusing on issues related to the humanities. Her teaching interests cover various topics related to Chicano/Latino literature and Chicana feminist politics across art and literature as they relate to new work in urban humanities.

Laura Elena Belmonte is an assistant professor of Chicana/o studies at the University of New Mexico. Professor Belmonte's research focus is spirituality and religious expression in border, transnational, and feminist literature and culture. She is currently working on a book manuscript entitled "Borderland Brutalities: Violence in the U.S.-Mexico Borderlands in Literature, Film, and Culture." This manuscript is an exploration of cultural production by people of color experiencing border violence perpetuated by the United States and Mexican governments.

Ayendy Bonifacio is an assistant professor of US ethnic literary studies at the University of Toledo. His areas of scholarship are American literature and culture, Latino/a/x studies, periodical studies, and the digital humanities. His work is published in *American Periodicals*, *Prose Studies*, and *American Literary Realism*. Bonifacio's research has been supported by the National Endowment for the Humanities (NEH), the Digital Media and Composition Institute (DMAC), and the Society for Nineteenth-Century Americanists (C19). He is currently at work on a book that sits at the intersection of nineteenth-century Latinidad and reprint culture.

Norma E. Cantú is the Norine R. and T. Frank Murchison Distinguished Professor of the Humanities at Trinity University in San Antonio. She teaches folklore, Latinx studies, and creative writing. Cantú's publications on border literature, the teaching of English, quinceañera celebration, and the matachines, a religious dance tradition, have earned her an international reputation as a scholar and folklorist.

Her most recent publications include *Cabañuelas: A Novel* and *Meditación Fronteriza: Poems of Love, Life, and Labor*, and the anthology *Teaching Gloria E. Anzaldúa: Pedagogy and Practice for Our Classrooms and Communities*.

Daniel Shank Cruz (he/they) is a queer Boricua who teaches English at Utica College in central New York. He received his PhD from Northern Illinois University. Cruz is the author of *Queering Mennonite Literature: Archives, Activism, and the Search for Community* (Penn State University Press, 2019). His writing has also appeared in venues such as *Crítica Hispánica*, *Mennonite Quarterly Review*, the *New York Times*, *Your Impossible Voice*, and several book collections. Follow him on Twitter: @shankcruz

Amelia María de la Luz Montes is an associate professor of English, ethnic studies, and creative writing at the University of Nebraska–Lincoln. She is an Americanist scholar, fiction writer, and memoirist who is interested in narrative contexts that complicate and contradict national, social, and personal identities. She has published edited books and several articles on the nineteenth-century Mexican American author María Amparo Ruiz de Burton. She has also published short stories and essays in journals such as the *Afro-Hispanic Review* and *Fifth Wednesday Journal*. Currently, she is finishing a book on her year as a Fulbright Scholar in the former Yugoslavia.

Araceli Esparza is an associate professor in the Department of English at California State University, Long Beach. She earned her PhD in American Studies and Ethnicity from the University of Southern California. Her teaching, research, and publications focus on representations of violence in Chicana/o/x and Latina/o/x literature and cultural production, women of color feminism, and gender studies. She is currently working on a book project that centers Chicana/o/x and US Central American representations of racial and ethnic identity formation with a focus on inter-Latina/o/x relations in the context of political violence in Central America and the United States.

Electra Gamón Fielding is an associate professor of Spanish at Weber State University in the Department of Foreign Languages. Fielding's main research interests include women writers in medieval and early modern Spain, and the presence of orientalized elements in Spanish cultural production, focusing especially on the representations of Jewish and Muslim women in the early modern picaresque novel. Her research interests also include Orientalism, race, cross-culturalism, and US Latino/a literature and culture.

Francisco J. Galarte is an assistant professor of American Studies and Gender, Women and Sexuality Studies at the University of New Mexico, where he teaches courses in Chicanx/Latinx studies and transgender studies. He is the newly appointed director of the Feminist Research Institute at UNM. He also serves as general coeditor for *TSQ: Transgender Studies Quarterly* and is the author of *Brown Trans Figurations: Rethinking Race, Gender, and Sexuality in Chicanx/Latinx Studies* published by University of Texas Press.

Liliana C. González is assistant professor of Gender and Women's Studies at California State University, Northridge. She earned her PhD from the University of Arizona in Latin American literature and culture. Her work is at the crossroads of Chicanx, Latinx, and Latin American cultural and literary studies, with an emphasis on narco studies, border studies, and queer theory. She is currently working on a book project titled "Narcosphere: The Intimate Politics of Narco Culture."

Bernadine M. Hernández is an assistant professor of American Literary Studies at the University of New Mexico. She specializes in transnational feminism and sexual economies of the US borderlands, along with American literary studies/empire, border, and migration history and theory, and Chicana/Latina literature and sexualities. Her forthcoming book, *Border Bodies: Racialized Sexuality, Sexual Capital, and Violence in the Nineteenth Century Borderlands*, is the first book-length study that focuses on gender and sexual violence on the borderlands in the nineteenth and early twentieth centuries through recovered archival work.

Ellie D. Hernández is an associate professor of Chican@ studies at the University of California, Santa Barbara. She specializes in twentieth century American literature, US minority and ethnic literature, cultural studies and critical theory, Chicana/o and US Latina/o studies, gender and sexuality studies, sexual minorities, and immigration. She is the author of *Postnationalism in Chicana/o Literature and Culture* (University of Texas Press, 2009). She is currently working on a coedited book with Eddy Alvarez: "Transmovimientos: The LGBTQ Immigrant Experience."

Olga L. Herrera is an associate professor of English at the University of St. Thomas. Her research examines the literary making of Chicago as a mythic place of work and opportunity for migrants and immigrants alike, with a focus on Chicanx and Latinx writers. Her work has been published in *Bridges, Borders, Breaks: History, Narrative, and Nation in Twenty-First Century Chicano/a Literary Criticism*; *MELUS: Multi-Ethnic Literature of the US*; *The Oxford Encyclopedia of Latino/a Literature*; and *The Cambridge History of Chicago Literature*.

Leigh Johnson is an associate professor of English at Marymount University, where she directs the Gender Studies Program and teaches courses on Latinx literature, gender and society, composition, and American literature. She views pedagogy as one of the most important ways in which the profession can arm students with tools they need to confront injustice, support their communities, and live meaningful lives. Her work appears in *Meridians, Rejoinder,* and edited collections.

Rebecca A. Kennedy de Lorenzini is a cultural historian of the Americas who specializes in the African Diaspora. She is currently an assistant professor in the Interdisciplinary General Education Department at the California State Polytechnic University, Pomona (Cal Poly Pomona), and she previously taught at Harvard University in the History & Literature program. She holds a PhD in history (University of Colorado, Boulder), an MA in Latin American studies (University of Texas, Austin), and an MA in modern history (University of St Andrews, Scotland).

Ximena Keogh Serrano is an assistant professor of Spanish and Latinx studies at Pacific University in Oregon. Her areas of specialization lie at the intersection of Latin American and US Latinx literary and cultural studies, and studies in gender and sexuality. A poet and scholar committed to crossings, her writing moves across genres of literary criticism, visual culture, and performance. She is currently working on a collection of essays that center on the politics of transnational identity, belonging, and quests for decolonizing desire.

Danizete Martínez received her PhD in twentieth-century American literature, specializing in Chicana/o literature, from the University of New Mexico. She spent the past nine years as an English faculty member at the UNM–Valencia branch campus and is currently a member of the English faculty at Central New Mexico Community College, the largest community college in the Southwest, where she continues to teach on a cross-cultural and regionally driven pedagogy.

Emma Pérez is a research social scientist at the Southwest Center and a professor in Gender and Women's Studies at the University of Arizona. Pérez has published fiction, essays, and the history monograph *The Decolonial Imaginary: Writing Chicanas into History* (1999). She is the author of three novels: *Gulf Dreams* (1996); *Forgetting the Alamo, or Blood Memory* (2009); and *Electra's Complex* (2015). Her latest project is a dystopic novel, "Chronicle of a Sex-Shifter," which probes a colonial global order run by the wealthy one percent.

Karen R. Roybal is an assistant professor of Southwest Studies at Colorado College. Her specializations include Southwest studies, Chicanx and Latinx literature and history, and cultural studies. She is the author of *Archives of Dispossession: Recovering the Testimonios of Mexican American Herederas, 1848–1960* (University of North Carolina Press, 2017). Her work has been published in *Southwestern American Literature*; *Aztlán: A Journal of Chicano Studies*; *Culture, Theory and Critique*; and *Chicana/Latina Studies*, among others.

Sandra Ruiz is an associate professor of Spanish and Chicana/o/x studies as well as vice chair of Modern Languages and Cultures at West Los Angeles College, having earned her PhD in Hispanic languages and literatures from University of California, Los Angeles. She specializes in twentieth- and twenty-first-century Mexican, US Chicana/o, and Latina/o literatures, specifically focusing on transborder feminist detective-crime fictions. Her current project explores Mexicana and Chicana crime narratives.

Shanna M. Salinas is an associate professor in the English Department and co-director of the Critical Ethnic Studies program at Kalamazoo College, where she teaches nineteenth-, twentieth-, and twenty-first-century American literary and cultural studies, with an emphasis on American race and ethnicity and Chicanx literature. She received her PhD in English from the University of California, Santa Barbara. Her work focuses on the constitutive relationship between US national identity and Chicanx racialized identity.

Gabriela Spears-Rico is an assistant professor in Chicano Latino Studies and American Indian Studies at the University of Minnesota. She received her PhD in ethnic studies from UC Berkeley and is a Mellon Fellow and a Woodrow Wilson Fellow. Spears-Rico's research interests include Latinx indigeneities, colonial violence, and mestizaje. She has been published in Indigenous studies and Chicano studies collections.

Tereza M. Szeghi is an associate professor of comparative literature and social justice at the University of Dayton in Ohio. Her research focuses on ways Indigenous writers use literature to effect social and political change pertaining to their human rights and land claims. Her publications have appeared in such journals as *Aztlán*, *Comparative Literature*, *MELUS*, and *Western American Literature*.

INDEX